THE CATHOLIC
SPIRIT

An Anthology for Discovering Faith Through Literature,
Art, Film, and Music

A fine introduction to Catholic literature and culture in a time that greatly needs just this. I give this collection for young Catholics a strong endorsement.

Fr. Benedict J. Groeschel, C.F.R.
Author of *The Tears of God*

This book understands fully that the Catholic tradition is incarnational. The judicious selection of texts drawn from literary and artistic sources will illuminate that fact superbly.

Lawrence S. Cunningham
John A. O'Brien Professor of Theology
University of Notre Dame

It is easy to see how *The Catholic Spirit* will serve as an essential resource for the high school theology class. This book will no doubt instill a lifelong love of God and the arts for both students and teachers alike.

Patricia Gallagher
Teacher of Religion
Cardinal Gibbons High School

This book is just what the Catholic community needs at this moment. Those of us teaching Catholic literature and studying films for ideas and insights that either explicitly present or implicitly point toward truths of the Catholic faith will welcome this new volume.

Rev. Robert E. Lauder
Author of *Magnetized by God*

Michel Bettigole, O.S.F., and James D. Childs

THE CATHOLIC
SPIRIT

An Anthology for Discovering Faith Through Literature,
Art, Film, and Music

AVE MARIA PRESS AVE Notre Dame, Indiana

© 2010 by Ave Maria Press

Founded in 1865, Ave Maria Press is a ministry of the United States Province of Holy Cross.

www.avemariapress.com

ISBN-10 1-59471-182-8   ISBN-13 978-1-59471-182-4

Cover images © Scala/Art Resource, NY and John Collier/Hillstream LLC

Cover and text design by Andy Wagoner.

Printed and bound in the United States of America.

Contents

Preface

The impetus for this book, which uses literature, art, film, and music for teaching about the Catechism and traditions of the Catholic Church, came from the editors' many years of experience as teachers and administrators in Catholic schools. We are grateful to the Trustees, Administrations, and Faculties of: St. Francis Preparatory School, Fresh Meadows, New York; St. Anthony's High School, South Huntington, New York; Bishop Ford High School, Brooklyn, New York; Marian High School, Mishawaka, Indiana; Mission College Preparatory Catholic High School, San Luis Obispo, California; and Cardinal Gibbons High School, Raleigh, North Carolina, for their encouragement, insights, and friendship.

Special thanks are due to the Franciscan Brothers of Brooklyn for their ongoing support of this project. We are particularly thankful to Br. Richard Pinkes, O.S.F., for his contribution on technical computer issues; Br. Hugh McGrath, O.S.F., and Br. Damian Novello, O.S.F., for their suggestions regarding literary works; Br. Franciscus Rowles, O.S.F., for his advice on sacred music; Rev. Robert Lauder for his advice on film; and Br. Jeremy Sztabnik, O.S.F., for his insights concerning visual art.

We are profoundly grateful to our editor at Ave Maria Press, Michael Amodei, for his advice, support, and encouragement.

On a personal note, we wish to convey our love and gratitude to Kate and to the children for their understanding and good humor while Daddy worked on the book with Brother.

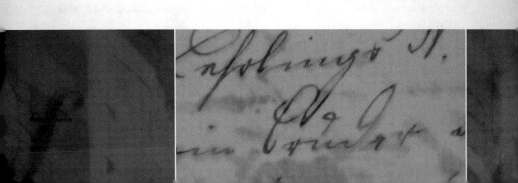

GENERAL INTRODUCTION

How to Use this Sourcebook

Conveying the Catholic Vision

The purpose of this collection of classic and modern readings and works of visual and performance art is to help students understand the teachings of Catholicism in a personal way, to bring the tradition of the faith to life, and to make real the life of grace. In this anthology, students and teachers will be exposed to classic expressions of faith that convey the richness of the Catholic religious vision. This vision has an intellectual content, a series of beliefs that have been passed down throughout history from one generation to the next. As St. Paul said when instructing the Church of Corinth about the Mystery of the Eucharist, "For I received from the Lord what I also handed on to you . . ." (1 Cor 11:23).

The efficacy of using the literary and visual arts to present the experience of belief was stated clearly by Pope John Paul II in his *Letter to Artists* (April 1999), in which he pointed out that it is through the arts that religious truths are made tangible, "making perceptible . . .the world of the spirit, of the invisible, of God." In emphasizing the critical role of the arts on the development of the moral imagination and the formation of conscience, Pope John Paul II was echoing the insights of philosophers and theologians throughout the ages who have always stressed their role in the formation of minds attuned to the good, the true, and the beautiful.

Great literature and art play a significant role in moral and religious education. Men and women of letters have continuously stressed the role of reading and storytelling for the proper inculcation of religious and spiritual values. In every generation, parents, grandparents, clergy, and teachers have told tales of faith and showed religious imagery to make real the teachings of our faith. Thus they have passed on those eternal values that are exemplified in the stories and legends and paintings of heroes and saints. It is primarily through stories and other imaginative activities that people become aware of the divine universe that surrounds them and learn to distinguish between right and wrong, good and evil.

Today we live in an age whose visual and literary arts often glorify the secular, not the religious. The sensuality, materialism, and utilitarianism that mark so much of present-day adult painting, film, writing, and music

2

find their reflection in modern tales. One finds in so much contemporary writing stories that exalt material success and fame. Rarely does the student find a well-written story, see a painting, view a film, or listen to a piece of music that portrays the world of the spirit and the life of grace. The lack of the divine in so much contemporary artistic expression and its utter denial of spiritual realities have resulted in a shrinking of the imagination and a closing of the mind for people of all ages. Society and individuals have been reduced to the purely measurable and functional instead of being open to the unseen—but all so real—world of the eternal and the miraculous.

The purpose of *The Catholic Spirit*, therefore, is to make available to contemporary Catholics some great literary and artistic works that take God, religion, and spirituality seriously. The expectation is that by joining together the teaching of the Church as outlined in the *Catechism of the Catholic Church* with works of art and literature that express that tradition in a personal way, you will able to understand your faith not only with your mind but with all the strength and power of your heart and soul. Following the thought of St. Bonaventure, we believe that, like angels, the human soul becomes transformed into whatever it intently gazes upon (St. Bonaventure, *Homily 8, "Such Love"*), and that therefore, through exposure to great works of religious art and literature, you will more closely reflect the goodness and beauty of God.

The *Catechism of the Catholic Church* presents the articles of faith in a precise and systematic fashion. By its very nature it is meant to teach rather than inspire. In the following pages you are going to read stories and poems, view works of art, and listen to music that are organized around the four pillars of the *Catechism* in order to assist you in understanding the revelation that God has made to his people in an imaginative and emotional way, and how these expressions can impact your own personal experience of God. These stories, poems, works of art, films, and musical selections are meant to convey a range of imaginative experiences of knowing and loving God. Perhaps you will experience the loving kindness of God in a new way through your study.

How this Book Is Organized

The four units of *The Catholic Spirit* parallel the four parts of the *Catechism of the Catholic Church*. These units are:

1. The Profession of Faith (What We Believe)
2. The Celebration of the Christian Mystery (How We Touch God and How God Touches Us)
3. Life in Christ (How We Should Live)
4. Prayer (How We Talk to God and How God Talks to Us).

When studying a particular Catholic belief or tradition, it is helpful to first examine Church teaching. A teaching from the *Catechism* introduces each section and provides the context for the material that follows. Selections from literature, biography, the visual arts, film, and music then express how that teaching is lived.

Examining Literature

Each literary selection includes the following elements:

- The title of the piece and name of the author.
- A relevant quotation for further consideration.
- *Author Background:* Brief biographical information on the person who created the entry.
- *Before the Reading:* The cultural and historical context of the piece is introduced.
- The actual text of the literature.
- *Reading for Comprehension:* A series of objective questions to help you accurately account for the information presented.
- *Reading for Understanding:* These personal reflection questions help you to apply the reading in a personal way. They are appropriate for both journal writing and discussion.
- *Activity:* The reading spurs new creativity. The activity is meant to challenge you to explore several opportunities.

Examining Art, Film, and Music

Besides literature, examining art, film, and music can help you make deeper connections with truths of faith. Special features within each unit introduce works of art, film, and music. Additionally, there are assignments and projects that enable the student to more fully understand a teaching of the Church through a particular work of art, or to connect art, film, and music to the readings in the text. Examples of visual art are introduced with a section called "Seeing with the Artist." Supplementing the examples of film included with each unit, the section "Looking at Film" provides background for how religious truths are manifested in the cinematic arts.

A special note about the films suggested in this book: Films are recommended by two ratings systems. They are:

1. *Vatican Best Films List:* On the occasion of the centennial anniversary of cinema in 1995, the Vatican compiled a list of forty-five "great" films.

2. *United States Conference of Catholic Bishops Ratings:* The classifications are as follows: A-l —general patronage; A-ll—adults and adolescents; A-lll—adults; L—limited adult audience (films whose problematic content many adults would find troubling); A-IV—discontinued rating, originally adults, with reservations (an A-IV classification designates problematic films that, while not morally offensive in themselves, require caution and some analysis and explanation as a safeguard against wrong interpretations and false conclusions); O—morally offensive.

Each film suggested in this text will include a reference to one of these rating systems.

"Listening to Sacred Music" sections demonstrate how this artistic form is essential for the full expression of the Church's worship. The tradition of using music as a vehicle to praise God is as old as revelation itself. In Psalm 71:21–22, the psalmist sings: "Restore my honor; turn and comfort me, that I may praise you with the lyre for your faithfulness, my God, and sing to you with the harp, O Holy One of Israel!" The Gospel of Matthew points out that the Lord and the Apostles concluded the Last Supper with a hymn; then, after singing a hymn, they went out to the Mount of Olives (Mt 26: 30).

The early Church Fathers also stressed the role of music as a vehicle for proclaiming the Word of Scripture and the Liturgy. Therefore, they encouraged only that music which allowed the congregation to clearly understand the words that were being sung. They opposed the use of instruments and polyphonic music because it did not allow the congregation to clearly understand what the choir was singing. The classic example of this type of music is *Gregorian Chant*, a form of music that is not accompanied by instruments and allows the congregation to clearly understand what is being sung. Until the Second Vatican Council, this form of chant was always performed in Latin with the exception of the Greek, *Kyrie*, and the Hebrew, *Alleluia*. Today there are many forms of contemporary chant that also stress the importance of understanding the words and thus emphasize simple, unadorned musical expressions.

During the Renaissance, composers and liturgists introduced musical instruments and polyphonic singing into the Church's worship. The purpose of this elaborate and brilliant musical style was to create a sense of awe in the congregation by filling the church with a sound of excessive beauty, and thus point the hearts and minds of worshippers to God himself, the source and essence of all beauty.

In the modern age, many composers have used contemporary secular music as a means to engage the congregation with music that is easily sung and easily understood. Thus many liturgies use the musical vocabulary of jazz, rhythm and blues, and country folk tunes as a vehicle for music about God.

Although the music used for the worship of God has changed over time, all forms of liturgical music have the same goal: to involve the congregation in a musical experience that assists them in raising their hearts and minds to God.

This text has been compiled in the spirit of the philosophic work *The Grammar of Assent*, in which John Cardinal Newman attempted to show what is meant by the words "I believe." Newman distinguished between *notional assent*, which was a saying of "yes" by the mind to abstract truths, and *real assent*, which was a saying of "yes" with one's whole being to a living encounter with God. One objective of this collection of stories, biography, music, and visual art is to encourage your *real assent* to the teachings and traditions of the Church.

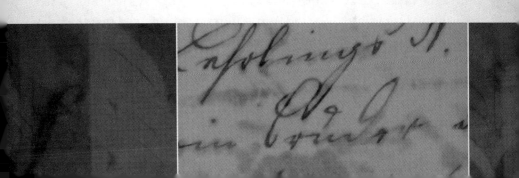

UNIT 1

What We Believe

(The Profession of Faith)

Beliefs Handed Down

Because God made us for himself in his own image, our goal is to know and love him throughout our earthly lives and to live with him for eternity in Heaven. By his very nature, God is totally above human comprehension: He is eternal, almighty, and all-knowing. And while we are mortal and limited in our knowledge and power, through the gift of his Son Jesus Christ, and in the Scriptures, God has revealed to us certain truths about his being and nature and his plan for humankind. Over many centuries, saints and theologians have reflected on God's revelation to his people, and so we have come to a fuller knowledge of who he is and how he loves us.

The handing on of this revelation from generation to generation, coupled with a deepening reflection upon it by the Church over the course of time, is known as the Sacred Tradition of the Church. Occasionally, to clarify matters and to summarize our beliefs about God, the bishops from all over the world gather together in meetings called ecumenical councils to assert fundamental truths of the faith in a clear and systematic way. These truths are expressed in dogmatic statements about our faith are called creeds (beliefs). These creeds reflect the teaching of the Church as revealed to the prophets and apostles and passed on from generation to generation to the entire Church. The most well known of these creeds was formulated in AD 325 by the bishops at the Council of Nicaea. The Nicene Creed was slightly modified in AD 385 at the Council of Constantinople. We recite this creed at each Sunday liturgy to strengthen us in our beliefs and to remind us of our communion with the Christians who have preceded us, as well as those who are still to come.

The Nicene Creed expresses our desire for God, the subject of belief, and the nature of God himself. God has revealed that he is One and that he is a Trinity of Persons—Father, Son, and Holy Spirit. God has revealed that he is the Creator of all that is. He has made known that His only Son, Jesus Christ, has come into the world to save us from our sins, and that the Holy Spirit is present to guide and teach us always through the Church.

Introducing the Unit

Each section in Unit 1 focuses on the lived experience of creative persons who, through their work, bring imaginative access to the Christian beliefs detailed by the Nicene Creed. These beliefs are highlighted by the following selections:

Creation and the Nature of God

- Gerard Manley Hopkins's beautiful poem "God's Grandeur" lauds God in his role as Creator, Redeemer, and Sanctifier.
- Oscar Wilde's story "The Teacher of Wisdom" tells of our need to know and love God.
- "Pigeon Feathers" by John Updike shows how God reveals himself to a teenager in a most unexpected way.
- The poems "The Creation" and "The Burning Babe" by James Weldon Johnson and Robert Southwell, respectively, focus our reflections on the mystery of God's creation and the precious gift of his Son, who entered the world as a vulnerable infant.
- The unsettling story "Parker's Back" by Flannery O'Connor shows how Jesus reveals himself in time and space as our brother.
- The philosophical selection taken from St. Bonaventure's *The Journey of the Mind into God* provides witness to the revelation of God through creation.

God's Ongoing Revelation

- The transfiguring revelation of God in history is clearly expressed in Madeleine L'Engle's poem, "The Bethlehem Explosion." In the life, Passion, Death, and Resurrection of Jesus, God shows us that Jesus truly is the perfect expression of God's love for his people.
- In his short story "Where Love Is, God Is," the great Russian writer Leo Tolstoy shows how the manifestation of God's love is made known to a humble shoemaker.

- In Dostoyevsky's "A Woman of Little Faith," Father Zosima calls on the 'woman of little faith' to reform her life, to love passionately the individual human persons who are a part of her life, and not to waste her spiritual energy in the pursuit of grandiose dreams of universal love. Only by doing this will she be able to believe.

- Pope Leo XIII said that "truth cannot contradict Truth." The methodology for investigating the apparent conflict between the divinely inspired Scriptures and the discoveries of science is explored in the readings of both the great physicist Galileo Galilei and Pope John Paul II.

The Uniqueness of Mary, the Mother of God

- In the poem "The Blessed Virgin Mary Compared to a Window," Thomas Merton uses the image of a window to highlight Mary's special role in the history of salvation, her union with God as his Bride, her humility, and her concern for her children on Earth.

- By looking toward Mary, we see through her toward the Lord. In the short story "Our Lady's Juggler" by Anatole France, we see how the Blessed Virgin Mary expresses maternal love for her children.

The Communion of Saints

- That the Church is a visible society made up of various persons and groups, each of whom plays a specific and vital role in the life and governance of the Church, is clearly seen in the poem "Marble Floor," by Karol Wojtyla (Pope John Paul II).

- Martyrs and saints are witnesses to the presence of God's Kingdom on Earth. An Account of the Martyrdom of St. Blandine and Her Companions in AD 177 is a second century account of the steadfast bravery demonstrated by exemplars of the Christian life.

Life Everlasting

- How we should prepare for the Second Coming at the end of time—when God will judge the entire world—is beautifully explained in two letters to a young priest written by St. Thérèse of Lisieux.

Creation and Nature of God

"God's Grandeur"

Gerard Manley Hopkins

We believe in the Holy Spirit, the lord, the giver of life,
who proceeds from the Father and the Son . . .

—Nicene Creed

Author Background

Gerard Manley Hopkins (1844–1889) was a Jesuit priest who never saw a single one of his poems published during his lifetime; his poetry was not published until twenty years after his death. He was an innovator in the use of poetic language, and the originality of his work has made him very influential among modern writers. Hopkins is not an easy poet to read. In his works, he compresses language, eliminates modifiers, and even invents new words in order to better express his meaning. This intensification of language, however, gives his poetry (especially when it is read aloud) an explosive power that can be matched by very few writers. The following selection, "God's Grandeur," is Hopkins's most well-known poem.

Before the Reading

This poem by Hopkins can be called a "creedal" poem, because it contains within it the essential articles of Christian faith: The world has been created by God; the world has fallen into sin through human choice; but it is redeemed through the love of God and the abiding presence of the Holy Spirit. The poem is an example of how the believer is called to look upon all creation with the vision of faith and an attitude of hopeful realism. From that perspective, we are empowered to view the world in all its defects, and yet also see the saving grace of God, who makes all things new.

"God's Grandeur"

The world is charged with the grandeur of God.
    It will flame out, like shining from shook foil;
    It gathers to a greatness, like the ooze of oil
Crushed. Why do men then now not reck his rod?
Generations have trod, have trod, have trod;
    And all is seared with trade; bleared, smeared with toil;
    And wears man's smudge and shares man's smell: the soil
Is bare now, nor can foot feel, being shod.

And for all this, nature is never spent;
    There lives the dearest freshness deep down things;
And though the last lights off the black West went
    Oh, morning, at the brown brink eastward, springs—
Because the Holy Ghost over the bent
World broods with warm breast and with ah! bright wings.

Reading for Comprehension

1. What words connote electricity in this poem?

2. What images does Hopkins use to describe humanity's destruction of nature?

3. Why are feet no longer able to feel?

4. Easter is associated with the dawn, the coming of light. What images in the poem express resurrection?

5. What is the colorful image of the divine that Hopkins uses at the conclusion of the poem?

Reading for Understanding

1. Reflect on moments in your life when you have experienced and been swept away by the sight of natural beauty. In what way do these experiences give you insights about the existence of God, or about his nature?

2. Reflect on ecological disasters, such as oil spills, the destruction of the rain forests, forest fires, or global warming. What do these occurrences tell us about our role as stewards of God's creation?

3. What is Hopkins's commentary about the modern world that explains our inability to see God in nature?

4. What ideas about the nature of God is Hopkins trying to convey by describing how the Holy Spirit "over the bent world broods with warm breast and ah! bright wings"?

Activity

The following are some of the essential beliefs expressed in the Nicene Creed:

- God has created the world;
- humanity has fallen through sin and has become estranged from God;
- God has not abandoned humankind but has sent his Son for our salvation;
- the Holy Spirit will remain with humankind and protect us until the end of time.

Locate the places in the Nicene Creed where these beliefs are stated and then match them with the images and descriptions found in Hopkins's poem.

Creation and Nature of God

"The Teacher of Wisdom"

Oscar Wilde

"You have made us for yourself, O Lord, and our hearts are restless until they rest in Thee."

—St. Augustine

Author Background

Oscar Wilde (1854–1900) is regarded as one of the greatest British writers of the nineteenth century. His comedy of manners, *The Importance of Being Earnest*, is a masterpiece of the modern theater. Wilde had a lifelong attraction to Catholicism and was received into the Church immediately before his death in France at the age of forty-six. A writer who worked in a variety of genres, his works have never been out of print. His book, *The Happy Prince and Other Tales*, his lengthy dramatic poem, "The Ballad of Reading Gaol," and his novel, *The Picture of Dorian Gray*, are of special interest to those who would like to read other literary works that reflect his religious sensibilities. However, controversy followed Wilde as well; "The Ballad of Reading Gaol" was based on his imprisonment for "gross indecency." The following selection, "The Teacher of Wisdom," is from his collection, *Poems in Prose*. The tale is representative of Wilde's religious stories; it is classic in structure, filled with lush and evocative imagery, and animated by a profound religious vision.

Before the Reading

God calls us "to seek him, to know him, to love him with all his strength" (*CCC*, Prologue, 1). In the following reading, Oscar Wilde portrays the yearning for the knowledge and love of God. Through this short story, Wilde explores the psychological reality that our response to God must be a response of love as well as a response of knowledge. The story points out that no matter how theologically educated a person is, it is only in loving God that one comes to know him.

"The Teacher of Wisdom"

From his childhood he had been as one filled with the perfect knowledge of God, and even while he was yet but a lad many of the saints, as well as certain holy women who dwelt in the free city of his birth, had been stirred to much wonder by the grave wisdom of his answers.

And when his parents had given him the robe and the ring of manhood he kissed them, and left them and went out into the world, that he might speak to the world about God. For there were at that time many in the world who either knew not God at all, or had but an incomplete knowledge of Him, or worshipped the false gods who dwell in groves and have no care of their worshippers.

And he set his face to the sun and journeyed, walking without sandals, as he had seen the saints walk, and carrying at his girdle a leathern wallet and a little water-bottle of burnt clay.

And as he walked along the highway he was full of the joy that comes from the perfect knowledge of God, and he sang praises unto God without ceasing; and after a time he reached a strange land in which there were many cities.

And he passed through eleven cities. And some of these cities were in valleys, and others were by the banks of great rivers, and others were set on hills. And in each city he found a disciple who loved him and followed him, and a great multitude also of people followed him from each city, and the knowledge of God spread in the whole land, and many of the rulers were converted, and the priests of the temples in which there were idols found that half of their gain was gone, and when they beat upon their drums at noon none, or but a few, came with peacocks and with offerings of flesh as had been the custom of the land before his coming.

Yet the more the people followed him, and the greater the number of his disciples, the greater became his sorrow. And he knew not why his sorrow was so great. For he spake ever about God, and out of the fullness of that perfect knowledge of God which God had Himself given to him.

And one evening he passed out of the eleventh city, which was a city of Armenia, and his disciples and a great crowd of people followed after him; and he went up on to a mountain and sat down on a rock that was on the mountain, and his disciples stood round him, and the multitude knelt in the valley.

And he bowed his head on his hands and wept, and said to his Soul, "Why is it that I am full of sorrow and fear, and that each of my disciples is as an enemy that walks in the noonday?"

And his Soul answered him and said, "God filled thee with the perfect knowledge of Himself, and thou hast given this knowledge away to others. The pearl of great price thou hast divided, and the vesture without seam thou hast parted asunder. He who giveth away wisdom robbeth himself. He is as one who giveth his treasure to a robber. Is not God wiser than thou art? Who art thou to give away the secret that God hath told thee? I was rich once, and thou hast made me poor. Once I saw God, and now thou hast hidden Him from me."

And he wept again, for he knew that his Soul spake truth to him, and that he had given to others the perfect knowledge of God, and that he was as one clinging to the skirts of God, and that his faith was leaving him by reason of the number of those who believed in him.

And he said to himself, I will talk no more about God. He who giveth away wisdom robbeth himself.

And after the space of some hours his disciples came near him and bowed themselves to the ground and said, "Master, talk to us about God, for thou hast the perfect knowledge of God, and no man save thee hath this knowledge."

And he answered them and said, "I will talk to you about all other things that are in heaven and on earth, but about God I will not talk to you. Neither now, nor at any time, will I talk to you about God." And they were wroth with him and said to him, "Thou hast led us into the desert that we might hearken to thee. Wilt thou send us away hungry, and the great multitude that thou hast made to follow thee?"

And he answered them and said, "I will not talk to you about God."

And the multitude murmured against him and said to him, "Thou hast led us into the desert, and hast given us no food to eat. Talk to us about God and it will suffice us."

But he answered them not a word. For he knew that if he spake to them about God he would give away his treasure.

And his disciples went away sadly, and the multitude of people returned to their own homes. And many died on the way.

And when he was alone he rose up and set his face to the moon, and journeyed for seven moons, speaking to no man nor making any answer. And when the seventh moon had waned he reached that desert which is the desert of the Great River. And having found a cavern in which a Centaur had once dwelt, he took it for his place of dwelling, and made himself a mat of reeds on which to lie, and became a hermit. And every hour the Hermit praised God that He had suffered him to keep some knowledge of Him and of His wonderful greatness.

Now, one evening, as the Hermit was seated before the cavern in which he had made his place of dwelling, he beheld a young man of evil and beautiful face who passed by in mean apparel and with empty hands. Every evening with empty hands the young man passed by, and every morning he returned with his hands full of purple and pearls. For he was a Robber and robbed the caravans of the merchants.

And the Hermit looked at him and pitied him. But he spake not a word. For he knew that he who speaks a word loses his faith.

And one morning, as the young man returned with his hands full of purple and pearls, he stopped and frowned and stamped his foot upon the sand, and said to the Hermit: "Why do you look at me ever in this manner as I pass by? What is it that I see in your eyes? For no man has looked at me before in this manner. And the thing is a thorn and a trouble to me."

And the Hermit answered him and said, "What you see in my eyes is pity. Pity is what looks out at you from my eyes."

And the young man laughed with scorn, and cried to the Hermit in a bitter voice, and said to him, "I have purple and pearls in my hands, and you have but a mat of reeds on which to lie. What pity should you have for me? And for what reason have you this pity?"

"I have pity for you," said the Hermit, "because you have no knowledge of God."

"Is this knowledge of God a precious thing?" asked the young man, and he came close to the mouth of the cavern.

"It is more precious than all the purple and the pearls of the world," answered the Hermit.

"And have you got it?" said the young Robber, and he came closer still.

"Once, indeed," answered the Hermit, "I possessed the perfect knowledge of God. But in my foolishness I parted with it, and divided it amongst others. Yet even now is such knowledge as remains to me more precious than purple or pearls."

And when the young Robber heard this he threw away the purple and the pearls that he was bearing in his hands, and drawing a sharp sword of curved steel he said to the Hermit, "Give me, forthwith, this knowledge of God that you possess, or I will surely slay you. Wherefore should I not slay him who has a treasure greater than my treasure?"

And the Hermit spread out his arms and said, "Were it not better for me to go unto the uttermost courts of God and praise Him, than to live in the world and have no knowledge of Him? Slay me if that be your desire. But I will not give away my knowledge of God."

And the young Robber knelt down and besought him, but the Hermit would not talk to him about God, nor give him his Treasure, and the young Robber rose up and said to the Hermit, "Be it as you will. As for myself, I will go to the City of the Seven Sins, that is but three days' Journey from this place, and for my purple they will give me pleasure, and for my pearls they will sell me joy." And he took up the purple and the pearls and went swiftly away.

And the Hermit cried out and followed him and besought him. For the space of three days he followed the young Robber on the road and entreated him to return, nor to enter into the City of the Seven Sins.

And ever and anon the young Robber looked back at the Hermit and called to him, and said, "Will you give me this knowledge of God which is more precious than purple and pearls? If you will give me that, I will not enter the city."

And ever did the Hermit answer, "All things that I have I will give thee, save that one thing only. For that thing it is not lawful for me to give away."

And in the twilight of the third day they came nigh to the great scarlet gates of the City of the Seven Sins. And from the city there came the sound of much laughter.

And the young Robber laughed in answer, and sought to knock at the gate. And as he did so the Hermit ran forward and caught him by the skirts of his raiment, and said to him: "Stretch forth your hands, and set your arms around my neck, and put your ear close to my lips, and I will give you what remains to me of the knowledge of God." And the young Robber stopped.

And when the Hermit had given away his knowledge of God, he fell upon the ground and wept, and a great darkness hid from him the city and the young Robber, so that he saw them no more.

And as he lay there weeping he was aware of One who was standing beside him; and He who was standing beside him had feet of brass and hair like fine wool. And He raised the Hermit up, and said to him: "Before this time thou hadst the perfect knowledge of God. Now thou shalt have the perfect love of God. Wherefore art thou weeping?" And He kissed him.

Reading for Comprehension

1. What reason does his Soul give the Teacher for his feelings of sorrow and fear?

2. What does the Teacher do to make sure that he does not lose his knowledge of God?

3. Who does the Hermit see each day passing by his cave?

4. What does the young Robber say that he is going to do when the Hermit tells him that he cannot share with him the knowledge of God?

5. What is God's response to the Hermit when the Hermit has given away the last of his knowledge of God?

Reading for Understanding

1. In this story, Oscar Wilde portrays two ways of knowing God: with one's intellect and with one's heart. Reflect on the people in your life who know you primarily either with their intellects or their hearts. Both of these groups of people have a certain true knowledge about you. Give examples of each and discuss the value of each type of knowledge to explain and express who you truly are.

2. Who in your life knows you most completely? Why? Which type of knowledge most adequately expresses who you are?

3. In the spirit of this story list three ways that you know God with your head and three ways that you know him with your heart.

4. Discuss the possible dangers of seeking God solely with one's head or solely with one's heart.

Activity

The desire to know God is built into the very fabric of our being. However, there are many ways to know and love God. Select your patron saint using your baptismal or Confirmation name. Research how this saint came to the knowledge and love of God.

Creation and Nature of God

"Pigeon Feathers"
John Updike

I am the Way, the Truth, and the Life;
He who believes in me will never die . . .
—John 14:6

Author Background
John Updike (1932–2009) was a contemporary American writer who was
twice-awarded the Pulitzer Prize. His body of work shows a profound interest in the spiritual life. In the following short story, "Pigeon Feathers,"
Updike shows how the God of all creation manifests himself in a surprising
way to a teenager who is seeking him.

Before the Reading
God is eternal, all good, and all-loving. He reveals himself to humankind
through the wondrous work of his creation. The encounter with God, however, takes place in the individual soul and is different for each person.
Moreover, the encounter with God calls for a response from the individual;
that is, an act of faith. In John Updike's short story, "Pigeon Feathers," a
teenager confronts his own mortality and his desire to truly have faith in
the words of Jesus.

"Pigeon Feathers"

When they moved to Firetown, things were upset, displaced, re-
arranged. A red cane-back sofa that had been the chief piece in the
living room at Olinger was here banished, too big for the narrow
country parlor, to the barn, and shrouded under a tarpaulin. Never
again would David lie on its length all afternoon eating raisins and

reading mystery novels and science fiction and P. G. Wodehouse. The blue wing chair that had stood for years in the ghostly, immaculate guest bedroom, gazing through the windows curtained with dotted swiss toward the telephone wires and horse-chestnut trees and opposite houses, was here established importantly in front of the smutty little fireplace that supplied, in those first cold April days, their only heat. As a child, David had been afraid of the guest bedroom—it was there that he, lying sick with the measles, had seen a black rod the size of a yardstick jog along at a slight slant beside the edge of the bed and vanish when he screamed—and it was disquieting to have one of the elements of its haunted atmosphere basking by the fire, in the center of the family, growing sooty with use. The books that at home had gathered dust in the case beside the piano were here hastily stacked, all out of order, in the shelves that the carpenters had built along one wall below the deep-silled windows. David, at thirteen, had been more moved than a mover; like the furniture, he had to find a new place, and on the Saturday of the second week he tried to work off some of his disorientation by arranging the books.

It was a collection obscurely depressing to him, mostly books his mother had acquired when she was young: college anthologies of Greek plays and Romantic poetry, Will Durant's *The Story of Philosophy*, a soft-leather set of Shakespeare with string bookmarks sewed to the bindings, *Green Mansions* boxed and illustrated with woodcuts, *The Tiger*, by Manuel Komroff, novels by names like Galsworthy and Ellen Glasgow and Irvin S. Cobb and Sinclair Lewis and "Elizabeth." The odor of faded taste made him feel the ominous gap between himself and his parents, the insulting gulf of time that existed before he was born. Suddenly he was tempted to dip into this time. From the heaps of books piled around him on the worn old floorboards, he picked up Volume II of a four-volume set of *The Outline of History*, by H. G. Wells. Once David had read *The Time Machine*; this gave him a small grip on the author. The book's red binding had faded to orange-pink on the spine. When he lifted the cover, there was a sweetish, moldy smell, and his mother's maiden name written in unfamiliar handwriting on the flyleaf—an upright, bold, yet careful signature, bearing a faint relation to the quick scrunched backslant that flowed with marvelous consistency across her shopping lists and budget accounts and Christmas cards to college friends from this same, vaguely menacing long ago.

He leafed through, pausing at drawings, done in an old-fashioned stippled style, of bas-reliefs, masks, Romans without pupils in their eyes, articles of ancient costume, fragments of pottery found in unearthed homes. He knew it would be interesting in a magazine, sandwiched between ads and jokes, but in this undiluted form history was somehow sour. The print was determinedly legible, and smug, like a lesson book. As he bent over the pages, yellow at the edges, they seemed rectangles of dusty glass through which he looked down into unreal and irrelevant worlds. He could see things sluggishly move, and an unpleasant fullness came into his throat. His mother and grandmother fussed in the kitchen; the puppy, which they had just acquired, as a watchdog in the country, was cowering, with a sporadic panicked scrabble of claws, under the dining table that in their old home had been reserved for special days but that here was used for every meal.

Then, before he could halt his eyes, David slipped into Wells's account of Jesus. He had been an obscure political agitator, a kind of hobo, in a minor colony of the Roman Empire. By an accident impossible to reconstruct, he (the small h horrified David) survived his own crucifixion and presumably died a few weeks later. A religion was founded on the freakish incident. The credulous imagination of the times retrospectively assigned miracles and supernatural pretensions to Jesus; a myth grew, and then a church, whose theology at most points was in direct contradiction of the simple, rather communistic teachings of the Galilean.

It was as if a stone that for months and even years had been gathering weight in the web of David's nerves snapped them and plunged through the page and a hundred layers of paper underneath. These fantastic falsehoods—plainly untrue: churches stood everywhere, the entire nation was founded "under God"—did not at first frighten him; it was the fact that they had been permitted to exist in an actual human brain. This was the initial impact—that at a definite spot in time and space a brain black with the denial of Christ's divinity had been suffered to exist. The universe had not spat out this ball of tar but allowed it to continue in its blasphemy, to grow old, win honors, wear a hat, write books that, if true, collapsed everything into a jumble of horror. The world outside the deep-silled windows—a rutted lawn, a whitewashed barn, a walnut tree frothy with fresh green—seemed a haven from which David was forever sealed off. Hot washrags seemed pressed against his cheeks.

He read the account again. He tried to supply out of his ignorance objections that would defeat the complacent march of these black words, and found none. Survivals and misunderstandings more far-fetched were reported daily in the papers. But none of them caused churches to be built in every town. He tried to work backwards through the churches, from their brave high fronts through their shabby, ill-attended interiors back into the events at Jerusalem, and felt himself surrounded by shifting gray shadows, centuries of history, where he knew nothing. The thread dissolved in his hands. Had Christ ever come to him, David Kern, and said, "Here. Feel the wound in My side"? No; but prayers had been answered. What prayers? He had prayed that Rudy Mohn, whom he had purposely tripped so he cracked his head on their radiator, not die, and he had not died. But for all the blood, it was just a cut; Rudy came back the same day, wearing a bandage and repeating the same teasing words. He could never have died. Again, David had prayed for two separate war-effort posters he had sent away for to arrive tomorrow, and though they did not, they did arrive, some days later, together, popping through the clacking letter slot like a rebuke from God's mouth: I answer your prayers in My way, in My time. After that, he had made his prayers less definite, less susceptible of being twisted into a scolding. But what a tiny, ridiculous coincidence this was, after all, to throw into battle against H. G. Wells's engines of knowledge! Indeed, it proved the enemy's point: Hope bases vast premises on foolish accidents, and reads a word where in fact only a scribble exists.

His father came home. Though Saturday was a free day for him, he had been working. He taught school in Olinger and spent his free days performing, with a kind of panic, needless errands. A city boy by birth, he was frightened of the farm and seized any excuse to get away. The farm had been David's mother's birthplace; it had been her idea to buy it back. With a determination unparalleled in her life, she had gained that end, and moved them all here—her son, her husband, her mother. Granmom, in her prime, had worked these fields alongside her husband, but now she dabbled around the kitchen, her hands waggling with Parkinson's disease. She was always in the way. Strange, out in the country, amid eighty acres, they were crowded together. His father expressed his feelings of discomfort by conducting with Mother an endless argument about organic farming. All through dusk, all through supper, it rattled on.

"Elsie, I know, I know from my education, the earth is nothing but chemicals. It's the only damn thing I got out of four years of college, so don't tell me it's not true."

"George, if you'd just walk out on the farm you'd know it's not true. The land has a soul."

"Soil, has, no, soul," he said, enunciating stiffly, as if to a very stupid class. To David he said, "You can't argue with a femme. Your mother's a real femme. That's why I married her, and now I'm suffering for it."

"This soil has no soul," she said, "because it's been killed with superphosphate. It's been burned bare by Boyer's tenant farmers." Boyer was the rich man they had bought the farm from. "It used to have a soul, didn't it, Mother? When you and Pop farmed it?"

"Ach, yes; I guess." Granmom was trying to bring a forkful of food to her mouth with her less severely afflicted hand. In her attempt she brought the other hand up from her lap. The crippled fingers, dull red in the orange light of the kerosene lamp in the center of the table, were welded by disease into one knobbed hook.

"Only human individuals have souls," his father went on, in the same mincing, lifeless voice. "Because the Bible tells us so." Done eating, he crossed his legs and dug into his ear with a match; to get at the thing inside his head he tucked in his chin, and his voice came out low-pitched at David. "When God made your mother, He made a real femme."

"George, don't you read the papers? Don't you know that between the chemical fertilizers and the bug sprays we'll all be dead in ten years? Heart attacks are killing every man in the country over forty-five."

He sighed wearily; the yellow skin of his eyelids wrinkled as he hurt himself with the match. "There's no connection," he stated, spacing his words with pained patience, "between the heart and chemical fertilizers. It's alcohol that's doing it. Alcohol and milk. There is too much cholesterol in the tissues of the American heart. Don't tell me about chemistry, Elsie; I majored in the damn stuff for four years."

"Yes, and I majored in philosophy and I'm not a penny wiser. Mother, put your waggler away!" The old woman started, and the food dropped from her fork. For some reason, the sight of her bad hand at the table cruelly irritated her daughter. Granmom's eyes widened behind her cockeyed spectacles. Circles of silver as fine as thread, the frames clung to the red notches they had carved over the years into her little white beak. In the orange flicker of the kerosene lamp, her dazed misery seemed infernal. David's mother began, without noise, to cry. His father did not seem to have eyes at all, just jaundiced sockets of wrinkled skin. The steam of food clouded the scene, which was grim but familiar and distracted David from the formless dread that worked, sticky and sore, within him, like a too-large wound trying to heal.

He had to go to the bathroom. He took a flashlight down through the wet grass to the outhouse. For once, his fear of spiders there felt trivial. He set the flashlight, burning, beside him, and an insect alighted on its lens, a tiny insect, a mosquito or flea, made so fine that the weak light projected its X-ray onto the wall boards: the faint rim of its wings, the blurred strokes, magnified, of its long hinged legs, the dark cone at the heart of its anatomy. The tremor must be its heart beating.

Without warning, David was visited by an exact vision of death: a long hole in the ground, no wider than your body, down which you are drawn while the white faces above recede. You try to reach them but your arms are pinned. Shovels pour dirt into your face. There you will be forever, in an upright position, blind and silent, and in time no one will remember you, and you will never be called by any angel. As strata of rock shift, your fingers elongate, and your teeth are distended sideways in a great underground grimace indistinguishable from a strip of chalk. And the earth tumbles on, and the sun expires, and unaltering darkness reigns where once there were stars.

Sweat broke out on his back. His mind seemed to rebound off a solidness. Such extinction was not another threat, a graver sort of danger, a kind of pain; it was qualitatively different. It was not even a conception that could be voluntarily pictured; it entered him from outside. His protesting nerves swarmed on its surface like lichen on a meteor. The skin of his chest was soaked with the effort of rejection. At the same time that the fear was dense and internal, it was dense and all around him; a tide of clay had swept up to the stars; space was crushed into a mass. When he stood up, automatically hunching his shoulders to keep his head away from the spiderwebs, it was with a numb sense of being cramped between two huge, rigid masses. That he had even this small freedom to move surprised him. In the narrow shelter of that rank shack, adjusting his pants, he felt—his first spark of comfort—too small to be crushed.

But in the open, as the beam of the flashlight skidded with frightened quickness across the remote surfaces of the barn and the grape arbor and the giant pine that stood by the path to the woods, the terror descended. He raced up through the clinging grass pursued, not by one of the wild animals the woods might hold, or one of the goblins his superstitious grandmother had communicated to his childhood, but by spectres out of science fiction, where gigantic cinder moons fill half the turquoise sky. As David ran, a gray planet rolled inches behind his neck. If he looked back, he would be buried. And in the momentum of his terror, hideous possibilities—the dilation of the sun, the triumph of the insects, the crabs on the shore in The Time Machine—wheeled out of the vacuum of make-believe and added their weight to his impending oblivion.

He wrenched the door open; the lamps within the house flared. The wicks burning here and there seemed to mirror one another. His mother was washing the dishes in a little pan of heated pump-water; Granmom hovered near her elbow. In the living room—the downstairs of the little square house was two long rooms—his father sat in front of the black fireplace restlessly folding and unfolding a newspaper as he sustained his half of the argument. "Nitrogen, phosphorus, potash: these are the three replaceable constituents of the soil. One crop of corn carries away hundreds of pounds of"—he dropped the paper into his lap and ticked them off on three fingers—"nitrogen, phosphorus, potash."

"Boyer didn't grow corn."

"Any crop, Elsie. The human animal—

"You're killing the earthworms, George!"

"The human animal, after thousands and thousands of years, learned methods whereby the chemical balance of the soil may be maintained. Don't carry me back to the Dark Ages."

"When we moved to Olinger the ground in the garden was like slate. Just one summer of my cousin's chicken dung and the earthworms came back."

"I'm sure the Dark Ages were a fine place to the poor devils born in them, but I don't want to go there. They give me the creeps." Daddy stared into the cold pit of the fireplace and clung to the rolled newspaper in his lap as if it alone were keeping him from slipping backwards and down, down.

Mother came into the doorway brandishing a fistful of wet forks. "And thanks to your DDT there soon won't be a bee left in the country. When I was a girl here you could eat a peach without washing it."

31

"It's primitive, Elsie. It's Dark Age stuff."

"Oh, what do you know about the Dark Ages?"

"I know I don't want to go back to them."

David took from the shelf, where he had placed it this afternoon, the great unabridged Webster's Dictionary that his grandfather had owned. He turned the big thin pages, floppy as cloth, to the entry he wanted, and read

> soul . . . 1. An entity conceived as the essence, sub-stance, animating principle, or actuating cause of life, or of the individual life, esp. of life manifested in psy-chical activities; the vehicle of individual existence, separate in nature from the body and usually held to be separable in existence.

The definition went on, into Greek and Egyptian conceptions, but David stopped short on the treacherous edge of antiquity. He needed to read no further. The careful overlapping words shingled a tempo-rary shelter for him. "Usually held to be separable in existence"—what could be fairer, more judicious, surer?

His father was saying, "The modern farmer can't go around sweeping up after his cows. The poor devil has thousands and thou-sands of acres on his hands. Your modern farmer uses a scientifically arrived-at mixture, like five-ten-five, or six-twelve-six, or three-twelve-six, and spreads it on with this wonderful modern machinery which of course we can't afford. Your modern farmer can't afford medieval methods."

Mother was quiet in the kitchen; her silence radiated waves of anger.

"No, now, Elsie: don't play the femme with me. Let's discuss this calmly like two rational twentieth-century people. Your organic-farming nuts aren't attacking five-ten-five; they're attacking the chemical-fertilizer crooks. The monster firms."

A cup clinked in the kitchen. Mother's anger touched David's face; his cheeks burned guiltily. Just by staying in the living room he associated himself with his father. She appeared in the doorway with red hands and tears in her eyes, and said to the two of them, "I knew you didn't want to come here but I didn't know you'd torment me like this. You talked Pop into his grave and now you'll kill me. Go ahead, George, more power to you; at least I'll be buried in good ground." She tried to turn and met an obstacle and screamed, "Mother, stop hanging on my back! Why don't you go to bed?"

"Let's all go to bed," David's father said, rising from the blue wing chair and slapping his thigh with a newspaper. "This reminds me of death." It was a phrase of his that David had heard so often he never considered its sense.

Upstairs, he seemed to be lifted above his fears. The sheets on his bed were clean. Granmom had ironed them with a pair of flatirons saved from the Olinger attic; she plucked them hot off the stove alternately, with a wooden handle called a goose. It was a wonder, to see how she managed. In the next room, his parents grunted peaceably; they seemed to take their quarrels less seriously than he did. They made comfortable scratching noises as they carried a little lamp back and forth. Their door was open a crack, so he saw the light shift and swing. Surely there would be, in the last five minutes, in the last second, a crack of light, showing the door from the dark room to another, full of light. Thinking of it this way vividly frightened him. His own dying, in a specific bed in a specific room, specific walls mottled with a particular wallpaper, the dry whistle of his breathing, the murmuring doctors, the dutiful relatives going in and out, but for him no way out but down, into that hole. Never walk again, never touch a doorknob again. A whisper, and his parents' light was blown out. David prayed to be reassured. Though the experiment frightened him, he lifted his hands high into the darkness above his face and begged Christ to touch them. Not hard or long: The faintest, quickest grip would be final for a lifetime. His hands waited in the air, itself a substance, which seemed to move through his fingers; or was it the pressure of his pulse? He returned his hands to beneath the covers, uncertain if they had been touched or not. For would not Christ's touch be infinitely gentle?

Through all the eddies of its aftermath, David clung to this thought about his revelation of extinction: that there, in the outhouse, he had struck a solid something qualitatively different, a base terror dense enough to support any height of construction. All he needed was a little help; a word, a gesture, a nod of certainty, and he would be sealed in, safe. The reassurance from the dictionary had melted in the night. Today was Sunday, a hot fair day. Across a mile of clear air the church bells called, celebrate, celebrate. Only Daddy went. He put on a coat over his rolled-up shirtsleeves and got into the little old black Plymouth parked by the barn and went off, with the same pained hurried grimness of all his actions. His churning wheels, as he shifted too hastily into second, raised plumes of red dust on the dirt road. Mother walked to the far field, to see what bushes needed cutting. David, though he usually preferred to stay in the house, went with her. The puppy followed at a distance, whining as it picked its way through the stubble but floundering off timidly if one of them went back to pick it up and carry it. When they reached the crest of the far field, his mother asked, "David, what's troubling you?"

"Nothing. Why?"

She looked at him sharply. The greening woods crosshatched the space beyond her half-gray hair. Then she showed him her profile, and gestured toward the house, which they had left a half-mile behind them. "See how it sits in the land? They don't know how to build with the land any more. Pop always said the foundations were set with the compass. We must get a compass and see. It's supposed to face due south; but south feels a little more that way to me." From the side, as she said these things, she seemed handsome and young. The smooth sweep of her hair over her ear had a calm that made her feel foreign to him. He had never regarded his parents as consolers of his troubles; from the beginning they had seemed to have more troubles than he. Their frailty had flattered him into an illusion of strength; so now on this high clear ridge he jealously guarded the menace all around them, blowing like an invisible breeze—the possibility of all this wide scenery's sinking into everlasting darkness. The strange fact that, though she came to look at the brush, she carried no clippers, for she had a fixed prejudice against working on Sundays, was the only comfort he allowed her to offer.

As they walked back, the puppy whimpering after them, the rising dust behind a distant line of trees announced that Daddy was speeding home from church. When they reached the house he was there. He had brought back the Sunday paper and the vehement remark, "Dobson's too intelligent for these farmers. They just sit there with their mouths open and don't hear a thing the poor devil's saying."

"What makes you think farmers are unintelligent? This country was made by farmers. George Washington was a farmer."

"They are, Elsie. They are unintelligent. George Washington's dead. In this day and age only the misfits stay on the farm. The lame, the halt, the blind. The morons with one arm. Human garbage. They remind me of death, sitting there with their mouths open."

"My father was a farmer."

"He was a frustrated man, Elsie. He never knew what hit him. The poor devil meant so well, and he never knew which end was up. Your mother'll bear me out. Isn't that right, Mom? Pop never knew what hit him?"

"Ach, I guess not," the old woman quavered, and the ambiguity for the moment silenced both sides.

David hid in the funny papers and sports section until one-thirty. At two, the catechetical class met at the Firetown church. He had transferred from the catechetical class of the Lutheran church in Olinger, a humiliating comedown. In Olinger they met on Wednesday nights, spiffy and spruce, in a very social atmosphere. Afterwards, blessed by the brick-faced minister on whose lips the word "Christ" had a pugnacious juiciness, the more daring of them went with their Bibles to a luncheonette and gossiped and smoked. Here in Firetown, the girls were dull white cows and the boys narrow-faced brown goats in old men's suits, herded on Sunday afternoons into a threadbare church basement that smelled of stale hay. Because his father had taken the car on one of his endless errands to Olinger, David walked, grateful for the open air, the lonely dirt road, and the silence. The catechetical class embarrassed him, but today he placed hope in it, as the source of the nod, the gesture, that was all he needed.

Reverend Dobson was a delicate young man with great dark eyes and small white shapely hands that nickered like protesting doves when he preached; he seemed a bit misplaced in the Lutheran ministry. This was his first call. It was a split parish; he served another rural church twelve miles away. His iridescent-green Ford, new six months ago, was spattered to the windows with red mud and rattled from bouncing on the rude back roads, where he frequently got lost, to the malicious satisfaction of some parishioners. But David's mother liked him, and, more pertinent to his success, the Haiers, the sleek family of feed merchants and tractor salesmen who dominated the Firetown church, liked him. David liked him, and felt liked in turn; sometimes in class, after some special stupidity, Dobson directed toward him out of those wide black eyes a mild look of disbelief, a look that, though flattering, was also delicately disquieting.

Catechetical instruction consisted of reading aloud from a work booklet answers to problems prepared during the week, problems like, "I am the _____, the _____, and the _____, saith the Lord." Then there was a question period in which no one ever asked any questions. Today's theme was the last third of the Apostles' Creed. When the time came for questions, David blushed and asked, "About the Resurrection of the Body—are we conscious between the time when we die and the Day of Judgment?"

Dobson blinked, and his fine small mouth pursed, suggesting that David was making difficult things more difficult. The faces of the other students went blank, as if an indiscretion had been committed.

"No, I suppose not," Reverend Dobson said.

"Well, where is our soul, then, in this gap?"

The sense grew, in the class, of a naughtiness occurring. Dobson's shy eyes watered, as if he were straining to keep up the formality of attention, and one of the girls, the fattest, simpered toward her twin, who was a little less fat. Their chairs were arranged in a rough circle. The current running around the circle panicked David. Did everybody know something he didn't know?

"I suppose you could say our souls are asleep," Dobson said.

"And then they wake up, and there is the earth like it always is, and all the people who have ever lived? Where will Heaven be?"

Anita Haier giggled. Dobson gazed at David intently, but with an awkward, puzzled flicker of forgiveness, as if there existed a secret between them that David was violating. But David knew of no secret. All he wanted was to hear Dobson repeat the words he said every Sunday morning. This he would not do. As if these words were unworthy of the conversational voice.

"David, you might think of Heaven this way: as the way in which the goodness Abraham Lincoln did lives after him."

"But is Lincoln conscious of it living on?" He blushed no longer with embarrassment but in anger; he had walked here in good faith and was being made a fool.

"Is he conscious now? I would have to say no. But I don't think it matters." His voice had a coward's firmness; he was hostile now.

"You don't."

"Not in the eyes of God, no." The unction, the stunning impudence, of this reply sprang tears of outrage in David's eyes. He bowed them to his workbook, where short words like Duty, Love, Obey, Honor were stacked in the form of a cross.

"Were there any other questions, David?" Dobson asked, more softly. The others were rustling, collecting their books.

"No." David made his voice firm, though he could not look up at the man.

"Did I answer your question fully enough?"

"Yes."

In the minister's silence the shame that should have been his crept over David: The burden and fever of being a fraud were placed upon him, who was innocent, and it seemed, he knew, a confession of this guilt that on the way out he was unable to face Dobson's stirred gaze, though he felt it probing the side of his head.

Anita Haier's father gave him a ride down the highway as far as the dirt road. David said he wanted to walk the rest, and figured that his offer was accepted because Mr. Haier did not want to dirty his dark new Oldsmobile with dust. This was all right; everything was all right, as long as it was clear. His indignation at being betrayed, at seeing Christianity betrayed, had hardened him. The road reflected his hardness. Pink stones thrust up through its packed surface. The April sun beat down from the center of the afternoon half of the sky; already it had some of summer's heat. Already the fringes of weeds at the edges of the road were bedraggled with dust. From the reviving grass and scruff of the fields that he walked between, insects were sending up a monotonous, automatic chant. In the distance a tiny figure in his father's coat was walking along the edge of the woods. His mother. He wondered what joy she found in such walks; to him the brown stretches of slowly rising and falling land expressed only a huge exhaustion.

Flushed with fresh air and happiness, she returned from her walk earlier than he had expected, and surprised him at his grandfather's Bible. It was a stumpy black book, the boards worn thin where the old man's fingers had held them; the spine hung by one weak hinge of fabric. David had been looking for the passage where Jesus says to the good thief on the cross, "Today shalt thou be with Me in paradise." He had never tried reading the Bible for himself before. What was so embarrassing about being caught at it was that he detested the apparatus of piety. Fusty churches, creaking hymns, ugly Sunday-school teachers and their stupid leaflets—he hated everything about them but the promise they held out, a promise that in the most perverse way, as if the homeliest crone in the kingdom were given the prince's hand, made every good and real thing, ball games and jokes and big-breasted girls, possible. He couldn't explain this to his mother. There was no time. Her solicitude was upon him.

"David, what are you doing?"

"Nothing."

"What are you doing at your grandfather's Bible?"

"Trying to read it. This is supposed to be a Christian country, isn't it?"

She sat down beside him on the green sofa, which used to be in the sun parlor at Olinger, under the fancy mirror. A little smile still lingered on her face from the walk. "David, I wish you'd talk to me."

"What about?"

"About whatever it is that's troubling you. Your father and I have both noticed it."

"I asked Reverend Dobson about Heaven and he said it was like Abraham Lincoln's goodness living after him."

He waited for the shock to strike her. "Yes?" she said, expecting more.

"That's all."

"And why didn't you like it?"

"Well—don't you see? It amounts to saying there isn't any Heaven at all."

"I don't see that it amounts to that. What do you want Heaven to be?"

"Well, I don't know. I want it to be something. I thought he'd tell me what it was. I thought that was his job." He was becoming angry, sensing her surprise. She had assumed that Heaven had faded from his head years ago. She had imagined that he had already entered, in the secrecy of silence, the conspiracy that he now knew to be all around him.

"David," she asked gently, "don't you ever want to rest?"

"No. Not forever."

"David, you're so young. When you get older, you'll feel differently."

"Grandpa didn't. Look how tattered this book is."

"I never understood your grandfather."

"Well, I don't understand ministers who say it's like Lincoln's goodness going on and on. Suppose you're not Lincoln?"

"I think Reverend Dobson made a mistake. You must try to forgive him."

"It's not a question of his making a mistake! It's a question of dying and never moving or seeing or hearing anything ever again."

"But"—in exasperation—"darling, it's so greedy of you to want more. When God has given us this wonderful April day, and given us this farm, and you have your whole life ahead of you—"

"You think, then, that there is a God?"

"Of course I do"—with deep relief, that smoothed her features into a reposeful oval. He had risen in his unease; he was afraid she would reach out and touch him.

"He made everything? You feel that?"

"Yes."

"Then who made Him?"

"Why, Man. Man." The happiness of this answer lit up her face radiantly, until she saw his gesture of disgust. She was so simple, so illogical; such a femme.

"Well, that amounts to saying He doesn't exist."

Her hand reached for his wrist but he backed away. "David, it's a mystery. A miracle. It's a miracle more beautiful than any Reverend Dobson could have told you about. You don't say houses don't exist because Man made them."

"No. God has to be different."

"But, David, you have the evidence. Look out the window at the sun; at the fields."

"Mother, good grief. Don't you see"—he rasped away the roughness in his throat—"if when we die there's nothing, all your sun and fields and whatnot are all, ah, horror? It's just an ocean of horror."

"But, David, it's not. It's so clearly not that." And she made an urgent, opening gesture with her hands that expressed a willingness to receive his helplessness; all her grace and maternal nurturing were gathered into a passive intensity that intensely repelled him. He would not be wooed away from the truth. I am the Way, the Truth . . .

"No," he told her. "Just let me alone."

He found his tennis ball behind the piano and went outside to throw it against the side of the house. There was a patch high up where the brown stucco laid over the sandstone masonry was crumbling away; he kept trying with the tennis ball to chip more pieces off. It was difficult, aiming up; the ball kept falling short.

Superimposed upon his deep ache was a smaller but more immediate worry—that he had hurt his mother. He heard his father's car rattling on the straightaway, and went into the house, to make peace before he arrived. To his relief, she was not giving off the stifling damp heat of her anger, but instead was cool, decisive, maternal. She handed him an old green book, her college text of Plato.

"I want you to read the Parable of the Cave," she said.

"All right," he said, though he knew it would do no good. Some story by a dead Greek just vague enough to please her. "Don't worry about it, Mother."

"I am worried. Honestly, David, I'm sure there will be something for us. As you get older, these things seem to matter a great deal less."

"That may be. It's a dismal thought, though."

His father bumped at the door. The locks and jambs stuck here. But before Granmom could totter to the latch and let him in, he had knocked it open. He had been in Olinger dithering with track-meet tickets. Although Mother usually kept her talks with David a secret between them, she called instantly, "George, David is worried about death!"

Daddy came to the doorway of the living room, his shirt pocket bristling with pencils, holding in one hand a pint box of melting ice cream and in the other the knife with which he was about to divide it into four sections, their Sunday treat. "Is the kid worried about death? Don't give it a thought, David. I'll be lucky if I live till tomorrow, and I'm not worried. If they'd taken a buckshot gun and shot me in the cradle I'd be better off. The world'd be better off. Hell, I think death is a wonderful thing. I look forward to it. Get the garbage

41

out of the way. If I had the man here who invented death, I'd pin a medal on him."

"Hush, George. You'll frighten the child worse than he is."

This was not true; he never frightened David. There was no harm in his father, no harm at all. Indeed, in the man's lively self-disgust the boy felt a kind of ally. A distant ally. He saw his position with a certain strategic coldness. Nowhere in the world of other people would he find the hint, the nod, he needed to begin to build his fortress against death. They none of them believed. He was alone. In that deep hole.

In the months that followed, his position changed little. School was some comfort. All those sexy, perfumed people, wisecracking, chewing gum, all of them doomed to die, and none of them noticing. In their company David felt that they would carry him along into the bright, cheap paradise reserved for them. In any crowd, the fear ebbed a little; he had reasoned that somewhere in the world there must exist a few people who believed what was necessary, and the larger the crowd, the greater the chance that he was near such a soul, within calling distance, if only he was not too ignorant, too ill-equipped, to spot him. The sight of clergymen cheered him; whatever they themselves thought, their collars were still a sign that somewhere, at some time, someone had recognized that we cannot, cannot, submit to death. The sermon topics posted outside churches, the flip, hurried pieties of disc jockeys, the cartoons in magazines showing angels or devils—on such scraps he kept alive the possibility of hope.

For the rest, he tried to drown his hopelessness in clatter and jostle. The pinball machine at the luncheonette was a merciful distraction; as he bent over its buzzing, flashing board of flippers and cushions, the weight and constriction in his chest lightened and loosened. He was grateful for all the time his father wasted in Olinger. Every delay postponed the moment when they must ride together down the dirt road into the heart of the dark farmland, where the only light was the kerosene lamp waiting on the dining-room table, a light that drowned their food in shadow and made it sinister.

He lost his appetite for reading. He was afraid of being ambushed again. In mystery novels people died like dolls being discarded; in science fiction immensities of space and time conspired to annihilate the human beings; and even in P. G. Wodehouse there was a threat, a bland mockery that acquired bite in the comic figures of futile clergymen. All gaiety seemed minced out on the skin of a void. All quiet hours seemed invitations to dread.

Even on weekends, he and his father contrived to escape the farm; and when, some Saturdays, they did stay home, it was to do something destructive—tear down an old henhouse or set huge brush fires that threatened, while Mother shouted and flapped her arms, to spread to the woods. Whenever his father worked, it was with rapt violence; when he chopped kindling, fragments of the old henhouse boards flew like shrapnel and the ax-head was always within a quarter of an inch of flying off the handle. He was exhilarating to watch, sweating and swearing and sucking bits of saliva back into his mouth.

School stopped. His father took the car in the opposite direction, to a highway construction job where he had been hired for the summer as a timekeeper, and David was stranded in the middle of acres of heat and greenery and blowing pollen and the strange, mechanical humming that lay invisibly in the weeds and alfalfa and dry orchard grass.

For his fourteenth birthday his parents gave him, with jokes about him being a hillbilly now, a Remington .22. It was somewhat like a pinball machine to take it out to the old kiln in the woods where they dumped their trash, and set up tin cans on the kiln's sandstone shoulder and shoot them off one by one. He'd take the puppy, who had grown long legs and a rich coat of reddish fur—he was part chow. Copper hated the gun but loved the boy enough to accompany him. When the flat, acrid crack rang out, he would race in terrified circles that would tighten and tighten until they brought him, shivering, against David's legs. Depending upon his mood, David would shoot again or drop to his knees and comfort the dog. Giving this comfort returned some comfort to him. The dog's ears, laid flat against his skull in fear, were folded so intricately, so—he groped for the concept—surely. Where the dull-studded collar made the fur stand up, each hair showed a root of soft white under the length, black-tipped, of the metal color that had lent the dog its name. In his agitation Copper panted through nostrils that were elegant slits, like two healed cuts, or like the keyholes of a dainty lock of black, grained wood. His whole whorling, knotted, jointed body was a wealth of such embellishments. And in the smell of the dog's hair David seemed to descend through many finely differentiated layers of earth: mulch, soil, sand, clay, and the glittering mineral base.

But when he returned to the house, and saw the books arranged on the low shelves, fear dully returned. The four adamant volumes of Wells like four thin bricks, the green Plato that had puzzled him with its dialogue form and hard-to-picture shadow show, the dead Galsworthy and "Elizabeth," Grandpa's mammoth dictionary, Grandpa's old Bible, the limp-covered Bible that he himself had received on becoming confirmed a member of the Firetown Lutheran Church—at the sight of these, the memory of his fear reawakened and came around him. He had grown stiff and stupid in its embrace. His parents tried to think of ways to entertain him.

"David, I have a job for you to do," his mother said one evening at the table.

"What?"

"If you're going to take that tone perhaps we'd better not talk."

"What tone? I didn't take any tone."

"Your grandmother thinks there are too many pigeons in the barn."

"Why?" David turned to look at his grandmother, but she sat there staring at the burning lamp with her usual expression of bewilderment. Her irises were pale discs of crazed crystal.

Mother shouted, "Mom, he wants to know why!"

Granmom made a jerky, irritable motion with her bad hand, as if generating the force for utterance, and said, "They foul the furniture."

"That's right," Mother said. "She's afraid for that old Olinger furniture that we'll never use. David, she's been after me for a month about those poor pigeons. She wants you to shoot them."

"I don't want to kill anything especially," David said.

Daddy said, "The kid's like you are, Elsie. He's too good for this world. Kill or be killed, that's my motto."

His mother said loudly, "Mother, he doesn't want to do it."

"Not?" The old lady's eyes distended as if in alarm, and her claw descended slowly to her lap.

"Oh, I'll do it, I'll do it tomorrow," David snapped, and a pleasant crisp taste entered his mouth with the decision.

"And I had thought, when Boyer's men made the hay, it would be better if the barn doesn't look like a rookery," his mother added needlessly.

A barn, in day, is a small night. The splinters of light between the dry shingles pierce the high roof like stars, and the rafters and cross-beams and built-in ladders seem, until your eyes adjust, as mysterious as the branches of a haunted forest. David entered silently, the gun in one hand. Copper whined desperately at the door, too frightened to come in with the gun yet unwilling to leave the boy. David stealthily turned, said "Go away," shut the door on the dog, and slipped the bolt across. It was a door within a door; the double door for wagons and tractors was as high and wide as the face of a house.

The smell of old straw scratched his sinuses. The red sofa, half hidden under its white-splotched tarpaulin, seemed assimilated into this smell, sunk in it, buried. The mouths of empty bins gaped like caves. Rusty oddments of farming—coils of baling wire, some spare tines for a harrow, a handleless shovel—hung on nails driven here and there in the thick wood. He stood stock-still a minute; it took a while to separate the cooing of the pigeons from the rushing in his ears. When he had focused on the cooing, it flooded the vast interior with

45

its throaty, bubbling outpour: there seemed no other sound. They
were up behind the beams. What light there was leaked through
the shingles and the dirty glass windows at the far end and the small
round holes, about as big as basketballs, high on the opposite stone
side walls, under the ridge of the roof.

A pigeon appeared in one of these holes, on the side toward
the house. It flew in, with a battering of wings, from the outside,
and waited there, silhouetted against its pinched bit of sky, preen-
ing and cooing in a throbbing, thrilled, tentative way. David tiptoed
four steps to the side, rested his gun against the lowest rung of a
ladder pegged between two upright beams, and lowered the gun-
sight into the bird's tiny, jauntily cocked head. The slap of the report
seemed to come off the stone wall behind him, and the pigeon did
not fall. Neither did it fly. Instead it stuck in the round hole, pirouet-
ting rapidly and nodding its head as if in frantic agreement. David
shot the bolt back and forth and had aimed again before the spent
cartridge had stopped jingling on the boards by his feet. He eased
the tip of the sight a little lower, into the bird's breast, and took care
to squeeze the trigger with perfect evenness. The slow contraction
of his hand abruptly sprang the bullet; for a half-second there was
doubt, and then the pigeon fell like a handful of rags, skimming
down the barn wall into the layer of straw that coated the floor of
the mow on this side.

Now others shook loose from the rafters, and whirled in the dim
air with a great blurred hurtle of feathers and noise. They would go
for the hole; he fixed his sight on the little moon of blue, and when
a pigeon came to it, shot him as he was walking the twenty inches
of stone that would have carried him into the open air. This pigeon
lay down in that tunnel of stone, unable to fall either one way or the
other, although he was alive enough to lift one wing and cloud the
light. The wing would sink back, and he would suddenly lift it again,
the feathers flaring. His body blocked that exit. David raced to the
other side of the barn's main aisle, where a similar ladder was sym-
metrically placed, and rested his gun on the same rung. Three birds

came together to this hole; he got one, and two got through. The rest resettled in the rafters.

There was a shallow triangular space behind the crossbeams supporting the roof. It was here they roosted and hid. But either the space was too small, or they were curious, for now that his eyes were at home in the dusty gloom David could see little dabs of gray popping in and out. The cooing was shriller now; its apprehensive tremolo made the whole volume of air seem liquid. He noticed one little smudge of a head that was especially persistent in peeking out; he marked the place, and fixed his gun on it, and when the head appeared again, had his finger tightened in advance on the trigger. A parcel of fluff slipped off the beam and fell the barn's height onto a canvas covering some Olinger furniture, and where its head had peeked out there was a fresh prick of light in the shingles.

Standing in the center of the floor, fully master now, disdaining to steady the barrel with anything but his arm, he killed two more that way. Out of the shadowy ragged infinity of the vast barn roof these impudent things dared to thrust their heads, presumed to dirty its starred silence with their filthy timorous life, and he cut them off, tucked them back neatly into the silence. He felt like a creator; these little smudges and flickers that he was clever to see and even cleverer to hit in the dim recesses of the rafters—out of each of them he was making a full bird. A tiny peek, probe, dab of life, when he hit it blossomed into a dead enemy, falling with good, final weight.

The imperfection of the second pigeon he had shot, who was still lifting his wing now and then up in the round hole, nagged him. He put a new clip into the stock. Hugging the gun against his body, he climbed the ladder. The barrel sight scratched his ear; he had a sharp, garish vision, like a color slide, of shooting himself and being found tumbled on the barn floor among his prey. He locked his arm around the top rung—a fragile, gnawed rod braced between uprights—and shot into the bird's body from a flat angle. The wing folded, but the impact did not, as he had hoped, push the bird out of the hole. He fired again, and again, and still the little body, lighter than air when alive, was too heavy to budge from its high grave. From up here he could see green trees and a brown corner of the house through the hole. Clammy with the cobwebs that gathered between the rungs, he pumped a full clip of eight bullets into the stubborn shadow, with no success. He climbed down, and was struck by the silence in the barn. The remaining pigeons must have escaped out the other hole. That was all right; he was tired of it.

He stepped with his rifle into the light. His mother was coming to meet him, and it tickled him to see her shy away from the carelessly held gun. "You took a chip out of the house," she said. "What were those last shots about?"

"One of them died up in that little round hole and I was trying to shoot it down."

"Copper's hiding behind the piano and won't come out. I had to leave him."

"Well, don't blame me. I didn't want to shoot the poor devils."

"Don't smirk. You look like your father. How many did you get?"

"Six."

She went into the barn, and he followed. She listened to the silence. Her hair was scraggly, perhaps from tussling with the dog. "I don't suppose the others will be back," she said wearily. "Indeed, I don't know why I let Mother talk me into it. Their cooing was such a comforting noise." She began to gather up the dead pigeons. Though he didn't want to touch them, David went into the mow and picked up by its tepid, horny, coral-colored feet the first bird he had killed. Its wings unfolded disconcertingly, as if the creature had been held together by threads that now were slit. It did not weigh much. He retrieved the one on the other side of the barn; his mother got the three in the middle and led the way across the road to the little south-facing slope of land that went down toward the foundations of the vanished tobacco shed. The ground was too steep to plant and mow; wild strawberries grew in the tangled grass. She put her burden down and said, "We'll have to bury them. The dog will go wild."

He put his two down on her three; the slick feathers let the bodies slide liquidly on one another. David asked, "Shall I get you the shovel?"

"Get it for yourself; you bury them. They're your kill. And be sure to make the hole deep enough so Copper won't dig them up." While he went to the tool shed for the shovel, she went into the house. Unlike his usual mother, she did not look up, either at the orchard to the right of her or at the meadow on her left, but instead held her head rigidly, tilted a little, as if listening to the ground.

He dug the hole, in a spot where there were no strawberry plants, before he studied the pigeons. He had never seen a bird this close before. The feathers were more wonderful than dog's hair, for each filament was shaped within the shape of the feather, and the feathers in turn were trimmed to fit a pattern that flowed without error across the bird's body. He lost himself in the geometrical tides as the feathers now broadened and stiffened to make an edge for flight, now softened and constricted to cup warmth around the mute flesh. And across the surface of the infinitely adjusted yet somehow effortless mechanics of the feathers played idle designs of color, no two alike, designs executed, it seemed, in a controlled rapture, with a joy that hung level in the air above and behind him. Yet these birds bred in the millions and were exterminated as pests. Into the fragrant open earth he dropped one broadly banded in slate shades of blue, and on top of it another, mottled all over in rhythms of lilac and gray. The next was almost wholly white, but for a salmon glaze at its throat. As he fitted the last two, still pliant, on the top, and stood up, crusty coverings were lifted from him, and with a feminine, slipping sensation along his nerves that seemed to give the air hands, he was robed in this certainty: that the God who had lavished such craft upon these worthless birds would not destroy His whole Creation by refusing to let David live forever.

Reading for Comprehension

1. What is the name of the book in which David reads an account of the life of Jesus that denies his divinity and resurrection from the dead?

2. Identify the reason why David feels so anxious about the thought of his own death.

3. What was the question that David asked Mr. Dobson in Catechism class?

4. What does David's father say about David's fear of death?

5. What gift does David receive for his birthday?

Reading for Understanding

1. Why does David lift his hands in the air when he is going to bed? What does he want to happen? How does he eventually receive what he's looking for?

2. Why did David find the Reverend Dobson's and his mother's explanations about the afterlife so unsatisfying?

3. Why is the number of pigeons David kills in the barn significant? What other descriptions in that same section reinforce the significance of the number of pigeons David kills?

4. A theory for the existence of God is called "the argument from design." This argument states that the order and symmetry of the universe gives evidence of an Intelligent Creator. How did David experience the "argument from design" for the existence of God in his examination of the dead pigeons?

5. In light of this story, how is the revelation of God made to David through the pigeon feathers an example of knowledge by both head and heart?

Activities

1. The most famous series of rational and philosophical arguments for the existence of God were constructed by St. Thomas Aquinas in his *Summa Theologica*. Review the five arguments for the existence of God found in the *Summa* (www.fordham.edu/halsall/source/aquinas3.html) and select the argument that you find most satisfactory and persuasive.

2. The experience of the absence of God, a difficulty of sensing his Presence, even a difficulty in believing in him and his promises, is not an unknown occurrence in the lives of people of faith. St. John of the Cross, one of the greatest writers on the spiritual life, called this experience of God's absence, "the dark night of the soul." Read selections from the letters of Mother Teresa of Calcutta found in the book *Come Be My Light,* by Mother Teresa and Brian Kolodiejchuk. Write a report that traces how Mother Teresa experienced a sense of the absence of God and what she came to see as the reason why God gave her this trial of an experience of darkness.

Creation and Nature of God

"The Creation"

James Weldon Johnson

We believe in one God, the Father, the almighty, maker of Heaven
and earth, of all that is, visible and invisible.

—Nicene Creed

Author Background

James Weldon Johnson (1871–1938) was a writer, poet, journalist, civil
rights activist, diplomat, and songwriter. He was the most prominent representative of the Harlem Renaissance, a term that is used to describe the
outpouring of artistic, literary, and musical genius that took place among
the African-American community in New York City during the 1920s and
30s. The following selection is Mr. Johnson's most famous poem. It is taken
from his book of poetry, *God's Trombones: Seven Negro Sermons in Verse*.

Before the Reading

The Nicene Creed states, "We believe in one God, the Father, the Almighty,
maker of Heaven and earth, of all that is, seen and unseen." In the following poem, James Weldon Johnson looks at the account of creation from
Genesis and transforms that account into a sermon by a preacher to his
congregation. The preacher uses language and imagery that relates the creation story to the lived experience of his listeners. He makes the Scriptures
"come alive." He shows them through his sermon that they, like the first
man, are made in the image and likeness of God and that they have been
created to know and love their Creator.

"The Creation"

And God stepped out on space,
And he looked around and said:

I'm lonely.
I'll make me a world.

And far as the eye of God could see
Darkness covered everything,
Blacker than a hundred midnights
Down in a cypress swamp.

Then God smiled,
And the light broke,
And the darkness rolled up on one side,
And the light stood shining on the other,
And God said: *That's good!*

Then God reached out and took the light in his hands,
And God rolled the light around in his hands
Until he made the sun;
And he set that sun a-blazing in the heavens.

And the light that was left from making the sun
God gathered it up in a shining ball
And flung it against the darkness,
Spangling the night with the moon and stars.
Then down between
The darkness and the light
He hurled the world;
And God said: *That's good!*

Then God himself stepped down.
And the sun was on his right hand,
And the moon was on his left;
The stars were clustered about his head,
And the earth was under his feet.
And God walked, and where he trod

His footsteps hollowed the valleys out
And bulged the mountains up.

Then he stopped and looked and saw
That the earth was hot and barren.
So God stepped over to the edge of the world
And he spat out the seven seas—
He batted his eyes, and the lightnings flashed—
He clapped his hands, and the thunders rolled—
And the waters above the earth came down,
The cooling waters came down.

Then the green grass sprouted,
And the little red flowers blossomed,
The pine tree pointed his finger to the sky,
And the oak spread out his arms,
The lakes cuddled down in the hollows of the ground,
And the rivers ran down to the sea;
And God smiled again,
And the rainbow appeared,
And curled itself around his shoulder.

Then God raised his arm and he waved his hand
Over the sea and over the land,
And he said: *Bring forth! Bring forth!*
And quicker than God could drop his hand,
Fishes and fowls
And beasts and birds
Swam the rivers and the seas,
Roamed the forests and the woods,
And split the air with their wings.
And God said: *That's good!*

Then God walked around,
And God looked around
On all that he had made.
He looked at his sun,
And he looked at his moon,
And he looked at his little stars;
He looked on his world
With all its living things,
And God said: *I'm lonely still.*

Then God sat down—
On the side of a hill where he could think;
By a deep, wide river he sat down;
With his head in his hands,
God thought and thought,
Till he thought: *I'll make me a man!*

Up from the bed of the river
God scooped the clay;
And by the bank of the river
He kneeled him down;
And there the great God Almighty
Who lit the sun and fixed it in the sky,
Who flung the stars to the most far corner of the night,
Who rounded the earth in the middle of his hand;
This great God,
Like a mammy bending over her baby,
Kneeled down in the dust
Toiling over a lump of clay
Till he shaped it in is his own image;

Then into it he blew the breath of life,
And man became a living soul.
Amen. Amen.

"The Burning Babe"
Robert Southwell

We believe in One Lord, Jesus Christ, the only Son of God. . . .
For us men and for our salvation he came down from Heaven:
by the power of the Holy Spirit he was born of the Virgin Mary
and became man. For our sake He was crucified under Pontius
Pilate, He suffered, died, and was buried. On the third day
He rose again in fulfillment of the Scriptures.

—Nicene Creed

Author Background
Robert Southwell (1561–1595) was born in England to a family of Catholic
aristocrats at a time when the English Reformation was at its most violent stage. He was educated in France where he joined the Society of Jesus
(Jesuits) and he was ordained a priest in Rome in 1584. Upon her acces-
sion to the throne, Queen Elizabeth I decreed that any English born subject who had become a priest was forbidden to stay in England on pain of
death. Southwell requested to be sent to England where he could minister in secret to the Catholic community. He served in England as a priest
for six years before he was captured. He was executed as a traitor in 1595,
being hanged and drawn and quartered. He was canonized by Pope Paul VI
in 1970.

Southwell wrote poems throughout his life, many of which were written
while he was in prison. None of his poems were published in his lifetime.
Once his poems had been collected and published, they were immediately
recognized as masterpieces of English poetry. The following selection, "The
Burning Babe," is his best-known poem.

Before the Reading
In "The Burning Babe," Robert Southwell reflects on the love of the Son of
God for fallen humanity. Through poetic imagery he combines the story
of Christ's birth found with accounts of his Passion and Death. His poem

succeeds in giving us an unforgettable portrait of Jesus Christ, true God and true man.

The Burning Babe

As I in hoary winter's night
    Stood shivering in the snow,
Surprised I was with sudden heat
    Which made my heart to glow;
And lifting up a fearful eye
    To view what fire was near,
A pretty babe all burning bright
    Did in the air appear;
Who, scorched with excessive heat,
    Such floods of tears did shed,
As though His floods should quench His flames,
    Which with His tears were bred:
'Alas!' quoth He, 'but newly born
    In fiery heats I fry,
Yet none approach to warm their hearts
    Or feel my fire but I!
'My faultless breast the furnace is;
    The fuel, wounding thorns;
Love is the fire, and sighs the smoke;
    The ashes, shames and scorns;
The fuel Justice layeth on,
    And Mercy blows the coals,
The metal in this furnace wrought
    Are men's defiled souls:
For which, as now on fire I am
    To work them to their good,
So will I melt into a bath,
    To wash them in my blood'

With this He vanish'd out of sight
  And swiftly shrunk away,
And straight I called unto mind
  That it was Christmas Day.

Reading for Comprehension

1. What image does Johnson use for the creation of the sun, moon, and stars?

2. What image does Johnson use for the creation of the seven seas and water?

3. What image does Johnson use for the creation of man?

4. Why does the Babe weep in Southwell's poem?

Reading for Understanding

1. Why does the preacher in "The Creation" find it necessary to use vernacular language rather than theological language to explain the creation account from the Book of Genesis to his congregation?

2. How does Southwell's poem represent Christ as true God and true man?

3. God is a pure Spirit; however, Scripture usually refers to him as masculine. How is the feminine nature of God represented in the poem by Johnson?

Activity

After you read the poem by Johnson, read the first creation account in the book of Genesis (Gn 1–2). Also, look carefully at the portrayal of the creation of Adam in Michelangelo's great fresco in the Sistine Chapel. Write an essay that explains how the poem and the painting give us an enlarged understanding of the account found in Scripture.

Creation and Nature of God

"Parker's Back"

Flannery O'Connor

In the beginning was the Word, and the Word was with God, and the Word was God.

—John 1:1

Author Background

Flannery O'Connor (1925–1964) is regarded as the greatest American Catholic writer. Her voice is unique and is founded on a singular and compelling religious faith. A collection of her letters edited by Sally Fitzgerald under the title, *The Habit of Being*, shows the depth of her religious knowledge and illustrates how fundamental Catholic theology and spirituality were to her writing.

Despite the high admiration for her art, to include her writing in this text is controversial. This is because the focus of her writings is on humankind's fall from grace and the very tangible effects of Original Sin, with its resulting estrangement of men and women from their Creator. Her stories are frontal assaults on our complacency in the face of sin and evil.

In her depiction of racism, she shows evil and sin in all its ugliness. During her lifetime, O'Connor was criticized for the graphic and violent description of sin in her stories. Her response was that, in a world that was deaf to spiritual realities, one had to scream in order to be heard.

Mary Flannery O'Connor was born and raised in Georgia, and most of her stories and novels are set in the Deep South in a period when racial prejudice was deep and prevalent. Her use of racial and class epithets by characters in her stories, such as "nigger" and "white trash," grate on our modern ears. We want to turn away from this ignorance and moral ugliness. O'Connor, however, was not one to write pretty stories or to hide unpleasant truths from our eyes. Many religious tales stress the love and peace that can be found from one's relationship to God. They are "feel good" stories. Flannery O'Connor's stories, on the other hand, confront us with the reality of sin and evil in our lives. They are "wake-up" stories; instead of giving us comfort, they hit us like a slap in the face.

Before the Reading

God is pure Spirit, eternal, infinite, and almighty; "He dwells in unapproachable light." The One God is a Trinity of Persons: Father, Son, and Holy Spirit. It was because of God's loving kindness that he chose to reveal his name to Moses on Mount Sinai and to reveal himself perfectly in his only begotten Son, Jesus Christ. Jesus is "the image of the invisible God." Thus, in the Catholic tradition God is at the same time a pure Spirit and a Person of flesh and blood revealed in the man, Jesus Christ. God is at the same time "transcendent," above and beyond nature, and "immanent," found in the very substance of the material world.

In a letter to a friend, Flannery O'Connor explained that this story was in essence the working out of the implications of a heresy. A heresy is an erroneous idea about the nature of God or other teachings of the Church. She wrote to her friend who had inquired about the nature of the heresy, "Sarah Ruth (Parker's wife) was the heretic (because she held) the notion that you can worship in pure spirit." Catholics believe in a transcendent God who is infinitely above them, but we also believe that Jesus Christ in becoming man has truly become our brother and has made known to us the face of the Father.

"Parker's Back"

Parker's wife was sitting on the front porch floor, snapping beans. Parker was sitting on the step, some distance away, watching her sullenly. She was plain, plain. The skin on her face was thin and drawn as tight as the skin on an onion and her eyes were gray and sharp like the points of two ice picks. Parker understood why he had married her—he couldn't have got her any other way—but he couldn't understand why he stayed with her now. She was pregnant and pregnant women were not his favorite kind. Nevertheless, he stayed as if she had him conjured. He was puzzled and ashamed of himself.

The house they rented sat alone save for a single tall pecan tree on a high embankment overlooking a highway. At intervals a car would shoot past below and his wife's eyes would swerve suspiciously after the sound of it and then come back to rest on the newspaper full of beans in her lap. One of the things she did not approve of was automobiles. In addition to her other bad qualities, she was forever sniffing up sin. She did not smoke or dip, drink whiskey, use bad language or paint her face, and God knew some paint would have improved it, Parker thought. Her being against color, it was the more remarkable she had married him. Sometimes he supposed that she had married him because she meant to save him. At other times he had a suspicion that she actually liked everything she said she didn't. He could account for her one way or another; it was himself he could not understand.

She turned her head in his direction and said, "It's no reason you can't work for a man. It don't have to be a woman."

"Aw shut your mouth for a change," Parker muttered.

If he had been certain she was jealous of the woman he worked for he would have been pleased but more likely she was concerned with the sin that would result if he and the woman took a liking to each other. He had told her that the woman was a hefty young blonde; in fact she was nearly seventy years old and too dried up to have an interest in anything except getting as much work out of him as she could. Not that an old woman didn't sometimes get an interest in a young man, particularly if he was as attractive as Parker felt he was, but this old woman looked at him the same way she looked at her old tractor—as if she had to put up with it because it was all she had. The tractor had broken down the second day Parker was on it and she had set him at once to cutting bushes, saying out of the side of her mouth to the nigger, "Everything he touches, he breaks." She also asked him to wear his shirt when he worked; Parker had removed it even though the day was not sultry; he put it back on reluctantly.

This ugly woman Parker married was his first wife. He had had other women but he had planned never to get himself tied up legally. He had first seen her one morning when his truck broke down on the highway. He had managed to pull it off the road into a neatly swept yard on which sat a peeling two-room house. He got out and opened the hood of the truck and began to study the motor. Parker had an extra sense that told him when there was a woman nearby watching him. After he had leaned over the motor a few minutes, his neck began to prickle. He cast his eye over the empty yard and porch of the house. A woman he could not see was either nearby beyond a clump of honeysuckle or in the house, watching him out the window.

Suddenly Parker began to jump up and down and fling his hand about as if he had mashed it in the machinery. He doubled over and held his hand close to his chest. "God dammit!" he hollered, "Jesus Christ in hell! Jesus God Almighty damm! God dammit to hell!" he went on, flinging out the same few oaths over and over as loud as he could.

Without warning a terrible bristly claw slammed the side of his face and he fell backwards on the hood of the truck. "You don't talk no filth here!" a voice close to him shrilled.

Parker's vision was so blurred that for an instant he thought he had been attacked by some creature from above, a giant hawk-eyed angel wielding a hoary weapon. As his sight cleared, he saw before him a tall raw-boned girl with a broom.

"I hurt my hand," he said. "I HURT my hand." He was so incensed that he forgot that he hadn't hurt his hand. "My hand may be broke," he growled although his voice was still unsteady.

"Lemme see it," the girl demanded.

Parker stuck out his hand and she came closer and looked at it. There was no mark on the palm and she took the hand and turned it over. Her own hand was dry and hot and rough and Parker felt himself jolted back to life by her touch. He looked more closely at her. I don't want nothing to do with this one, he thought.

The girl's sharp eyes peered at the back of the stubby reddish hand she held. There emblazoned in red and blue was a tattooed eagle perched on a cannon. Parker's sleeve was rolled to the elbow. Above the eagle a serpent was coiled about a shield and in the spaces between the eagle and the serpent there were hearts, some with arrows through them. Above the serpent there was a spread hand of cards. Every space on the skin of Parker's arm, from wrist to elbow, was covered in some loud design. The girl gazed at this with an almost stupefied smile of shock, as if she had accidentally grasped a poisonous snake; she dropped the hand.

"I got most of my other ones in foreign parts," Parker said. "These here I mostly got in the United States. I got my first one when I was only fifteen year old."

"Don't tell me," the girl said, "I don't like it. I ain't got any use for it."

"You ought to see the ones you can't see," Parker said and winked.

Two circles of red appeared like apples on the girl's cheeks and softened her appearance. Parker was intrigued. He did not for a minute think that she didn't like the tattoos. He had never yet met a woman who was not attracted to them.

Parker was fourteen when he saw a man in a fair, tattooed from head to foot. Except for his loins which were girded with a panther hide, the man's skin was patterned in what seemed from Parker's distance—he was near the back of the tent, standing on a bench—a single intricate design of brilliant color. The man, who was small and sturdy, moved about on the platform, flexing his muscles so that the arabesque of men and beasts and flowers on his skin appeared to have a subtle motion of its own. Parker was filled with emotion, lifted up as some people are when the flag passes. He was a boy whose mouth habitually hung open. He was heavy and earnest, as ordinary as a loaf of bread. When the show was over, he had remained standing on the bench, staring where the tattooed man had been, until the tent was almost empty.

63

Parker had never before felt the least motion of wonder in himself. Until he saw the man at the fair, it did not enter his head that there was anything out of the ordinary about the fact that he existed. Even then it did not enter his head, but a peculiar unease settled in him. It was as if a blind boy had been turned so gently in a different direction that he did not know his destination had been changed.

He had his first tattoo some time after—the eagle perched on the cannon. It was done by a local artist. It hurt very little, just enough to make it appear to Parker to be worth doing. This was peculiar too for before he had thought that only what did not hurt was worth doing. The next year he quit school because he was sixteen and could. He went to the trade school for a while, then he quit the trade school and worked for six months in a garage. The only reason he worked at all was to pay for more tattoos. His mother worked in a laundry and could support him, but she would not pay for any tattoo except her name on a heart, which he had put on, grumbling. However, her name was Betty Jean and nobody had to know it was his mother. He found out that the tattoos were attractive to the kind of girls he liked but who had never liked him before. He began to drink beer and get in fights. His mother wept over what was becoming of him. One night she dragged him off to a revival with her, not telling him where they were going. When he saw the big lighted church, he jerked out of her grasp and ran. The next day he lied about his age and joined the Navy.

Parker was large for the tight sailor's pants but the silly white cap, sitting low on his forehead, made his face by contrast look thoughtful and almost intense. After a month or two in the Navy, his mouth ceased to hang open. His features hardened into the features of a man. He stayed in the Navy five years and seemed a natural part of the gray mechanical ship, except for his eyes, which were the same pale slate-color as the ocean and reflected the immense spaces around him as if they were a microcosm of the mysterious sea. In port Parker wandered about comparing the run-down places he was in to Birmingham, Alabama. Everywhere he went he picked up more tattoos.

He had stopped having lifeless ones like anchors and crossed rifles. He had a tiger and a panther on each shoulder, a cobra coiled about a torch on his chest, hawks on his thighs, Elizabeth II and Philip over where his stomach and liver were respectively. He did not care much what the subject was so long as it was colorful; on his abdomen he had a few obscenities but only because that seemed the proper place for them. Parker would be satisfied with each tattoo about a month, then something about it that had attracted him would wear off. Whenever a decent-sized mirror was available, he would get in front of it and study his overall look. The effect was not of one intricate arabesque of colors but of something haphazard and botched. A huge dissatisfaction would come over him and he would go off and find another tattooist and have another space filled up. The front of Parker was almost completely covered but there were no tattoos on his back. He had no desire for one anywhere he could not readily see it himself. As the space on the front of him for tattoos decreased, his dissatisfaction grew and became general.

After one of his furloughs, he didn't go back to the Navy but remained away without official leave, drunk, in a rooming house in a city he did not know. His dissatisfaction, from being chronic and latent, had suddenly become acute and raged in him. It was as if the panther and the lion and the serpents and the eagles and the hawks had penetrated his skin and lived inside him in a raging warfare. The Navy caught up with him, put him in the brig for nine months and then gave him a dishonorable discharge.

After that Parker decided that country air was the only kind fit to breathe. He rented the shack on the embankment and bought the old truck and took various jobs which he kept as long as it suited him. At the time he met his future wife, he was buying apples by the bushel and selling them for the same price by the pound to isolated homesteaders on back country roads.

65

"All that there," the woman said, pointing to his arm, "is no better than what a fool Indian would do. It's a heap of vanity." She seemed to have found the word she wanted. "Vanity of vanities," she said.

Well what the hell do I care what she thinks of it? Parker asked himself, but he was plainly bewildered. "I reckon you like one of these better than another anyway," he said, dallying until he thought of something that would impress her. He thrust the arm back at her. "Which you like best?"

"None of them," she said, "but the chicken is not as bad as the rest."

"What chicken?" Parker almost yelled.

She pointed to the eagle.

"That's an eagle," Parker said. "What fool would waste their time having a chicken put on themself?"

"What fool would have any of it?" the girl said and turned away. She went slowly back to the house and left him there to get going. Parker remained for almost five minutes, looking agape at the dark door she had entered.

The next day he returned with a bushel of apples. He was not one to be outdone by anything that looked like her. He liked women with meat on them, so you didn't feel their muscles, much less their old bones. When he arrived, she was sitting on the top step and the yard was full of children, all as thin and poor as herself; Parker remembered it was Saturday. He hated to be making up to a woman when there were children around, but it was fortunate he had brought the bushel of apples off the truck. As the children approached him to see what he carried, he gave each child an apple and told it to get lost; in that way he cleared out the whole crowd.

The girl did nothing to acknowledge his presence. He might have been a stray pig or goat that had wandered into the yard and she too tired to take up the broom and send it off. He set the bushel of apples down next to her on the step. He sat down on a lower step.

"Hep yourself," he said, nodding at the basket; then he lapsed into silence.

She took an apple quickly as if the basket might disappear if she didn't make haste. Hungry people made Parker nervous. He had always had plenty to eat himself. He grew very uncomfortable. He reasoned he had nothing to say so why should he say it? He could not think now why he had come or why he didn't go before he wasted another bushel of apples on the crowd of children. He supposed they were her brothers and sisters.

She chewed the apple slowly but with a kind of relish of concentration, bent slightly but looking out ahead. The view from the porch stretched off across a long incline studded with ironweed and across the highway to a vast vista of hills and one small mountain. Long views depressed Parker. You look out into space like that and you begin to feel as if someone were after you, the Navy or the government or religion.

"Who them children belong to, you?" he said at length.

"I ain't married yet," she said. "They belong to momma." She said it as if it were only a matter of time before she would be married.

Who in God's name would marry her? Parker thought.

A large barefooted woman with a wide gap-toothed face appeared in the door behind Parker. She had apparently been there for several minutes.

"Good evening," Parker said.

The woman crossed the porch and picked up what was left of the bushel of apples. "We thank you," she said and returned with it into the house.

"That your old woman?" Parker muttered.

The girl nodded. Parker knew a lot of sharp things he could have said like "You got my sympathy," but he was gloomily silent. He just sat there, looking at the view. He thought he must be coming down with something.

"If I pick up some peaches tomorrow I'll bring you some," he said.

"I'll be much obliged to you," the girl said.

Parker had no intention of taking any basket of peaches back there but the next day he found himself doing it. He and the girl had almost nothing to say to each other. One thing he did say was, "I ain't got any tattoo on my back."

"What you got on it?" the girl said.

"My shirt," Parker said. "Haw."

"Haw, haw," the girl said politely.

Parker thought he was losing his mind. He could not believe for a minute that he was attracted to a woman like this. She showed not the least interest in anything but what he brought until he appeared the third time with two cantaloupes. "What's your name?" she asked.

"O. E. Parker," he said.

"What does the O. E. stand for?"

"You can just call me O. E.," Parker said. "Or Parker. Don't nobody call me by my name."

"What's it stand for?" she persisted.

"Never mind," Parker said. "What's yours?"

"I'll tell you when you tell me what them letters are the short of," she said. There was just a hint of flirtatiousness in her tone and it went rapidly to Parker's head. He had never revealed the name to any man or woman, only to the files of the Navy and the government, and it was on his baptismal record which he got at the age of a month; his mother was a Methodist. When the name leaked out of the Navy files, Parker narrowly missed killing the man who used it.

"You'll go blab it around," he said.

"I'll swear I'll never tell nobody," she said. "On God's holy word I swear it."

Parker sat for a few minutes in silence. Then he reached for the girl's neck, drew her ear close to his mouth and revealed the name in low voice.

"Obadiah," she whispered. Her face slowly brightened as if the name came as a sign to her. "Obadiah," she said.

The name still stank in Parker's estimation.

"Obadiah Elihue," she said in a reverent voice.

"If you call me that aloud, I'll bust your head open," Parker said. "What's yours?"

"Sarah Ruth Gates," she said.

"Glad to meet you, Sarah Ruth," Parker said.

Sarah Ruth's father was a Straight Gospel preacher but he was away, spreading it in Florida. Her mother did not seem to mind his attention to the girl so long as he brought a basket of something with him when he came. As for Sarah Ruth herself, it was plain to Parker after he had visited three times that she was crazy about him. She liked him even though she insisted that pictures on the skin were vanity of vanities and even after hearing him curse, and even after she had asked him if he was saved and he had replied that he didn't see it was anything in particular to save him from. After that, inspired, Parker had said, "I'd be saved enough if you was to kiss me."

She scowled. "That ain't being saved," she said.

Not long after that she agreed to take a ride in his truck. Parker parked it on a deserted road and suggested to her that they lie down together in the back of it.

"Not until after we're married," she said—just like that.

"Oh that ain't necessary," Parker said and as he reached for her, she thrust him away with such force that the door of the truck came off and he found himself flat on his back on the ground. He made up his mind then and there to have nothing further to do with her.

They were married in the County Ordinary's office because Sarah Ruth thought churches were idolatrous. Parker had no opinion about that one way or the other. The Ordinary's office was lined with cardboard file boxes and record books with dusty yellow slips of paper hanging on out of them. The Ordinary was an old woman with red hair who had held office for forty years and looked as dusty as her books. She married them from behind the iron-grill of a stand-up desk and when she finished, she said with a flourish, "Three dollars and fifty cents and till death do you part!" and yanked some forms out of a machine.

Marriage did not change Sarah Ruth a jot and it made Parker gloomier than ever. Every morning he decided he had had enough and would not return that night; every night he returned. Whenever Parker couldn't stand the way he felt, he would have another tattoo, but the only surface left on him now was his back. To see a tattoo on his own back he would have to get two mirrors and stand between them in just the correct position and this seemed to Parker a good way to make an idiot of himself. Sarah Ruth who, if she had had better sense, could have enjoyed a tattoo on his back, would not even look at the ones he had elsewhere. When he attempted to point out especial details of them, she would shut her eyes tight and turn her back as well. Except in total darkness, she preferred Parker dressed and with his sleeves rolled down.

"At the judgment seat of God, Jesus is going to say to you, 'What you been doing all your life besides have pictures drawn all over you?'" she said.

"You don't fool me none," Parker said, "you're just afraid that hefty girl I work for'll like me so much she'll say, 'Come on, Mr. Parker, let's you and me . . .'"

"You're tempting sin," she said, "and at the judgment seat of God you'll have to answer for that too. You ought to go back to selling the fruits of the earth."

Parker did nothing much when he was at home but listen to what the judgment seat of God would be like for him if he didn't change his ways. When he could, he broke in with tales of the hefty girl he worked for. "'Mr. Parker,'" he said she said, 'I hired you for your brains.'" (She had added, "So why don't you use them?")

"And you should have seen her face the first time she saw me without my shirt," he said. "'Mr. Parker,' she said, 'you're a walking panner-rammer!'" This had, in fact, been her remark but it had been delivered out of one side of her mouth.

Dissatisfaction began to grow so great in Parker that there was no containing it outside of a tattoo. It had to be his back. There was no help for it. A dim half-formed inspiration began to work in his mind.

He visualized having a tattoo put there that Sarah Ruth would not be able to resist—a religious subject. He thought of an open book with "Holy Bible" tattooed under it and an actual verse printed on the page. This seemed just the thing for a while; then he began to hear her say, "Ain't I already got a real Bible? What you think I want to read the same verse over and over for when I can read it all?" He needed something better even than the Bible! He thought about it so much that he began to lose sleep. He was already losing flesh—Sarah Ruth just threw food in the pot and let it boil. Not knowing for certain why he continued to stay with a woman who was both ugly and pregnant and no cook made him generally nervous and irritable, and he developed a little tic in the side of his face.

Once or twice he found himself turning around abruptly as if someone were trailing him. He had had a granddaddy who had ended in the state mental hospital, although not until he was seventy-five, but as urgent as it might be for him to get a tattoo, it was just as urgent that he get exactly the right one to bring Sarah Ruth to heel. As he continued to worry over it, his eyes took on a hollow preoccupied expression. The old woman he worked for told him that if he couldn't keep his mind on what he was doing, she knew where she could find a fourteen-year-old colored boy who could. Parker was too preoccupied even to be offended. At any time previous, he would have left her then and there, saying dryly, "Well, you go ahead on and get him then."

Two or three mornings later he was baling hay with the old woman's sorry baler and her broken down tractor in a large field, cleared save for one enormous old tree standing in the middle of it. The old woman was the kind who would not cut down a large old tree because it was a large old tree. She had pointed it out to Parker as if he didn't have eyes and told him to be careful not to hit it as the machine picked up hay near it. Parker began at the outside of the field and made circles inward toward it. He had to get off the tractor every now and then and untangle the baling cord or kick a rock out of the way. The old woman had told him to carry the rocks to the edge of the field, which he did when she was there watching. When he thought he could make it, he ran over them. As he circled the field his mind was on a suitable design for his back. The sun, the size of a golf ball, began to switch regularly from in front to behind him, but he appeared to see it both places as if he had eyes in the back of his head. All at once he saw the tree reaching out to grasp him. A ferocious thud propelled him into the air, and he heard himself yelling in an unbelievably loud voice, "GOD ABOVE!"

He landed on his back while the tractor crashed upside down into the tree and burst into flame. The first thing Parker saw were his shoes, quickly being eaten by the fire; one was caught under the tractor, the other was some distance away, burning by itself. He was not in them. He could feel the hot breath of the burning tree on his face. He scrambled backwards, still sitting, his eyes cavernous, and if he had known how to cross himself he would have done it.

His truck was on a dirt road at the edge of the field. He moved toward it, still sitting, still backwards, but faster and faster; halfway to it he got up and began a kind of forward-bent run from which he collapsed on his knees twice. His legs felt like two old rusted rain gutters. He reached the truck finally and took off in it, zigzagging up the road. He drove past his house on the embankment and straight for the city, fifty miles distant.

Parker did not allow himself to think on the way to the city. He only knew that there had been a great change in his life, a leap forward into a worse unknown, and that there was nothing he could do about it. It was for all intents accomplished.

The artist had two large cluttered rooms over a chiropodist's office on a back street. Parker, still barefooted, burst silently in on him at a little after three in the afternoon. The artist, who was about Parker's own age—twenty-eight—but thin and bald, was behind a small drawing table, tracing a design in green ink. He looked up with an annoyed glance and did not seem to recognize Parker in the hollow-eyed creature before him.

"Let me see the book you got with all the pictures of God in it," Parker said breathlessly. "The religious one."

The artist continued to look at him with his intellectual, superior stare. "I don't put tattoos on drunks," he said.

"You know me!" Parker cried indignantly. "I'm O. E. Parker! You done work for me before and I always paid!"

The artist looked at him another moment as if he were not altogether sure. "You've fallen off some," he said. "You must have been in jail."

"Married," Parker said.

"Oh," said the artist. With the aid of mirrors the artist had tattooed on the top of his head a miniature owl, perfect in every detail. It was about the size of a half-dollar and served him as a show piece. There were cheaper artists in town but Parker had never wanted anything but the best. The artist went over to a cabinet at the back of the room and began to look over some art books. "Who are you interested in?" he said, "saints, angels, Christs or what?"

"God," Parker said.

"Father, Son or Spirit?"

"Just God," Parker said impatiently. "Christ. I don't care. Just so it's God."

The artist returned with a book. He moved some papers off another table and put the book down on it and told Parker to sit down and see what he liked. "The up-to-date ones are in the back," he said.

Parker sat down with the book and wet his thumb. He began to go through it, beginning at the back where the up-to-date pictures were. Some of them he recognized—The Good Shepherd, Forbid Them Not, The Smiling Jesus, Jesus the Physician's Friend, but he kept turning rapidly backwards and the pictures became less and less reassuring. One showed a gaunt green dead face streaked with blood. One was yellow with sagging purple eyes. Parker's heart began to beat faster and faster until it appeared to be roaring inside him like a great generator. He flipped the pages quickly, feeling that when he reached the one ordained, a sign would come. He continued to flip through until he had almost reached the front of the book. On one of the pages a pair of eyes glanced at him swiftly. Parker sped on, then stopped. His heart too appeared to cut off; there was absolute silence. It said as plainly as if silence were a language itself, "go back."

Parker returned to the picture—the haloed head of a flat stern Byzantine Christ with all-demanding eyes. He sat there trembling; his heart began slowly to beat again as if it were being brought to life by a subtle power.

"You found what you want?" the artist asked.

Parker's throat was too dry to speak. He got up and thrust the book at the artist, opened at the picture.

"That'll cost you plenty," the artist said. "You don't want all those little blocks though, just the outline and some better features."

"Just like it is," Parker said, "just like it is or nothing."

"It's your funeral," the artist said, "but I don't do that kind of work for nothing."

"How much?" Parker asked.

"It'll take maybe two days work."

"How much?" Parker said.

"On time or cash?" the artist asked. Parker's other jobs had been on time, but he had paid.

"Ten down and ten for every day it takes," the artist said.

Parker drew ten dollar bills out of his wallet; he had three left in.

"You come back in the morning," the artist said, putting the money in his own pocket. "First I'll have to trace that out of the book."

"No no!" Parker said. "Trace it now or gimme my money back," and his eyes blared as if he were ready for a fight.

The artist agreed. Any one stupid enough to want a Christ on his back, he reasoned, would be just as likely as not to change his mind the next minute, but once the work was begun he could hardly do so.

While he worked on the tracing, he told Parker to go wash his back at the sink with the special soap he used there. Parker did it and returned to pace back and forth across the room, nervously flexing his shoulders. He wanted to go look at the picture again but at the same time he did not want to. The artist got up finally and had Parker lie down on the table. He swabbed his back with ethyl chloride and then began to outline the head on it with his iodine pencil. Another hour passed before he took up his electric instrument. Parker felt no particular pain. In Japan he had had a tattoo of the Buddha done on his upper arm with ivory needles; in Burma, a little brown root of a man had made a peacock on each of his knees using thin pointed sticks, two feet long; amateurs had worked on him with pins and soot. Parker was usually so relaxed and easy under the hand of the artist that he often went to sleep, but this time he remained awake, every muscle taut.

At midnight the artist said he was ready to quit. He propped one mirror, four feet square, on a table by the wall and took a smaller mirror off the lavatory wall and put it in Parker's hands. Parker stood with his back to the one on the table and moved the other until he saw a flashing burst of color reflected from his back. It was almost completely covered with little red and blue and ivory and saffron squares; from them he made out the lineaments of the face—a mouth, the beginning of heavy brows, a straight nose, but the face was empty; the eyes had not yet been put in. The impression for the moment was almost as if the artist had tricked him and done the Physician's Friend.

"It don't have eyes," Parker cried out.

"That'll come," the artist said, "in due time. We have another day to go on it yet."

Parker spent the night on a cot at the Haven of Light Christian Mission. He found these the best places to stay in the city because they were free and included a meal of sorts. He got the last available cot and because he was still barefooted, he accepted a pair of secondhand shoes which, in his confusion, he put on to go to bed; he was still shocked from all that had happened to him. All night he lay awake in the long dormitory of cots with lumpy figures on them. The only light was from a phosphorescent cross glowing at the end of the room. The tree reached out to grasp him again, then burst into flame; the shoe burned quietly by itself; the eyes in the book said to him distinctly GO BACK and at the same time did not utter a sound. He wished that he were not in this city, not in this Haven of Light Mission, not in a bed by himself. He longed miserably for Sarah Ruth. Her sharp tongue and icepick eyes were the only comfort he could bring to mind. He decided he was losing it. Her eyes appeared soft and dilatory compared with the eyes in the book, for even though he could not summon up the exact look of those eyes, he could still feel their penetration. He felt as though, under their gaze, he was as transparent as the wing of a fly.

The tattooist had told him not to come until ten in the morning, but when he arrived at that hour, Parker was sitting in the dark hallway on the floor, waiting for him. He had decided upon getting up that, once the tattoo was on him, he would not look at it, that all his sensations of the day and night before were those of a crazy man and that he would return to doing things according to his own sound judgment.

The artist began where he left off. "One thing I want to know," he said presently as he worked over Parker's back, "why do you want this on you? Have you gone and got religion? Are you saved?" he asked in a mocking voice.

Parker's throat felt salty and dry. "Naw," he said, "I ain't got no use for none of that. A man can't save his self from whatever it is he don't deserve none of my sympathy." These words seemed to leave his mouth like wraiths and to evaporate at once as if he had never uttered them.

"Then why . . ."

"I married this woman that's saved," Parker said. "I never should have done it. I ought to leave her. She's done gone and got pregnant."

"That's too bad," the artist said. "Then it's her making you have this tattoo."

"Naw," Parker said, "she don't know nothing about it. It's a surprise for her."

"You think she'll like it and lay off you a while?"

"She can't hep herself," Parker said. "She can't say she don't like the looks of God." He decided he had told the artist enough of his business. Artists were all right in their place but he didn't like them poking their noses into the affairs of regular people. "I didn't get no sleep last night," he said. "I think I'll get some now."

That closed the mouth of the artist but it did not bring him any sleep. He lay there, imagining how Sarah Ruth would be struck speechless by the face on his back and every now and then this would be interrupted by a vision of the tree of fire and his empty shoe burning beneath it.

The artist worked steadily until nearly four o'clock, not stopping to have lunch, hardly pausing with the electric instrument except to wipe the dripping dye off Parker's back as he went along. Finally he finished. "You can get up and look at it now," he said.

Parker sat up but he remained on the edge of the table.

The artist was pleased with his work and wanted Parker to look at it at once. Instead Parker continued to sit on the edge of the table, bent forward slightly but with a vacant look. "What ails you?" the artist said. "Go look at it."

"Ain't nothing ail me," Parker said in a sudden belligerent voice. "That tattoo ain't going nowhere. It'll be there when I get there." He reached for his shirt and began gingerly to put it on.

The artist took him roughly by the arm and propelled him between the two mirrors. "Now *look,*" he said, angry at having his work ignored.

Parker looked, turned white and moved away. The eyes in the reflected face continued to look at him—still, straight, all-demanding, enclosed in silence.

"It was your idea, remember," the artist said. "I would have advised something else."

Parker said nothing. He put on his shirt and went out the door while the artist shouted, "I'll expect all of my money!"

Parker headed toward a package shop on the corner. He bought a pint of whiskey and took it into a nearby alley and drank it all in five minutes. Then he moved on to a pool hall nearby which he frequented when he came to the city. It was a well-lighted barn-like place with a bar up one side and gambling machines on the other and pool tables in the back. As soon as Parker entered, a large man in a red and black checkered shirt hailed him by slapping him on the back and yelling, "Yeyyyyyy boy! O. E. Parker!"

Parker was not yet ready to be struck on the back. "Lay off," he said, "I got a fresh tattoo there."

"What you got this time?" the man asked and then yelled to a few at the machines. "O. E.'s got him another tattoo."

"Nothing special this time," Parker said and slunk over to a machine that was not being used.

"Come on," the big man said, "let's have a look at O. E.'s tattoo," and while Parker squirmed in their hands, they pulled up his shirt. Parker felt all the hands drop away instantly and his shirt fell again like a veil over the face. There was a silence in the pool room which seemed to Parker to grow from the circle around him until it extended to the foundations under the building and upward through the beams in the roof.

Finally some one said, "Christ!" Then they all broke into noise at once. Parker turned around, an uncertain grin on his face.

"Leave it to O. E.!" the man in the checkered shirt said. "That boy's a real card!"

"Maybe he's gone and got religion," some one yelled.

"Not on your life," Parker said.

"O. E.'s got religion and is witnessing for Jesus, ain't you, O. E.?" a little man with a piece of cigar in his mouth said wryly. "An o-riginal way to do it if I ever saw one."

"Leave it to Parker to think of a new one!" the fat man said.

"Yyeeeeeeyyyyyyy boy!" someone yelled and they all began to whistle and curse in compliment until Parker said, "Aaa shut up."

"What'd you do it for?" somebody asked.

"For laughs," Parker said. "What's it to you?"

"Why ain't you laughing then?" somebody yelled. Parker lunged into the midst of them and like a whirlwind on a summer's day there began a fight that raged amid overturned tables and swinging fists until two of them grabbed him and ran to the door with him and threw him out. Then a calm descended on the pool hall as nerve shattering as if the long barnlike room were the ship from which Jonah had been cast into the sea.

Parker sat for a long time on the ground in the alley behind the pool hall, examining his soul. He saw it as a spider web of facts and lies that was not at all important to him but which appeared to be necessary in spite of his opinion. The eyes that were now forever on his back were eyes to be obeyed. He was as certain of it as he had ever been of anything. Throughout his life, grumbling and some-times cursing, often afraid, once in rapture, Parker had obeyed what-ever instinct of this kind had come to him—in rapture when his spirit had lifted at the sight of the tattooed man at the fair, afraid when he had joined the Navy, grumbling when he had married Sarah Ruth.

The thought of her brought him slowly to his feet. She would know what he had to do. She would clear up the rest of it, and she would at least be pleased. It seemed to him that, all along, that was what he wanted, to please her. His truck was still parked in front of the building where the artist had his place, but it was not far away. He got in it and drove out of the city and into the country night. His head was almost clear of liquor and he observed that his dissatisfac-tion was gone, but he felt not quite like himself. It was as if he were himself but a stranger to himself, driving into a new country though everything he saw was familiar to him, even at night.

He arrived finally at the house on the embankment, pulled the truck under the pecan tree and got out. He made as much noise as possible to assert that he was still in charge here, that his leaving her for a night without word meant nothing except it was the way he did things. He slammed the car door, stamped up the two steps and across the porch and rattled the door knob. It did not respond to his touch. "Sarah Ruth!" he yelled, "let me in."

There was no lock on the door and she had evidently placed the back of a chair against the knob. He began to beat on the door and rattle the knob at the same time.

He heard the bed springs creak and bent down and put his head to the keyhole, but it was stopped up with paper. "Let me in!" he hollered, bamming on the door again. "What you got me locked out for?"

A sharp voice close to the door said, "Who's there?"

"Me," Parker said, "O. E."

He waited a moment.

"Me," he said impatiently, "O. E."

Still no sound from inside.

He tried once more. "O. E.," he said, bamming the door two or three more times. "O. E. Parker. You know me."

There was a silence. Then the voice said slowly, "I don't know no O. E."

"Quit fooling," Parker pleaded. "You ain't got any business doing me this way. It's me, old O. E., I'm back. You ain't afraid of me."

"Who's there?" the same unfeeling voice said.

Parker turned his head as if he expected someone behind him to give him the answer. The sky had lightened slightly and there were two or three streaks of yellow floating above the horizon. Then as he stood there, a tree of light burst over the skyline.

Parker fell back against the door as if he had been pinned there by a lance.

"Who's there?" the voice from inside said and there was a quality about it now that seemed final. The knob rattled and the voice said peremptorily, "Who's there, I ast you?"

Parker bent down and put his mouth near the stuffed keyhole. "Obadiah," he whispered and all at once he felt the light pouring through him, turning his spider web soul into a perfect arabesque of colors, a garden of trees and birds and beasts.

"Obadiah Elihue!" he whispered.

The door opened and he stumbled in. Sarah Ruth loomed there, hands on her hips. She began at once, "That was no hefty blonde woman you was working for and you'll have to pay her every penny on her tractor you busted up. She don't keep insurance on it. She came here and her and me had us a long talk and I . . ."

Trembling, Parker set about lighting the kerosene lamp.

"What's the matter with you, wasting that kerosene this near daylight?" she demanded. "I ain't got to look at you."

A yellow glow enveloped them. Parker put the match down and began to unbutton his shirt.

"And you ain't going to have none of me this near morning," she said.

"Shut your mouth," he said quietly. "Look at this and then I don't want to hear no more out of you." He removed the shirt and turned his back to her.

"Another picture," Sarah Ruth growled. "I might have known you was off after putting some more trash on yourself."

Parker's knees went hollow under him. He wheeled around and cried, "Look at it! Don't just say that! *Look* at it!"

"I done looked," she said.

"Don't you know who it is?" he cried in anguish.

"No, who is it?" Sarah Ruth said. "It ain't anybody I know."

"It's him," Parker said.

"Him who?"

"God!" Parker cried.

"God? God don't look like that!"

"What do you know how he looks?" Parker moaned. "You ain't seen him."

"He don't *look*," Sarah Ruth said. "He's a spirit. No man shall see his face."

"Aw listen," Parker groaned, "this is just a picture of him."

"Idolatry!" Sarah Ruth screamed. "Idolatry! Enflaming yourself, with idols under every green tree! I can put up with lies and vanity but I don't want no idolater in this house!" and she grabbed up the broom and began to thrash him across the shoulders with it.

Parker was too stunned to resist. He sat there and let her beat him until she had nearly knocked him senseless and large welts had formed on the face of the tattooed Christ. Then he staggered up and made for the door.

She stamped the broom two or three times on the floor and went to the window and shook it out to get the taint of him off it. Still gripping it, she looked toward the pecan tree and her eyes hardened still more. There he was—who called himself Obadiah Elihue—leaning against the tree, crying like a baby.

Reading for Comprehension

1. How does the description of Parker's wife in the first two paragraphs of the story give us an insight into her psychology?
2. What does Parker's wife do to him after he begins swearing when he hurts his hand?
3. What was the first tattoo that Parker got?
4. What happens to Parker when driving the tractor?
5. Describe the tattoo that Parker chooses to have imprinted on his back.
6. What does Parker's wife do when she sees the tattoo on his back?

Reading for Understanding

1. What do the initials O. E. in Parker's name stand for? What is their significance for the story?
2. Identify the imagery in the story that parallels the account of God's revelation to Moses found in the Book of Exodus.
3. How do the welts on Parker's back demonstrate O'Connor's judgment that the wife's view of God is deficient? What theological belief about the nature of God is being expressed by this incident?

Activities

1. An early heretical movement in the history of the Church was Iconoclasm. This heresy held that it was not permissible for Christians to use images of God in their places of worship. Investigate the history of this movement and then write a report that lists the main tenets of the iconoclasts. Also include in your report the response of the Church to this heresy.

2. Explain why art for the Roman Catholic is essential to an understanding of the Incarnation.

Creation and Nature of God

The Journey of the Mind into God

St. Bonaventure

The heavens declare the glory of God;
the sky proclaims its builder's craft.
—Psalm 19:1

Author Background

St. Bonaventure (1221–1274) was a Franciscan friar who became the leader of the religious order founded by St. Francis of Assisi. A brilliant philosopher, theologian, and mathematician, Bonaventure was one of the leading professors at the University of Paris when that school was the center of intellectual life in the Christian world. He was beatified in 1482. In his masterpiece, *The Journey of the Mind into God*, Bonaventure lays out a guide for prayerful travelers, one that can aid us in gaining a mystical vision and union with God.

Before the Reading

St. Bonaventure was tremendously influenced by the life of St. Francis of Assisi. St. Francis had tremendous experiences of union with God. He was so inflamed with the love of God that he could see the manifestation of God in all of nature. St. Francis's great poem, "The Canticle of Creatures," portrays God's presence in all His creatures. Unlike St. Francis, St. Bonaventure was a most learned man. He was a doctor of philosophy and a renowned teacher. His greatest philosophical work, *The Journey of the Mind into God*, is his way of describing in the terms of science and philosophy the mystical experiences of Francis. For St. Bonaventure the road to the vision of God starts with the presence of God in the world of created things; it then proceeds to the presence of God within ourselves; and finally, the journey ends when we are raised to see the presence of God above us, to have the experience of union with a Being who is eternal, wholly immaterial, and the source and the goal of all that is good, true, and beautiful. In the following brief excerpt from *The Journey of the Mind into God*, St. Bonaventure offers instruction about the presence of God in creation and how creation itself speaks to us about God.

The Journey of the Mind into God

From these first two steps by which we are led to behold God in vestiges . . . we can gather that all creatures in this visible world lead the spirit of the contemplative and wise man to the eternal God. For creatures are shadows, echoes, and pictures of that first, most powerful, most wise, and most perfect Principle, of that first eternal Source, Light, Fullness, of that first efficient, exemplary and ordering Art. They are the vestiges, images, and displays presented to us for the constitution of God, and of the divinely given signs wherein we can see God. These creatures are exemplars, or rather illustrations offered to souls as yet untrained, and immersed in the senses, so that through these sensible things that they see they may be transported to the intelligible which they do not see, as through signs to that which is signified (Chapter 2:11).

For creatures of this visible world signify the invisible things of God: partly, because God is the Origin, Exemplar, and End of every creature—and every effect is a sign of its cause; every example a sign of its exemplar; and every way a sign of the end to which it leads—partly by their own power of representation; partly because of their prophetic prefiguring; partly because of angelic operation; partly also by virtue of supernatural institution. For every creature is by its very nature a figure and likeness of eternal Wisdom, but especially a creature that has been raised by the Spirit of Prophecy to prefigure spiritual things in the book of Scriptures; and more especially those creatures in whose figures it pleased God to appear through the ministry of the angels; and, finally, and most especially, any creature which he chose to institute for the purpose of signifying, and which not only has the character of sign in the ordinary sense of the term, but also the character of sacrament as well (Chapter 2:12).

From all this, one can gather that since the creation of the world his invisible attributes are clearly seen, being understood through the things that are made (Rom 1:20 cited in Chapter 2:13).

Therefore, whoever is not enlightened by such great splendor in created things is blind; whoever remains unheedful of such great outcries is deaf; whoever does not praise God in all these effects is dumb; whoever does not turn to the First Principle after so many signs is a fool. So, open your eyes, alert the ears of your spirit, unlock your lips, and apply your heart that you may see, hear, praise, love, and adore, magnify, and honor your God in every creature, lest perchance the entire universe rise against you. For because of this, the whole world shall fight against the unwise. But on the other hand, it will be a matter of glory for the wise, who can say with the prophet: For you have given me, O Lord, a delight in your doings, and in the work of your hands I shall rejoice (Ps 91:5). How great are your works, O Lord! You have made all things in wisdom; the earth is filled with your riches (Ps 103:24). (Chapter 1, 15).

Reading for Comprehension

1. Where does the observation of the created world lead the wise man?

2. How does Bonaventure describe people who do not see the traces of God in created things?

3. What does Bonaventure call the believer to do when he contemplates the presence of God in nature?

Reading for Understanding

1. Bonaventure teaches us that the created world speaks to us about God. What might each of the following works of creation tell us about the nature of God:

   • lightning;

   • mountains;

- the sea;
- the care of animals for their young;
- the intricacies of a spider's web?

2. Trappist monk and author Thomas Merton said that, in the quiet of prayerful contemplation, he was able to see God's presence in all things. He said that when he saw a rabbit running and hopping, he got a glimpse of the "rabbitness" of God. What do you think he meant?

3. Read Psalm 148. Show three ways that this psalm reflects the ideas found in *The Journey of the Mind into God*.

Activity

St. Francis of Assisi wrote the first great poem that was written in Italian, "The Canticle of the Creatures." Look for the poem online, read it, and write five ways that this poem expresses notion found in *The Journey of the Mind into God* that each creature is a reflection of God telling us about his nature.

WHAT WE BELIEVE
(The Profession of Faith)

SEEING WITH THE ARTIST

Just like writers, visual artists too have sought to portray the mystery of God to humans. In the following section, you will find suggestions for viewing an array of paintings from different epochs in history. Use an Internet search engine to find links for these paintings. Each selection presents a different dimension of the nature of God. As you view the paintings ask yourself:

- What is the message of the artist?
- Why do you think different artists see the same scenes so differently?
- Which painting speaks most forcefully to you? Why is this so?

The Paintings

Icon of the Holy Savior—Artist Unknown

This thirteenth-century mosaic found in the great Byzantine Church, Hagia Sophia, in Istanbul (once known as Constantinople) is based on a sixth-century icon from the Greek monastery of Mount Athos. The mosaic shows Jesus with his hand raised in benediction as he holds the Bible. This is no purely human Jesus. He is robed in Royal Purple and is surrounded by a halo that signifies his eternal nature. This icon is often called a visual representation of the teachings of the Council of Chalcedon, which said that Christ was true God and true man.

The Creation of Adam—Michelangelo Buonarroti (1475–1564)

This depiction of the creation of Adam is the centerpiece of the large fresco found on the ceiling of the Sistine Chapel. In this painting,

Michelangelo depicts the eternal nature of God, who creates man out of nothing by a gesture of his hand. God is seen as surrounded by angels. To stress his eternal nature, God is represented as a mature man with the muscular body of a youth.

Madonna and Child Enthroned with Saints —Raffaello (Raphael) Sanzio (1483–1520)

In this painting, the Infant Jesus and the Madonna are seen enthroned in Heaven as Jesus is worshipped by several saints, including the infant John the Baptist, Peter, Paul, Catherine, and Cecilia. The fact that these saints lived in different centuries stresses the fact that, for God, there is no past or future. His time is not chronological (measurable and sequential time) but *kairological* (time that is not bound by sequence or measurement but rather by emotional significance). He lives in an eternal "now," where all are alive for him.

And Veronica is still among us with her veil of compassion . . . (Et Véronique au tendre lin, passe encore sur le chemin . . .) —Georges Rouault (1871–1958)

Rouault was a devout Catholic and his artistic works stress the human sufferings of the Divine Christ.The artist was trained in producing stained glass. This medium is prominent in his paintings and etchings. Horrified by the devastation of World War I, Rouault constructed a series of fifty etchings from 1917–1927 that he titled *The Miserere* ("Have Pity on Me"). These etchings focus on the life of Christ and the horrors of contemporary war and exploitation of the poor. The particular etching cited here brings to life the legend of Veronica's veil. According to this legend, a young woman named Veronica wiped the bloody face of Jesus with her veil as he made his way on the road to crucifixion. In gratitude for her compassion, Christ left the imprint of his sorrowful face on her veil.

The Black Christ—Ronald Harrison

Harrison, a South African citizen, painted this image of Christ in 1962 during the worst days of violence of the apartheid regime in South Africa, which segregated blacks from the rest of the population. Harrison portrays Albert Luthuli, a South African leader of black Africans, in the image of Christ being crucified by the white political leaders of South Africa, John Vorster and Hendrik Verwoerd. The painting was once displayed in St. Paul's Cathedral in London. In this painting, Harrison emphasizes the human nature of Christ and His solidarity with the oppressed and marginalized.

Activities

1. The Shroud of Turin is an ancient piece of cloth that many people believe is the burial shroud of Jesus that has imprinted on it the face and body of the crucified Christ. People who believe that the shroud is authentic also believe that the face imprinted on the shroud accounts for the similarity of the images of Christ's face found on ancient icons. Look at the image of the face on the Shroud of Turin, paying special attention to certain features, like nose, forehead, hair color and length, shape of the face, eyes, etc. Compare it with five Byzantine icons of Christ. How are they similar?

2. Compare the different way that Michelangelo represents God the Creator in his painting of "The Creation of Adam," and how James Weldon Johnson represents God the Creator in his poem, "The Creation."

3. What are the similarities and differences in the depiction of the Infant Jesus in Raphael's painting, *The Madonna and Child Enthroned with Saints* and Southwell's poem, "The Burning Babe"?

4. Christ is true God and true man with both divine and human natures. Compare *The Icon of the Holy Savior* with Rouault's image *And Veronica is still among us with her veil of compassion. . . .* How does

each painting reflect and focus on the human and divine nature of Christ?

5. View Fra Angelico's great paintings *The Annunciation* and *Christ Crowned with Thorns*. Then read the following poem, "Questions for Fra Angelico," which tells how one sensitive viewer reacted to these masterpieces. The author of the poem, Annabelle Mosely, is an American poet who composed this work after a visit to the Museum of St. Mark in Florence. Fra Angelico was known and revered as one of the great artists of the Renaissance as much for his sanctity as for his brilliance. In the convent of San Marco in Florence, he decorated each monk's cell with frescos that portrayed the life of Christ, the Virgin Mary, and the saints. *The Annunciation*, perhaps the most famous painting of this episode in the life of the Virgin, is on display at this convent.

"Questions For Fra Angelico" by Annabelle Mosley

I imagine the face of Fra Angelico,
radiant and serene,
as he worked in wet plaster
on the walls of San Marco.
In that cloistered space,
amidst the sparseness and the quiet,
there was room for creation.
Guido di Pietro graced each monk's cell
with private frescoes free from time and place.
During his life, this painter-monk
rendered the Annunciation,
the Holy Yes,
with immaculate colors, joyous hues—
but painted *Christ Crowned With Thorns*
with eyes and lips of cherry blood,

red tears, searing brow.
What can you tell me, Brother Angel,
of passion and restraint?
Patron of Artists,
in what sacred conversation
may I speak with you?
You point to the light and the shadows,
mottled on San Marco's floors
and tell me, *Begin there.*

- How is the question about the origin of the paintings answered in Mosley's poem?

- How is the experience of dialogue with a work of art expressed in Mosley's poem? What questions does she ask the artist? What answers does she receive?

LOOKING AT FILM

Religious faith involves seeing life differently than people who have a more materialistic bent. A person of faith is able to transcend the senses and see the life of the spirit beneath the veil of the material world. Because films are a visual medium, they are an ideal vehicle for helping us to see with the eyes of faith. Two films are described below. Read the synopsis of each film. View the films in their entirety. Then do the following:

- Write your impressions of the films.

- Answer the following questions:

  1. What message do you think the directors were trying to communicate?

  2. How did the films help you connect with the mystery of God?

The Films

City Lights (1931)—Directed by Charles (Charlie) Chaplin
Rating: A1

City Lights is the last silent film made by Charles Chaplin. It was made just as talking pictures were replacing silent films. The cinematic techniques of silent films demanded that the primary medium of communication be totally visual. Without words, the narrative of the silent film had to be told completely through pictures. The plot is very simple. The Little Tramp (Chaplin's trademark hero) sees a beautiful but blind flower girl selling flowers on the street. He falls in love with her not only for her simple beauty, but because her blindness has protected her from seeing the evils of the world. She possesses an aura of innocence that enchants him. The Tramp courts the girl, leading her to believe that he is a man of great wealth and sophistication.

The Tramp also has an encounter with the other major character of the film: a wealthy man who is plagued by drunkenness. In one of the early scenes, the wealthy drunk tries to commit suicide while intoxicated but he is saved from death by the Tramp. The wealthy man rewards the Tramp with money, the use of his Rolls-Royce, and expensive parties. The problem is that he only sees the Tramp as his friend when he is drunk; when he is sober, he does not know him and has him thrown out of his mansion.

During his stay with the wealthy man, the Tramp had been seeing the blind girl regularly. She falls in love with him, and her simple goodness increases his love for her. When he finds out that her blindness can be cured, Chaplin asks the rich man (now drunk) for money. He gives the money to the girl for an operation but he himself is sent to jail because, in his sober state, the rich man no longer remembers him. He says farewell to the girl, who is left alone and heartbroken.

The final scene of the film shows the blind girl as the owner of a flower shop; she can now see. She is made up with cosmetics and wears the most fashionable clothes. Now that she can see, she pursues the goals of wealth and beauty and pleasure. She fantasizes about the Tramp as a young, handsome man of wealth and refinement. She has gained her physical sight but has lost the moral sight that made her so enchanting.

The Tramp is released from jail. He wanders the city in shabby clothes, the picture of the homeless man of poverty. One day he passes the flower shop and sees the girl. When he indicates his affection for her, the girl and her companions are amused. She thinks that it is comical that such a poor and unkempt person would be attracted to her. In a moment of pity she offers him a coin. As she places the coin in his hand, her sense of touch tells her that this homeless, impoverished tramp is her benefactor. In one of the most acclaimed scenes in cinema, her face registers her recognition of her benefactor. In the closing sequence, the tramp points to her eyes and says to her, "You can see now." Clasping his hand the flower girl regains her moral vision and says to him, "Yes, I can see now."

The Gospel According to St. Matthew (1966) —Directed by Pier Paolo Pasolini

Rating: Vatican Forty-Five Films

This film seeks to illustrate events in the Life, Death, and Resurrection of Jesus. The film attempts to be as true as possible to the accounts of the life of Jesus found in Scripture. The filmmaker sought authenticity in clothing, set decoration, and artistic design in order to faithfully represent pivotal events in the Gospel story. The film is in no way a glamorous Hollywood-style production. Rather, it is a thoughtful film that gives the viewer an opportunity to meditate and reflect on the meaning and mission of Jesus.

God's Ongoing Revelation

"The Bethlehem Explosion"

Madeleine L'Engle

God has revealed himself to man by gradually communicating his own mystery in deeds and in words.

—*Catechism of the Catholic Church*, 69

Author Background

Madeleine L'Engle (1918–2007) was a prolific writer of more than sixty books in a variety of forms, including fiction, fantasy, biography, poetry, and prose. She is best known, however, for her children's books. Her book of fantasy, *A Wrinkle in Time*, won the distinguished Newberry Medal for Children's Literature. Madeleine L'Engle was a woman of profound religious faith. She felt strongly that all writers, especially Christian writers, had a vocation from God to bring hope and light into a darkened world. As she said in her book *Walking on Water*, the writer has a duty "to further the coming of the kingdom and to turn our feet toward home."

Before the Reading

It is God's will to reveal himself and his purpose for humankind. However, God has not made his revelation known all at once. He has revealed himself to humanity in stages. First he spoke to Adam and Eve, and made a covenant with them to send a Redeemer who would defeat death and sin. Next, God spoke to Noah, Abraham and the Patriarchs, and to Moses and made an everlasting covenant with the people of Israel. Finally, the Lord made himself most perfectly known through the revelation of his Son, Jesus Christ. "In times past. God spoke in partial and various ways to our ancestors through the prophet; in these last days, he spoke to us through a son, whom he made heir of all things and through whom he created the universe" (Heb 1:1–2). All Salvation History leads up to the moment when

Christ comes into the world as true God and true man. In her poem "The Bethlehem Explosion," Madeleine L'Engle writes about a common experiment in a chemistry class. Because she sees the world with the eyes of faith, this common experiment becomes a sign and a metaphor for the coming of Jesus into the world.

"The Bethlehem Explosion"

In those days a decree went out from Caesar Augustus that the world should be enrolled. And Joseph too went up from the town of Nazareth to Judea, to the city of David that is called Bethlehem, because he was of the house and family of David, to be enrolled with Mary, his betrothed, who was with child (Lk 1:1, 4–5).

The chemistry lab at school
was in an old greenhouse
surrounded by ancient live oaks
garnished with Spanish moss.

The experiment I remember best
was pouring a quart of clear fluid
into a glass jar, and dropping into it,
grain by grain, salt-sized crystals,
until they layered
like white sand on the floor of the jar.

One more grain—and suddenly—
water and crystal burst
into a living, moving pattern,
a silent, quietly violent explosion.
The teacher told us that only when
we supersaturated the solution,
would come the precipitation.

The little town
was like the glass jar in our lab.
One by one they came, grain by grain,
all those of the house of David,
like grains of sand to be counted.

The inn was full. When Joseph knocked,
his wife was already in labour; there was no room
even for compassion. Until the barn was offered.
That was the precipitating factor. A child was born,
and the pattern changed forever, the cosmos
shaken with that silent explosion.

Reading for Comprehension

1. Where was the chemistry laboratory located?
2. What does the student do with the individual grains of salt-sized crystals?
3. What is meant by "supersaturation"?
4. What happened when the final grain was dropped into the solution?
5. What is the final event that causes "the silent explosion in the cosmos" that completes God's plan?

Reading for Understanding

1. What aspects of the birth of Jesus are represented in the poem by: the glass jar, the grains of crystal, the silent and violent explosion in the glass jar?
2. An explosion destroys the surface order of things to reveal the power that lies beneath. Read John 1:1–3. Explain how Christ's birth reveals the dynamic love of God that was present from the beginning of creation.
3. God speaks to us as individuals at various stages of our life. In a gradual manner or by a sudden event, he makes himself known to us and enables us to see people, events, and God himself in a clearer way.

Examine a decisive moment in your life. What did it tell you about yourself or the world? How would your life be different if that event had never occurred? How did God speak to you in this event? What was the Lord trying to tell you?

Activity

God revealed himself to Israel, his Chosen People, over a long period of time. Read the following stories from the Bible:

- the creation of Adam and Eve (Gn 2:4–24)
- the freeing of the Israelites from Egypt (Ex 14)
- the prophecies about the Suffering Servant (Is 52:13–53:12)

How can each of these episodes be compared to the grains of crystal described in L'Engle's poem? Read the account of the Transfiguration found in Matthew 17:1–8. How is this manifestation of Jesus in glory another example of a "silent explosion"?

God's Ongoing Revelation

"Where Love Is, God Is"

Leo Tolstoy

In Sacred Scripture, the Church constantly finds her
nourishment and her strength, for she welcomes it
not as a human word, 'but what it really is the word of God'
(1 Thes 2:13). In the sacred books, the father who is in heaven
comes lovingly to meet his children and talks with them.

—*Catechism of the Catholic Church*, **104**

Author Background

Leo Tolstoy (1828–1910) is world-renowned for his epic novels *War and Peace* and *Anna Karenina*. Throughout his long life and in virtually all his writings, we see a profound interest in religion and spirituality. During the last portion of his life, Tolstoy renounced wealth and privilege and sought to live on the land as a humble and poor peasant. During this time, he wrote a series of tales that were meant to be read to children and illiterate peasants so that they could better understand the teachings of Jesus. Many of these stories, like the one that follows, are classics of world literature.

Before the Reading

By looking at the life and actions of Jesus and taking his teachings into our hearts, we come to a fuller understanding of who God is and how he wants us to live. Most of what we know about Jesus' life is found in the Gospels. It is through the prayerful reading of the Gospels that God "speaks" to us. In the following story by Leo Tolstoy, we learn that God has revealed through his Son the fact that he identifies himself in a special way with the poor, the lowly, and the oppressed. In this tale we see how a poor shoemaker listens to the Word of God and comes to meet his Savior.

"Where Love Is, God Is"

In a certain town there lived a cobbler, Martin Avdéitch by name. He had a tiny room in a basement, the one window of which looked out on to the street. Through it one could only see the feet of those who passed by, but Martin recognized the people by their boots. He had lived long in the place and had many acquaintances. There was hardly a pair of boots in the neighborhood that had not been once or twice through his hands, so he often saw his own handiwork through the window. Some he had resoled, some patched, some stitched up, and to some he had even put fresh uppers. He had plenty to do, for he worked well, used good material, did not charge too much, and could be relied on. If he could do a job by the day required, he undertook it; if not, he told the truth and gave no false promises; so he was well known and never short of work.

Martin had always been a good man, but in his old age he began to think more about his soul and to draw nearer to God. While he still worked for a master, before he set up on his own account, his wife had died, leaving him with a three-year-old son. None of his elder children had lived, they had all died in infancy. At first Martin thought of sending his little son to his sister's in the country, but then he felt sorry to part with the boy, thinking: "It would be hard for my little Kapitón to have to grow up in a strange family, I will keep him with me."

Martin left his master and went into lodgings with his little son. But he had no luck with his children. No sooner had the boy reached an age when he could help his father and be a support as well as a joy to him, than he fell ill and, after being laid up for a week with a burning fever, died. Martin buried his son, and gave way to despair so great and overwhelming that he murmured against God. In his sorrow he prayed again and again that he too might die, reproaching God for having taken the son he loved, his only son, while he, old as he was, remained alive. After that Martin left off going to church.

One day an old man from Martin's native village, who had been a pilgrim for the last eight years, called in on his way from the Troitsa Monastery. Martin opened his heart to him and told him of his sorrow.

"I no longer even wish to live, holy man," he said. "All I ask of God is that I soon may die. I am now quite without hope in the world."

The old man replied: "You have no right to say such things, Martin. We cannot judge God's ways. Not our reasoning, but God's will, decides. If God willed that your son should die and you should live, it must be best so. As to your despair—that comes because you wish to live for your own happiness."

"What else should one live for?" asked Martin.

"For God, Martin," said the old man. "He gives you life, and you must live for him. When you have learnt to live for him, you will grieve no more, and all will seem easy to you."

Martin was silent awhile, and then asked: "But how is one to live for God?"

The old man answered: "How one may live for God has been shown us by Christ. Can you read? Then buy the Gospels and read them: there you will see how God would have you live. You have it all there."

These words sank deep into Martin's heart, and that same day he went and bought himself a Testament in large print, and began to read.

At first he meant only to read on holidays, but having once begun, he found it made his heart so light that he read every day. Sometimes he was so absorbed in his reading that the oil in his lamp burnt out before he could tear himself away from the book. He continued to read every night, and the more he read the more clearly he understood what God required of him, and how he might live for God. And his heart grew lighter and lighter. Before, when he went to bed he used to lie with a heavy heart, moaning as he thought of his little Kapitón; but now he only repeated again and again: "Glory to Thee, glory to Thee, O Lord! Thy will be done!"

From that time Martin's whole life changed. Formerly, on holidays he used to go and have tea at the public-house and did not even refuse a glass or two of vodka. Sometimes, after having had a drop with a friend, he left the public-house not drunk, but rather merry, and would say foolish things: shout at a man, or abuse him. Now all that sort of thing passed away from him. His life became peaceful and joyful. He sat down to his work in the morning, and when he had finished his day's work he took the lamp down from the wall, stood it on the table, fetched his book from the shelf, opened it, and sat down to read. The more he read the better he understood and the clearer and happier he felt in his mind.

It happened once that Martin sat up late, absorbed in his book. He was reading Luke's Gospel; and in the sixth chapter he came upon the verses:

"To him that smiteth thee on the one cheek offer also the other; and from him that taketh away thy cloke withhold not thy coat also. Give to every man that asketh thee; and of him that taketh away thy goods ask them not again. And as ye would that men should do to you, do ye also to them likewise."

He also read the verses where our Lord says:

"And why call ye me, Lord, Lord, and do not the things which I say? Whosoever cometh to me, and heareth my sayings, and doeth them, I will shew you to whom he is like: He is like a man which built an house, and digged deep, and laid the foundation on a rock: and when the flood arose, the stream beat vehemently upon that house, and could not shake it: for it was founded upon a rock. But he that heareth, and doeth not, is like a man that without foundation built an house upon the earth, against which the stream did beat vehemently, and immediately it fell; and the ruin of that house was great."

When Martin read these words his soul was glad within him. He took off his spectacles and laid them on the book, and leaning his elbows on the table pondered over what he had read. He tried his own life by the standard of those words, asking himself:

"Is my house built on the rock, or on sand? If it stands on the rock, it is well. It seems easy enough while one sits here alone, and one thinks one has done all that God commands; but as soon as I cease to be on my guard, I sin again. Still I will persevere. It brings such joy. Help me, O Lord!"

He thought all this, and was about to go to bed, but was loth to leave his book. So he went on reading the seventh chapter—about the centurion, the widow's son, and the answer to John's disciples—and he came to the part where a rich Pharisee invited the Lord to his house; and he read how the woman who was a sinner anointed his feet and washed them with her tears, and how he justified her. Coming to the forty-fourth verse, he read:

"And turning to the woman, he said unto Simon, Seest thou this woman? I entered into thine house, thou gavest me no water for my feet: but she hath wetted my feet with her tears, and wiped them with her hair. Thou gavest me no kiss; but she, since the time I came in, hath not ceased to kiss my feet. My head with oil thou didst not anoint; but she hath anointed my feet with ointment."

He read these verses and thought: "He gave no water for his feet, gave no kiss, his head with oil he did not anoint. . . ." And Martin took off his spectacles once more, laid them on his book, and pondered.

"He must have been like me, that Pharisee. He too thought only of himself—how to get a cup of tea, how to keep warm and comfortable; never a thought of his guest. He took care of himself, but for his guest he cared nothing at all. Yet who was the guest? The Lord himself! If he came to me, should I behave like that?"

Then Martin laid his head upon both his arms and, before he was aware of it, he fell asleep.

"Martin!" he suddenly heard a voice, as if someone had breathed the word above his ear.

He started from his sleep. "Who's there?" he asked.

He turned round and looked at the door; no one was there. He called again. Then he heard quite distinctly: "Martin, Martin! Look out into the street tomorrow, for I shall come."

Martin roused himself, rose from his chair and rubbed his eyes, but did not know whether he had heard the words in a dream or awake. He put out the lamp and lay down to sleep.

Next morning he rose before daylight, and after saying his prayers he lit the fire and prepared his cabbage soup and buckwheat porridge. Then he lit the samovar, put on his apron, and sat down by the window to his work. As he sat working Martin thought over what had happened the night before. At times it seemed to him like a dream, and at times he thought that he had really heard the voice. "Such things have happened before now," thought he.

So he sat by the window, looking out into the street more than he worked, and whenever any one passed in unfamiliar boots he would stoop and look up, so as to see not the feet only but the face of the passerby as well. A house porter passed in new felt boots; then a water carrier. Presently an old soldier of Nicholas' reign came near the window, spade in hand. Martin knew him by his boots which were shabby old felt ones, goolashed with leather. The old man was called Stepánitch: a neighboring tradesman kept him in his house for charity, and his duty was to help the house porter. He began to clear away the snow before Martin's window. Martin glanced at him and then went on with is work.

"I must be going crazy with age," said Martin, laughing at his fancy. "Stepánitch comes to clean the snow, and I must needs imagine it's Christ coming to visit me. Old dotard that I am!"

Yet after he had made a dozen stitches he felt drawn to look out of the window again. He saw that Stepánitch had leaned his spade against the wall and was either resting himself or trying to get warm. The man was old and broken down, and had evidently not enough strength even to clear away the snow.

"What if I called him in and gave him some tea?" thought Martin. "The samovar is just on the boil."

He stuck his awl in its place, and rose; and putting the samovar on the table, made tea. Then he tapped the window with his fingers.

Stepánitch turned and came to the window. Martin beckoned to him to come in and went himself to open the door.

"Come in," he said, "and warm yourself a bit. I'm sure you must be cold."

"May God bless you!" Stepánitch answered. "My bones do ache to be sure." He came in, first shaking off the snow, and lest he should leave marks on the floor he began wiping his feet, but as he did so he tottered and nearly fell.

"Don't trouble to wipe your feet," said Martin; "I'll wipe up the floor—it's all in the day's work. Come, friend, sit down and have some tea."

Filling two tumblers, he passed one to his visitor, and pouring his own out into the saucer, began to blow on it.

Stepánitch emptied his glass, and, turning it upside down, put the remains of his piece of sugar on the top. He began to express his thanks, but it was plain that he would be glad of some more.

"Have another glass," said Martin, refilling the visitor's tumbler and his own. But while he drank his tea Martin kept looking out into the street.

"Are you expecting any one?" asked the visitor.

"Am I expecting any one? Well now, I'm ashamed to tell you. It isn't that I really expect any one; but I heard something last night which I can't get out of my mind. Whether it was a vision, or only a fancy, I can't tell. You see, friend, last night I was reading the Gospel, about Christ the Lord, how he suffered and how he walked on earth. You have heard tell of it, I dare say."

"I have heard tell of it," answered Stepánitch; "but I'm an ignorant man and not able to read."

"Well, you see, I was reading of how he walked on earth. I came to that part, you know, where he went to a Pharisee who did not receive him well. Well, friend, as I read about it, I thought how that man did not receive Christ the Lord with proper honor. Suppose such a thing could happen to such a man as myself, I thought, what would I not do to receive him! But that man gave him no reception at all.

Well, friend, as I was thinking of this I began to doze, and as I dozed I heard some one call me by name. I got up, and thought I heard some one whispering, 'Expect me; I will come to-morrow.' This happened twice over. And to tell you the truth, it sank so into my mind that, though I am ashamed of it myself, I keep on expecting him, the dear Lord!"

Stepánitch shook his head in silence, finished his tumbler and laid it on its side; but Martin stood it up again and refilled it for him.

"Here, drink another glass, bless you! And I was thinking, too, how he walked on earth and despised no one, but went mostly among common folk. He went with plain people, and chose his disciples from among the likes of us, from workmen like us, sinners that we are. 'He who raises himself,' he said, 'shall be humbled; and he who humbles himself shall be raised.' 'You call me Lord,' he said, 'and I will wash your feet.' 'He who would be first,' he said, 'let him be the servant of all; because,' he said, 'blessed are the poor, the humble, the meek, and the merciful.'"

Stepánitch forgot his tea. He was an old man, easily moved to tears, and as he sat and listened the tears ran down his cheeks.

"Come, drink some more," said Martin. But Stepánitch crossed himself, thanked him, moved away his tumbler, and rose.

"Thank you, Martin Avdéitch," he said, "you have given me food and comfort both for soul and body."

"You're very welcome. Come again another time. I am glad to have a guest," said Martin.

Stepánitch went away; and Martin poured out the last of the tea and drank it up. Then he put away the tea things and sat down to his work, stitching the back seam of a boot. And as he stitched he kept looking out of the window, waiting for Christ and thinking about him and his doing. And his head was full of Christ's sayings.

Two soldiers went by: one in Government boots, the other in boots of his own; then the master of a neighboring house, in shining galoshes; then a baker carrying a basket. All these passed on. Then a woman came up in worsted stockings and peasant-made shoes.

She passed the window, but stopped by the wall. Martin glanced up at her through the window and saw that she was a stranger, poorly dressed and with a baby in her arms. She stopped by the wall with her back to the wind, trying to wrap the baby up though she had hardly anything to wrap it in. The woman had only summer clothes on, and even they were shabby and worn. Through the window Martin heard the baby crying, and the woman trying to soothe it but unable to do so. Martin rose, and going out of the door and up the steps he called to her.

"My dear, I say, my dear!"

The woman heard and turned round.

"Why do you stand out there with the baby in the cold? Come inside. You can wrap him up better in a warm place. Come this way!"

The woman was surprised to see an old man in an apron, with spectacles on his nose, calling to her, but she followed him in.

They went down the steps, entered the little room, and the old man led her to the bed.

"There, sit down, my dear, near the stove. Warm yourself and feed the baby."

"Haven't any milk. I have eaten nothing myself since early morning," said the woman, but still she took the baby to her breast.

Martin shook his head. He brought a basin and some bread. Then he opened the oven door and poured some cabbage soup into the basin. He took out the porridge pot also, but the porridge was not yet ready, so he spread a cloth on the table and served only the soup and bread.

"Sit down and eat, my dear, and I'll mind the baby. Why, bless me, I've had children of my own; I know how to manage them."

The woman crossed herself, and sitting down at the table began to eat, while Martin put the baby on the bed and sat down by it. He chucked and chucked, but having no teeth he could not do it well and the baby continued to cry. Then Martin tried poking at him with his finger; he drove his finger straight at the baby's mouth and then quickly drew it back, and did this again and again. He did not let the baby take his finger in its mouth, because it was all black with cobbler's wax. But the baby first grew quiet watching the finger, and then began to laugh. And Martin felt quite pleased.

The woman sat eating and talking, and told him who she was, and where she had been.

"I'm a soldier's wife," said she. "They sent my husband somewhere, far away, eight months ago, and I have heard nothing of him since. I had a place as cook till my baby was born, but then they would not keep me with a child. For three months now I have been struggling, unable to find a place, and I've had to sell all I had for food. I tried to go as a wet-nurse, but no one would have me; they said I was too starved-looking and thin. Now I have just been to see a tradesman's wife (a woman from our village is in service with her) and she has promised to take me. I thought it was all settled at last, but she tells me not to come till next week. It is far to her place, and I am fagged out, and baby is quite starved, poor mite. Fortunately our landlady has pity on us, and lets us lodge free, else I don't know what we should do."

Martin sighed. "Haven't you any warmer clothing?" he asked.

"How could I get warm clothing?" said she. "Why, I pawned my last shawl for sixpence yesterday."

Then the woman came and took the child, and Martin got up. He went and looked among some things that were hanging on the wall, and brought back an old cloak.

"Here," he said, "though it's a worn-out old thing, it will do to wrap him up in."

The woman looked at the cloak, then at the old man, and taking it, burst into tears. Martin turned away, and groping under the bed brought out a small trunk. He fumbled about in it, and again sat down opposite the woman. And the woman said:

"The Lord bless you, friend. Surely Christ must have sent me to your window, else the child would have frozen. It was mild when I started, but now see how cold it has turned. Surely it must have been

Christ who made you look out of your window and take pity on me, poor wretch!"

Martin smiled and said, "It is quite true; it was He made me do it. It was no mere chance made me look out."

And he told the woman his dream, and how he had heard the Lord's voice promising to visit him that day.

"Who knows! All things are possible," said the woman. And she got up and threw the cloak over her shoulders, wrapping it round herself and round the baby. Then she bowed, and thanked Martin once more.

"Take this for Christ's sake," said Martin, and gave her sixpence to get her shawl out of pawn. The woman crossed herself, and Martin did the same, and then he saw her out.

After the woman had gone, Martin ate some cabbage soup, cleared the things away, and sat down to work again. He sat and worked, but did not forget the window, and every time a shadow fell on it he looked up at once to see who was passing. People he knew and strangers passed by, but no one remarkable.

After a while Martin saw an apple-woman stop just in front of his window. She had a large basket, but there did not seem to be many apples left in it; she had evidently sold most of her stock. On her back she had a sack full of chips, which she was taking home. No doubt she had gathered them at some place where building was going on. The sack evidently hurt her and she wanted to shift it from one shoulder to the other, so she put it down on the footpath and, placing her basket on a post, began to shake down the chips in the sack. While she was doing this a boy in a tattered cap ran up, snatched an apple out of the basket and tried to slip away; but the old woman noticed it and, turning, caught the boy by his sleeve. He began to struggle, trying to free himself, but the old woman held on with both hands, knocked his cap off his head, and seized hold of his hair. The boy screamed and the old woman scolded. Martin dropped his awl, not waiting to stick it in its place, and rushed out of the door. Stumbling up the steps, and dropping his spectacles in his hurry, he ran out into the street. The old woman was pulling the boy's hair and scolding him, and threatening to take him to the police. The lad was struggling and protesting, saying, "I did not take it. What are you beating me for? Let me go!"

Martin separated them. He took the boy by the hand and said, "Let him go, Granny. Forgive him for Christ's sake."

"I'll pay him out, so that he won't forget it for a year! I'll take the rascal to the police!"

Martin began entreating the old woman.

"Let him go, Granny. He won't do it again. Let him go for Christ's sake!"

The old woman let go, and the boy wished to run away, but Martin stopped him.

"Ask the Granny's forgiveness!" said he. "And don't do it another time. I saw you take the apple."

The boy began to cry and to beg pardon.

"That's right. And now here's an apple for you," and Martin took an apple from the basket and gave it to the boy, saying, "I will pay you, Granny."

"You will spoil them that way, the young rascals," said the old woman. "He ought to be whipped so that he should remember it for a week."

"Oh, Granny, Granny," said Martin, "that's our way—but it's not God's way. If he should be whipped for stealing an apple, what should be done to us for our sins?"

The old woman was silent.

And Martin told her the parable of the lord who forgave his servant a large debt, and how the servant went out and seized his debtor by the throat. The old woman listened to it all, and the boy, too, stood by and listened.

"God bids us forgive," said Martin, "or else we shall not be forgiven. Forgive every one, and a thoughtless youngster most of all."

The old woman wagged her head and sighed.

"It's true enough," said she, "but they are getting terribly spoilt."

"Then we old ones must show them better ways," Martin replied.

"That's just what I say," said the old woman. "I have had seven of them myself, and only one daughter is left." And the old woman began to tell how and where she was living with her daughter, and how many grandchildren she had. "There now," she said, "I have but little strength left, yet I work hard for the sake of my grandchildren; and nice children they are, too. No one comes out to meet me but the children. Little Annie, now, won't leave me for any one. 'It's grandmother, dear grandmother, darling grandmother.'" And the old woman completely softened, at the thought.

"Of course it was only his childishness, God help him," said she, referring to the boy.

As the old woman was about to hoist her sack on her back, the lad sprang forward to her, saying, "Let me carry it for you, Granny. I'm going that way."

The old woman nodded her head, and put the sack on the boy's back, and they went down the street together, the old woman quite forgetting to ask Martin to pay for the apple. Martin stood and watched them as they went along talking to each other. When they were out of sight Martin went back to the house. Having found his spectacles unbroken on the steps, he picked up his awl and sat down again to work. He worked a little, but could soon not see to pass the bristle through the holes in the leather; and presently he noticed the lamplighter passing on his way to light the street lamps.

"Seems it's time to light up," thought he. So he trimmed his lamp, hung it up, and sat down again to work. He finished off one boot and, turning it about, examined. It was all right. Then he gathered his tools together, swept up the cuttings, put away the bristles and the thread and the awls, and, taking down the lamp, placed it on the table. Then he took the Gospels from the shelf. He meant to open them at the place he had marked the day before with a bit of morocco, but the book opened at another place. As Martin opened it, his yesterday's dream came back to his mind, and no sooner had he thought of it than he seemed to hear footsteps, as though some one were moving behind him. Martin turned round, and it seemed to him as if people were standing in the dark corner, but he could not make out who they were. And a voice whispered in his ear: "Martin, Martin, don't you know me?"

"Who is it?" muttered Martin.

"It is I," said the voice. And out of the dark corner stepped Stepánitch, who smiled, and vanishing like a cloud was seen no more.

"It is I," said the voice again. And out of the darkness stepped the woman with the baby in her arms, and the woman smiled and the baby laughed, and they too vanished.

"It is I," said the voice once more. And the old woman and the boy with the apple stepped out and both smiled, and then they too vanished.

And Martin's soul grew glad. He crossed himself, put on his spectacles, and began reading the Gospel just where it had opened; and at the top of the page he read:

"I was an hungered, and ye gave me meat: I was thirsty, and ye gave me drink: I was a stranger, and ye took me in." And at the bottom of the page he read:

"Inasmuch as ye did it unto one of these my brethren, even these least, ye did it unto me" (Matt. xxv).

And Martin understood that his dream had come true; and that the Saviour had really come to him that day, and he had welcomed him.

Reading for Comprehension

1. Tolstoy writes at the beginning of the story that Martin was in a despair so great that he murmured against God. What caused Martin to be so despairing?

2. What advice does the pilgrim, the holy man from the monastery at Troitsa, give to Martin?

3. What words does Martin hear Jesus saying when he is dozing?

4. How does Martin help Stepánitch?

5. How does Martin learn that he has received a visit from the Savior?

Reading for Understanding

1. Think about the people you know. Who is hungry for affection; or thirsting for friendship; or seeking freedom from the prison of isolation; or is overwhelmed with despair and sorrow? How can you "welcome" them as Martin welcomed the Savior?

2. Christ revealed himself to Martin through the reading of Scripture. Throughout the history of Christianity, many people have sought advice from God by opening the Bible to a particular page, reading it, and reflecting on what it means for them. Open your Bible to a section of one of the Gospels. Read a passage on that page and reflect on its meaning for you.

3. What is meant by the term, "Incarnation"? What does this tale tell us about the nature of the Incarnation?

Activity

Search for and read the short story titled "The Happy Prince," by Oscar Wilde. List three ways that this story parallels the sentiments found in Tolstoy's "Where Love Is, God Is."

God's Ongoing Revelation

"A Woman of Little Faith"
from *The Brothers Karamazov*

Fyodor Dostoyevsky

Author Background

Russian Fyodor Dostoyevsky (1821–1881) is considered one of the greatest novelists of all time. In *Crime and Punishment*, *The Idiot*, *The Devils*, and *The Brothers Karamazov*, he investigated the issues of good and evil, belief and atheism, and violence and non-violence, as they manifested themselves in the lives of his characters. He also is known as the supreme "novelist of ideas," who was able to weave the thread of philosophical discussion into the fabric of his narratives. As a Christian he protested against the evils of the modern world. His calls for society's return to God ring as true today as when they were first written.

Before the Reading

The Brothers Karamazov was Dostoyevsky's last novel and is considered his masterpiece. In this story of the three brothers of the Karamazov family, Dostoyevsky compares the nature of belief to that of atheism, and the effect those opposing views have on human action and character. A major figure in the novel is the Elder Zosima, a Russian Monk of great holiness and wisdom. Zosima believes that only Christianity can save humans from demonism.

In this excerpt from the novel, Elder Zosima has an encounter with a woman who confesses to him her difficulty in believing in the afterlife. She also expresses her aspiration to love all humanity. Interestingly, Zosima does not answer her problems of belief with a rational argument for the existence of the afterlife, nor does he praise her for her idealism. Instead he calls on her to reform her life, to love passionately the people who are a part of her daily life, and not to waste her spiritual energy in the pursuit of grandiose dreams of universal love. Only by doing these things, he says, will she be able to believe.

"A Woman of Little Faith"

"It's not often I can see visitors. I am ill, and I know that my days are numbered."

"Oh, no, no! God will not take you from us. You will live a long, long time yet," cried the lady. "And in what way are you ill? You look so well, so gay and happy."

"I am extraordinarily better today. But I know that it's only for a moment. I understand my disease now thoroughly. If I seem so happy to you, you could never say anything that would please me so much. For men are made for happiness, and anyone who is completely happy has a right to say to himself, 'I am doing God's will on earth.' All the righteous, all the saints, all the holy martyrs were happy."

"Oh, how you speak! What bold and lofty words!" cried the lady. "You seem to pierce with your words. And yet—happiness, happiness—where is it? Who can say of himself that he is happy? Oh, since you have been so good as to let us see you once more today, let me tell you what I could not utter last time, what I dared not say, all I am suffering and have been for so long! I am suffering! Forgive me! I am suffering!"

And in a rush of fervent feeling she clasped her hands before him.

"From what specially?"

"I suffer . . . from lack of faith."

"Lack of faith in God?"

"Oh, no, no! I dare not even think of that. But the future life—it is such an enigma! And no one, no one can solve it. Listen! You are a healer, you are deeply versed in the human soul, and of course I dare not expect you to believe me entirely, but I assure you on my word of honor that I am not speaking lightly now. The thought of the life beyond the grave distracts me to anguish, to terror. And I don't know to whom to appeal, and have not dared to all my life. And now I am so bold as to ask you. Oh, God! What will you think of me now?"

She clasped her hands.

"Don't distress yourself about my opinion of you," said the elder. "I quite believe in the sincerity of your suffering."

"Oh, how thankful I am to you! You see, I shut my eyes and ask myself if everyone has faith, where did it come from? And then they do say that it all comes from terror at the menacing phenomena of nature, and that none of it's real. And I say to myself, 'What if I've been believing all my life, and when I come to die there's nothing but the burdocks growing on my grave?' as I read in some author. It's awful! How—how can I get back my faith? But I only believed when I was a little child, mechanically, without thinking of anything. How, how is one to prove it? I have come now to lay my soul before you and to ask you about it. If I let this chance slip, no one all my life will answer me. How can I prove it? How can I convince myself? Oh, how unhappy I am! I stand and look about me and see that scarcely anyone else cares; no one troubles his head about it, and I'm the only one who can't stand it. It's deadly—deadly!"

"No doubt. But there's no proving it, though you can be convinced of it."

"How?"

"By the experience of active love. Strive to love your neighbor actively and indefatigably. In as far as you advance in love you will grow surer of the reality of God and of the immortality of your soul. If you attain to perfect self-forgetfulness in the love of your neighbor, then you will believe without doubt, and no doubt can possibly enter your soul. This has been tried. This is certain."

"In active love? There's another question—and such a question! You see, I so love humanity that—would you believe it?—I often dream of forsaking all that I have, leaving Lise, and becoming a Sister of Mercy. I close my eyes and think and dream, and at that moment I feel full of strength to overcome all obstacles. No wounds, no festering sores could at that moment frighten me. I would bind them

117

up and wash them with my own hands. I would nurse the afflicted. I would be ready to kiss such wounds."

"It is much, and well that your mind is full of such dreams and not others. Sometime, unawares, you may do a good deed in reality."

"Yes. But could I endure such a life for long?" the lady went on fervently, almost frantically. "That's the chief question—that's my most agonizing question. I shut my eyes and ask myself, 'Would you persevere long on that path? And if the patient whose wounds you are washing did not meet you with gratitude, but worried you with his whims, without valuing or remarking your charitable services, began abusing you and rudely commanding you, and complaining to the superior authorities of you (which often happens when people are in great suffering)—what then? Would you persevere in your love, or not?' And do you know, I came with horror to the conclusion that, if anything could dissipate my love to humanity, it would be ingratitude. In short, I am a hired servant, I expect my payment at once— that is, praise, and the repayment of love with love. Otherwise I am incapable of loving anyone."

She was in a very paroxysm of self-castigation, and, concluding, she looked with defiant resolution at the elder.

"It's just the same story as a doctor once told me," observed the elder. "He was a man getting on in years, and undoubtedly clever. He spoke as frankly as you, though in jest, in bitter jest. 'I love humanity,' he said, 'but I wonder at myself. The more I love humanity in general, the less I love man in particular. In my dreams,' he said, 'I have often come to making enthusiastic schemes for the service of humanity, and perhaps I might actually have faced crucifixion if it had been suddenly necessary; and yet I am incapable of living in the same room with anyone for two days together, as I know by experience. As soon as anyone is near me, his personality disturbs my self-complacency and restricts my freedom. In twenty-four hours I begin to hate the best of men: one because he's too long over his dinner; another because he has a cold and keeps on blowing his nose. I become hostile to people the moment they come close to me. But it has always happened that the more I detest men individually the more ardent becomes my love for humanity.'"

"But what's to be done? What can one do in such a case? Must one despair?"

"No. It is enough that you are distressed at it. Do what you can, and it will be reckoned unto you. Much is done already in you since you can so deeply and sincerely know yourself. If you have been talking to me so sincerely, simply to gain approbation for your frankness, as you did from me just now, then, of course, you will not attain to anything in the achievement of real love; it will all get no further than dreams, and your whole life will slip away like a phantom. In that case you will naturally cease to think of the future life too, and will of yourself grow calmer after a fashion in the end."

"You have crushed me! Only now, as you speak, I understand that I was really only seeking your approbation for my sincerity when I told you I could not endure ingratitude. You have revealed me to myself. You have seen through me and explained me to myself."

"Are you speaking the truth? Well, now, after such a confession, I believe that you are sincere and good at heart. If you do not attain happiness, always remember that you are on the right road, and try not to leave it. Above all, avoid falsehood, every kind of falsehood, especially falseness to yourself. Watch over your own deceitfulness and look into it every hour, every minute. Avoid being scornful, both to others and to yourself. What seems to you bad within you will grow purer from the very fact of your observing it in yourself. Avoid fear, too, though fear is only the consequence of every sort of falsehood. Never be frightened at your own faint-heartedness in attaining love. Don't be frightened overmuch even at your evil actions. I am sorry I can say nothing more consoling to you, for love in action is a harsh and dreadful thing compared with love in dreams. Love in dreams is greedy for immediate action, rapidly performed and in the sight of all. Men will even give their lives if only the ordeal does not last long but is soon over, with all looking on and applauding as though on the stage. But active love is labor and fortitude, and for some people too, perhaps, a complete science. But I predict that just when you see with horror that in spite of all your efforts you are getting further from your goal instead of nearer to it—at that very moment I predict that you will reach it and behold clearly the miraculous power of the Lord who has been all the time loving, and mysteriously guiding you. Forgive me for not being able to stay longer with you. They are waiting for me. Good-bye."

The lady was weeping.

Reading for Comprehension

1. What does Elder Zosima say about people who are truly happy?

2. What does the woman say is the cause of her unhappiness?

3. What does Zosima say that the woman must do to regain her faith and end her unhappiness?

4. What did the doctor tell Zosima about his love for humanity?

5. What does the woman do at the conclusion of this episode with Elder Zosima?

Reading for Understanding

1. What does Elder Zosima mean when he says that love in reality is a harsh and dreadful thing?

2. Summarize Zosima's answer to a crisis of faith. What should one do to make faith come alive?

Activity

Research the life of Blessed Mother Teresa of Calcutta and the Missionaries of Charity. Answer the following questions:

- What is the charism of the Missionaries of Charity?

- What is the difference between what they do and what those who only talk about their love and concern for the poor do?

- How does this type of work help them fulfill Elder Zosima's prediction about how belief and love of God flow from active love?

God's Ongoing Revelation

Letter to the Grand Duchess Christina of Tuscany

Galileo Galilei

"... the intention of the Holy Ghost is to teach us how one goes to heaven, not how heaven goes."

—Galileo Galilei

Author Background

Galileo Galilei (1564–1642), a mathematician, astronomer, and physicist, is one of the greatest scientists of all time. He conducted the first system-atic studies of accelerated motion, made improvements to the telescope that led to new astronomical discoveries, and conducted observations that verified the Copernican theory that the earth and planets revolved around the sun (heliocentrism) rather than the earth being the center of the solar system with the sun revolving around it (geocentricism). He is one of the most important originators of the "scientific method," which depends on observation and experimentation to investigate the laws that govern the natural world. Galileo was a true believer who, by his life and work, inte-grated within himself the man of science and the man of faith.

Before the Reading

In 1543 Nicholas Copernicus, a Polish priest, published a book titled *On the Revolution of the Celestial Spheres*. In this book, Copernicus stated his theory that the earth was not the center of the solar system, but rather re-volved around the sun. Copernicus' ideas spread throughout the educated classes of Europe and were accepted by many, including scientists, bish-ops, and even popes. There was, however, opposition to the Copernican system. Some opposed it on scientific grounds claiming that it was sim-ply not true to the principles of physics. Others condemned it because it seemed to contradict passages in the Bible where the earth is spoken of as the center of the solar system and that the sun revolves around the earth. Finally, there were many who thought that Copernicus was correct but that it would be destructive to the faith of the simple if the Bible was seen to be in error about the movement of the heavenly spheres.

In 1633 Galileo published his epic work *The Dialogue of the Two Chief Systems of the World*, in which he promoted support of the Copernican system and backed up the heliocentric hypothesis with astronomical observation that he had made with his own telescopes. Due to a variety of reasons, which included scientific ignorance on the part of some members of the Church, political competition by various schools of physics, and Galileo's own stubbornness, Galileo was brought to trial by the Inquisition (a court of the Church) and convicted of heresy for holding that the earth is not the center of the universe. Galileo was forced by a Church court to recant his teachings that supported the Copernican theory. He was placed under house arrest and remained there until he died in 1642.

The Galileo case has become one of the most important symbols of the modern world. It has been used continuously by opponents of religion and Catholicism to show that faith and science cannot be reconciled, that a true scientist can never hold religious beliefs. This assertion, however, flies in the face of facts, common sense, and historical experience. In the first place, Galileo and Copernicus were both believers and practicing Catholics. Obviously they felt no irreconcilable opposition between faith and reason. Also, in his lifetime and during and after his trial, Galileo had the support of many prominent priests, bishops, and cardinals. The fact that there is no inherent antagonism between faith and reason, however, does not excuse the actions of theologians who were quick to condemn a great scientist without a real understanding of science or the scientific method. That they were close-minded and rushed to judgment presents a very sobering example to the contemporary Church of the need for openness to modern scholarship. Pope John Paul II specifically addressed the Galileo case in 1979 (see pages 127–134). The Galileo case is also a warning to people of science to understand that the material world is not the whole of reality, and that only religion and religious teaching is able to investigate and explain the spiritual aspect of the universe.

In these next two readings the following points are made: First, faith and science cannot be in conflict. Where there seems to be a conflict, then either the science itself or the religious interpretation is in error. As Pius XI said, "Truth cannot contradict truth." Second, these readings underscore the Church teaching that the Bible cannot be read literally. It must be interpreted by the Church in the light of the knowledge of the authors of the sacred text when it was written. "In order to discover the sacred authors' intention, the reader must consider the conditions of their time and the modes of feeling, speaking, and narrating then current" (*CCC*, 110).

Letter to the Grand Duchess Christina of Tuscany

The reason produced for condemning the opinion that the earth moves and the sun stands still in many places in the Bible one may read that the sun moves and the earth stands still. Since the Bible cannot err; it follows as a necessary consequence that anyone takes an erroneous and heretical position who maintains that the sun is inherently motionless and the earth movable.

With regard to this argument, I think in the first place that it is very pious to say and prudent to affirm that the holy Bible can never speak untruth whenever its true meaning is understood. But I believe nobody will deny that it is often very abstruse, and may say things which are quite different from what its bare words signify. Hence in expounding the Bible if one were always to confine oneself to the unadorned grammatical meaning, one might; fall into error. Not only contradictions and propositions far from true might thus be made to appear in the Bible, but even grave heresies and follies. Thus it would be necessary to assign to God feet, hands and eyes, as well as corporeal and human affections, such as anger, repentance, hatred, and sometimes even the forgetting of things past and ignorance of those to come. These propositions uttered by the Holy Ghost were set down in that manner by the sacred scribes in order to accommodate them to the capacities of the common people, who are rude and unlearned. For the sake of those who deserve to be separated from the herd, it is necessary that wise expositors should produce the true senses of such passages, together with the special reasons for which they were set down in these words. This doctrine is so widespread and so definite with all theologians that it would be superfluous to adduce evidence for it.

Hence I think that I may reasonably conclude that whenever the Bible has occasion to speak to any physical conclusion (especially those which are very abstruse and hard to understand), the rule has been observed of avoiding confusion in the minds of the common people which would render them contumacious toward the higher mysteries. Now the Bible, merely to condescend to popular capacity, has not hesitated to obscure some very important pronouncements, attributing to God himself some qualities extremely remote from (and even contrary to) his essence. Who, then, would positively declare that this principle has been set aside, and the Bible has confined itself rigorously to the bare and restricted sense of its words, when speaking but casually of the earth, of water, of the sun, or of any other created thing? Especially in view of the fact that these things in no way concern the primary purpose of the sacred writings, which is the service of God and the salvation of souls—matters infinitely beyond the comprehension of the common people.

This being granted, I think that in discussions of physical problems we ought to begin not from the authority of scriptural passages but from sense experiences and necessary demonstrations; for the holy Bible and the phenomena of nature proceed alike from the divine Word: the former as the dictate of the Holy Ghost and the latter as the observant executrix of God's commands. It is necessary for the Bible, in order to be accommodated to the understanding of every man, to speak many things which appear to differ from the absolute truth so far as the bare meaning of the words is concerned. But Nature, on the other hand, is inexorable and immutable; she never transgresses the laws imposed upon her, or cares a whit whether her abstruse reasons and methods of operation are understandable to men. For that reason it appears that nothing physical which sense experience sets before our eyes, or which necessary demonstrations prove to us, ought to be called in question (much less condemned) upon the testimony of biblical passages which may have some different meaning beneath their words. For the Bible is not chained in every expression to conditions as strict as those which govern all physical effects; nor is God any less excellently revealed in Nature's actions than in the sacred statements of the Bible. Perhaps this is what Tertullian meant by these words: "We conclude that God is known first through Nature, and then again, more particularly, by doctrine, by Nature in his works, and by doctrine in his revealed word."

From this I do not mean to infer that we need not have an extraordinary esteem for the passages of holy Scripture. On the contrary, having arrived at any certainties in physics, we ought to utilize these as the most appropriate aids in the true exposition of the Bible and in the investigation of those meanings which are necessarily contained therein, for these must be concordant with demonstrated truths. I should judge that the authority of the Bible was designed to persuade men of those articles and propositions which, surpassing all human reasoning could not be made credible by science, or by any other means than through the very mouth of the Holy Spirit.

But I do not feel obliged to believe that the same God who has endowed us with senses, reason and intellect has intended us to forego their use and by some other means to give us knowledge which we can attain by them. He would not require us to deny sense and reason in physical matters which are set before our eyes and minds by direct experience or necessary demonstrations. This must be especially true in those sciences of which but the faintest trace (and that consisting of conclusions) is to be found in the Bible. Of astronomy; for instance, so little is found that none of the planets except Venus are so much as mentioned, and this only once or twice under the name of "Lucifer." If the sacred scribes had had any intention of teaching people certain arrangements and motions of the heavenly bodies, or had they wished us to derive such knowledge from the Bible, then in my opinion they would not have spoken of these matters so sparingly in comparison with the infinite number of admirable conclusions which are demonstrated in that science. Far from pretending to teach us the constitution and motions of the heavens and other stars, with their shapes, magnitudes, and distances, the authors of the Bible intentionally forbore to speak of these things, though all were quite well known to them. . . .

From these things it follows as a necessary consequence that, since the Holy Ghost did not intend to teach us whether heaven moves or stands still, whether its shape is spherical or like a discus or extended in a plane, nor whether the earth is located at its center or off to one side, then so much the less was it intended to settle for us any other conclusion of the same kind. And the motion or rest of the earth and the sun is so closely linked with the things just named, that without a determination of the one, neither side can be taken in the other matters. Now if the Holy Spirit has purposely neglected to teach us propositions of this sort as irrelevant to the highest goal (that is, to our salvation), how can anyone affirm that it is obligatory to take sides on them, that one belief is required by faith, while the other side is erroneous? Can an opinion be heretical and yet have no concern with the salvation of souls? Can the Holy Ghost be asserted not to have intended teaching us something that does concern our salvation? I would say here something that was heard from an ecclesiastic of the most eminent degree: "That the intention of the Holy Ghost is to teach us how one goes to heaven, not how heaven goes."

"Address to the Pontifical Academy of Science"

Pope John Paul II

"Truth cannot contradict truth"

—Pope Leo XIII

Author Background

Pope John Paul II (1920–2005) reigned as pope for almost twenty-seven years. Throughout his long papacy, he spoke out against war, fascism, communism, materialism, abortion, and relativism. He termed many of the philosophies and actions of the twentieth century "a culture of death." He urged humankind to return to God and for modern thinkers to return to their Christian roots. He spoke for the Church's belief in a "culture of life," where all peoples would be treated with dignity because of their common humanity as children of God and brothers of Christ.

Pope John Paul II was a most learned man with a broad background in literature and culture who had earned a doctorate in philosophy. He considered a major task of his papacy to continue the work of the Second Vatican Council, which called the Church to enter into dialogue with the modern world and into conversation with men and women of science. He was a strong promoter and supporter of the Pontifical Academy of Science, which was established in 1936 to promote progress in mathematics, physics, and the natural sciences and to encourage dialogue where the discoveries of science seemed to conflict with religious thinking. Pope John Paul II presided over several sessions of the Pontifical Academy of Science, whose members (Catholics, non-Catholics, and non-believers) investigated the implications of scientific discoveries for culture and religion.

Before the Reading

In 1979, Pope John Paul II expressed the wish that the Pontifical Academy of Sciences would conduct an in-depth study of the celebrated and controversial "Galileo case," devoting its meeting to a study of the notion of complexity and the various methods of examining reality. A commission of scholars was established for this purpose in 1981, and it chose Cardinal Paul Poupard to present their conclusions to the pope that same year on the distinct but complementary roles that faith and science fulfill in human life.

The Galileo case teaches us that different branches of knowledge call for different methods of inquiry, each of which brings out various aspects of reality. In his remarks to the Pontifical Academy, the pope commended Galileo for his profound understanding of the interpretation of Scripture and directed contemporary theologians to keep themselves abreast of modern scientific research. He also warned scientists of the danger of *scientism*, a method of thinking that would deny all spiritual reality. In 1979 Pope John Paul II asked that the conviction of Galileo by the Church court be annulled, and in 1992 this event took place. Thus Galileo was seen in his true light, as a genius of science and as a loyal and devoted follower of Christ.

"Address to the Pontifical Academy of Science"

Your Eminences, Your Excellencies, Ladies and Gentlemen,

In the first place, I wish to congratulate the Pontifical Academy of Sciences for having chosen to deal, in its plenary session, with a problem of great importance and great relevance today: the problem of the emergence of complexity in mathematics, physics, chemistry and biology.

The emergence of the subject of complexity probably marks in the history of the natural sciences a stage as important as the stage that bears relation to the name of Galileo, when a univocal model of order seemed to be obvious. Complexity indicates precisely that, in order to account for the rich variety of reality, we must have recourse to a number of different models.

Contemporary culture demands a constant effort to synthesize knowledge and to integrate learning. Of course, the successes that we see are due to the specialization of research. But unless this is balanced by a reflection concerned with articulating the various branches of knowledge, there is a great risk that we shall have a "shattered culture," which would in fact be the negation of true culture. A true culture cannot be conceived of without humanism and wisdom.

I was moved by similar concerns on 10 November 1979, at the time of the first centenary of the birth of Albert Einstein, when I expressed the hope before this same Academy that "theologians, scholars and historians, animated by a spirit of sincere collaboration, will study the Galileo case more deeply and, in frank recognition of wrongs from whatever side they come, dispel the mistrust that still opposes, in many minds, a fruitful concord between science and faith.

One might perhaps be surprised that at the end of the Academy's study week on the theme of the emergence of complexity in the various sciences, I am returning to the Galileo case. Has not this case long been shelved and have not the errors committed been recognized?

That is certainly true. However, the underlying problems of this case concern both the nature of science and the message of faith. It is therefore not to be excluded that one day we shall find ourselves in a similar situation, one which will require both sides to have an informed awareness of the field and of the limits of their own competencies. The approach provided by the theme of complexity could provide an illustration of this.

A twofold question is at the heart of the debate of which Galileo was the center. The first is of the epistemological order and concerns biblical hermeneutics. In this regard, two points must again be raised. In the first place, like most of his adversaries, Galileo made no distinction between the scientific approach to natural phenomena and a reflection on nature, of the philosophical order, which that approach generally calls for. That is why he rejected the suggestion made to him to present the Copernican system as a hypothesis, inasmuch as it had not been confirmed by irrefutable proof. Such therefore, was an exigency of the experimental method of which he was the inspired founder.

Secondly the geocentric representation of the world was commonly admitted in the culture of the time as fully agreeing with the teaching of the Bible of which certain expressions, taken literally seemed to affirm geocentrism. The problem posed by theologians of that age was, therefore, that of the compatibility between heliocentrism and Scripture.

Thus the new science, with its methods and the freedom of research which they implied, obliged theologians to examine their own criteria of scriptural interpretation. Most of them did not know how to do so.

Paradoxically, Galileo, a sincere believer, showed himself to be more perceptive in this regard than the theologians who opposed him. "If Scripture cannot err," he wrote to Benedetto Castelli, "certain of its interpreters and commentators can and do so in many ways." We also know of his letter to Christine de Lorraine (1615) which is like a short treatise on biblical hermeneutics.

From this we can now draw our first conclusion. The birth of a new way of approaching the study of natural phenomena demands a clarification on the part of all disciplines of knowledge. It obliges them to define more clearly their own field, their approach, their methods, as well as the precise import of their conclusions. In other words, this new way requires each discipline to become more rigorously aware of its own nature.

It is necessary to repeat here what I said above. It is a duty for theologians to keep themselves regularly informed of scientific advances in order to examine if such be necessary, whether or not there are reasons for taking them into account in their reflection or for introducing changes in their teaching.

If contemporary culture is marked by a tendency to scientism, the cultural horizon of Galileo's age was uniform and carried the imprint of a particular philosophical formation. This unitary character of culture, which in itself is positive and desirable even in our own day, was one of the reasons for Galileo's condemnation. The majority of theologians did not recognize the formal distinction between Sacred Scripture and its interpretation, and this led them unduly to transpose into the realm of the doctrine of the faith a question which in fact pertained to scientific investigation.

In fact, as Cardinal Poupard has recalled, Robert Bellarmine, who had seen what was truly at stake in the debate personally felt that, in the face of possible scientific proofs that the earth orbited round the sun, one should "interpret with great circumspection" every biblical passage which seems to affirm that the earth is immobile and "say that we do not understand, rather than affirm that what has been demonstrated is false." Before Bellarmine, this same wisdom and same respect for the divine Word guided St Augustine when he wrote: "If it happens that the authority of Sacred Scripture is set in opposition to clear and certain reasoning, this must mean that the person who interprets Scripture does not understand it correctly. It is not the meaning of Scripture which is opposed to the truth but the meaning which he has wanted to give to it. That which is opposed to Scripture is not what is in Scripture but what he has placed there himself, believing that this is what Scripture meant." A century ago, Pope Leo XIII echoed this advice in his encyclical *Providentissimus Deus*: "Truth cannot contradict truth" and we may be sure that some mistake has been made either in the interpretation of the sacred words, or in the polemical discussion itself.

From the beginning of the Age of Enlightenment down to our own day, the Galileo case has been a sort of "myth," in which the image fabricated out of the events was quite far removed from reality. In this perspective, the Galileo case was the symbol of the Church's supposed rejection of scientific progress, or of "dogmatic" obscurantism opposed to the free search for truth. This myth has played a considerable cultural role. It has helped to anchor a number of scientists of good faith in the idea that there was an incompatibility between the spirit of science and its rules of research on the one hand and the Christian faith on the other. A tragic mutual incomprehension has been interpreted as the reflection of a fundamental opposition between science and faith. The clarifications furnished by recent historical studies enable us to state that this sad misunderstanding now belongs to the past.

From the Galileo affair we can learn a lesson which remains valid in relation to similar situations which occur today and which may occur in the future.

In Galileo's time, to depict the world as lacking an absolute physical reference point was, so to speak, inconceivable. And since the cosmos, as it was then known, was contained within the solar system alone, this reference point could only be situated in the earth or in the sun. Today, after Einstein and within the perspective of contemporary cosmology neither of these two reference points has the importance they once had. This observation, it goes without saying, is not directed against the validity of Galileo's position in the debate; it is only meant to show that often, beyond two partial and contrasting perceptions, there exists a wider perception which includes them and goes beyond both of them.

Another lesson which we can draw is that the different branches of knowledge call for different methods. Thanks to his intuition as a brilliant physicist and by relying on different arguments, Galileo, who practically invented the experimental method, understood why only the sun could function as the center of the world, as it was then known, that is to say, as a planetary system. The error of the theologians of the time, when they maintained the centrality of the earth, was to think that our understanding of the physical world's structure was, in some way, imposed by the literal sense of Sacred Scripture. In fact, the Bible does not concern itself with the details of the physical world, the understanding of which is the competence of human experience and reasoning. There exist two realms of knowledge, one which has its source in Revelation and one which reason can discover by its own power. To the latter belong especially the experimental sciences and philosophy. The distinction between the two realms of knowledge ought not to be understood as opposition. The two realms are not altogether foreign to each other, they have points of contact. The methodologies proper to each make it possible to bring out different aspects of reality.

Humanity has before it two modes of development. The first involves culture, scientific research and technology that is to say whatever falls within the horizontal aspect of man and creation which is growing at an impressive rate. In order that this progress should not remain completely external to man, it presupposes a simultaneous raising of conscience, as well as its actuation. The second mode of development involves what is deepest in the human being, when transcending the world and transcending himself, man turns to the One who is the Creator of all. It is only this vertical direction which can give full meaning to man's being and action, because it situates him in relation to his origin and his end. In this twofold direction, horizontal and vertical, man realizes himself fully as a spiritual being and as *homo sapiens*. But we see that development is not uniform and linear, and that progress is not always well ordered. This reveals the disorder which affects the human condition. The scientist who is conscious of this twofold development and takes it into account contributes to the restoration of harmony.

Those who engage in scientific and technological research admit as the premise of its progress, that the world is not a chaos but a "cosmos"—that is to say, that there exist order and natural laws which can be grasped and examined, and which, for this reason, have a certain affinity with the spirit. Einstein used to say: "What is eternally incomprehensible in the world is that it is comprehensible." This intelligibility, attested to by the marvelous discoveries of science and technology, leads us, in the last analysis, to that transcendent and primordial Thought imprinted on all things.

Reading for Comprehension

1. Who was Nicholas Copernicus?
2. What is meant by the terms *heliocentrism* and *geocentrism*?

3. What illustrations did Galileo give for showing that it was impossible to read the Bible in a literal fashion?

4. Why did Pope John Paul II praise Galileo?

5. What did Pope John Paul II mean when he referred to "the myth of the Galileo case"?

Reading for Understanding

1. Why were so many theologians threatened by heliocentrism?

2. An eminent, atheistic physician said, in support of his view, that he had performed thousands of autopsies but never discovered the soul in any of the corpses. What do you think Pope John Paul II would say is the error in this type of thinking?

3. What is meant by a "fundamentalist approach" to the interpretation of Scripture? What is the difficulty with this approach to the interpretation of Scripture? Why do Catholics have no difficulty with the discoveries of science as these discoveries relate to Scripture?

Activity

Today many people see a conflict between the Genesis creation stories (see Genesis 1:1–2:4) and the theories of evolution in accounting for the origins of the human race. Using the principles discussed in the readings from the Galileo case, what do you think the Catholic position is on this controversy? For further clarification of this issue, see Pope John Paul II's "Message to the Pontifical Academy of Sciences: On Evolution" (1996).

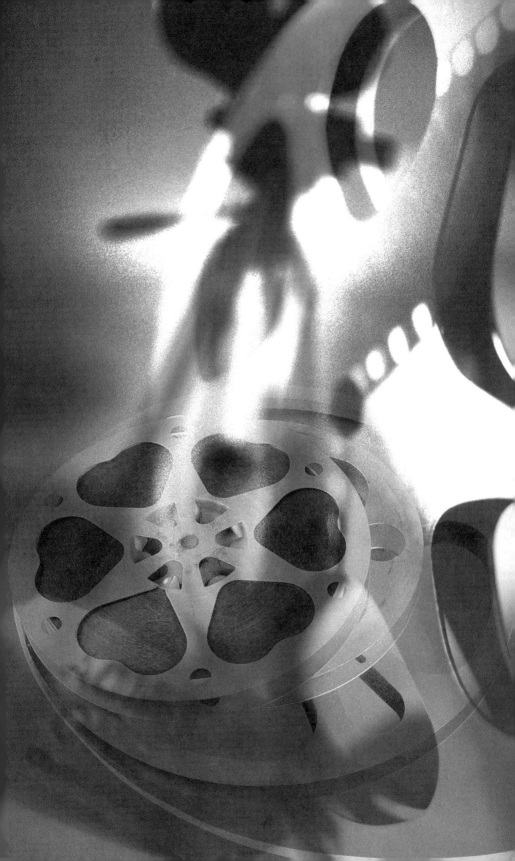

WHAT WE BELIEVE
(The Profession of Faith)

SEEING WITH THE ARTIST

Use an Internet search engine to locate the following artwork. After reading the background material below, write your impressions of the piece and complete the first assignment on page 140.

The Painting

Crucifixion (Corpus Hypercubus)—**Salvador Dali (1904–1989)**

In this painting, the great surrealist Salvador Dali shows a crucified Christ who is beyond time and space. There are no wounds on his body. This is truly Christ in his Divine nature. The painting is based on the mathematical form, the hypercube. To stress the mathematical nature of the painting, Dali portrays his wife looking adoringly at the crucified Christ as she stands on an enormous chess board. In this painting, Dali said that he wished to show that there was no conflict between religion and science, and that Christ existed not only in time but could be seen eternally in the laws of mathematics of the cosmos.

LOOKING AT FILM

God's revelation is ongoing. The Church's debate with Galileo on the compatibility between science and religion is expressed in the following film. Read the synopsis. Watch the film. Complete relevant assignments related to the film (see page 140).

The Film

2001: A Space Odyssey (1968)—Directed by Stanley Kubrick

Rating: Vatican Top Forty-five Films

This brilliant film is a wonderful vehicle for exploring the relationship between science and religion. The mechanical life of the astronauts as they travel through space shows the emptiness of a life without God. The guiding presence of the unnamed "monolith" allows the filmmaker to develop the idea of a divine guiding force that is intimately involved with the lives of human beings. The opening sequence of the film, which shows the transformation of apes with an animal soul into human-like creatures with the gift of thought, is an ideal vehicle by which to discuss the creation stories of the Book of Genesis and to examine the relationship between evolution versus creationism.

LISTENING TO SACRED MUSIC

Several types of music are traditional in the Church. The three types described below, as with others, help to initiate a sense of God's presence. Both lyrics and the music itself are able to reveal how God is near. Read the descriptions of chant, polyphonic, and contemporary religious music. Then search out an example of each type of music on the Internet or by purchasing a sample. After meditative listening, write your feelings about the music. Answer: "How did the music help to reveal God's presence in your life?"

The Music

Chant

This form of music stresses the importance of hearing and understanding the words that are being sung. The musical expression is simple, and unadorned with complex melodies. The most popular form of this type of music, which was used in the Church for over a thousand years, is *Gregorian chant*.

A contemporary setting for chanted music has been composed by Fr. Joseph Gelineau, S.J. Gelineau's psalms maintain the essence of chant by providing music that allows the words to be more easily understood. He sets these words, however, to modern music, which makes it much more accessible to congregational singing.

Another contemporary musical form of chant that stresses sung words and encourages congregational singing are the hymns produced at Taize, France, home of an ecumenical community of Christians.

Polyphonic

Liturgical music that makes use of musical instruments and multi-part choral settings is among the most beautiful musical settings ever composed. This music, with its complex instrumental patterns and a vocal arrangement that makes use of four, six, or eight different vocal groups, provides an awe-inspiring experience for the congregation. Examples of this music can be found in sacred music recordings by Johann Sebastian Bach, Thomas Tallis, Palestrina, and Gabrielli.

Contemporary Music

Examples of composers who use contemporary musical forms to create complex musical expressions are Henryk Gorecki, Arvo Part, and John Tavener.

Popular religious music that makes use of country and Western and rhythm and blues musical themes includes *Peace in the Valley: The Complete Gospel Recordings of Elvis Presley*, and *Gospels, Spirituals and Hymns* by Mahalia Jackson.

ACTIVITIES

1. For some people, the ultimate statement of a scientific truth is a mathematical formula. They give no credence to the truths of art or philosophy; they only believe in numbers. How does Dali use this obsession with mathematical truth to highlight the value of artistic and religious truth in his painting, *Corpus Hypercubus*?

2. How is the creation of human life visualized in the opening sequence of *2001: A Space Odyssey*?

3. Many of the Church Fathers, including St. Augustine and St. Jerome, were opposed to using contemporary secular music as a background for Christian hymns. They felt that such music made the congregation focus on the talent and energy of the performing artist and the rhythm of the music, rather than raising their hearts and minds to God. In essence, they believed that such music was not religious but secular. Listen to the hymns of Mahalia Jackson or Elvis Presley and then react to this type of music: Is it secular or religious? Provide reasons to support your view.

The Uniqueness of Mary, the Mother of God

"The Blessed Virgin Mary Compared to a Window"

Thomas Merton

> By the power of the Holy Spirit he was born of the Virgin Mary, and became man.
>
> **—Nicene Creed**

Author Background

Thomas Merton (1915–1968) led a very irreligious life in his younger days. While a student at Columbia University in New York City, Merton began to be attracted to Catholicism. After much prayer and many spiritual experiences, he became Catholic.

In 1941, Merton entered the Trappist Order and was later ordained with the name of Father Louis. The contemplative religious order that Merton entered is one of the most austere in the Church. The Trappists fast in every season of the year and live in almost perpetual silence. All of their energy is devoted to building up an intense interior life of union with God.

In 1948 Merton published his autobiography *The Seven Storey Mountain*, which told of his life as a layman and his beginnings as a Trappist. Merton wrote scores of books and articles on the life of prayer. He was also a pacifist and a firm believer in social justice; his writings tried to show the relationship between prayer and the life of Christian action. *Contemplation in a World of Action* is one of his most famous books.

Merton died in Bangkok, Thailand, in 1968 of accidental electrocution while attending a conference on contemplation.

Before the Reading

From the beginning of the Church, faithful believers have honored the Blessed Virgin Mary and understood the unique role she had in God's plan for the salvation of humankind. Because Mary has such a crucial role in our salvation and because Jesus gave her to the Church as our Mother, Catholics have always turned to her for guidance, protection, and love. Mary's special role in the history of salvation, her union with God, her humility, and her concern for her children on earth are strongly illustrated in the following poem.

"The Blessed Virgin Mary Compared to a Window"

Because my will is simple as a window
And knows no pride of original earth,
It is my life to die, like glass, by light:
Slain in the strong rays of the bridegroom sun.

Because my love is simple as a window
And knows no shame of original dust,
I longed all night, (when I was visible) for dawn my death:
When I would marry day, my Holy Spirit:
And die by transubstantiation into light.

For light, my lover, steals my life in secret.
I vanish into day, and leave no shadow
But the geometry of my cross,
Whose frame and structure are the strength
By which I die, but only to the earth,
And am uplifted to the sky my life.

When I become the substance of my lover,
(Being obedient, sinless glass)
I love all things that need my lover's life,
And live to give my newborn Morning to your quiet rooms,

Your rooms, that would be tombs,
Or vaults of night, and death, and terror,
Fill with the clarity of living Heaven,
Shine with the rays of God's Jerusalem:
O shine, bright Sions!

Because I die by brightness and the Holy Spirit,
The sun rejoices in your jail, my kneeling Christian,
(Where even now you weep and grin
To learn, from my simplicity, the strength of faith.)

Therefore do not be troubled at the judgments of the thunder.
Stay still and pray, still stay, my other son,
And do not fear the armies and black ramparts
Of the advancing and retreating rains:
I'll let no lightning kill your room's white order.

Although it is the day's last hour,
Look with no fear:
For the torn storm lets in, at the world's rim,
Three streaming rays as straight as Jacob's ladder:

And you shall see the sun, my Son, my Substance,
Come to convince the world of the day's end, and of the night,
Smile to the lovers of the day in smiles of blood:
For through my love, He'll be their Brother,
My light—the Lamb of their Apocalypse.

Reading for Comprehension

1. In the poem, what does Mary say would happen to our rooms if she were not transparent?

2. What happens to the "kneeling Christian" who dies by brightness and the Holy Spirit?

3. What does the Blessed Virgin say to Christians when they hear the thunder and are afraid?

Reading for Understanding

1. The Blessed Virgin Mary was preserved by God from all stain of Original Sin. This privilege of Mary is known as the "Immaculate Conception." In what ways does Merton describe this sinless quality of the Blessed Virgin Mary in stanzas one and two?

2. What does glass do for light? How is glass used as a symbol for the Virgin in the poem?

Activities

1. One of the most popular prayers of the Church is the *Salve Regina* (Hail, Holy Queen). Look up and recite this prayer slowly. Then explain how it reflects three qualities of the Blessed Virgin Mary.

2. Gerard Manley Hopkins wrote a long poem titled "The Blessed Virgin Compared to the Air We Breathe." Look up and read this poem. Then focus on three images that Hopkins uses to explain the special relationship that Mary has to the Church.

The Uniqueness of Mary, the Mother of God

"Our Lady's Juggler"

Anatole France

I am a flower of Sharon, a lily of the valley.
—**Song of Songs 2:1**

Author Background

Anatole France (1844–1924) was a prolific French writer and man of letters who was awarded the Nobel Prize for Literature in 1921. Most of France's writings are marked by pessimism and skepticism. The following tale shows a sweetness and a religious sensibility that are rarely found in his other writings.

Before the Reading

Throughout history, legends and tales have been used to deepen our understanding of historical events and human character. In American lore, the story of George Washington and the cherry tree comes to mind. When asked by his father about the destruction of the tree, young George reportedly replied: "Father, I cannot tell a lie. It was I who chopped down the tree." The story may or may not have happened as told in the legend. What remains true is that George Washington, throughout his life, was a man of truth, honor, and integrity, and that the tale illustrates the nobility of his character. In the same way, pious tales and legends have been told about Mary, the saints, and other devout people to illustrate their goodness, beauty, and service of God. God's care for even the most humble of his creatures is seen in this delightful retelling of a medieval legend.

"Our Lady's Juggler"

In the days of King Louis there was a poor juggler in France, a native of Compiegne, Barnaby by name, who went about from town to town performing feats of skill and strength.

On fair days he would unfold an old worn-out carpet in the public square, and when by means of jovial address, which he had learned of a very ancient juggler, and which he never varied in the least, he had drawn together the children and loafers, he assumed extraordinary attitudes, and balanced a tin plate on the tip of his nose. At first the crowd would feign indifference.

But when, supporting himself on his hands face downwards, he threw into the air six copper balls, which glittered in the sunshine, and caught them again with his feet; or when throwing himself backwards until his heels and the nape of the neck met, giving his body the form of a perfect wheel, he would juggle in this posture with a dozen knives, a murmur of admiration would escape the spectators, and pieces of money rain down upon the carpet.

Nevertheless, like the majority of those who live by their wits, Barnaby of Compiegne had a great struggle to make a living.

Earning his bread in the sweat of his brow, he bore rather more than his share of the penalties consequent upon the misdoings of our father Adam.

Again, he was unable to work as constantly as he would have been willing to do. The warmth of the sun and the broad daylight were as necessary to enable him to display his brilliant parts as to the trees if flower and fruit should be expected of them. In winter time he was nothing more than a tree stripped of its leaves, and as it were dead.

The frozen ground was hard to the juggler, and, like the grasshopper of which Marie de France tells us, the inclement season caused him to suffer both cold and hunger. But as he was simple-natured he bore his ills patiently.

He had never meditated on the origin of wealth, nor upon the inequality of human conditions. He believed firmly that if this life should prove hard, the life to come could not fail to redress the balance, and this hope upheld him. He did not resemble those thievish and miscreant Merry Andrews who sell their souls to the devil. He never blasphemed God's name; he lived uprightly, and although he had no wife of his own, he did not covet his neighbor's, since woman is ever the enemy of the strong man, as it appears by the history of Samson recorded in the Scriptures.

In truth, his was not a nature much disposed to carnal delights, and it was a greater deprivation to him to forsake the tankard than the Hebe who bore it. For whilst not wanting in sobriety, he was fond of a drink when the weather waxed hot. He was a worthy man who feared God, and was very devoted to the Blessed Virgin.

Never did he fail on entering a church to fall upon his knees before the image of the Mother of God, and offer up this prayer to her:

"Blessed Lady, keep watch over my life until it shall please God that I die, and when I am dead, ensure to me the possession of the joys of paradise."

Now on a certain evening after a dreary wet day, as Barnaby pursued his road, sad and bent, carrying under his arm his balls and knives wrapped up on his old carpet, on the watch for some barn where, though he might not sup, he might sleep, he perceived on the road, going in the same direction as himself, a monk, whom he saluted courteously. And as they walked at the same rate they fell into conversation with one another.

"Fellow traveller," said the monk, "how comes it about that you are clothed all in green? Is it perhaps in order to take the part a jester in some mystery play?" "Not at all, good Father," replied Barnaby. "Such as you see me, I am called Barnaby, and for my calling I am a juggler. There would be no pleasanter calling in the world if it would always provide one with daily bread."

"Friend Barnaby," returned the monk," be careful what you say. There is no calling more pleasant than the monastic life. Those who lead it are occupied with the praises of God, the Blessed Virgin, and the saints; and, indeed, the religious life is one ceaseless hymn to the Lord."

Barnaby replied—"Good Father, I own that I spoke like an ignorant man. Your calling cannot be in any respect compared to mine, and although there may be some merit in dancing with a penny balanced on a stick on the tip of one's nose, it is not a merit which comes within hail of your own. Gladly would I, like you, good Father, sing my office day by day, and especially the office of the most Holy Virgin, to whom I have vowed a singular devotion. In order to embrace the monastic life I would willingly abandon the art by which from Soissons to Beauvais I am well known in upwards of six hundred towns and villages."

The monk was touched by the juggler's simplicity, and as he was not lacking in discernment, he at once recognized in Barnaby one of those men of whom it is said in the Scriptures: Peace on earth to men of good will. And for this reason he replied—

"Friend Barnaby, come with me, and I will have you admitted into the monastery of which I am Prior. He who guided St. Mary of Egypt in the desert set me upon your path to lead you into the way of salvation."

It was in this manner, then, that Barnaby became a monk. In the monastery into which he was received the religious vied with one another in the worship of the Blessed Virgin, and in her honor each employed all the knowledge and all the skill which God had given him.

The prior on his part wrote books dealing according to the rules of scholarship with the virtues of the Mother of God. Brother Maurice, with a deft hand, copied out these treatises upon sheets of vellum.

Brother Alexander adorned the leaves with delicate miniature paintings. Here were displayed the Queen of Heaven seated upon Solomon's throne, and while four lions were on guard at her feet, around the nimbus which encircled her head hovered seven doves, which are the seven gifts of the Holy Spirit, the gifts, namely, of Fear, Piety, Knowledge, Strength, Counsel, Understanding, and

Wisdom. For her companions she had six virgins with hair of gold, namely, Humility, Prudence, Seclusion, Submission, Virginity, and Obedience.

At her feet were two little naked figures, perfectly white, in an attitude of supplication. These were souls imploring her all-powerful intercession for their soul's health, and we may be sure not imploring in vain.

Upon another page facing this, Brother Alexander represented Eve, so that the Fall and the Redemption could be perceived at one and the same time—Eve the Wife abased, and Mary the Virgin exalted.

Furthermore, to the marvel of the beholder, this book contained presentments of the Well of Living Waters, the Fountain, the Lily, the Moon, the Sun, and the Garden Enclosed of which the Song of Songs tells us, the Gate of Heaven and the City of God, and all these things were symbols of the Blessed Virgin.

Brother Marbode was likewise one of the most loving children of Mary.

He spent all his days carving images in stone, so that his beard, his eyebrows, and his hair were white with dust, and his eyes continually swollen and weeping; but his strength and cheerfulness were not diminished, although he was now well gone in years, and it was clear that the Queen of Paradise still cherished her servant in his old age. Marbode represented her seated upon a throne, her brow encircled with an orb-shaped nimbus set with pearls. And he took care that the folds of her dress should cover the feet of her, concerning whom the prophet declared: My beloved is as a garden enclosed.

Sometimes, too, he depicted her in the semblance of a child full of grace, and appearing to say, "Thou art my God, even from my mother's womb."

In the priory, moreover, were poets who composed hymns in Latin, both in prose and verse, in honor of the Blessed Virgin Mary, and amongst the company was even a brother from Picardy who sang the miracles of Our Lady in rhymed verse and in the vulgar tongue.

Being a witness of this emulation in praise and the glorious harvest of their labors, Barnaby mourned his own ignorance and simplicity.

"Alas!" he sighed, as he took his solitary walk in the little shelterless garden of the monastery, "wretched weight that I am, to be unable, like my brothers, worthily to praise the Holy Mother of God, to whom I have vowed my whole heart's affection. Alas! alas! I am but a rough man and unskilled in the arts, and I can render you in service, blessed Lady, neither edifying sermons, nor treatises set out in order according to rule, nor ingenious paintings, nor statues truthfully sculptured, nor verses whose march is measured to the beat of feet. No gift have I, alas!"

After this fashion he groaned and gave himself up to sorrow. But one evening, when the monks were spending their hour of liberty in conversation, he heard one of them tell the tale of a religious man who could repeat nothing other than the *Ave Maria*. This poor man was despised for his ignorance; but after his death there issued forth from his mouth five roses in honor of the five letters of the name Mary (Marie), and thus his sanctity was made manifest.

While he listened to this narrative Barnaby marvelled yet once again at the loving kindness of the Virgin; but the lesson of that blessed death did not avail to console him, for his heart overflowed with zeal, and he longed to advance the glory of his Lady, who is in heaven.

How to compass this he sought but could find no way, and day by day he became the more cast down, when one morning he awakened filled full with joy, hastened to the chapel, and remained there alone for more than an hour. After dinner he returned to the chapel once more.

And, starting from that moment, he repaired daily to the chapel at such hours as it was deserted, and spent within it a good part of the time which the other monks devoted to the liberal and mechanical arts. His sadness vanished, nor did he any longer groan.

A demeanor so strange awakened the curiosity of the monks.

These began to ask one another for what purpose Brother Barnaby could be indulging so persistently in retreat.

The prior, whose duty it is to let nothing escape him in the behavior of his children in religion, resolved to keep watch over Barnaby during his withdrawals to the chapel. One day, then when he was shut up there after his custom, the prior, accompanied by two of the older monks, went to discover through the chinks in the door what was going on within the chapel.

They saw Barnaby before the altar of the Blessed Virgin, head downwards, with his feet in the air, and he was juggling with six balls of copper and a dozen knives. In honor of the Holy Mother of God he was performing those feats, which aforetime had won him most renown. Not recognizing that the simple fellow was thus placing at the service of the Blessed Virgin his knowledge and skill, the two old monks exclaimed against the sacrilege.

The prior was aware how stainless was Barnaby's soul, but he concluded that he had been seized with madness. They were all three preparing to lead him swiftly from the chapel, when they saw the Blessed Virgin descend the steps of the altar and advance to wipe away with a fold of her azure robe the sweat which was dropping from her juggler's forehead.

"Blessed are the simple-hearted, for they shall see God."

"Amen!" responded the old brethren, and kissed the ground.

Reading for Comprehension

1. Why was Barnaby unable to work during the winter?

2. What did the monk that Barnaby met on the road do for him?

3. In what ways did Brothers Maurice, Alexander, and Marbode honor the Blessed Virgin?

4. What did the prior and the two other brothers see when they spied on Barnaby in the chapel?

5. What did the Blessed Virgin do for the juggler?

6. What are the seven gifts of the Holy Spirit that Brother Alexander represented in his drawing?

Reading for Understanding

1. Why is the Blessed Virgin Mary sometimes referred to as the "New Eve"?

2. In the parable of the Prayer of the Pharisee and the Publican, Jesus pointed out that the humble prayer of a poor man or a sinner may be more valuable in God's eyes than the self-righteous prayers of a highly educated man. How is this teaching of Jesus reflected in the story of "Our Lady's Juggler"?

Activity

Throughout history Jesus and Mary have appeared to individuals and made private revelations to them. The Church has recommended many of these revelations, but they are not part of the deposit of faith. They are meant to be aids to prayer and devotion. One of the most famous of these private revelations occurred when Our Lady appeared to a poor shepherd girl, Bernadette Soubirous, in 1858 in Lourdes, France. Read Franz Werfel's outstanding novel, *The Song of Bernadette*, and write a reflection on how Bernadette's simplicity and trust made her a kindred spirit to the character of Barnaby in "Our Lady's Juggler." Or, you can also answer the question by viewing the outstanding film based on the novel, *The Song of Bernadette* (see pages 176–177), which starred Jennifer Jones.

The Communion of Saints

"Marble Floor"
Karol Wojtyla (Pope John Paul II)

We believe in one holy catholic and apostolic Church
—Nicene Creed

Author Background

Pope John Paul II (see mini-biography on page 127) was also a respected poet. Most of his poems were written and published anonymously before he was elected to the papacy. These poems were later collected and published under his baptismal name, Karol Wojtyla, while he served as pope.

Before the Reading

The term "Church" derives from the Greek *ek-ka-lein* and the Latin word *ecclesia*. It refers to a convocation or assembly. Church has many theological meanings that point out the many ways that humankind encounters the divine. "The Church is essentially both human and divine, . . . so constituted that in her the human is directed toward and subordinated to the divine, the visible to the invisible, action to contemplation, and this present world to that city yet to come . . ." (St. Bernard of Clairvaux, *Cant. Srm*, 27:14).

In its visible aspect the Church is composed of bishops, priests, laity, and religious, each of whom play a specific role in making Christ present in the world. One of the primary responsibilities of bishops, the descendents of the Apostles, is to teach and to govern the Church. Christ himself appointed St. Peter to lead the apostles when he said, "And so I say to you, you are Peter, and upon this rock I will build my church"(Mt 16:18). The pope, therefore, is a descendent of St. Peter who is a sign of unity and stability for the entire Church—for all the People of God. The mystical meaning of the papacy is reflected in the following poem, which was written by Karol

Wojtyla during the Second Vatican Council in 1962, sixteen years before Wojtyla was elected pope and chose the name John Paul II.

"Marble Floor"

Our feet meet the earth in this place;
there are so many walls, so many colonnades,
yet we are not lost. If we find
meaning and oneness,
it is the floor that guides us. It joins the spaces
of this great edifice, and joins
the spaces within us,
who walk aware of our weakness and defeat.
Peter, you are the floor, that others
may walk over you (not knowing
where they go). You guide their steps
so that spaces can be one in their eyes,
and from them thought is born.
You want to serve their feet that pass
as rock serves the hooves of sheep.
The rock is a gigantic temple floor,
the cross a pasture.

Reading for Comprehension

1. What is it that guides us as we walk amidst the walls and colonnades of a church?

2. What Apostle does the floor represent?

3. One of the titles of the pope is "the servant of the servants of God." What portion of the poem represents this title of the pope?

Reading for Understanding

1. The poem states that in the Church, there are "so many walls, so many colonnades." What does this mean? What is the danger for the Christian who sees only one wall or one colonnade?

2. Christ named St. Peter the "rock" so that the Church would be built on a firm foundation and that the gates of hell would not prevail against it. God has given all of us "rocks" in our own lives, people whose stability and strength enable us to overcome difficulties and survive trials and temptations. Who are the foundations in your life? Are you a "rock" for anyone? In what way do you support and strengthen them? In what way must Christians be a "rock" for one another?

Activity

Read Matthew 16:5–20, the occasion when Jesus called Peter to lead his Church. Write a poem or draw an image that depicts this event.

The Communion of Saints

An Account of the Martyrdom of St. Blandine and Her Companions in AD 177, from *The Ecclesiastical History*

Eusebius of Caesarea

We believe in the holy Catholic Church, the communion of saints.

—The Apostles' Creed

Author Background

Eusebius of Caesarea, often called the "Father of Church History," lived from approximately 260–340. He was a highly learned man and had access to the magnificent library founded by Pamphilus in Caesarea (now a part of Syria). He used the manuscripts and texts found in that library as sources to write his masterpiece, *The Ecclesiastical History*. In this book, he not only recounts episodes of Church history, but he also includes long texts and quotations from the manuscripts that he consulted, many of which have been lost and no longer exist.

Before the Reading

The letter quoted in this passage is from Christians living in Lyons, Gaul (France) to their brethren living in Asia and Phrygia (Turkey). It was written in the second century and recounts the suffering and martyrdom of members of the Church in Lyons in the year AD 177 when Marcus Aurelius was the Roman emperor. Eusebius included this letter in his *Ecclesiastical History* (AD 326). The letter is also important because it contains a passage that commends the priest Irenaeus to Pope Eutherius. We know from other writings that St. Irenaeus was a disciple of St. Polycarp, who had been a disciple of St. John the Apostle. Thus we see in the Church of Lyons a community directly connected to the apostolic tradition of the Church and to the "communion of saints," a society made up of all living and dead, who hold to belief in Jesus. The passage also points out the unique witness of *martyrs*, those who endure death to be faithful to God.

An Account of the Martyrdom of St. Blandine and Her Companions in AD 177, from The Ecclesiastical History

The servants of Christ residing at Vienne and Lyons, in Gaul, to their brothers throughout Asia and Phrygia, who hold the same faith and hope of redemption, peace and grace and glory from God the Father and Christ Jesus our Lord.

The greatness of the persecution in this region, the fury of the pagans against the Christians, and the sufferings of the blessed martyrs we cannot recount accurately, nor indeed could they possibly be recorded. For with all his might the Adversary fell upon us, giving us a foretaste of his unbridled activity at his future coming. He endeavored in every manner to prepare and exercise his people against the servants of God, not only shutting us out from houses and baths and forum, but forbidding any of us to be seen in any place whatever.

But the grace of God led the conflict against him, and protected the weak, and set firm pillars, able through patience to endure all the attacks of the Evil One. They joined battle with him, undergoing all kinds of shame and injury; and regarding their great sufferings as little, they hastened to Christ, manifesting truly that "the sufferings of this present time are not worthy to be compared with the glory which shall be revealed to us."

Then the holy martyrs endured sufferings beyond description, Satan striving earnestly that also some of them might utter blasphemies. But the whole wrath of the populace, the governor, and the soldiers was aroused against Sanctus, the deacon from Vienne, against Maturus, a recent convert but a courageous athlete, against Attalus, a native of Pergamon who had always been a pillar and foundation for us here, and against Blandine, through whom Christ showed that things which appear mean, obscure and despicable to men are with God of great glory, because of love of him manifested in power to act, and not in boasting. For while we all trembled, as did her earthly mistress, who was herself also one of the martyrs, fearing that on account of the weakness of her body she would be unable to make her confession with self-assurance, Blandine was filled with such power as to exhaust and defeat those who took turns at torturing her in every manner from morning till dusk, that they acknowledged they were conquered, and could do nothing more to her. They were astonished at her endurance, since her entire body was mangled and broken; and they testified that one of these forms of torture was sufficient to destroy life, not to speak of so many and so great sufferings. But the blessed woman, like a brave athlete, renewed her strength in her confession; and her comfort and recreation and relief from the pain of her sufferings was in exclaiming: "I am a Christian, and in us there is no evil."

But Sanctus also endured marvelously and superhumanly all the outrages which he suffered. While the wicked men hoped by the continuing severity of their tortures to wring something from him which he ought not to say, he girded himself against them with such firmness that he would not even tell his name, nor the nation or city to which he belonged, nor whether he was slave or free, but answered in Latin all their questions: "I am a Christian." He confessed this instead of name and city and race and everything besides, and the pagans heard from him no other word.

The blessed Pothinus, who had been entrusted with the bishopric of Lyons, was dragged to the tribunal. He was more than ninety years old and very infirm, scarcely indeed able to breathe because of his weakness; but he was strengthened by spiritual zeal through his earnest desire for martyrdom. Though his body was worn out by old age and disease, his spirit was preserved so that Christ might triumph in it. When he was brought by the soldiers to the tribunal, accompanied by the magistrates and a multitude who shouted against him in every manner as if he were Christ himself, he bore noble witness.

Asked by the governor: Who is the God of the Christians? he replied: "If you are worthy, you will know." Then he was dragged away harshly, and received blows of every kind. Those near him struck him with their hands and feet, regardless of his age; and those at a distance hurled at him whatever they could seize, all of them thinking that they would be guilty of great wickedness and impiety if any possible abuse were omitted. For thus they thought to avenge their own deities. Scarcely able to breathe, he was cast into prison and died after two days.

Maturus, Sanctus, Blandine and Attalus were led to the amphitheatre to be given over to the beasts and provide the public with a spectacle of pagan cruelty during the day appointed for combat against wild animals. Maturus and Sanctus passed again through every torment in the amphitheatre, as if they had suffered nothing before, or rather, as if, having already conquered their antagonist in many contests, they were now striving for the crown itself. They endured again the customary running of the gauntlet and the violence of the beasts, and everything which the furious crowd called for or desired, and at last the iron chair on which their bodies were consumed in a cloud of smoke.

Not with this did the persecutors cease, but increased yet more their anger, determined to overcome their endurance. But even thus they did not hear a word from Sanctus, except the confession which he had uttered from the beginning. Since Maturus and Sanctus survived their long combat they were at last sacrificed. . . .

But Blandine was suspended from a stake, to be devoured by the beasts who were to attack her. Because she appeared as if hanging on a cross, and because of her earnest prayers, she inspired the combatants with great zeal: for they looked upon her in their combat, and beheld with their human eyes, in the form of their sister, him who was crucified for them to persuade those who believe in him, that everyone who suffers for the glory of Christ is always in communion with the living God. As none of the beasts touched her then, she was taken down from the stake and cast again into prison. Thus she was preserved for another contest, so that, being victorious in more conflicts, she might make irrevocable the condemnation of the faithless Serpent; and that, though small, weak and despised, yet clothed with Christ the mighty and conquering Athlete, she might arouse the brothers' zeal and, overcoming the Adversary many times, might receive through her combat the crown incorruptible. But Attalus was called for loudly by the people, because he was a person of distinction. He entered the arena like a wrestler trained in the Christian faith, as he had always practiced the veritable discipline of Christ and born witness to the truth among us. He was led around the amphitheatre, a tablet being carried before him on which was written in Latin: "This is Attalus the Christian," and the people were filled with indignation against him. But when the governor learned that he was a Roman citizen, he commanded him to be taken back to prison with the others.

Caesar commanded that the Christians should be put to death, but that those who abjured should be set free. Therefore, at the beginning of the public festival which was attended by crowds of men from all of Gaul, the governor brought the martyrs to his tribunal, to make a show of them and a spectacle for the crowd. He examined them again, and had those beheaded who appeared to possess Roman citizenship, but sent the others to the beasts.

After all this, on the last day of the single contests Blandine was again brought in with Ponticus, a boy about fifteen years old. They had been brought every day to witness the sufferings of the others, and had been urged to swear by the idols. But because they remained steadfast, the multitude became furious and had no compassion for the youth of the boy, nor respect for the woman.

Therefore they took them through the entire round of tortures, repeatedly urging them, one after the other, to abjure, but being unable to effect this; for Ponticus, encouraged by his sister so that even the pagans could see that she was confirming and strengthening him, having nobly endured every torture, gave up the ghost. But the blessed Blandine, last of all, having, as a noble mother, encouraged her children and sent them before her victorious to the King, endured herself all the combats undertaken by her children and hastened after them, glad and rejoicing in her departure as if called to a marriage feast and not to the beasts. After the scourging, after the beasts, after the roasting seat, she was finally enclosed in a net and thrown to a bull. Being tossed about by the animal, but feeling none of the things which were happening to her because of her hope and firm hold upon her faith and her communion with Christ, she also was sacrificed. The pagans themselves confessed that never among them had a woman endured such tortures.

But not even then were their madness and cruelty toward the saints satisfied. Incited by the Beast, those wild and barbarous tribes were not easily appeased, and their violence found another opportunity in the bodies of their victims. To be vanquished did not put them to shame, since they lacked all human feeling; on the contrary, this kindled their anger yet more, like that of a wild beast, and aroused the hatred of governor and people alike to treat us unjustly, so that Scripture might be fulfilled: "He who is lawless, let him be yet more lawless, and he who is righteous, yet more righteous." They cast to the dogs those who had died of suffocation in the prison, carefully guarding them night and day, lest we should bury any of them. And they exposed without burial the remains left by the beasts and the fire, mangled and charred, and the heads and bodies of those who had been decapitated, and soldiers guarded them for many days.

Some raged and gnashed their teeth against the martyrs, desiring to execute upon them some additional vengeance; others laughed and mocked them, magnifying their own idols, to whom they imputed the punishment of the Christians. Even the more reasonable, and those who seemed to sympathize somewhat, still criticized the martyrs vehemently, saying: "Where is their God, and what has their religion, which they have chosen rather than life, profited them?" Such were the different attitudes of the pagans; but we were in deep affliction, because we could not bury the bodies. Neither did night avail to us, nor did money persuade the soldiers, nor entreaty move them to compassion; they kept watch in every way, as if prevention of burial would be of some great advantage to them.

The bodies of the martyrs, thus exposed in different manners for six days to serve as an example, were then burned and reduced to ashes and swept into the Rhone by the wicked men, so that no trace of them might remain on earth. And this they did, as if able to conquer God, and prevent their rebirth; "in order that," as they said, "they may have no hope of a resurrection, by trust in which they bring to us this new foreign religion, and despise terrible things, and are ready even to go to death with joy. Now let us see if they will rise again, and if their God is able to help them and deliver them out of our hands."

Such things happened to the churches of Christ under this emperor, from which we may reasonably conjecture what occurred in the other provinces. It is proper to add other selections from the same letter, in which the moderation and compassion of these martyrs is recorded in the following words:

They reminded us of the martyrs who had already departed, and said, "Those are martyrs whom Christ deemed worthy to be taken up in their confession, sealing their testimony by their departure; but we are lowly and humble confessors." They beseeched their brothers with tears, that earnest prayers be offered that they might reach their goal.

They showed in their deeds the power of their testimony, manifesting great boldness towards the pagans, and they made plain their nobility through patience, fearlessness and courage, but they refused the title of martyrs as distinguishing them from their brothers, being filled with the fear of God.

They humbled themselves under the mighty hand by which they are now greatly exalted. They defended all, but accused none. They absolved all, but bound none. They prayed for those who inflicted cruelties upon them, just as did Stephen, the perfect martyr: "Lord, lay not this sin to their charge." But if he prayed for those who stoned him, how much more for his brothers!

Moved by veritable charity, their greatest contest was against the Adversary, to stifle the Beast and make him cast out alive those whom he supposed he had swallowed. For they did not boast over the fallen, but helped them in their need with those things in which they themselves abounded, showing the compassion of a mother, and shedding many tears on their account before the Father. They asked him for life, and he gave it to them, and they shared it with their neighbors. Victorious in every fashion, they departed to God. Having always loved peace, and having commended peace to us, they went in peace to God, leaving no sorrow to their mother the Church, nor division or strife to their brothers, but joy, peace, concord and love.

Letter of the Martyrs Recommending Irenaeus

"We pray, Father Eleutherius, that you may rejoice in God in all things and always. We have requested our brother and comrade Irenaeus to carry this letter to you, and we ask you to hold him in esteem, as zealous for the covenant of Christ. For if we thought that office could confer righteousness upon any one, we should commend him among the first as a presbyter of the church, which is his position."

Reading for Comprehension

1. What did Blandine cry out when she and her companions were being tortured?
2. How did Bishop Pothinus die?
3. What were three of the tortures endured by the martyrs?
4. Why was Attalus beheaded rather than killed by beasts?
5. How was Blandine finally slain?
6. What was done with the bodies of the martyrs?

Reading for Understanding

1. How was Blandine a "rock" for her companions, especially Ponticus?

2. Imagine a situation in which you were called to give up your life for Christ. What would that be like?

Activities

1. We live is a society that has many of the characteristics of paganism. Name a situation today in which actions in accordance with Christian beliefs have resulted in hostility, ridicule, and persecution?

2. Giving up one's life because of persecution for one's Christian beliefs is not limited to the ancient world. It has happened throughout history. It is happening today. Research the life of Archbishop Oscar Romero of San Salvador or view the film, *Romero* (see page 375). Explain how Romero is a contemporary Christian martyr.

Life Everlasting

Two Letters of St. Thérèse of Lisieux to Abbe Belliere

Thérèse of Lisieux

I will spend my heaven doing good on earth.

—**St. Thérèse of Lisieux**

Author Background

Thérèse of Lisieux (Thérèse Martin, 1873–1897) was born to a middle class French family in 1873. At age sixteen she received special permission to enter the Carmelites, a religious order of nuns devoted to prayer who lead an austere life of fasting and silence. Thérèse lived only ten years in the Convent of Lisieux. She died of tuberculosis in 1897 when she was only twenty-four. After her death, a series of personal writings intended for her religious superiors was published under the title *The Story of a Soul.* Thérèse's autobiography took the world by storm and in a few short years had sold millions of copies. She was canonized in 1925, only twenty-eight years after her death. Pope John Paul II named her a Doctor of the Church in 1997.

Before the Reading

Pope Pius XI called Thérèse "the greatest saint of modern times." What is it that made the life and teaching of this young, obscure nun so attractive to Catholics and non-Catholics alike? It may be that Thérèse speaks to the modern person because of her anonymity and humbleness. She is a representative of those millions of people who toil and live in obscurity as factory workers, day laborers, office workers, and homemakers. In her, the common person can find a model for great sanctity. Thérèse also suffered throughout her life with bouts of depression and darkness. She had to witness the mental breakdown of her beloved father and try to come to grips with the evil and pain that exists in the world. In meeting these challenges to faith and life, St. Thérèse serves as a model and guide to the modern world.

As a Carmelite sister, Thérèse lived in a cloister and had virtually no face-to-face contact with anyone other than the sisters living in her convent. However, she was permitted to correspond with people outside the convent and her letters to her relatives and friends sparkle with wit and charm. Toward the end of her life, a young priest, Abbe Maurice Belliere, wrote to the Carmel of Lisieux asking if a sister could devote her prayers for the success of his activities as a missionary priest. Thérèse was chosen to assist him and she wrote to him a series of letters that spell out her spiritual teaching, her "little way," in which she offers the most ordinary actions and events or her day to God.

Like most of us, Abbe Belliere lacked confidence in his abilities to serve God; he dwelt on and suffered guilt over his sins, and feared the judgment of the Lord. In her letters, Thérèse points out that she does not fear the judgment of God precisely because he is just. She knows that he is her Father and, therefore, will forgive her faults and failing because of his intense love for her.

St. Thérèse never met Abbe Belliere, but the love for him reflected in these letters, written as she was dying of tuberculosis, is a sign of the love that God has for each of us, especially when we are weak, afraid, and lonely.

Two Letters of St. Thérèse of Lisieux to Abbe Belliere

J. M. J. T.
Carmel, Lisieux,
21 June 1897
My dear little Brother,

With you I have thanked Our Lord for the great grace he deigned to give you on the day of Pentecost; it was also on that great feast (ten years ago) that I obtained—not from my Director but from my

Father—permission to become an apostle in Carmel. That is one more link between our souls.

O Brother, please, never think you "weary me or distract me," by talking much of yourself. Would it be possible for a sister not to take interest in all that concerns her brother? As to distracting me, you have nothing to fear; on the contrary, your letters unite me still closer to the good God, bringing the marvels of His mercy and love very near for my contemplation. Sometimes Jesus delights "to reveal His secrets to the little ones": as an example, when I had read your first letter of 15 October 1895, I thought the same thing as your Director. You cannot be half a saint, you must be a whole saint or no saint at all. I felt that you must have a soul of great energy, and I was happy to become your sister. Don't think you can frighten me with talk of "your best years wasted." I simply thank Jesus for looking on you with a look of love, as once he looked on the young man in the Gospel. More fortunate than he, you loyally answered the Master's call, you left all to follow him, and that at the best age of life, eighteen.

Ah! my Brother, like me you can hymn the mercies of the Lord! They shine in you in all their splendor. . . . You love St. Augustine, St. Magdalen, those souls to whom "many sins have been forgiven because they loved much"; I love them too, love their repentance and above all . . . their daring in love! When I see Magdalen come forward in face of the crowd of guests, and water with her tears the feet of her adored Master as she touches him for the first time, I feel that her heart realized the fathomless depths of love and mercy in Jesus' Heart, realized, despite her sins, that that Heart was ready not only to pardon her but actually to lavish on her the treasures of His divine intimacy and raise her to the highest summits of contemplation.

Ah! my dear little Brother, since it has been given me too to realize the love of Jesus' Heart, I own that it has driven from my own heart all fear! The remembrance of my faults humiliates me, leads me never to rely at all on my strength, which is only weakness; but the remembrance speaks to me still more of mercy and love. When one

167

casts one's faults into the consuming flame of Love, how could they fail to be consumed past return?

I know there are saints who spent their lives in the practice of astonishing mortifications to expiate their sins, but what of it?—"In my Father's house there are many mansions." Jesus has told us so, which is why I follow the path He marks out for me. I try not to think about myself in anything whatsoever; and what Jesus in his goodness effects in my soul, I give over to him; for I chose an austere life, not to expiate my own sins but the sins of others.

I have just read over my brief note and I wonder if you will understand me, for I have put it very badly. Do not think I am blaming you for repenting of your sins and wanting to expiate them. Oh, no! far from it; but you know, now that there are two of us the work will go faster (and I, with my way, will get more done than you), so I hope that one day Jesus will set you on the same way as me.

Forgive me, Brother, I don't know what is the matter with me today, I hadn't really meant to say all this. I have no more room to answer your letter. I shall do so another time. Thank you for the dates of your life. I have already celebrated your twenty-third birthday. I am praying for your dear parents whom God has taken from this world, and I am not forgetting the mother you love. Your unworthy little Sister,

Thérèse of the Child Jesus of the Holy Face rel. carm. ind.

J. M. J. T.
18 July 1897
My poor dear little Brother,

Your grief touches me deeply; but you see how good Jesus is. He permits me still to be able to write and try to console you, probably not for the last time. That loving Savior understands your grief and your prayers: that is why He leaves me still on earth. Do not think I mind. Oh, no! my dear little Brother, very much the reverse, for in this conduct of Jesus I see how much He loves you!

I have never asked God to let me die young, it would have seemed to me cowardice; but from my childhood He has deigned to give me the intimate conviction that my course here below would be brief. So that the one cause of all my joy is the thought of doing the Lord's will.

O Brother! how I wish I could pour the balm of consolation into your soul! I can only borrow Jesus' words at the Last Supper. He will not object, because I am his little bride and therefore all his goods are mine. I say to you then, as he to his friends, "I go to my Father . . . but because I have spoken these things to you, sorrow has filled your heart. But I tell you the truth: it is expedient to you that I go. You now have sorrow, but I will see you again and you shall rejoice; and your joy no man will take from you."

Yes, of this I am sure, after my entry into life, my dear little Brother's sorrow will be turned into a serene joy that no creature can wrest from him. I feel that we must go to Heaven by the same road-suffering joined with love. When I am come into harbor, I shall instruct you, dear little Brother of my soul, how you must navigate on the tempestuous sea of the world: with the love and utter trustfulness of a child who knows that his father loves him too much to forsake him in the hour of peril.

Ah! how I wish I could make you realize the tenderness of Jesus' heart, what It expects of you. As I read your letter of the fourteenth, my heart thrilled tenderly. More than ever I realized the degree to which your love is sister to mine, since it is called to go up to God by the elevator of love, not to climb the rough stairway of fear. I am not surprised that the practice of "familiarity" with Jesus seems to you not at all easy to manage; you cannot come to it in a day, but I am certain that I shall aid you better to walk that delightful way when I am free of my mortal envelope, and soon you will be saying with St. Augustine "Love is the weight that draws me."

But why do I speak to you of the life of trust and love? I explain myself so badly that I must wait till Heaven to talk with you of that blissful life. What I wanted to do today was console you. Ah! how happy I should be if you could take my death as Mother Agnes of Jesus is taking it. . . . She speaks of my death as of a feast, and this is a great consolation to me.

Please, dear little Brother, try like her to realize that you will not be losing me but finding me, and that I shall never more leave you. . . .

In view of my approaching death, a sister has photographed me for our Mother's feast. When the novices saw me they cried that I had put on my grand look; it seems that I am ordinarily more smiling; but take my word for it, Brother, that if my photograph does not smile at you, my soul will never cease to smile on you when it is close by you.

Goodbye, dear little Brother, be assured that for eternity I shall be your true little sister.

Thérèse of the Child Jesus r.c.i.

Reading for Comprehension

1. How does Thérèse respond to Abbe Belliere's fears of tiring her with talk about himself?

2. What does Thérèse say to Belliere about her premonition about the length of her life?

3. Abbe Belliere was sorrowful about her approaching death. What did Thérèse say she would do for him after she died?

4. What did Thérèse most admire about St. Mary Magdalene?

Reading for Understanding

1. Why do so many of us have a fear of silence? Why must we always be talking or watching television or listening to music? What would happen if we spent a full hour in total silence? Why do spiritual masters tell us that times of silence are essential to any profound life of prayer?

2. Abbe Belliere believed that St. Thérèse would guide and protect him personally after her death. Select a saint that appeals to you and

over a period of several weeks, ask that saint to help you in whatever endeavor that you select. Journal daily on this experience.

Activities

1. St. Thérèse's form of life as a vowed cloistered nun is not one to which all are called. There are many ways of serving God, and hers is one of them. However, does her form of life, her silence and fasting, have anything to say to those of us who live in the world? Was her vocation just for herself, or does it say something to members of the Church in the modern world?

2. Soren Kierkegaard, the great Danish theologian and philosopher who is considered one of the founders of the school of philosophy called Existentialism, once said that if he were a physician and asked for one type of medicine to cure the ills of humankind, he would prescribe silence. What do you think he meant by that statement?

3. Read and report on St. Thérèse's autobiography, *The Story of a Soul*.

WHAT WE BELIEVE
(The Profession of Faith)

SEEING WITH THE ARTIST

Use an Internet search engine to locate the following artwork. After reading the background material below, note how the pieces relate to the text readings on these subjects. Complete the related assignments on page 177.

The Paintings

The Annunciation (Castillo Annunciation)—Sandro Botticelli (1445–1510)

This tempura painting on a wood panel is found in the Uffizi Gallery in Florence, Italy. The painting depicts the Angel Gabriel who, after having made a dramatic entry into Mary's home, greets her with the words, "Hail, favored one! The Lord is with you" (Lk 1:28). Botticelli inscribed these words on the bottom of the original frame. The Virgin Mary is depicted as a young girl looking up from a book that she has been reading. Traditionally, Renaissance painters represented the book used in scenes of the Annunciation as the Book of Isaiah, which speaks of the coming of the Savior of Israel. In his left hand, the angel holds a lily, the symbol of purity. Mary's room looks out on a Tuscan landscape. The landscape and the even squares of the floor on which the angel is kneeling point to the Renaissance artist's love of symmetry and perspective.

The Annunciation—John Collier

In this present day representation of the classic paintings of the Annunciation, the Virgin wears contemporary dress and is represented as a young teenager. Mary may have been fifteen to eighteen years old at the time of her betrothal to St. Joseph. She is portrayed as looking up from the Bible that she has been reading and looking at the angel in Renaissance garb who has just greeted her with the words, "Hail, full of grace." A potted lily is in the foreground of the picture and Mary's house is situated in a typical American suburban development. The artist, John Collier, is an American artist who works in painting, illustrations, and sculpture. He was chosen from a long list of competitors to design and sculpt the Catholic Memorial at Ground Zero.

The Christ of the Breadline—Fritz Eichenberg (1901–1990)

This black and white print portrays Christ as one of the needy seeking bread from an urban charity house. Eichenberg was born in Germany to Jewish parents. He was a successful artist in Germany and an outspoken critic of the Nazis. He fled Germany to the United States in 1933. He was a world-renowned engraver and taught at the New School for Social Research and Pratt Institute in New York City before heading the art department at the University of Rhode Island. In the 1940s, Eichenberg met the co-founder of the Catholic Worker movement, Dorothy Day, who was a passionate pacifist and advocate for the rights of the poor and oppressed throughout the world. Under her influence he did a series of illustrations for the newspaper, *The Catholic Worker*, that spoke to the issues of non-violence and social justice. This print was done during that period of his life.

"Photograph of St. Thérèse of Lisieux" and *Painting of St. Thérèse of Lisieux*—Celine Martin

Celine Martin was one of St. Thérèse's older sisters. She followed Thérèse into the Convent of Carmel in Lisieux, France, in 1894. Celine had remained at home and delayed entering the convent while caring for her father. She was an accomplished artist and photographer who had received several important artistic commissions. When she became a nun, she brought her photographic equipment into the convent with her and took several groups of pictures of Thérèse and the other members of the Carmelite community that could be shared with families and friends. When St. Thérèse was canonized in 1925, Celine was asked to do an official portrait of the saint. In her lifetime, she did numerous painting of St. Thérèse. Like many of her contemporaries, Celine Martin did not feel that photography could compare with painting as an art form. Late in her life she said, "I would like to say a word about the physical portraits of the saint. Sheer mechanical processes of reproduction, showing only the plastic structure of her face, cannot capture her soul, any more than they can capture refinement of manners or the perfume of a rose. What I have always tried to do is to capture and communicate that indefinable quality which shows the true picture of her soul beneath her features." Because of this philosophy of art, the images that we had of St. Thérèse were based on paintings rather than photographs. Celine's untouched photographs have only recently been published.

LOOKING AT FILM

The films listed below are well-made biographical accounts of famous saints. Read a short biography of each saint prior to viewing the film connected with his or her life stories. Research discrepancies in detail and note them in short written summaries.

The Films
....

Becket (1964)—Directed by Peter Glenville

Rating: A-II

Becket tells the story of the early friendship and later conflict between Thomas à Becket, the Archbishop of Canterbury, and Henry II, King of England. This film is an outstanding example of man's restlessness and unhappiness until he rests in God. At the beginning of the film, Becket is a cynical hedonist who finds no meaning in life except for power and pleasure. It is only when he is ordained a bishop that he comes to realize that he is responsible for maintaining and protecting the honor of God. This film is a fine illustration of the sacramental meaning of the priesthood and the divine authority given to bishops to rule and govern the Church. It is also a moving story of a man who was lost and then found, returning to God.

A Man for All Seasons (1966)—Directed by Fred Zinneman

Rating: Vatican Top Forty-Five Films

The Church is a supernatural entity that cannot be ruled by earthly powers. To insure the protection of the Church, God has ordained the Magisterium to care for the Church throughout the ages. Throughout history there have been monarchs, dictators, and parliaments who have sought to treat the Church as a purely human society, to subject it to the state, and deny its authority to teach and guide its members. These rulers have persecuted the Church, and opposition to such rulers by clergy and laypeople has often led to suffering and death. *A Man for All Seasons* explores the divine nature of the Church and introduces St. Thomas More, a family man, writer, scholar, statesmen, and martyr.

The Song of Bernadette (1943)—Directed by Henry King

Rating: AI

Devotion to the Blessed Virgin Mary, the Mother of God, has been a signifying element of Catholicism from the earliest days of the Church. Apparitions of the Virgin to young people, where she has explained to them her love for all of God's people and her prayer that humankind will turn away from sin and come back to the God who loves them, have taken place throughout history. One of the most famous of these apparitions is that of the Virgin appearing to Bernadette Soubirous in

Lourdes, France, in 1858. The striking testimony of the Virgin, the simple piety of St. Bernadette, and the miraculous cures associated with the shrine of Lourdes are beautifully rendered in this film that is based on the best-selling novel by Franz Werfel.

ACTIVITIES

1. What symbols of Mary are common to both the *Annunciation* by Botticelli and the *Annunciation* by Collier?

2. What do you think John Collier was trying to say by painting Mary as a contemporary teenager?

3. How can Eichenberg's *The Christ of the Breadline* be seen as a visual representation of the ideas expressed in Tolstoy's story "Where Love Is, God Is" (pages 101–113)?

4. What aspects of St. Thérèse's personality are represented by her photograph? What aspects are represented by the painting?

5. Read St. Thérèse's letters to Abbe Belliere. Does the photograph or the painting best express her personality? Offer three reasons to support your opinion.

6. Look up the meaning of the word *excommunication*. How is the rite of excommunication portrayed in the film *Becket*?

7. How is the character of Richard Rich in the film *A Man for All Seasons* similar to the character of Judas?

8. At the end of the film *The Song of Bernadette*, the dying Imperial Commissioner visits the shrine of Lourdes and asks Bernadette Soubirous to pray for him. Why is this action in many ways the greatest of the miracles portrayed in the film?

How We Touch God and How God Touches Us

(The Celebration of the Christian Mystery)

A Sacramental View of the World

Because God is the source of all beauty and goodness, the material universe possesses its own innate goodness. Furthermore, by becoming flesh, Christ has given to the world of matter an innate dignity and sanctity. This belief in the goodness of creation is echoed throughout Scripture. Moreover, the material world tells us about the nature of the Creator. For those who view the universe with the eyes of faith, this world reflects God in all his majesty, power, goodness, and beauty.

The origin of the word *sacrament* comes from the Latin word for mystery. The sacraments help us to encounter the mystery of God and offer the ability to see that the material world represents the attributes of the Creator. The entire universe is a series of signs leading us to knowledge of God. Our understanding of a world viewed through the sacraments can also refer to the experience of a journey, whereby we learn how to truly see and move beyond creatures and creation to the God whom they signify. The material in this unit reflects these two aspects of the universe.

During his life on earth, Christ made use of material things and symbolic actions to make manifest the presence of God and the actions of the Holy Spirit. He preached, he allowed himself to be baptized by St. John the Baptist, and he commanded his followers to also baptize. He called forth certain men to act as leaders and evangelists. He healed with the touch of his hands. He forgave sins. He gave the gift of the Holy Spirit to his disciples. He sanctified marriage and family life. He blessed bread and wine and gave it to his disciples as spiritual food and commanded them to follow his example in doing this. In the Catholic Church, we continue these actions of Jesus in the seven sacraments. We are a sacramental Church, and central to our liturgical life are priestly ministers who are given the authority and power to perform certain ritual actions that have the effect of making God present in special and concrete ways. These actions, these signs and symbols, are called the sacraments. "The seven sacraments touch all the stages and all the important moments of Christian life: they give birth and increase healing and mission to the Christian's life of faith" (*CCC*, 1210).

Introducing the Unit

The sacraments are of the Church. They literally make the Church since they communicate the mystery of our communion with God, who is love. Also, the gift of the Holy Spirit manifests in creation more of God's mystery and goodness.

In the following selections, you will discover how writers and thinkers have expressed the truth of God's presence in creation and how the experience of viewing can be transformed instantly into the experience of ecstatic prayer.

Sacred Times and Spaces

- In the reading about St. Francis of Assisi, "St. Francis and the Animals," we see how the saint saw God's presence even in the brute beasts of the forest.

- In the poems "Welcome Morning" by Anne Sexton and "i thank you God for most this amazing" by e e cummings, we see the ecstasy of an encounter with God.

- The reading from *The Cathedral,* about the Cathedral of Chartres, shows how certain places are "sacred spaces" where all the arts are used to mediate an encounter with God's holy presence.

The Seven Sacraments and Their Effects

The following readings will illustrate the personal effect of five of the sacraments:

- "She Went by Gently" tells us about the nature of Baptism.

- "The Hint of an Explanation" concentrates on the Sacrament of the Eucharist.

- "The Gift of the Magi" shows the effect and grace given by the Sacrament of Matrimony.

- The excerpt from *The Diary of a Country Priest* provides an insight into the Sacraments of Penance and Holy Orders.

Sacred Times and Sacred Spaces

"St. Francis and the Animals," from *The Writings of Thomas of Celano*

Adapted by John Feister

God looked at everything he had made, and he found it very good.
—Genesis 1:31

Author Background

Thomas of Celano (ca. 1200–ca. 1255) was a companion of St. Francis of Assisi. He wrote two biographies of St. Francis and a book on the miracles of St. Francis. It is from Celano's works that we learn about St. Francis's love of nature and how he interacted with the creatures of the land, sky, and sea.

Before the Reading

St. Francis had the ability to see the presence of God in all things. He authored the first great poem written in Italian vernacular. St. Francis's poem, "The Canticle of the Creatures," expresses his ability to find God even in the humblest of circumstances. Similarly, the following reading is a wonderful example of how St. Francis communicated with his "brothers and sisters" in the animal world. St. Francis is the patron saint of animals and the environment. Many people place status of St. Francis in their gardens, yards, or wherever nature is nearby.

"St. Francis and the Animals"

St. Francis Preaches to the Birds

Father Francis and his companions were making a trip through the Spoleto Valley near the town of Bevagna. Suddenly, Francis spotted a great number of birds of all varieties. There were doves, crows, and all sorts of birds. Swept up in the moment, Francis left his friends in the road and ran after the birds, who patiently waited for him. He greeted them in his usual way, expecting them to scurry off into the air as he spoke. But they moved not.

Filled with awe, he asked them if they would stay awhile and listen to the Word of God. He said to them: "My brother and sister birds, you should praise your Creator and always love him: He gave you feathers for clothes, wings to fly. and all other things that you need. It is God who made you noble among all creatures, making your home in thin, pure air. Without sowing or reaping, you receive God's guidance and protection."

At this the birds began to spread their wings, stretch their necks and gaze at Francis, rejoicing and praising God in a wonderful way according to their nature. Francis then walked right through the middle of them, turned around and came back, touching their heads and bodies with his tunic.

Then he gave them his blessing, making the Sign of the Cross over them. At that they flew off and Francis, rejoicing and giving thanks to God, went on his way. Later, Francis wondered aloud to his companions why he had never preached to birds before. And from that day on, Francis made it his habit to solicitously invoke all birds, all animals and reptiles to praise and love their Creator. And many times during Francis' life there were remarkable events of Francis speaking to the animals. There was even a time when St. Francis quieted a flock of noisy birds that were interrupting a religious ceremony! Much to the wonder of all present, the birds remained quiet until Francis' sermon was complete.

St. Francis and the Rabbits and Fish

One day a brother brought a rabbit who had been caught in a trap to St. Francis. Francis advised the rabbit to be more alert in the future, then released the rabbit from the trap and set it on the ground to go its way. But the rabbit hopped back up onto Francis' lap, desiring to be close to the saint.

Francis took the rabbit a few steps into the woods and set it down. But it followed Francis back to his seat and hopped on his lap again! Finally Francis asked one of his fellow friars to take the rabbit far into the woods and let it go. That worked. This type of thing happened repeatedly to Francis—which he saw as an opportunity to praise the glory of God. If the simplest creatures could be so endowed with God's wonder, how much the more so we humans!

Fish were also known to obey Francis. Whenever a fish was caught and Francis was nearby, he would return the fish to the water, warning it not to be caught again. On several occasions the fish would linger awhile near the boat, listening to Francis preach, until he gave them permission to leave. Then they would swim off. In every work of art, as St. Francis called all creation, he would praise the artist, our loving Creator.

St. Francis and the Wolf

Perhaps the most famous story of St. Francis is when he tamed the wolf that was terrorizing the people of Gubbio. While Francis was staying in that town he learned of a wolf so ravenous that it was not only killing and eating animals, but people, too. The people took up arms and went after it, but those who encountered the wolf perished at its sharp teeth. Villagers became afraid to leave the city walls.

Francis had pity on the people and decided to go out and meet the wolf. He was desperately warned by the people, but he insisted that God would take care of him. A brave friar and several peasants accompanied Francis outside the city gate. But soon the peasants lost heart and said they would go no farther.

Francis and his companion began to walk on. Suddenly the wolf, jaws agape, charged out of the woods at the couple. Francis made the Sign of the Cross toward it. The power of God caused the wolf to slow down and to close its mouth.

Then Francis called out to the creature: "Come to me, Brother Wolf. In the name of Christ, I order you not to hurt anyone." At that moment the wolf lowered its head and lay down at St. Francis' feet, meek as a lamb.

St. Francis explained to the wolf that he had been terrorizing the people, killing not only animals, but humans who are made in the image of God. "Brother Wolf," said Francis, "I want to make peace between you and the people of Gubbio. They will harm you no more and you must no longer harm them. All past crimes are to be forgiven."

The wolf showed its assent by moving its body and nodding its head. Then to the absolute surprise of the gathering crowd, Francis asked the wolf to make a pledge. As St. Francis extended his hand to receive the pledge, so the wolf extended its front paw and placed it into the saint's hand. Then Francis commanded the wolf to follow him into town to make a peace pact with the townspeople. The wolf meekly followed St. Francis.

By the time they got to the town square, everyone was there to witness the miracle. With the wolf at his side, Francis gave the town a sermon on the wondrous and fearful love of God, calling them to repent from all their sins. Then he offered the townspeople peace, on behalf of the wolf. The townspeople promised in a loud voice to feed the wolf. Then Francis asked the wolf if he would live in peace under those terms. He bowed his head and twisted his body in a way that convinced everyone he accepted the pact. Then once again the wolf placed its paw in Francis' hand as a sign of the pact.

From that day on the people kept the pact they had made. The wolf lived for two years among the townspeople, going from door to door for food. It hurt no one and no one hurt it. Even the dogs did not bark at it. When the wolf finally died of old age, the people of Gubbio were sad. The wolf's peaceful ways had been a living re-minder to them of the wonders, patience, virtues and holiness of St. Francis. It had been a living symbol of the power and providence of the living God.

Reading for Comprehension

1. How did the birds react to St. Francis's sermon?
2. What did the rabbit do when St. Francis set it free?
3. What did St. Francis do with the fish that had been caught?
4. How did St. Francis stop the wolf when he charged violently at the saint?
5. Why did the people of Gubbio mourn when the wolf died?

Reading for Understanding

1. Who are "human wolves" that commit crimes and disrupt the community? How does God want us to teach such people?
2. When was a time when you saw how reconciliation and forgiveness took place among classmates? What was the result of that experience?
3. How effective are stories like these in teaching truths of faith? Why do you think parents and teachers use stories to teach young children about the wonders of God?

Activity

Jesus also used stories to instruct his followers. Read the Parable of the Lost Son (Lk 15:11–32). What lesson was Jesus trying to impart when he told this story to the Pharisees?

Sacred Times and Sacred Spaces

"Welcome Morning"
Anne Sexton

The manifold perfections of creatures—their truth, their goodness,
their beauty—all reflect the infinite perfection of God.
—Catechism of the Catholic Church, **41**

Author Background
Anne Sexton (1928–1974) continually struggled with depression. Several
times she attempted suicide, and she underwent many treatments to help
improve her mental illness. Writing poetry helped her deal with her emotions in a creative way. Her poems reflect the joys, sorrows, and struggles
of her personal life. Anne Sexton was awarded the Pulitzer Prize for poetry
in 1967. Near the end of her life, she was drawn to Catholicism, and her religious interest is seen in many of these later poems, especially those found
in the collection *The Awful Rowing Toward God.*

Before the Reading
"Welcome Morning" is one of the most joyous poems in American literature. Like Gerard Manley Hopkins, Anne Sexton experienced God's presence in the simplest pleasures, as is represented in the verses that follow.

"Welcome Morning"
There is joy
in all:
in the hair I brush each morning,
in the Cannon towel, newly washed,
that I rub my body with each morning,
in the chapel of eggs I cook
each morning,

The Catholic Spirit

in the outcry from the kettle
that heats my coffee
each morning,
in the spoon and the chair
that cry "hello there, Anne"
each morning,
in the godhead of the table
that I set my silver, plate, cup upon
each morning.

All this is God,
right here in my pea-green house
each morning
and I mean,
though often forget,
to give thanks,
to faint down by the kitchen table
in a prayer of rejoicing
as the holy birds at the kitchen window
peck into their marriage of seeds.

So while I think of it,
Let me paint a thank-you on my palm
For this God, this laughter of the morning,
Lest it go unspoken.

The joy that isn't shared, I've heard,
Dies young.

"i thank You God for most this amazing"

e e cummings

God speaks to man through the visible creation.
—*Catechism of the Catholic Church*, **1147**

Author Background

Poet e e cummings (1894–1962) is known for his unique use (and non-use) of capitalization in grammar. He was born in Massachusetts to a middle class family who had great appreciation for the arts. His father was a Unitarian minister. Cummings was educated at Harvard and then served as an ambulance volunteer in France during World War I. He was enormously popular as both a poet and a painter during his lifetime.

Before the Reading

Familiarity often prevents us from seeing. Try to remember your excitement about first seeing the ocean, or flying in a plane, or tasting an ice cream cone. Compare those experiences to your experiences of the same events today. Why has the sense of wonder and joy gone? By using grammar and the lack of capitalization in his own idiosyncratic way, e e cummings takes the worn phrase, "thank you, God," and makes us see that act of gratitude in a new and explosive way.

"i thank You God for most this amazing"

i thank You God for most this amazing
day: for the leaping greenly spirits of trees
and a blue true dream of sky; and for everything
which is natural which is infinite which is yes

(i who have died am alive again today,
and this is the sun's birthday; this is the birth

day of life and of love and wings: and of the gay
great happening illimitably earth)

how should tasting touching hearing seeing
breathing any—lifted from the no
of all nothing—human merely being
doubt unimaginable You?

(now the ears of my ears awake and
now the eyes of my eyes are opened)

Reading for Comprehension

1. How is God known to Anne Sexton as she grooms herself upon awakening? As she eats her breakfast?

2. What does Anne feel called to do when she realizes that God is present everywhere?

3. What does the poet feel called to do with the experiences that she has had?

4. What are the only words that are capitalized in Cummings's poem?

Reading for Understanding

1. How does the choice of capitalization provide a clue for getting at the main idea of Cummings's poem?

2. Philosophers and theologians tell us that God reveals himself through our senses. Give four examples of how this is expressed in the poems by Sexton and Cummings.

3. In the Gospel of Luke, Jesus says, "Whoever has ears to hear ought to hear" (Lk 8:8). What lines in Cummings's poem refer to this biblical text?

4. Is it possible for one to look without seeing or to hear without listening? How are racial, religious, and gender prejudices examples of this?

5. Ecstatic joy is a common phenomenon among saints. What is it about their "seeing" that causes this joy?

Activity

In many ways, Anne Sexton's poem is a modern version of the Magnificat, the Blessed Virgin Mary's song of praise found in the Gospel of Luke (1:46–55). Read the Magnificat and Sexton's poem, and then compose your own "song of praise," listing several things for which you are grateful to God.

Sacred Times and Sacred Spaces

The Cathedral

J. K. Huysmans

The beauty of the images moves me to contemplation as a meadow delights the eyes and subtly infuses the soul with the glory of God.
—**St. John Damascene, *De Image*, I, 16**

Author Background

Joris-Karl Huysmans (1848–1907) was a nineteenth-century French novelist who wrote *À Rebours* (Against Nature) and *Là-Bas* (Down There) which glorify sensuality and the occult. As a result of these novels, Huysmans was called the father of the Decadents, an artistic movement in France that depicted sin and the unnatural. In the course of his research, however, Huysmans had a religious conversion and returned to the Catholic Church. He spent the remainder of his life writing novels that explored the workings of grace in the soul of the believer. Huysmans had a great appreciation for art, and he was struck by the beauty of churches, especially Gothic cathedrals. His book, *The Cathedral*, which describes the beauty of Chartres Cathedral, is still used today as a guidebook for those who visit there.

Before the Reading

The Cathedral by Huysmans is a novel that traces the thoughts of his main character, Durtal, as Durtal compares the glory of a Gothic cathedral with the vulgar and sensualized art of the modern world. As you read the following descriptions of Chartres Cathedral, remember that material beauty is not an end in itself, but is rather an image and reflection of eternal beauty that allows those who view it properly to ascend to a greater knowledge of God.

The Cathedral

"It must constantly be repeated; every part of a church and every material object used in divine worship is representative of some theological truth. In the script of architecture everything is a reminiscence, an echo, a reflection, and every part is connected to form a whole.

"For instance, the altar, which is the Image of Our Lord, must be draped with white linen in memory of the winding-sheet in which Joseph of Arimathea wrapped his body. . . ."

"When I tell you further," added the Abbe, "that according to Saint Nilus, the columns signify the divine dogmas, or, according to Durand of Mende, the Bishops and the Doctors of the Church, that the capitals are the words of Scripture, that the pavement of the church is the foundation of faith and humility, that the ambos and rood-loft, almost everywhere destroyed, figure the pulpit of the gospel, the mountain on which Christ preached; again, that the seven lamps burning before the altar are the seven gifts of the Spirit, that the steps to the altar are the steps to perfection; that the alternating choirs represent on the one side the angels, and on the other the righteous, combining to do homage with their voices to the glory of the Most High, I have pretty well explained to you the general meaning and detailed symbolism of the interior of the cathedral, and more particularly that of Chartres. . . ."

But Durtal was not listening; far away from this architectural exegesis, he was admiring the amazing structure without even trying to analyze it. . . . The church appeared as a supreme effort of matter striving for lightness, rejecting, as though it were a burden, the diminished weight of its walls and substituting a less ponderous and more lucent matter, replacing the opacity of stone by the diaphanous texture of glass.

It grew more spiritual—wholly spiritual, purely prayer, as it sprang towards the Lord to meet Him; light and slender, as it were imponderable, it remained the most glorious expression of Beauty escaping from its earthly dross, Beauty become seraphic.

The Middle Ages, knowing that everything on earth is a Sign and a figure, that the only value of things visible is in so far as they correspond to things invisible—the Middle Ages, when consequently men were not, as we are, the dupes of appearances—made a profound study of this science, and made it the nursing mother and the handmaid of mysticism.

Jesus was seen in everything—in the fauna, the flora, the structure of buildings, in every decoration, in the use of colour, whichever way man could turn, he still saw him. . . .

"And this church above all!" sighed Durtal.

The Soul, distraught by the joy of union, heart-broken at having still to live, only aspires now to escape forever from the Gehenna of the flesh; thus it beseeches the Bridegroom with the uplifted arms of its towers, to take pity on it, to come to fetch it, to take it by the clasped hands of its spires and snatch it from earth, to carry it up with Him into Heaven.

In short, this church is the finest expression of art bequeathed to us by the Middle Ages.

Reading for Comprehension

1. What is the symbolism of the altar in Chartres Cathedral?
2. What is the symbolism of the floor?
3. What is the symbolism of the ambos (pulpits)?
4. What does the narrator say is the symbolism of the lamps and the steps?
5. What is the symbolism of the spires on the exterior of the building?

Reading for Understanding

1. Medieval cathedrals like Chartres were noted for their stained glass windows and were built to be "bibles in glass" for the illiterate masses of peasants. What do you think is meant by the phrase "bibles in glass"?

2. What do you think is the purpose of designing cathedrals and churches in splendor and beauty?

Activities

1. View the website of the recently built Cathedral of Our Lady of the Angels in Los Angeles. Explain what the builders were trying to convey. What were some of the visual elements they used to raise the hearts and minds of the worshippers to God? Compare the Cathedral in Los Angeles with another example of twentieth-century church architecture; for example: *Sagrada Familia*, designed by Antonio Gaudi, in Barcelona, Spain. Are there thematic similarities between the two structures? What are the most profound differences? What influences do Gaudi's artistic and religious sensibilities have on his design choices?

2. Visit a local Catholic church, speak to one of the priests or pastoral associates, and request an explanation of the symbolism of three structural or artistic elements found in that church. Report back to your classmates about your findings.

The Seven Sacraments and Their Effects

"She Went by Gently"
Paul Vincent Carroll

Go, therefore, and make disciples of all nations, baptizing them in the name of the Father, and of the Son, and of the holy Spirit.
—Matthew 28:19

Author Background

Paul Vincent Carroll (1900–1968) was born and raised in Ireland and is primarily known as a dramatist. Many of his plays were performed at the famous Abbey Theater in Dublin. Two of his plays, *Shadow and Substance*, and *The White Steed*, were produced on Broadway and received the prestigious New York Drama Critics Circle Award. Speaking of the philosophy behind his writing, he said: "I believe obstinately in a divine plan, and I am convinced that all plays should be written against such a background." The following story shows how he adapted this idea of writing to the short story.

Before the Reading

"Baptism is the basis of the whole Christian life, the gateway to life in the Spirit, and the doorway which gives access to the other sacraments" (*CCC*, 1213). From its earliest days, the Church has practiced the baptism of infants so that they may be freed from the realm of sin and darkness and incorporated into the life of the Church as children of God. The practice of infant baptism signifies that salvation is a pure gift from God and that life in the Church is a communal affair where the faith is taught, practiced, and transmitted from one generation to the next. In normal circumstances, the minister of Baptism is a bishop, priest, or deacon. In an emergency, however, any person, even an un-baptized person, who has the right intention may baptize. This reading tells of a midwife called to deliver the baby of an unmarried mother in the middle of the night, and then to baptize the baby too.

"She Went by Gently"

It was close on three when the knock came in the night. She was out of bed on the instant in her old flannelette nightgown, with her silver-grey hair tossed down her back. The night-light was flickering quietly as, in the shadows by the elm tree outside, she discerned Manahan's unshaven face under the battered hat.

"The pains is bad on the girl," came his voice. "I think maybe it's surely her time."

"Go before me fast and have plenty of hot water," she answered. "I'll be at your heels with Frank."

She heard his foot in the night hurrying off as she drew on her heavy dress over the nightgown. Himself stirred and put his beard irascibly outside the blankets.

"You'll go none," he snapped. "A slut like that, that gets her child outside of priest and law. Four miles uphill on a mountain road and the mists swarmin'."

"I'll go," she said quietly, and crossing, she ruffled Frank's unruly hair on the little camp bed. "Be risin', Frank, and let you carry the lantern for me to Manahan's."

"If there was just a drop o' tay before we'd start, ma," he protested sleepily.

"There's no time, son."

"A grand pass we've come to, in this country," grumbled himself. "Encouragin' the huzzies and the sluts to be shameless. I'd let her suffer. A good bellyful o' sufferin' would keep her from doin' it again."

He moved coughingly into the deep warm hollow she had vacated in the bed. The strictures of his uncharitable piety followed her into the silver and ebony of the mountainy night. She went gently . . . her feet almost noiseless. There was an inward grace in her that spilt out and over her physical lineaments, lending them a strange

197

litheness and beauty of movement. Frank was a little ahead of her, swinging the storm lantern. He was munching a currant scone plastered with butter. His sturdy little legs took the steep sharp-pebbled incline with careless grace. Now and again, he mannishly kicked a stone from his path and whistled in the dark.

"Careful now, Frank, in case you'd slip over the bank in the dark," she admonished.

"Och, ma," he protested, "the way you talk! You'd think I wasn't grew up. It makes little of a fella."

She smiled and watched him lovingly in the silver dark. He was her youngest. The others had all followed the swallows into the mighty world. Martin was in America, Annie in England, Matthew in Glasgow, Paddy in the Navy, Mary Kate a nursemaid in Canada, Michael was at rest somewhere in Italy. His C.O. had said in a letter that he had died well. If that meant that he had had the priest in his last hours, then God be praised, for he was her wayward one. She preferred him dying full of grace to dying full of glory. . . . But Frank was still with her. He had her eyes and gentleness and the winning tilt of the head. It would be good to have him to close her weary eyes at the end of all.

They had now crossed the cockeyed little bridge over a dashing tawny stream and the mountains came near her and about her like mighty elephants gathered in a mystic circle for some high purpose. Everywhere in the vast silvery empire of the dark there was the deep silence of the eternal, except for the rebellious chattering of the mountain streams racing with madcap abandon to the lough below. They were the *enfants terribles* of the mighty house, keeping it awake and uneasy. Now and again a cottage lifted a sleepy eye out of its feathery thatch, smiled at her knowingly and slumbered again. All of them knew her . . . knew of her heroism, her quiet skilled hands, her chiding, coaxing voice in the moments of peril. . . . In each of them she had been the leading actress in the great primitive drama of birth.

The climb was now grueling and Frank took her arm pantingly. The lantern threw its yellow ray merrily ahead. All would be well.

She ruffled his hair playfully, and smiled secretively under the black mask of the night.

At a mischievous bend on the mountain path, the Manahan cottage suddenly jumped out of the mist like a sheep dog and welcomed them with a blaze of wild, flowering creepers. Inside, the middle-aged labourer was bending over a dark deep chimney nook. A turf fire burned underneath on the floor. From a sooty hook far up, a rude chain hung down and supported a large pot of boiling water. She nodded approvingly and donning her overalls moved away in the direction of the highly-pitched cries from an inner room.

"If there's anythin' else I can do . . ." he called, half-shyly, after her.

"Keep a saucepan of gruel thin and hot," she answered. "And put the bottle of olive oil on the hob in case we'd need it. Play about, Frank, and behave yourself till I call you."

She went smilingly to the bed and looked down at the flushed tearful face, the big bloodshot eyes and the glossy tossed hair of the girl. No more than eighteen, she thought, but a well-developed little lass with a full luscious mouth and firm shapely breasts. Jim Cleary who skipped to England in time had had a conquest worth his while. . . . The little rebel, caught in the ruthless trap of Nature, grabbed her hands beseechingly, held on to them hysterically and yelled.

"Oh, Maura, ma'am, please, please, please . . ." she sobbed.

Maura chaffed her hands, soothed her gently, clacked her tongue admonishingly and pretended to be very disappointed at her behaviour.

"Now, now, now, Sadie," she reproved her. "A fine soldier you are! When I was here at your comin', your mother, God rest her, bit her lip hard and said no word at all. Come on now, and be your mother's daughter."

"Ah, sure how could I be like me poor dead mother, and me like this, and all agin me?" sobbed Sadie.

"Am I agin ye, child?" soothed Maura, "and I after walkin' four miles of darkness to be with you!"

The tears came now but silently, as Maura's skilful hands warmed to her work . . .

Frank remained in the kitchen at a loss until suddenly the door opened and a large nanny goat sailed in with perfect equanimity and balefully contemplated this stranger on home ground. Frank looked askance at her full-length beard and her formidable pair of horns, but this was of small consequence to the goat which advanced on Frank and in the wink of an eye had whipped his handkerchief out of his top pocket and stuffed it in her mouth. Frank's protest brought an assurance from Manahan who was stooped over the fire bringing the gruel to the boil.

"She'll not touch you," he said without turning his head.

"But she has me handkerchief," protested Frank.

"Ah, sure isn't she only playing with you!" returned Manahan heedlessly.

But by this time the goat had consumed the handkerchief with terrific relish, and was about to make a direct attack on the sleeve of his jersey. Frank dashed for the door with the goat after him. In the little yard he dived behind the water barrel that caught the rain-water from the roof. The goat snuffed past him in the darkness, and Frank hastily retraced his steps to the kitchen and barred the door.

He was just in time to see his mother put a generous spoonful of butter into a bowl of thin steaming gruel.

"Go in and feed this to your daughter, and coax her to take it," she directed Manahan. "She's quiet and aisy now and all will be well." He obeyed her shyly and without a word.

"You must be a big grown-up fella tonight and help your ma, Frank," she said.

"Anythin' you say, ma," he answered. "What is it?"

The baby had come forth without a cry. It was limp and devoid of any sign of life. She carried it quickly but calmly to the open peat fire, as close to the grimy chain as the heat would allow. It was naked and upside down. Frank, under her calm directions, held it firmly by its miniature ankles.

"Be a good son now and don't let it fall," she warned him, and plastering her own hands with the warm olive oil, she started to work methodically on the tiny body. Up, down and across the little chest, lungs and buttocks went the skilful fingers rhythmically until the new-born skin glistened like a silver-wrought piece of gossamer. The long minutes went by heavily. The oil lamp flickered and went out, leaving the dancing rays and shadows of the fire to light this crude drama with its eternal theme. Five minutes, seven, ten . . . without fruit or the promise of fruit. . . . But the moving fingers went on with rhythmic ruthlessness, searching for the spark that must surely be hidden there in a fold of the descending darkness. Frank's face was flushed, his eyes gathered up with the pain of exertion, his breath coming in spasms. On his mother's forehead beads of sweat gathered, rivulett-ed down the gray gentle face and flowed on to the newborn body to be ruthlessly merged in the hot oily waves of her massaging.

Then suddenly, as the tension had reached almost to the un-bearable, a thin, highly-pitched cry came from the tiny spume-filled lips. She seized the baby, pushed Frank from her, turned it upright, grabbed a chipped, handleless cup of cold water and even as the flut-tering life hesitated on the miniature features for one solitary second to receive its divine passport and the symbol of its eternal heritage, she poured a little of the water on the tiny skull and said, "I bap-tize you, in the Name of the Father and of the Son and of the Holy Ghost."

She wrapped the little corpse in the remnant of a torn sheet, without tear or trace of any sentiment, placed it in a drawer she took from the crazy wardrobe, and having made the Sign of the Cross over it gave it no further attention.

When she saw that the bowl was almost empty of gruel, she chased Manahan out with a gesture and settled the little mother comfortably. She was adjusting her wet, tearstained hair over her pil-low when suddenly she felt Sadie's arms tightly about her neck. Her big eyes were quiet now and the pain and the travail were gone, but the tears came rushing from them again as Maura kissed and soothed her.

"I wish I had me mother," she sobbed. "Maura, ma'am, I'm goin' to be a good girl from now on."

"You have never been a bad one, darlin'," coaxed Maura, tucking the faded bedclothes into her back. "A wee bit foolish maybe, but the world and the years will learn ye. Sleep now and I'll see you tonight."

She re-donned her old black cloak in the kitchen.

"I'll tell Maloney to bring you up a white box," she said to Manahan. "It will save you the journey down."

On the mountain path she went noiselessly, with Frank a little ahead, carrying the extinguished lantern. The dawn greeted her from the heights with far-flung banners of amber and amethyst. The heights themselves ceased from their eternal brooding for a brief moment of rime and gave her a series of benign obeisances. The racing rivulets tossed her name from one to the other on the Lord's commendation. The sun himself, new-risen and generous, sent a very special ray of light that caught up her tossed hair and rolled it in priceless silver.

"Why do men lie prone in their beds," she murmured, "and the great glory of God washin' the hills with holy fire?"

Shamus Dunne was taking in his two nanny goats for the milking as she passed his cottage.

"The blessin' o' God light on ye, woman," he said, touching his wind-swept hat.

"And on yourself too, Shamus," she answered. "How is the little fella now?"

"Ah, sure isn't he over a stone weight already. Ah, woman-oh, wasn't it the near thing that night? Ah, sure only for yourself, wasn't me whole world lost?"

"Arrah, men always think the worst at such times," she answered smilingly. "Sure, there was never any great fear of the worst that night! Herself, within, is much too good a soldier for that!"

Frank had now discovered a salmon tin and was kicking it vigorously before him. She took out her rosary at the bend where the path dips perilously between two ageless boulders, and as she trudged along, she began counting the beads effortlessly. There on the heights at dawn, caught between the gold and the deepening blue of day, she might have been a pilgrim out of a Europe that has long since vanished, or maybe a Ruth garnering the lost and discredited straws of the age-old Christian thought.

Frank had now lobbed his salmon tin on the lofty fork of a tree, and when she caught up with him, he took her arm undemonstratively. Himself would be up now, she thought, with his braces hanging, and maybe a hole in his sock that she had overlooked. He wouldn't be able to find the soap and the towel even if they were both staring at him, and of course if he blew the fire, even with a thousand breaths, it would never light for him. . . . But no matter now. Thanks be to God, there was an egg left in the cracked bowl that would do his breakfast. If the little white pullet in the barn laid in the old butter box, Frank would have one, too, with the help o' God. . . . When the cock himself laid an egg, Glory be, she'd get one all to herself!

They crossed the rickety bridge, as the dawn was losing its virgin colour. Frank saw a squirrel and rushed ahead of her. She paused for a moment and contemplated the restless waters. They took to her like a rich tawny wine poured out of some capacious barrel by some high ruthless hand who had suddenly discovered the futility of all riches. A May blossom rushed under the incongruous arch and emerged to get caught between a moss-covered stone and a jagged piece of rock. There was a turmoil and pain for a moment, and then it freed itself and rushed on. She wondered if it was the little soul she had lately saved, rushing on in a virgin panic to the eternal waters. . . . Maybe it was. . . . Maybe she was just an imaginative old fool. . . . Ah, sure what harm anyway to be guessing at infinite mysteries, and she so small on a mountain road?

Himself met her in the stone-floored kitchen. Indeed, yes, he was trailing his braces, and the sulky fire was just giving a last gasp before expiring.

"I suppose you saved the slut's bastard," he commented acidly.

She bent on her knees to blow the fire aflame again.

"I saved him," she answered, and a flame leaped suddenly upwards and made a sweet and unforgettable picture of her face.

Reading for Comprehension

1. What is the woman's wish for her son, Michael?

2. Why is the girl so sad and frightened?

3. What does the women do when the baby is born?

4. What happens to the baby?

5. What is her husband's comment about the child when she returns home?

Reading for Understanding

1. A gift of Baptism is the ability to love others as God loves us. How is this ability seen in the women's treatment of the girl?

2. At the end of the story the woman says in regard to the infant, "I saved him." What does she mean by that statement?

3. The author describes the journey of the woman to her own home. What is the purpose of this section of the story? What is he trying to convey about the woman through his descriptions?

Activity

"The Lord himself affirms that baptism is necessary for salvation" (*CCC*, 1257). Research and report on the Church's teaching about the salvation of infants who have died before receiving the Sacrament of Baptism.

The Seven Sacraments and Their Effects

The Hint of An Explanation

Graham Greene

Jesus said to them, "Amen, Amen I say to you,
unless you eat the flesh of the Son of Man and drink his blood,
you do not have life within you. . . . For my flesh is true food,
and my blood is true drink."

—John 6:53, 55

Author Background

Graham Greene (1904–1991) wrote some of the most gripping novels and dramas of the twentieth century. For example, the novels *The Heart of the Matter* and *The End of the Affair* and his play, *The Potting Shed*, deal in a brilliant manner with specifically Catholic themes of grace and redemption. His novel *The Power and the Glory* is one of the greatest novels ever written treating the subject of the Catholic priesthood. Greene was haunted by questions of faith and has expressed this concern most effectively in the following story.

Before the Reading

Christ is truly present in the Eucharist under the appearance of bread and wine. This truth was reaffirmed by the Council of Trent where the Fathers of the Council wrote: ". . . it has always been the conviction of the Church of God, and this Council now declares again, that by the consecration of the bread and wine there takes place a change of the bread into the body of Christ our Lord and of the whole substance of the wine into the substance of his blood" (*CCC*, 1376). It is in the potential desecration of the Eucharist in the following story that a young boy comes to understand the meaning of this great mystery.

The Hint of an Explanation

A long train journey on a late December evening, in this new version of peace, is a dreary experience. I suppose that my fellow traveler and I could consider ourselves lucky to have a compartment to ourselves, even though the heating apparatus was not working, even though the lights went out entirely in the frequent Pennine tunnels and were too dim anyway for us to read our books without straining the eyes, and though there was no restaurant car to give at least a change of scene. It was when we were trying simultaneously to chew the same kind of dry bun bought at the same station buffet that my companion and I came together. Before that we had sat at opposite ends of the carriage, both muffled to the chin in overcoats, both bent low over type we could barely make out, but as I threw the remains of my cake under the seat our eyes met, and he laid his book down.

By the time we were halfway to Bedwell Junction we had found an enormous range of subjects for discussion; starting with buns and the weather, we had gone on to politics, the government, foreign affairs, the atom bomb, and by an inevitable progression, God. We had not, however, become either shrill or acid. My companion, who now sat opposite me, leaning a little forward, so that our knees nearly touched, gave such an impression of serenity that it would have been impossible to quarrel with him, however much our views differed, and differ they did profoundly.

I had soon realized I was speaking to a Roman Catholic—to someone who believed—how do they put it?—in an omnipotent and omniscient Deity, while I am what is loosely called an agnostic. I have a certain intuition (which I do not trust, founded as it may well be on childish experiences and needs) that a God exists, and I am surprised occasionally into belief by the extraordinary coincidences that beset our path like the traps set for leopards in the jungle, but intellectually I am revolted at the whole notion of such a God who can so abandon his creatures to the enormities of Free Will. I found myself expressing this view to my companion who listened quietly and with respect. He made no attempt to interrupt—he showed none of the impatience or the intellectual arrogance I have grown to expect from Catholics; when the lights of a wayside station flashed across his face which had escaped hitherto the rays of the one globe working in the compartment, I caught a glimpse suddenly of—what? I stopped speaking, so strong was the impression. I was carried back ten years, to the other side of the great useless conflict, to a small town, Gisors in Normandy. I was again, for a moment, walking on the ancient battlements and looking down across the grey roofs, until my eyes for some reason lit on one stony "back" out of the many where the face of a middle-aged man was pressed against a window pane (I suppose that face has ceased to exist now, just as perhaps the whole town with its medieval memories has been reduced to rubble). I remembered saying to myself with astonishment, "that man is happy—completely happy." I looked across the compartment at my fellow traveller, but his face was already again in shadow. I said weakly, "When you think what God—if there is a God—allows. It's not merely the physical agonies, but think of the corruption, even of children . . ."

He said. "Our view is so limited," and I was disappointed at the conventionality of his reply. He must have been aware of my disappointment (it was as though our thoughts were huddled as closely as ourselves for warmth), for he went on, "Of course there is no answer here. We catch hints . . ." and then the train roared into another tunnel and the lights again went out. It was the longest tunnel yet; we went rocking down it and the cold seemed to become more intense with the darkness, like an icy fog (when one sense—of sight—is robbed, the others grow more acute). When we emerged into the mere grey of night and the globe lit up once more, I could see that my companion was leaning back on his seat.

I repeated his last word as a question, "Hints?"

"Oh, they mean very little in cold print—or cold speech," he said, shivering in his overcoat. "And they mean nothing at all to another human being than the man who catches them. They are not scientific evidence—or evidence at all for that matter. Events that don't, somehow, turn out as they were intended—by the human actors, I mean, or by the thing behind the human actors."

"The thing?"

"The word Satan is so anthropomorphic." I had to lean forward now: I wanted to hear what he had to say. I am—I really am, God knows—open to conviction. He said, "One's words are so crude, but I sometimes feel pity for that thing. It is so continually finding the right weapon to use against its Enemy and the weapon breaks in its own breast. It sometimes seems to me so—powerless. You said something just now about the corruption of children. It reminded me of something in my own childhood. You are the first person—except for one—that I have thought of telling it to, perhaps because you are anonymous. It's not a very long story, and in a way it's relevant."

I said, "I'd like to hear it."

"You mustn't expect too much meaning. But to me there seems to be a hint. That's all. A hint."

He went slowly on turning his face to the pane, though he could have seen nothing in the whirling world outside except an occasional signal lamp, a light in a window, a small country station torn backwards by our rush, picking his words with precision. He said, "When I was a child they taught me to serve at Mass. The church was a small one, for there were very few Catholics where I lived. It was a market town in East Anglia, surrounded by flat chalky fields and ditches—so many ditches. I don't suppose there were fifty Catholics all told, and for some reason there was a tradition of hostility to us. Perhaps it went back to the burning of a Protestant martyr in the sixteenth century—there was a stone marking the place near where the meat stalls stood on Wednesdays. I was only half aware of the enmity, though I knew that my school nickname of Popey Martin had something to do with my religion and I had heard that my father was very nearly excluded from the Constitutional Club when he first came to the town.

"Every Sunday I had to dress up in my surplice and serve Mass. I hated it—I have always hated dressing up in any way (which is funny when you come to think of it), and I never ceased to be afraid of losing my place in the service and doing something which would put me to ridicule. Our services were at a different hour from the Anglican, and as our small, far-from-select band trudged out of the hideous chapel the whole of the townsfolk seemed to be on the way past to the proper church—I always thought of it as the proper church. We had to pass the parade of their eyes—indifferent, supercilious, mocking; you can't imagine how seriously religion can be taken in a small town—if only for social reasons.

"There was one man in particular; he was one of the two bakers in the town, the one my family did not patronize. I don't think any of the Catholics patronized him because he was called a free-thinker—an odd title, for, poor man, no one's thoughts were less free than his. He was hemmed in by his hatred—his hatred of us. He was very ugly to look at, with one wall-eye and a head the shape of a turnip, with the hair gone on the crown, and he was unmarried. He had no interests, apparently, but his baking and his hatred, though now that I am older I begin to see other sides of his nature—it did contain, perhaps, a certain furtive love. One would come across him suddenly, sometimes, on a country walk, especially if one was alone and it was Sunday. It was as though he rose from the ditches and the chalk smear on his clothes reminded one of the flour on his working overalls. He would have a stick in his hand and stab at the hedges, and if his mood were very black he would call out after you strange abrupt words that were like a foreign tongue—I know the meaning of those words, of course, now. Once the police went to his house because of what a boy said he had seen, but nothing came of it except that the hate shackled him closer. His name was Blacker, and he terrified me.

"I think he had a particular hatred of my father—I don't know why. My father was manager of the Midland Bank, and it's possible that at some time Blacker may have had unsatisfactory dealings with the bank—my father was a very cautious man who suffered all his life from anxiety about money—his own and other people's. If I try to picture Blacker now I see him walking along a narrowing path between high windowless walls, and at the end of the path stands a small boy often—me. I don't know whether it's a symbolic picture or the memory of one of our encounters—our encounters somehow got more and more frequent. You talked just now about the corruption of children. That poor man was preparing to revenge himself on everything he hated—my father, the Catholics, the God whom people persisted in crediting—by corrupting me. He had evolved a horrible and ingenious plan.

"I remember the first time I had a friendly word from him. I was passing his shop as rapidly as I could when I heard his voice call out with a kind of sly subservience as though he were an under-servant. 'Master David,' he called, 'Master David,' and I hurried on. But the next time I passed that way he was at his door (he must have seen me coming) with one of those curly cakes in his hand that we called Chelsea buns. I didn't want to take it, but he made me, and then I couldn't be other than polite when he asked me to come into his parlor behind the shop and see something very special.

"It was a small electric railway—a rare sight in those days, and he insisted on showing me how it worked. He made me turn the switches and stop and start it, and he told me that I could come in any morning and have a game with it. He used the word 'game' as though it were something secret, and it's true that I never told my family of this invitation and of how, perhaps twice a week those holidays, the desire to control that little railway became overpowering, and looking up and down the street to see if I were observed. I would dive into the shop."

Our larger, dirtier, adult train drove into a tunnel and the light went out. We sat in darkness and silence, with the noise of the train blocking our ears like wax. When we were through we didn't speak at once and I had to prick him into continuing.

"An elaborate seduction," I said.

"Don't think his plans were as simple as that," my companion said, "or as crude. There was much more hate than love, poor man in his makeup. Can you hate something you don't believe in? And yet he called himself a free-thinker. What an impossible paradox, to be free and to be so obsessed. Day by day all through those holidays his obsession must have grown, but he kept a grip; he bided his time. Perhaps that thing I spoke of gave him the strength and the wisdom. It was only a week from the end of the holidays that he spoke to me of what concerned him so deeply.

"I heard him behind me as I knelt on the floor, coupling two coaches. He said, 'You won't be able to do this, Master David, when school starts.' It wasn't a sentence that needed any comment from me any more than the one that followed. 'You ought to have it for your own, you ought,' but how skillfully and unemphatically he had sowed the longing, the idea of a possibility I was coming to his parlor every day now; you see I had to cram every opportunity in before the hated term started again, and I suppose I was becoming accustomed to Blacker, to that wall-eye, that turnip head, that nauseating subservience. The Pope, you know, describes himself as 'The servant of the servants of God,' and Blacker—I sometimes think, that Blacker was 'the servant of the servants of . . .' Well, let it be.

"The very next day, standing in the doorway watching me play, he began to talk to me about religion. He said with what untruth even I recognized, how much he admired the Catholics; he wished he could believe like that, but how could a baker believe? He accented 'a baker' as one might say a biologist. And the tiny train spun round the gauge track. He said, 'I can bake the things you eat just as well as any Catholic can,' and disappeared into his shop. I hadn't the faintest idea what he meant. Presently he emerged again, holding in his hand a little wafer. 'Here,' he said, 'eat that and tell me . . .' When I put it in my mouth I could tell that it was made in the same way as our wafers for communion—he had got the shape a little wrong, that was all, and I felt guilty and irrationally scared. 'Tell me,' he said, 'what's the difference?'

"'Difference?' I asked.

"'Isn't that just the same as you eat in church?'

"I said smugly, 'It hasn't been consecrated.'

"He said. 'Do you think if I put the two of them under a microscope, you could tell the difference?' But even at ten I had the answer to that question. 'No,' I said. 'The—accidents don't change,' stumbling a little on the word 'accidents' which had suddenly conveyed to me the idea of death and wounds.

"Blacker said with sudden intensity, 'How I'd like to get one of yours in my mouth—just to see . . .'

"It may seem odd to you, but this was the first time that the idea of transubstantiation really lodged in my mind. I had learnt it all by rote; I had grown up with the idea. The Mass was as lifeless to me as the sentences in *De Bella Gallico*, communion a routine like drill in the schoolyard, but here suddenly I was in the presence of a man who took it seriously, as seriously as the priest whom naturally one didn't count—it was his job. I felt more scared than ever.

"He said. 'It's all nonsense, but I'd just like to have it in my mouth.'

"'You could if you were a Catholic,' I said naively. He gazed at me with his one good eye like a Cyclops. He said. "You serve at Mass, don't you? It would be easy for you to get at one of those things. I tell you what I'd do—I'd swap this electric train set for one of your wafers—consecrated, mind. It's got to be consecrated.'

"'I could get you one out of the box,' I said. I think I still imagined that his interest was a baker's interest—to see how they were made.

"'Oh, no,' he said. 'I want to see what your God tastes like.'

"'I couldn't do that.'

"'Not for a whole electric train, just for yourself? You wouldn't have any trouble at home. I'd pack it up and put a label inside that your Dad could see— "For my bank manager's little boy from a grateful client." He'd be pleased as Punch with that.'

"Now that we are grown men it seems a trivial temptation, doesn't it? But try to think back to your own childhood. There was a whole circuit of rails on the floor at our feet, straight rails and curved rails, and a little station with porters and passengers, a tunnel, a footbridge, a level crossing, two signals, buffers, of course—and above all, a turntable. The tears of longing came into my eyes when I looked at the turntable. It was my favorite piece—it looked so ugly and practical and true. I said weakly. 'I wouldn't know how.'

"How carefully he had been studying the ground. He must have slipped several times into Mass at the back of the church. It would have been no good, you understand, in a little town like that, presenting himself for communion. Everybody there knew him for what he was. He said to me, 'When you've been given communion you could just put it under your tongue a moment. He serves you and the other boy first, and I saw you once go out behind the curtain straight afterwards. You'd forgotten one of those little bottles.'

"'The cruet,' I said.

"'Pepper and salt.' He grinned at me jovially, and I—well, I looked at the little railway which I could no longer come and play with when term started. I said, 'You'd just swallow it, wouldn't you?'

"'Oh, yes,' he said. 'I'd just swallow it.'

"Somehow I didn't want to play with the train any more that day. I got up and made for the door, but he detained me, gripping my lapel. He said, 'This will be a secret between you and me. Tomorrow's Sunday. You come along here in the afternoon. Put it in an envelope and post it in. Monday morning the train will be delivered bright and early.'

"'Not tomorrow.' I implored him.

"'I'm not interested in any other Sunday,' he said. 'It's your only chance.' He shook me gently backwards and forwards. 'It will always have to be a secret between you and me,' he said. 'Why, if anyone knew they'd take away the train and there'd be me to reckon with. I'd bleed you something awful. You know how I'm always about on Sunday walks. You can't avoid a man like me. I crop up. You wouldn't even be safe in your own house. I know ways to get into houses when people are asleep.' He pulled me into the shop after him and opened a drawer. In the drawer was an odd-looking key and a cut-throat razor. He said, 'That's a master key that opens all locks and that—that's

213

what I bleed people with.' Then he patted my cheek with his plump floury fingers and said. 'Forget it. You and me are friends.'

"That Sunday Mass stays in my head, every detail of it, as though it had happened only a week ago. From the moment of the Confession to the moment of Consecration it had a terrible importance; only one other Mass has ever been so important to me—perhaps not even one, for this was a solitary Mass which could never happen again. It seemed as final as the last Sacrament, when the priest bent down and put the wafer in my mouth where I knelt before the altar with my fellow server.

"I suppose I had made up my mind to commit this awful act—for, you know, to us it must always seem an awful act—from the moment when I saw Blacker watching from the back of the church. He had put on his best Sunday clothes, and as though he could never quite escape the smear of his profession, he had a dab of dried talcum on his cheek, which he had presumably applied after using that cut-throat razor of his. He was watching me closely all the time, and I think it was fear—fear of that terrible undefined thing called bleeding—as much as covetousness that drove me to carry out my instructions.

"My fellow server got briskly up and taking the communion plate preceded Father Carey to the altar rail where the other Communicants knelt. I had the Host lodged under my tongue: it felt like a blister. I got up and made for the curtain to get the cruet that I had purposely left in the sacristy. When I was there I looked quickly round for a hiding-place and saw an old copy of the Universe lying on a chair. I took the Host from my mouth and inserted it between two sheets—a little damp mess of pulp. Then I thought: perhaps Father Carey has put the paper out for a particular purpose and he will find the Host before I have time to remove it, and the enormity of my act began to come home to me when I tried to imagine what punishment I should incur. Murder is sufficiently trivial to have its appropriate punishment, but for this act the mind boggled at the thought of any retribution at all. I tried to remove the Host, but it had stuck clammily between the pages and in desperation I tore out a piece of the

Georges Rouault's *Et Véronique au tendre lin (And Veronica with the soft linen)*

Michelangelo Merisi da Caravaggio's *Supper at Emmaus*

Andy Warhol's *The Last Supper*

Salvador Dali's *The Sacrament of the Last Supper*

2001: A Space Odyssey

Paul Newman in a scene from *Cool Hand Luke*

Paul Gauguin's *Ia Orana Maria (Hail Mary)*

Giotto Di Bondone's *St. Francis of Assisi Preaching to the Birds*

Michelangelo Buonarroti's *Creation of Adam*

Giovanni Bellini's *The Agony in the Garden*

Scene from Alfred Hitchcock's *I Confess*

Edvard Munch's *The Scream*

Raymond Massey, Julie Harris, and James Dean in *East of Eden*

Gian Lorenzo Bernini's *Ecstasy of St. Theresa*

On the Waterfront movie poster

newspaper and screwing the whole thing up, stuck it in my trouser pocket. When I came back through the curtain carrying the cruet my eyes met Blacker's. He gave me a grin of encouragement and unhappiness—yes, I am sure, unhappiness. Was it perhaps that the poor man was all the time seeking something incorruptible?

"I can remember little more of that day. I think my mind was shocked and stunned and I was caught up too in the family bustle of Sunday. Sunday in a provincial town is the day for relations. All the family are at home and unfamiliar cousins and uncles are apt to arrive packed in the back seats of other people's cars. I remember that some crowd of that kind descended on us and pushed Blacker temporarily out of the foreground of my mind. There was somebody called Aunt Lucy with a loud hollow laugh that filled the house with mechanical merriment like the sound of recorded laughter from inside a hall of mirrors, and I had no opportunity to go out alone even if I had wished to. When six o'clock came and Aunt Lucy and the cousins departed and peace returned, it was too late to go to Blacker's and at eight it was my own bedtime.

"I think I had half forgotten what I had in my pocket. As I emptied my pocket the little screw of newspaper brought quickly back the Mass, the priest bending over me, Blacker's grin. I laid the packet on the chair by my bed and tried to go to sleep, but I was haunted by the shadows on the wall where the curtains blew, the squeak of furniture, the rustle in the chimney, haunted by the presence of God there on the chair. The Host had always been to me—well, the Host. I knew theoretically, as I have said, what I had to believe, but suddenly, as someone whistled in the road outside, whistled secretively, knowingly, to me, I knew that this which I had beside my bed was something of infinite value—something a man would pay for with his whole peace of mind, something that was so hated one could love it as one loves an outcast or a bullied child. These are adult words and it was a child often who lay scared in bed, listening to the whistle from the road, Blacker's whistle, but I think he felt fairly clearly what I am describing now. That is what I meant when I said this Thing, whatever it is, that seizes every possible weapon against God, is always, everywhere, disappointed at the moment of success. It must have felt as certain of me as Blacker did. It must have felt certain, too, of Blacker. But I wonder, if one knew what happened later to that poor man, whether one would not find again that the weapon had been turned against its own breast.

"At last I couldn't bear that whistle any more and got out of bed. I opened the curtains a little way, and there right under my window, the moonlight on his face, was Blacker. If I had stretched my hand down, his fingers reaching up could almost have touched mine. He looked up at me, flashing the one good eye, with hunger—I realize now that near-success must have developed his obsession almost to the point of madness. Desperation had driven him to the house. He whispered up at me. 'David, where is it?'

"I jerked my head back at the room. 'Give it me,' he said, 'quick. You shall have the train in the morning.'

"I shook my head. He said, 'I've got the bleeder here, and the key. You'd better toss it down.'

"'Go away.' I said. But I could hardly speak with fear.

"'I'll bleed you first and then I'll have it just the same.

"'Oh no, you won't,' I said. I went to the chair and picked it—Him—up. There was only one place where He was safe. I couldn't separate the Host from the paper, so I swallowed both. The newsprint stuck like a prune to the back of my throat, but I rinsed it down with water from the ewer. Then I went back to the window and looked down at Blacker. He began to wheedle me. 'What have you done with it, David? What's the fuss? It's only a bit of bread,' looking so longingly and pleadingly up at me that even as a child I wondered whether he could really think that, and yet desire it so much.

"'I swallowed it.' I said.

"'Swallowed it?'

"'Yes,' I said. 'Go away.' Then something happened which seems to me now more terrible than his desire to corrupt or my thoughtless act: he began to weep—the tears ran lopsidedly out of the one good eye and his shoulders shook. I only saw his face for a moment before he bent his head and strode off, the bald turnip head shaking, into the dark. When I think of it now, it's almost as if I had seen that Thing weeping for its inevitable defeat. It had tried to use me as a weapon and now I had broken in its hands and it wept its hopeless tears through one of Blacker's eyes."

The black furnaces of Bedwell Junction gathered around the line. The points switched and we were tossed from one set of rails to another. A spray of sparks, a signal light changed to red, tall chimneys jetting into the grey night sky, the fumes of steam from stationary engines—half the cold journey was over and now remained the long wait for the slow cross-country train. I said. "It's an interesting story. I think, should I have given Blacker what he wanted, I wonder what he would have done with it?"

"I really believe," my companion said, "that he would first of all have put it under his microscope—before he did all the other things I expect he had planned."

"And the hint?" I said. "I don't quite see what you mean by that."

"Oh, well," he said vaguely, "you know for me it was an odd beginning, that affair, when you come to think of it," but I should never have known what he meant had not his coat, when he rose to take his bag from the rack, come open and disclosed the collar of a priest.

I said, "I suppose you think you owe a lot to Blacker.'"

"Yes," he said. "You see, I am a very happy man."

Reading for Comprehension

1. What is the narrator's objection about belief in the existence of God?
2. What was the status of Catholics in the village where the boy was raised?
3. Describe Blacker's physical appearance.
4. What does Blacker ask the boy to do in exchange for the toy train set?

5. What does the boy do when Blacker demands he give him the communion host?

6. What does the narrator learn about the identity of his companion at the end of the story?

7. What is "the thing" the author described?

Reading for Understanding

1. In a philosophic work titled *The Grammar of Assent*, John Henry Cardinal Newman investigated what it means when a person says, "I believe." Newman distinguished between two forms of assent: "Notional" assent refers to saying "yes" with one's mind alone; "Real" assent means saying "yes" to something or someone with one's whole heart, soul, mind, and emotions. It is saying "yes" to something that is real. How does his stealing of the Eucharist reveal to the boy the true meaning of the presence of Jesus in the Eucharist?

2. An ancient proverb states that "God writes straight with crooked lines." How is the truth of that statement seen in the vocation to the priesthood of the boy in the story?

3. What do you think Graham Greene wanted to say about how God reveals himself to us by titling this story, "The Hint of an Explanation"?

Activities

1. Read the scriptural account of the experience of the disciples on the road to Emmaus (Lk 24:13–35). Next, look at Caravaggio's painting *The Disciples at Emmaus* (see page 241). How do both the painting and "The Hint of an Explanation" depict the emotional moment when people truly understand that God is being revealed to them?

2. Research the bizarre incident involving a University of Minnesota Morris biology professor, Paul Zachary Myers, who asked people to send him the consecrated host from Mass so that he could desecrate it. What is your reaction to this story? What do you think should be the Church's response to an incident like this? The government's response?

The Seven Sacraments and Their Effects

The Gift of the Magi

O. Henry

But do not be afraid because she was set apart for you before the world existed. . . . When Tobias heard Raphael say that she was his kinswoman, of his own family's lineage, he fell deeply in love with her, and his heart became set on her.

—Tobit 6:18

Author Background

O. Henry was the penname for William Sydney Porter, who was born in 1862. He focused his short stories—many of which were published in New York City newspapers—on the lives of New Yorkers at the beginning of the twentieth century. Porter had a great gift for illuminating the lives of the working class citizens who made the riches of a great city possible. He died in 1910 from complications due to alcoholism.

Before the Reading

Matrimony is a sign and a symbol of God's love for his Church. Just as spouses give themselves in love to each other, so does Christ give himself to the People of God. The *Catechism of the Catholic Church* also teaches: "Since God created him man and woman, their mutual love becomes an image of the absolute and unfailing love with which God loves man" (*CCC*, 1604). In the following story we see an illustration of the self-giving nature of matrimonial love.

The Gift of the Magi

One dollar and eighty-seven cents. That was all. And sixty cents of it was in pennies. Pennies saved one and two at a time by bulldozing the grocer and the vegetable man and the butcher until one's cheeks burned with the silent imputation of parsimony that such close dealing implied. Three times Delia counted it. One dollar and eighty-seven cents. And the next day would be Christmas.

There was clearly nothing to do but flop down on the shabby little couch and howl. So Delia did it. Which instigates the moral reflection that life is made up of sobs, sniffles, and smiles, with sniffles predominating.

While the mistress of the home is gradually subsiding from the first stage to the second, take a look at the home. A furnished flat at $8 per week. It did not exactly beggar description, but it certainly had that word on the lookout for the mendicancy squad.

In the vestibule below was a letter-box into which no letter would go, and an electric button from which no mortal finger could coax a ring. Also appertaining thereunto was a card bearing the name "Mr. James Dillingham Young."

The "Dillingham" had been flung to the breeze during a former period of prosperity when its possessor was being paid $30 per week. Now, when the income was shrunk to $20, though, they were thinking seriously of contracting to a modest and unassuming D. But whenever Mr. James Dillingham Young came home and reached his flat above he was called "Jim" and greatly hugged by Mrs. James Dillingham Young, already introduced to you as Delia. Which is all very good.

Delia finished her cry and attended to her cheeks with the powder rag. She stood by the window and looked out dully at a gray cat walking a gray fence in a gray backyard. Tomorrow would be Christmas Day, and she had only $1.87 with which to buy Jim a present. She had been saving every penny she could for months, with this result. Twenty dollars a week doesn't go far. Expenses had been greater than she had calculated. They always are. Only $1.87 to buy a present for Jim. Her Jim. Many a happy hour she had spent planning for something nice for him. Something fine and rare and sterling—something just a little bit near to being worthy of the honor of being owned by Jim.

There was a pier-glass between the windows of the room. Perhaps you have seen a pier-glass in an eight dollar flat. A very thin and very agile person may, by observing his reflection in a rapid sequence of longitudinal strips, obtain a fairly accurate conception of his looks. Delia, being slender, had mastered the art.

Suddenly she whirled from the window and stood before the glass, her eyes were shining brilliantly, but her face had lost its color within twenty seconds. Rapidly she pulled down her hair and let it fall to its full length.

Now, there were two possessions of the James Dillingham Youngs in which they both took a mighty pride. One was Jim's gold watch that had been his father's and his grandfather's. The other was Delia's hair. Had the queen of Sheba lived in the flat across the airshaft, Delia would have let her hair hang out the window some day to dry just to depreciate Her Majesty's jewels and gifts. Had King Solomon been the janitor, with all his treasures piled up in the basement, Jim would have pulled out his watch every time he passed, just to see him pluck at his beard from envy.

So now Delia's beautiful hair fell about her rippling and shining like a cascade of brown waters. It reached below her knee and made itself almost a garment for her. And then she did it up again nervously and quickly. Once she faltered for a minute and stood still while a tear or two splashed on the worn red carpet.

On went her old brown jacket; on went her old brown hat. With a whirl of skirts and with the brilliant sparkle still in her eyes, she fluttered out the door and down the stairs to the street.

Where she stopped the sign read: "Mne. Sofronie. Hair Goods of All Kinds." One flight up Delia ran, and collected herself, panting. Madame, large, too white, chilly, hardly looked the "Sofronie."

"Will you buy my hair?" asked Delia.

"I buy hair," said Madame. "Take yer hat off and let's have a sight at the looks of it."

Down rippled the brown cascade.

"Twenty dollars," said Madame, lifting the mass with a practised hand.

"Give it to me quick," said Delia.

Oh, and the next two hours tripped by on rosy wings. Forget the hashed metaphor. She was ransacking the stores for Jim's present.

She found it at last. It surely had been made for Jim and no one else. There was no other like it in any of the stores, and she had turned all of them inside out. It was a platinum fob chain simple and chaste in design, properly proclaiming its value by substance alone and not by meretricious ornamentation—as all good things should do. It was even worthy of The Watch. As soon as she saw it she knew that it must be Jim's. It was like him. Quietness and value—the description applied to both. Twenty-one dollars they took from her for it, and she hurried home with the eighty-seven cents. With that chain on his watch Jim might be properly anxious about the time in any company. Grand as the watch was, he sometimes looked at it on the sly on account of the old leather strap that he used in place of a chain.

When Delia reached home her intoxication gave way a little to prudence and reason. She got out her curling irons and lighted the gas and went to work repairing the ravages made by generosity added to love. Which is always a tremendous task, dear friends—a mammoth task.

Within forty minutes her head was covered with tiny, close-lying curls that made her look wonderfully like a truant schoolboy. She looked at her reflection in the mirror long, carefully, and critically.

"If Jim doesn't kill me," she said to herself, "before he takes a second look at me, he'll say I look like a Coney Island chorus girl. But what could I do—oh! what could I do with a dollar and eighty-seven cents?"

At seven o'clock the coffee was made and the frying-pan was on the back of the stove hot and ready to cook the chops.

Jim was never late. Delia doubled the fob chain in her hand and sat on the comer of the table near the door that he always entered. Then she heard his step on the stair away down on the first flight, and she turned white for just a moment. She had a habit for saying little silent prayer about the simplest everyday things, and now she whispered: "Please God, make him think I am still pretty."

The door opened and Jim stepped in and closed it. He looked thin and very serious. Poor fellow, he was only twenty-two—and to be burdened with a family! He needed a new overcoat and he was without gloves.

Jim stopped inside the door, as immovable as a setter at the scent of quail. His eyes were fixed upon Delia, and there was an expression in them that she could not read, and it terrified her. It was not anger, nor surprise, nor disapproval, nor horror, nor any of the sentiments that she had been prepared for. He simply stared at her fixedly with that peculiar expression on his face.

Delia wriggled off the table and went for him.

"Jim, darling," she cried, "don't look at me that way. I had my hair cut off and sold because I couldn't have lived through Christmas without giving you a present. It'll grow out again—you won't mind, will you? I just had to do it. My hair grows awfully fast. Say 'Merry Christmas!' Jim, and let's be happy. You don't know what a nice—what a beautiful, nice gift I've got for you."

"You've cut off your hair?" asked Jim, laboriously, as if he had not arrived at that patent fact yet even after the hardest mental labor.

"Cut it off and sold it," said Delia. "Don't you like me just as well, anyhow? I'm me without my hair, ain't I?"

Jim looked about the room curiously.

"You say your hair is gone?" he said, with an air almost of idiocy.

"You needn't look for it," said Delia. "It's sold, I tell you—sold and gone, too. It's Christmas Eve, boy. Be good to me, for it went for you. Maybe the hairs of my head were numbered," she went on with

223

sudden serious sweetness, "but nobody could ever count my love for you. Shall I put the chops on, Jim?"

Out of his trance Jim seemed quickly to wake. He enfolded his Delia. For ten seconds let us regard with discreet scrutiny some inconsequential object in the other direction. Eight dollars a week or a million a year—what is the difference? A mathematician or a wit would give you the wrong answer. The magi brought valuable gifts, but that was not among them. This dark assertion will be illuminated later on.

Jim drew a package from his overcoat pocket and threw it upon the table.

"Don't make any mistake, Dell," he said, "about me. I don't think there's anything in the way of a haircut or a shave or a shampoo that could make me like my girl any less. But if you'll unwrap that package you may see why you had me going a while at first."

White fingers and nimble tore at the string and paper. And then an ecstatic scream of joy; and then, alas! a quick feminine change to hysterical tears and wails, necessitating the immediate employment of all the comforting powers of the lord of the flat.

For there lay The Combs—the set of combs, side and back, that Delia had worshipped long in a Broadway window. Beautiful combs, pure tortoise shell, with jewelled rims—just the shade to wear in the beautiful vanished hair. They were expensive combs, she knew, and her heart had simply craved and yearned over them without the least hope of possession. And now, they were hers, but the tresses that should have adorned the coveted adornments were gone.

But she hugged them to her bosom, and at length she was able to look up with dim eyes and a smile and say: "My hair grows so fast, Jim!"

And them Delia leaped up like a little singed cat and cried, "Oh, oh!"

Jim had not yet seen his beautiful present. She held it out to him eagerly upon her open palm. The dull precious metal seemed to flash with a reflection of her bright and ardent spirit.

"Isn't it a dandy, Jim? I hunted all over town to find it. You'll have to look at the time a hundred times a day now. Give me your watch. I want to see how it looks on it."

Instead of obeying, Jim tumbled down on the couch and put his hands under the back of his head and smiled.

"Dell," said he, "let's put our Christmas presents away and keep 'em a while. They're too nice to use just at present. I sold the watch to get the money to buy your combs. And now suppose you put the chops on."

The magi, as you know, were wise men—wonderfully wise men—who brought gifts to the Babe in the manger. They invented the art of giving Christmas presents. Being wise, their gifts were no doubt wise ones, possibly bearing the privilege of exchange in case of duplication. And here I have lamely related to you the uneventful chronicle of two foolish children in a flat who most unwisely sacrificed for each other the greatest treasures of their house. But in a last word to the wise of these days let it be said that of all who give gifts these two were the wisest. Of all who give and receive gifts, such as they are wisest. Everywhere they are wisest. They are the magi.

Reading for Comprehension

1. How much had Jim's salary been reduced?
2. What were the most precious possessions of the married couple?
3. How much was the wife paid for the sale of her hair?
4. What did the wife do with the money she received for her hair?
5. Why was the husband dumbfounded when he saw his Christmas gift—the platinum chain for his watch?

Reading for Understanding

1. What do the actions of the husband and wife tell us about real love?
2. Why does O. Henry compare this husband and wife to the magi of Scripture?

Activity

Each sacrament has a specific minister. In six of the sacraments, the ordinary minister is a man who has received the Sacrament of Holy Orders. The exception is the Sacrament of Matrimony. Find out who the ministers of the Sacrament of Matrimony are. What is the role of a priest at a wedding ceremony?

The Seven Sacraments and Their Effects

The Diary of a Country Priest
Georges Bernanos

"Amen, I say to you, whatever you bind on earth shall be bound in heaven, and whatever you loose on earth shall be loosed in heaven."
—Matthew 18:18

Author Background

Georges Bernanos (1888–1948) was one of the greatest Catholic novelists of the twentieth century. A native of France, Bernanos's novels deal with the themes of sin, grace, and redemption. He had a unique ability to describe the inner life of the person and the action of grace on the life of humans. This is especially seen in his novels *Under the Sun of Satan*, *The Imposter*, and *Joy*. His most famous novel is *The Diary of a Country Priest*, which was awarded the Le Grand Prix du Roman, given by L'Académie française in 1936.

Before the Reading

The Diary of a Country Priest recounts the actions and thoughts of a poor but pious priest as he performs his duties in an obscure French village. The priest's sanctity and his transparent devotion to God have an unsettling effect on all who come in contact with him. In this excerpt, one of the central incidents in the novel, he visits a noblewoman whose aristocratic family owns the chateau that dominates the village. In the course of his conversation with her, he unearths the secret of her inner life—her bitterness and alienation from her husband and daughter, and her intense anger and opposition to God because of the death of her infant son. The dialogue between the priest and the noblewoman illustrate three of the major theological themes developed by Bernanos: the personal and unique relationship that God has with each human soul, the possibility of redemption, and the supernatural nature of the vocation to the priesthood.

The Diary of a Country Priest

Her eyes never left mine. "You must rest a bit. Why you're not fit to walk a yard. I'm stronger than you. Come now! This is hardly what we're taught, you know. It's all moonshine, poetry, nothing more! I don't believe you're really unkind. I'm certain when you think it over, you'll be hot with shame at this wretched blackmail. Nothing, either in this world or the next, can separate us from what we've loved more than ourselves, more than life, more than getting into heaven."

"Madame," I answered, "even in this world, the slightest thing, a mere stroke, can make us cease to know the people whom we've loved best of all."

"Death isn't like madness—"

"No, indeed. We know even less about it."

"Love is stronger than death—that stands written in your books."

"But it isn't we who invented love. Love has its own order, its own laws."

"God is love's master."

"No, not its master. God is love itself. . . . If you want to love don't place yourself beyond love's reach."

She rested both hands on my arm, her face was almost touching mine: "This is absurd. You talk to me as though I were a criminal. So all my husband's unfaithfulness goes for nothing—and my daughter's coldness, her rebellion, all that goes for nothing, nothing, nothing!"

"Madame, I speak to you as a priest, and according to the light which God has given me. You'd be wrong to think me a callow idealist. I know quite well there are many other homes like this—or still more unhappy. But an evil which spares one may kill another, and I think God has allowed me to see the perils which threatens you, and you alone."

"Why not say at once that it's all my doing?"

"Oh, madame, nobody can see in advance what one bad thought may have as its consequence. Evil thoughts are like good ones: thousands may be scattered by the wind, or overgrown or dried up by the sun. Only one takes root. The seeds of good and evil are everywhere. Our great misfortune is that human justice always intervenes too late. We only repress or brand the act, without ever being able to go back further than the culprit. But hidden sins poison the air which others breathe, and without such corruption at the source, many a wretched man, tainted unconsciously, would never have become a criminal."

"That's all rubbish—sheer rubbish, morbid dreaming!" (Her face was livid.) "We couldn't go on living if we thought of such things."

"No, madame, I don't think we could. I don't suppose if God had given us the clear knowledge of how closely we are bound to one another both in good and evil, that we could go on living, as you say."

No doubt the above suggests all this had been thought out beforehand, that my words were part of a general plan. I swear they were not. I was defending myself and that was all.

She answered after a long pause: "Would you deign to show me my hidden sin? The worm in the fruit?"

"You must resign yourself to—to God. Open your heart to him."

I dared not speak more plainly of her dead child, and the word "resign" seemed to astonish her.

"Resign myself? To what?" Then suddenly she understood.

I sometimes meet a "hardened" sinner. Usually they defend themselves against God by a mere species of blind instinct. It is even pitiful to watch an old man pleading for his vice, with the silly fierce sulkiness of a child. But now I saw rebellion, authentic rebellion, flash out upon a human face. Neither the eyes, fixed and dim, expressed it, nor the mouth, nor even the head itself which far from being proudly raised, drooped over her shoulder, appeared to sag as under an invisible load. Oh, not all the rhetoric of blasphemy has anything to approach such dire simplicity! It was as though a sudden flaming up of will had left her body inert, impassive, utterly void from this great expenditure of being.

"Resign myself?" Her gentle voice froze. "What do you mean? Don't you think me resigned enough? If I hadn't been resigned! It makes me ashamed." (Her tone was as soft as ever and yet her words had a strange intonation, a queer, metallic ring in them.) "I tell you I've often envied weaker women who haven't the strength to toil up these hills. But we're such a tough lot! I should have killed my wretched body, so that it shouldn't forget. Not all of us can manage to kill ourselves.

"That's not the resignation I mean, as you well know," I said to her.

"Well then—what? I go to mass, I make my Easter. I might have given up going to church altogether—I did think of it at one time. But I considered that sort of thing beneath me."

"Madame, no blasphemy you could utter would be as bad as what you've just said! Your words have all the callousness of hell in them." She stared at the wall and did not answer. "How dare you treat God in such a way? You close your heart against him and you—

"At least I've lived in peace—and I might have died in it—"

"That's no longer possible."

She reared like a viper: "I've ceased to bother about God. When you've forced me to admit that I hate him, will you be any better off, you idiot?"

"You no longer hate him. Hate is indifference and contempt. Now at last you're face to face with him."

She still stared into space and would not reply. At that moment I was seized with unnamable fear. All I had said, all she had answered, this whole endless dialogue became meaningless. Would any sensible man have viewed it otherwise? I had let myself be tricked by a girl enraged with jealousy and pride, and that was all. I had imagined I saw suicide in her eyes, as distinct in them, as clearly written, as a word scribbled on a wall. It had been no more than the kind of thoughtless impulse whose very violence makes it suspect. And this woman, standing as though to be judged by me, had doubtless lived for many years in that horrible quietness of the desolate, which of all forms of despair is the most atrocious, the most incurable, the least human. But such suffering is precisely of the kind which priests should only approach in fear and trembling. I had tried to liven this frozen heart in an instant, bring light into the innermost recess of a conscience which perhaps God's mercy intended still to leave in the pitiful dark. What was I to say? Or do? I felt like a man who has scrambled to the summit of a peak without once stopping to draw breath; he stands in amazement, his head reels, he opens his eyes and looks below him, unable to climb further or go back. It was then that—no, there are no words for it!—that while I struggled with all my might against doubt and terror, a spirit of prayer came back to my heart. Let me put it quite clearly: from the very start of this strange interview I never once had ceased to "pray" in the sense which shallow Christians give to the word. A wretched creature into which air is being pumped may look exactly as though it were breathing. That is nothing. Then air suddenly whistles through the lungs, inflates each separate delicate tissue already shrivelled, the arteries throb to the first violent influx of new blood—the whole being is like a ship creaking under swollen sails.

She had sunk into a chair, her head rested between her hands. The torn lace of her mantilla trailed from her shoulders; with a gentle movement she slipped it off and dropped it quietly at her feet. I watched each gesture closely, yet I had a strange feeling that we were neither of us there, in this arid little drawing-room, that the room was empty.

I watched her draw out a medallion worn round her neck on a plain silver chain; and then, as quietly as ever, with a gentleness more devastating than any violence, she pressed open the cover with her finger-nail. The glass tinkled down on to the carpet, but she paid no heed. A lock of yellow hair curled round her fingers, like a band of gold.

"Will you swear to me—" she began. But instantly she read in my eyes that I understood and would swear to nothing.

"My daughter," I said (the word came from me spontaneously), "God is not to be bargained with. We must give ourselves up to him unconditionally. Give him everything. He will give you back even more—I am neither a prophet nor a sage, and He alone has ever returned from the place to which we all are going." She did not protest. She only bent a little nearer to earth, and I saw her shoulders twitching with every word. "But at least I can assure you of this: there are not two separate kingdoms, one for the living, and one for the dead. There is only God's Kingdom and, living or dead, we are all therein." I said this, I could have said something else. Words seemed so trivial at that moment. I felt as though a mysterious hand had struck a breach in who knows what invisible rampart, so that peace flowed in from every side, majestically finding its level, peace unknown to the earth, the soft peace of the dead, like deep water.

"It seems quite plain to me," she said in a voice miraculously different, yet very calm. "Do you know what I was thinking just now, a moment ago? Perhaps I oughtn't to tell you what I was thinking. Well, I said to myself: Suppose that in this world or the next, somewhere was a place where God doesn't exist: though I had to die a thousand deaths there, to die stoically, every second—well, if it existed, I'd take my boy to that place" (she dared not call her dead child by his name) "and I'd say to God: 'Now, stamp us out! Now do your worst!' I suppose that sounds horrible to you?"

"No, madame."

"No? How do you mean?"

"Because I too, madame, sometimes I—" I could find no more words. I could see Dr. Delbende there before me: His old, tired, inflexible eyes were set on mine, eyes I feared to read. And I heard, or thought I heard, the groaning of so many men, their dry sobs, their sighs, the rattle of their grief, grief of our wretched humanity pressed to earth, its fearsome murmurings.

"Listen," she said gently, "how can one possibly—? Even children, even good little children whose hearts are true. . . . Have you ever seen a child die?"

"No, madame."

"He was so good all the time he was dying. He folded his little hands, he looked so serious and—and I tried to make him drink just before it happened—and a drop of milk was left on his mouth." She was trembling now. I seemed to be standing there alone between God and this tortured human being. It was like a huge throbbing in my breast, but our Lord gave me strength to face her.

"Madame," I said, "if our God were a pagan god or the god of intellectuals—and for me it comes to much the same—He might fly to his remotest heaven and our grief would force him down to earth again. But you know that our God came to be among us. Shake your fist at him, spit in his face, scourge him, and finally crucify him: what does it matter? My daughter, it's already been done to him." She dared not look at the medallion, which she still held. But how little I realized what she would do.

"Repeat what you said just now about hell. Hell is—not to love any more."

"Yes, madame."

"Well, say it again!"

"Hell is not to love any more. As long as we remain in this life we can still deceive ourselves, think that we love by our own will, that we love independently of God. But we're like madmen stretching our hands to clasp the moon reflected in water. I'm sorry: I express it so clumsily!"

An odd smile came into her face, but the taut look was in no way broken—a deathly smile. She had closed her fingers on the medallion, with her other hand she was pressing this clenched fist against her breast.

"What is it you want me to say?"

"Say: 'Thy Kingdom come.'"

"Thy Kingdom come."

"'Thy will be done on earth.'"

"Thy will be done—" She sprang to her feet, her clenched hand still over her breast.

"Listen! You must often have said it! Now you must say it with all your heart."

"I've never said the "Our Father" since—since— But you know that! You know things before you're told them." She shrugged her shoulders, and now she was angry. Then she did something I didn't understand till later. Her forehead was wet and shining. "I can't," she was muttering, "I seem to be losing him twice over."

"The kingdom that you have prayed will come, is yours too, and his," I said to her.

"All right then: Thy kingdom come." She looked up at me and I met her eyes. So we remained for a few seconds, and then she said: "It's to you I surrender."

"To me!"

"Yes, to you. I've sinned against God. I must have hated him. Yes, I know now that I should have died with this hate still in my heart, but I won't surrender—except to you."

"I'm too stupid and insignificant. It's as though you were to put a gold coin in a pierced hand."

"An hour ago my life seemed so perfectly arranged, everything in its proper place. And you've left nothing standing—nothing at all."

"Give it to God, just as it is!"

I'll either give him all or nothing. My people are made that way."

"Give everything."

"Oh, you don't understand! You think you've managed to make me docile. The dregs of my pride would still be enough to send you to hell."

"Give your pride with all the rest! Give everything!"

Then I saw her eyes shining strangely, but it was too late to stop her. She flung her medallion straight into the midst of the glowing logs. I scrambled down on to my knees and plunged my arm into the fire. I could not feel any burning. For one second I fancied my fingers had closed round a wisp of pale gold hair, but it slipped away from them, fell into the heart of the fire. Behind me there arose a terrible silence, and I did not dare turn round. The cloth of my sleeve was charred right up to the elbow.

"What madness," I stammered, "how could you dare?"

She had retreated to the wall against which she leaned, and pressed her hands. "I'm sorry." Her voice was humble.

"Do you take God for an executioner? God wants us to be merciful with ourselves. And besides, our sorrows are not our own. He takes them on himself, into his heart. We have no right to seek them there, mock them, outrage them. Do you understand?"

"What's done is done. I can't help it now."

"My daughter, you must be at peace," I said. And then I blessed her.

My fingers were beginning to bleed a little, the skin had blistered. She tore up a handkerchief and bandaged them. We exchanged no words. The peace I had invoked for her had descended also upon me; and it was so ordinary, so simple, that no outsider could ever have shaken it. For indeed we had returned so quietly to everyday life, that not the most attentive onlooker could have gauged the mystery of this secret, which already was no longer ours.

She has asked me to hear her confession tomorrow. I have made her promise to tell nobody of what passed between us, and on my side I have vowed absolute silence. "No matter what may happen," I said; and my heart sank with these last words, and again sadness overcame me, "God's will be done." . . .

Half-past six. Madame la Comtesse died last night. . . .

I went back for the last time to look at her. The nuns were saying the last decade of the rosary. Flowers and wreaths were piled up along the wall, brought by friends and relations who all day long have never stopped coming to the Chateau, and whose almost cheerful voices fill the house. Each minute brought a flare of headlights, a car would come flashing past the window, I heard the gravel crunch on the drive, the chauffeurs shouting to one another, the sound of motor-horns. None of all this interrupted the monotonous purr of the two good nuns; they might have been spinning. The candle-light showed me her face through the gauze better than daylight. These few hours had appeased and softened it, and the larger rings round her closed eyelids gave her eyes a kind of pensiveness. Certainly it was still a proud face. But now it seemed to have turned away from an enemy faced and braved for so long, to sink gradually into infinite meditation, too deep to share. How far it was from us, and beyond our power! Suddenly I saw her poor thin hands crossed on her breast, very slim, very delicate, far more truly dead than her face. I even saw a little mark, a scratch which I had noticed yesterday, as she pressed the medallion to her heart. The thin strip of lint was still attached to it. I don't know why that broke my heart. The memory of her struggle before my eyes, that fight for eternal life from which she emerged exhausted, victorious, became painfully vivid, shattering. . . . How could I have known that such a day would have no tomorrow, that she and I had faced each other on the very verge of the visible world, over the gulf of All Light? Why could we not have crossed together? "Be at peace," I told her. And she had knelt to receive this peace. May she keep it forever. It will be I that gave it her. Oh, miracle—thus to be able to give what we ourselves do not possess, sweet miracle of our empty hands! Hope which was shrivelling in my heart flowered again in hers; the spirit of prayer which I thought lost in me for ever was given back to her by God and—who can tell—perhaps in my name! Lord, I am stripped bare of all things, as you alone can strip us bare, whose fearful care nothing escapes, nor your terrible love! I lifted the muslin from her face, and stroked her high, pure forehead, full of silence. And poor as I am, an insignificant little priest, looking upon this woman only yesterday so far my superior in age, birth, fortune, intellect, I still knew—yes, knew—what fatherhood means.

Reading for Comprehension

1. How does the woman defend herself against the accusation that she has not resigned herself and opened her heart to God?

2. What admission does the woman make to the priest about her true feelings toward God?

3. What does the woman keep in the medallion that she wears about her neck?

4. What does the woman do with the medallion?

5. What happens to the woman at the conclusion of the story?

Reading for Understanding

1. What does the priest mean when he says that an evil that may spare one person, and may kill another?

2. Why has the woman been unable to say the Our Father since the death of her son?

3. What does the priest mean when he says, "Hell is not to love anymore"?

4. Describe how the priest in this story helps the noblewoman fully turn away from what was keeping her from God. How does the woman's final action with the medallion show her total change of heart and her total abandonment to God?

Activity

Bernanos shows us the insight that each of us has a unique relationship with God that is like that of no other person, and that each of us, like the noblewoman in the passage above, has some fundamental inclination that keeps us from God. Seat yourself in a quiet place and look deeply into your own soul. Is there something, some basic inclination, that separates you from God? Turn from that inclination, and prayerfully offer it to the God who made you and loves you more than you love yourself.

HOW WE TOUCH GOD AND HOW GOD TOUCHES US

(The Celebration of the Christian Mystery)

SEEING WITH THE ARTIST

Use an Internet search engine to locate the following artwork. Research each piece beginning with the information below. Write a journal entry answering the following question: "How does the piece connect me with nature, creation, and God?" Also, answer questions 1–5 on page 246.

The Paintings

St. Francis Preaching to the Birds—**Giotto di Bondone (ca. 1267–1337)**

Giotto was an Italian painter who was the first artist of the Italian Renaissance to paint in a realistic style. In this fresco, which is part of a series of frescos found in the upper portion of the Basilica of St. Francis in Assisi, we see St. Francis explaining to the birds why they should be grateful to for all the gifts that he has given them, and why they should never cease to praise him with their songs. None of the birds that are represented are exotic or highly colored. They are ordinary birds that represent the poor people of the world who were so open to the teachings of St. Francis.

The Baptism of Jesus—**Giovanni Bellini (1426–1516)**

The painting shows John administering Jesus' Baptism while a dove representing the Holy Spirit hovers over the head of Christ. God the

Father is seen in the heavens surrounded by angels who are quoted in Scripture as saying, "This is my beloved son, with whom I am well pleased" (Mt 3:17).

The Betrothal of the Virgin—Raphael (1483–1520)

An event in the life of the Blessed Virgin, not found in the Gospels, but nevertheless a popular legend in the Middle Ages and the Renaissance, is depicted in this painting by Raphael. According to this legend, when it came time for the Virgin to wed, she was approached by a group of suitors. It was revealed to her that the man that she should marry would be made known to her by a sign from heaven. In the painting we see St. Joseph at the forefront placing the ring of betrothal on Mary's finger. His flowering staff, crowned by a lily that represents his purity, is held in his left hand, while the other suitors with barren staffs look away. The painting is done in the framework of a Renaissance temple and the geometric lines leading to the temple represent the Renaissance artists' love of perspective and symmetry.

St. Mary Magdalene in Penitence with the Crucifix —El Greco (1541–1614)

Mary Magdalene is named in the Gospels as the first witness to the Resurrection of Christ. She has been associated with the penitent woman of the Gospel of John who bathed Christ's feet with her tears of repentance and dried them with her long, flowing hair. In this painting, her hair is cut short and she holds her garment pressed to her bosom in an attempt to minimize the beauty that was the cause of her sins while she gazes with love on the image of the Savior.

The Last Supper—Leonardo da Vinci (1452–1519)

Jesus and the bread and wine at the Last Supper are the central elements in this painting. Art critics disagree about what part of the event is being depicted. Some believe that it represents the institution of the Eucharist at the Last Supper. Others claim that it refers to the moment during the Last Supper when Jesus said to his disciples, "One of you will betray me," and the disciples attempt to discover who he is talking about. If the first claim is true, this is the most iconic representation of the institution of the Eucharist, emphasizing the identification of Jesus with the Blessed Sacrament.

The Disciples at Emmaus—Caravaggio (1571–1610)

This painting represents the event in Luke 24:13–32 where two of the disciples, having not recognized the Risen Christ on a walk with him, suddenly do know him when he blesses the bread in the same manner described in the institution of the Eucharist at the Last Supper. The drama of the moment is captured in the painting by the outstretched arms of one disciple and the motion of the other disciple to rise from his seat. They are seeing the Savior alive whom they thought was dead.

The Last Supper—Andy Warhol (1928–1987)

Warhol was an Eastern rite Catholic who attended Mass on a regular basis. He was the originator of the school of painting called "pop art" that took common objects like soup cans and photos of celebrities and treated them artistically in a similar way that Renaissance artists had once treated the lives of Christ and the saints. More than sixty silk-screens, paintings, and works on paper are included in Andy Warhol's last great cycle of work, *The Last Supper*. Warhol felt that viewing a sacred subject over and over again diminished our ability to fully recognize what was happening. In these paintings of the Last Supper he takes Leonardo's famous work and represents it in a myriad of different ways so that we can see that great painting in a fresh and vital manner. He also takes the subject of Christ instituting the Eucharist and counterpoises it with the emblem of the owl in the brand of Wise

Potato Chips. He hoped that the shock of seeing these two images side by side would jolt the viewer into realizing just what was happening when Christ said, "This is My Body."

The Sacrament of the Last Supper—Salvador Dali (1904–1989)

The entire painting is a mystic vision of the transformation of the elements of bread and wine into the Body and Blood of Jesus. It combines classical motifs with surrealist imagery. The action of the painting takes place in a twelve-sided space called a dodecahedron. This mathematical aspect of the painting represents Dali's idea that God is to be found in the energy and clarity of physics and mathematics. The figure of Christ points to the torso behind him and represents the presence of God the Father, whose face no one can see and still live. Both the figure of Christ and the gigantic torso behind him are transparent. The figures of the disciples, on the other hand, are concrete and materialized. The disciples are pictured looking at the elements of actual bread and wine that are placed on the table.

South Rose Window—Stained Glass Window in Chartres Cathedral (ca. 1220)

In this mammoth stained glass window, with representations of the lives of saints below it, we see the height of medieval art. The purpose of this and other stained glass windows of the period was to inspire the congregation to be lifted by the artistic display to a greater understanding and awareness of the life of the spirit and grace.

The Chapel of Saint Mary of the Rosary—Henri Matisse (1869–1954)

This small chapel found in the village of Vence in Southern France was designed by the great French painter Henri Matisse, and built between

242

1949–1951. Matisse built it for a congregation of French nuns who had nursed him during a severe illness. He designed every aspect of the chapel, including the altar, the vestments, the sacred vessels, the Stations of the Cross, and the murals of the saints. This photograph shows a stained glass window that Matisse titled, "The Tree of Life." In the front portion of the photograph stands the altar with its candlesticks and a mural of St. Dominic, the founder of the Dominican Order, to which the nuns belonged.

LOOKING AT FILM

The films introduced below have the common theme of the Catholic priesthood. But just as the life and ministry of priests encompass a variety of challenges and rewards, so too do these films reveal more about the multi-faceted life of priests. Watch at least one of the films. Answer the question that applies to the film on page 247. Also, consider developing a study from film of the ways Catholic priests have been portrayed. What conclusions can you reach from your study?

The Films

I Confess (1953)—Directed by Alfred Hitchcock

Rating: All

Hitchcock was a Catholic. In *I Confess*, he addresses the sacramental seal of Confession (the obligation of the priest not to reveal the sins that have been confessed to him). In the film, Montgomery Clift plays a priest who hears the confession of a murderer. Because the murderer disguised himself as a priest, Montgomery Clift is falsely accused and brought to trial for the killing. The film also addresses the authority of the priest by his ordination to grant absolution in the name of God.

Angels with Dirty Faces (1938)—Directed by Michael Curtiz

Rating: All

This film operates on many levels. On a superficial level it is a typical period movie featuring the antics of the group of young actors known as the Dead End Kids. On a deeper level, it explores the mystery of sin and how the sinful actions of one man can influence others. On a profound level, it shows the struggle between good and evil in one man's soul and how, in one of the most dramatic execution scenes in cinema, the priest in the story asks the criminal to make a final gift of repentance and conversion to God.

The Hoodlum Priest (1961)—Directed by Irvin Kirshner

Not Rated

The film brings up issues of social justice, prison reform, and capital punishment. It tells the story of Fr. Charles Dismas Clark (played by Don Murray), a Jesuit priest who ministered to prisoners and ex-convicts in St. Louis. At the heart of the film is Clark's relationship with a young ex-convict (Keir Dullea) who becomes embroiled in a crime and is eventually executed for murder. Be aware that the final scene of the man's execution is portrayed in a very realistic and visual way. Neither the United States Catholic Bishops nor the film industry has reviewed *The Hoodlum Priest*.

LISTENING TO SACRED MUSIC

The celebration of the Holy Eucharist is the source and summit of Catholic worship. There are five major parts of the Mass to be celebrated in a musical setting. These parts of the mass are: the *Kyrie* (Lord, have mercy); the *Gloria* (Glory to God in the Highest); the Creed (We believe in one God); the *Sanctus* (Holy, Holy, Holy); and the *Agnus Dei* (Lamb of God). Listed below you will find how composers from different periods of history have sought to combine music with the liturgical celebration of the Eucharist. Search out different examples of these types of music as they are connected with the Eucharist. Answer the question: "How did this music further my appreciation of the Real Presence of Christ in the Eucharist?" Also answer question 9 on page 247.

The Music

Chant

Listen to the classic Gregorian Mass, *Missa de Angelis* ("Mass of the Angels"). *Missa de Angelis* was written in the ninth century. It was written as a plain song Mass to be sung in unison and a cappella.

Polyphonic

This music stresses complex choral and orchestral elements to provide a music that seems to be the very voice of angels. Giovanni Palestrina is one of the greatest of the Renaissance composers. A compilation of his Masses is called *Palestrina*: *Missa Papae Marcelli, Missa Aetern*. Another great Renaissance composer is the Venetian, Giovanni Gabrieli.

Contemporary Music

Many modern composers have made use of jazz themes as a basis for the musical celebration of the Eucharist. Mary Lou Williams was a practicing Catholic and one of the great jazz musicians of our time. Her jazz mass is called "Mary Lou's Mass."

World Music

One of the "marks" of the Church found in the Nicene Creed is that it is "catholic" (universal). A splendid example of liturgical music written in the style of African Chant is *Missa Luba*, by the Troubadours du Roi Baudouin.

Popular Music

Examples of music sung specifically at the offertory or during communion are: "Gift of Finest Wheat" by Robert Kreutz; "Let Us Break Bread Together," a traditional spiritual; and "One Bread, One Body" by John Foley, S.J. Another example for the communion rite is "*Panis Angelicus* (Bread of Angels) by César Franck. This hymn is very operatic in structure and is popular at weddings and other liturgies of celebration.

ACTIVITIES

1. Reread the selection from Bonaventure's *The Journey of the Mind into God* (pages 85–86). How is the fresco *St. Francis Preaching to the Birds* a visual representation of Bonaventure's teaching?

2. In the painting *The Betrothal of the Virgin* by Raphael, St. Joseph is represented as a young man. Look up pictures of the Holy Family by Federico Barocci (1526–1612). In these paintings and many other similar paintings, St. Joseph is represented as an old man. What theological point was the painter trying to make by making Joseph so aged?

3. In the painting *St. Mary Magdalene in Penitence with the Crucifix*, a skull is seen beneath the Crucifix. Early Christian legend stated that Christ was crucified on the grave of Adam by whom sin and death were brought into the world. Read 1 Corinthians 15:22 and explain why Christ is often called the "New Adam."

4. What do you think that Andy Warhol would say to people who regard his portrayal of potato chips in a representation of the Last Supper as blasphemous?

5. Both the artists who constructed the Cathedral at Chartres and Matisse in his Chapel of the Rosary used art to bring us closer to God. Why is stained glass an ideal medium for use in sacred spaces? Which of these, the cathedral or the chapel, most assists you in coming closer to God? Why?

6. What is meant by the term, "the seal of confession"? How is the seal referred to in the film *I Confess*?

7. In the film *Angels with Dirty Faces*, the priest asks his friend who is about to be executed to be courageous with a type of courage that comes from heaven. What did he mean by that statement?

8. A central role of the priest is to bring the presence of Christ to the most lost and lonely souls in the world. How is this aspect of the priesthood portrayed in the film *The Hoodlum Priest*?

9. The purpose of liturgical music is to assist the congregation to raise its hearts and minds to God, to have an encounter with God who is pure beauty. Beautiful music brings us into the presence of God. What happens when the music at the liturgy is not adequate? What effect can poorly chosen or performed music have on the worshiping community?

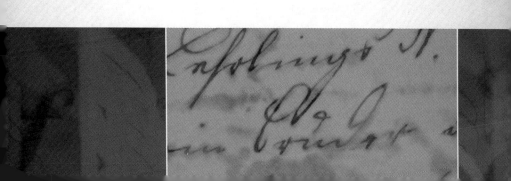

UNIT 3

How We Should Live

(Life in Christ)

"Put on Jesus Christ"

How should I live? What must I do to be happy? How does God speak to me about the decisions that I must make in my life? Through the Scriptures, in the moral and social teaching tradition of the Church, and in the voice of our conscience, we find the answers to these questions.

Catholic morality is based on reality, the way things are, on how God made them, and how he intends them to be. The Old Testament provided a moral code, summarized in the Ten Commandments, to aid us in making good choices. Jesus himself is the perfect norm for moral living. St. Paul taught to "put on the Lord Jesus Christ" (Rom 13:14) and this advice is the best and most succinct for how we should live.

Jesus' life and the events of the Paschal Mystery give further witness to how we should live. He pointed out that "This is the time of fulfillment. The kingdom of God is at hand. Repent, and believe in the Gospel" (Mk 1:15).

Introducing the Unit

In the Hebrew Scriptures, specifically in the Books of Exodus and Deuteronomy, God gave to Moses and the Chosen People the revelation of his law, which was intended to help them conduct their lives in accordance with his will.

In the Sermon on the Mount, Jesus revealed to his disciples a higher law, a law based on love that enabled all people to see that his disciples were truly children of God.

Another source for making good choices and living a moral life is following our conscience. The voice of God, speaking to us through our conscience, is a constant reminder of the way that God wishes us to act.

When people take the teachings of Jesus to heart and attempt to follow those teachings to establish a safer and more just society, a society that does not forget the poor and the oppressed, dramatic stories are told. In all of these readings, we learn that right action is not just a matter of pious thoughts: To truly do God's will, we must love our neighbor as our brother and sister. Examples for living a Christ-centered life abound and are communicated through the ages in many ways. Some of these expressions form the subjects of this unit.

Living Out God's Law

- The poem "Richard Cory" stands as a rebuke to those who would live their lives as if material wealth is all that matters.

- In the stories "The Sniper" and "The Filipino and the Drunkard," we witness what happens when people transgress the Ten Commandments.

Law of Love

- In "The Story of the Other Wise Man," and in the excerpt from *Les Misérables*, "The Bishop's Candlesticks," we see how two different men live out their lives in accordance with Jesus' teachings.

- The excerpt "Helen," from *The Junkie Priest: Father Daniel Eagan, S.A.,* tells how one young New York City priest made a decision for dealing with the young drug abusers who became part of his life.

The Voice of Conscience

- "The Merit of a Young Priest" from *Hasidic Tales of the Holocaust* details the story of a young Pope John Paul II and his response to a request to baptize a Jewish child.

- The excerpt about "The Mysterious Visitor" from *The Brothers Karamazov*, details how the voice of God speaks to our conscience and tells us what it is that we must do.

Right Judgment and Action

- In the stories "The Little Match Girl," "Vanka," and "The Trouble," we see that the command for right action and good conduct applies to our society as well as to individuals, and that there is such a thing as social justice.

- The poem "On Opening a Page in *Time Magazine*" contrasts the pages of an American magazine during a time when there was especially large contrast between consumerism of the advertisements and the news being photographed and reported.
- The excerpt from *Salvador Witness: The Life and Calling of Jean Donovan* tells the story of one woman who stood up to injustice.

Living Out God's Law

"Richard Cory"

Edward Arlington Robinson

The devil said to him, "If you are the Son of God, command this stone to become bread." Jesus answered him, "It is written, 'One does not live by bread alone.'"

—Luke 4:3–4

Author Background

Edwin Arlington Robinson (1869–1935) was born and raised in Maine, but spent most of his creative years writing poetry while living in poverty in New York City. The focus of much of Robinson's poetry was his past; he wrote of citizens of small-town America of the late nineteenth century. Robinson had a pessimistic view of life, and in many ways his poems are tales of the failure of the American dream. Although he endured many years of non-recognition, he was awarded the Pulitzer Prize for poetry three times in the waning years of his life (1922, 1925, 1928).

Before the Reading

In this poem, Robinson explores two aspects of human nature. First, he focuses on the unique mystery of each individual person. Second, he points out that personal happiness involves much more than the accumulation of material wealth, good looks, or education and refinement. The ultimate fate of the character Richard Cory proves the emptiness of the philosophy that sees happiness only in the possession of material things. The poem forces us to answer what we believe to be the meaning of true happiness.

"Richard Cory"

Whenever Richard Cory went down town,
We people on the pavement looked at him:

He was a gentleman from sole to crown,
Clean favored, and imperially slim.
And he was always quietly arrayed,
And he was always human when he talked,
But still he fluttered pulses when he said,
"Good-morning," and he glittered when he walked.

And he was rich—yes, richer than a king—
And admirably schooled in every grace;
In fine we thought that he was everything
To make us wish that we were in his place

So on we worked, and waited for the light,
And went without the meat, and cursed the bread;
And Richard Cory, one calm summer night,
Went home and put a bullet through his head.

Reading for Comprehension

1. How does the poet describe Richard Cory's appearance?

2. What did the townspeople think when they saw Richard Cory?

3. What did Richard Cory do on the final evening of his life?

Reading for Understanding

1. How does this poem represent the adage that "you can't judge a book by its cover"?

2. How might this poem lead you to a new understanding of peers who you and others believe "have it all together"?

Activities

1. Research the problem of suicide among teenagers in the United States. What are the most common causes of suicide among young people? What does the Church teach about suicide (see *Catechism of the Catholic Church*, 2280)?

2. The poem "Richard Cory" ultimately is a poem about the nature of happiness. Dolores Hart was one of the most beautiful and famous young movie stars of the 1950s. A brilliant career lay before her. She shocked her fellow actors and the public by leaving it all and by becoming a nun in a cloistered Benedictine convent where life is spent in silence, prayer, and simple labor. Dolores Hart has lived as a nun for more than fifty years and has written of her happiness as a religious sister and her lack of regret for giving up her Hollywood career. Research and summarize some of Dolores Hart's musings. What do you think about her decision to give up a life of fame for the religious life?

Living Out God's Law

"The Sniper"
Liam O'Flaherty

"You shall not kill."
—Exodus 20:13

Author Background
Liam O'Flaherty (1896–1984) wrote extensively about life in Ireland. He lived through the Irish Civil War in the early 1920s and he knew from personal experience the scars inflicted on Irish families during the days of the "uprising." His most successful work was the novel *The Informer*, which was made into a classic film by American director John Ford.

Before the Reading
Many people understand the Fifth Commandment as a prohibition against murder. We do not often equate the prohibition against killing to war, as killing in a just war is not an offense against that commandment. Nevertheless, killing in war can still have painful consequences and cause much hurt. In the following story, Liam O'Flaherty uses the context of the Irish Civil War to show how one man comes to a true understanding of the evil of killing.

"The Sniper"
The long June twilight faded into night. Dublin lay enveloped in darkness but for the dim light of the moon that shone through fleecy clouds, casting a pale light as of approaching dawn over the streets and the dark waters of the Liffey. Around the beleaguered Four Courts the heavy guns roared. Here and there through the city, machine-guns and rifles broke the silence of the night, spasmodically, like dogs

barking on lone farms. Republicans and Free Staters were waging civil war.

On a rooftop near O'Connell Bridge, a Republican sniper lay watching. Beside him lay his rifle and over his shoulders were slung a pair of field glasses. His face was the face of a student, thin and ascetic, but his eyes had the cold gleam of the fanatic. They were deep and thoughtful, the eyes of a man who is used to looking at death.

He was eating a sandwich hungrily. He had eaten nothing since morning. He had been too excited to eat. He finished the sandwich, and, taking a flask of whiskey from his pocket, he took a short draught. Then he returned the flask to his pocket. He paused for a moment, considering whether he should risk a smoke. It was dangerous. The flash might be seen in the darkness and there were enemies watching. He decided to take the risk.

Placing the cigarette between his lips, he struck a match. There was a flash and a bullet whizzed over his head. He dropped immediately. He had seen the flash. It came from the opposite side of the street.

He rolled over the roof to a chimney-stack in the rear, and slowly drew himself up behind it, until his eyes were level with the top of the parapet. There was nothing to be seen—just the dim outline of the opposite housetop against the blue sky. His enemy was under cover.

Just then an armored car came across the bridge and advanced slowly up the street. It stopped on the opposite side of the street, fifty yards ahead. The sniper could hear the dull panting of the motor. His heart beat faster. It was an enemy car. He wanted to fire, but he knew it was useless. His bullets would never pierce the steel that covered the gray monster.

Then round the corner of a side street came an old woman, her head covered by a tattered shawl. She began to talk to the man in the turret of the car. She was pointing to the roof where the sniper lay. An informer.

The turret opened. A man's head and shoulders appeared, looking toward the sniper. The sniper raised his rifle and fired. The head fell heavily on the turret wall. The woman darted toward the side street. The sniper fired again. The woman whirled round and fell with a shriek into the gutter.

Suddenly from the opposite roof a shot rang out and the sniper dropped his rifle with a curse. The rifle clattered to the roof. The sniper thought the noise would wake the dead. He stooped to pick the rifle up. He couldn't lift it. His forearm was dead.

"Christ," he muttered, "I'm hit."

Dropping flat onto the roof, he crawled back to the parapet. With his left hand he felt the injured right forearm. There was no pain—just a deadened sensation, as if the arm had been cut off.

Quickly he drew his knife from his pocket, opened it on the breast-work of the parapet, and ripped open the sleeve. There was a small hole where the bullet had entered. On the other side there was no hole. The bullet had lodged in the bone. It must have fractured it. He bent the arm below the wound. The arm bent back easily. He ground his teeth to overcome the pain.

Then, taking out the field dressing, he ripped open the packet with his knife. He broke the neck of the iodine bottle and let the bitter fluid drip into the wound. A paroxysm of pain swept through him. He placed the cotton wadding over the wound and wrapped the dressing over it. He tied the ends with his teeth.

Then he lay against the parapet, and, closing his eyes, he made an effort of will to overcome the pain.

In the street beneath all was still. The armored car had retired speedily over the bridge, with the machine-gunner's head hanging lifelessly over the turret. The woman's corpse lay still in the gutter.

The sniper lay still for a long time nursing his wounded arm and planning escape. Morning must not find him wounded on the roof. The enemy on the opposite roof covered his escape. He must kill that enemy and he could not use his rifle. He had only a revolver to do it. Then he thought of a plan.

Taking off his cap, he placed it over the muzzle of his rifle. Then he pushed the rifle slowly over the parapet, until the cap was visible from the opposite side of the street. Almost immediately there was a report, and a bullet pierced the center of the cap. The sniper slanted the rifle forward. The cap slipped down into the street. Then catching the rifle in the middle, the sniper dropped his left hand over the roof and let it hang, lifelessly. After a few moments he let the rifle drop to the street. Then he sank to the roof, dragging his hand with him.

Crawling quickly to the left, he peered up at the corner of the roof. His ruse had succeeded. The other sniper, seeing the cap and rifle fall, thought he had killed his man. He was now standing before a row of chimney pots, looking across, with his head clearly silhouetted against the western sky.

The Republican sniper smiled and lifted his revolver above the edge of the parapet. The distance was about fifty yards—a hard shot in the dim light, and his right arm was paining him like a thousand devils. He took a steady aim. His hand trembled with eagerness. Pressing his lips together, he took a deep breath through his nostrils and fired. He was almost deafened with the report and his arm shook with the recoil.

Then when the smoke cleared he peered across and uttered a cry of joy. His enemy had been hit. He was reeling over the parapet in his death agony. He struggled to keep his feet, but he was slowly falling forward, as if in a dream. The rifle fell from his grasp, hit the parapet, fell over, bounded off the pole of a barber's shop beneath and then clattered on the pavement.

Then the dying man on the roof crumpled up and fell forward. The body turned over and over in space and hit the ground with a dull thud. Then it lay still.

The sniper looked at his enemy falling and he shuddered. The lust of battle died in him. He became bitten by remorse. The sweat stood out in beads on his forehead. Weakened by his wound and the long summer day of fasting and watching on the roof, he revolted from the sight of the shattered mass of his dead enemy. His teeth chattered, he began to gibber to himself, cursing the war, cursing himself, cursing everybody.

He looked at the smoking revolver in his hand, and with an oath he hurled it to the roof at his feet. The revolver went off with the concussion and the bullet whizzed past the sniper's head. He was frightened back to his senses by the shock. His nerves steadied. The cloud of fear scattered from his mind and he laughed.

Taking the whiskey flask from his pocket, he emptied it at a draught. He felt reckless under the influence of the spirit. He decided to leave the roof now and look for his company commander, to report. Everywhere around was quiet. There was not much danger in going through the streets. He picked up his revolver and put it in his pocket. Then he crawled down through the sky-light to the house underneath.

When the sniper reached the laneway on the street level, he felt a sudden curiosity as to the identity of the enemy sniper whom he had killed. He decided that he was a good shot, whoever he was. He wondered did he know him. Perhaps he had been in his own company before the split in the army. He decided to risk going over to have a look at him. He peered round the corner into O'Connell Street. In the upper part of the street there was heavy firing, but around here all was quiet.

The sniper darted across the street. A machine-gun tore up the ground around him with a hail of bullets, but he escaped. He threw himself face downward beside the corpse. The machine-gun stopped.

Then the sniper turned over the dead body and looked into his brother's face.

Reading for Comprehension

1. What happens when the sniper lights a cigarette?
2. Why does the sniper not fire on the armored car?
3. What happens to the old lady who speaks to the driver of the armored car?
4. What does the sniper do to fool his enemy?

5. What does the sniper discover when he investigates the body of the man he has killed?

Reading for Understanding

1. Why does the author keep all the characters in the story unnamed?

2. What do you think is the significance of the slaying of the old lady?

3. What point is Liam O'Flaherty making by having the sniper kill his own brother?

Activity

Read the selections in the *Catechism of the Catholic Church* pertaining to Original Sin (388–395). Then read the story of Cain and Abel in Genesis 4:1–16. How do the stories of Cain and Abel and "The Sniper" provide us with an understanding of man's fallen nature?

Living Out God's Law

"The Filipino and the Drunkard"
William Saroyan

I have sinned through my own fault . . . in what I have done and in what I have failed to do.
—Penitential Rite from the Eucharistic Liturgy

Author Background
William Saroyan (1908–1981) wrote several award-winning short stories and successful novels. His best-known work is his collection of short stories, *My Name is Aram*, which recount the tales of his childhood growing up in an Armenian-American family. In 1940 he was awarded the Pulitzer Prize for Drama for his play, *The Time of Your Life*. Saroyan was a believer in the basic goodness of people, and much of his work is optimistic and filled with a spirit of compassion. The following is one of his few stories that explores the darker side of human nature.

Before the Reading
The words of the penitential rite at Mass call us to ask God to have mercy on us and to forgive us for the evil we have done and the good that we have failed to do. In the following story, William Saroyan portrays an incident where the failure of bystanders to speak out for the right thing results in a terrible tragedy.

"The Filipino and the Drunkard"
This loud-mouthed guy in the brown camel-hair coat was not really mean, he was drunk. He took a sudden dislike to the small well-dressed Filipino and began to order him around the waiting room, telling him to get back, not to crowd up among the white people. They were waiting to get on the boat and cross the bay to Oakland.

If he hadn't been drunk no one would have bothered to notice him at all, but as it was, he was making a commotion in the waiting room, and while everyone seemed to be in sympathy with the Filipino, no one seemed to want to bother about coming to the boy's rescue, and the poor Filipino was becoming very frightened.

He stood among the people, and this drunkard kept pushing up against him and saying, I told you to get back. Now get back. Go away back. I fought twenty-fours month in France. I'm a real American. I don't want you standing up here among white people.

The boy kept squeezing nimbly and politely out of the drunkard's way, hurrying through the crowd, not saying anything and trying his best to be as decent as possible. He kept dodging in and out, with the drunkard stumbling after him, and as time went on the drunkard's dislike grew and he began to swear at the boy. He kept saying, You fellows are the best-dressed men in San Francisco, and you make your money washing dishes. You've got no right to wear such fine clothes.

He swore a lot, and it got so bad that a lot of ladies had to imagine they were deaf and weren't hearing any of the things he was saying.

When the big door opened, the young Filipino moved swiftly among the people, fleeing from the drunkard, reaching the boat before anyone else. He ran to a corner, sat down for a moment, then got up and began looking for a more hidden place. At the other end of the boat was the drunkard. He could hear the man swearing. He looked about for a place to hide, and rushed into the lavatory. He went into one of the open compartments and bolted the door.

The drunkard entered the lavatory and began asking others in the room if they had seen the boy. He was a real American, he said. He had been wounded twice in the War.

In the lavatory he swore more freely, using words he could never use where women were present. He began to stoop and look beyond the shut doors of the various compartments. I beg your pardon, he said to those he was not seeking, and when he came to the compartment where the boy was standing, he began swearing and demanding that the boy come out.

You can't get away from me, he said. You got no right to use a place white men use. Come out or I'll break the door.

Go away, the boy said.

The drunkard began to pound on the door.

You got to come out sometime, he said. I'll wait here till you do.

Go away, said the boy. I've done nothing to you.

He wondered why none of the men in the lavatory had the decency to calm the drunkard and take him away, and then he realized there were no other men in the lavatory.

Go away, he said.

The drunkard answered with curses, pounding the door.

Behind the door, the boy's bitterness grew to rage. He began to tremble, not fearing the man but fearing the rage growing in himself. He brought the knife from his pocket and drew open the sharp blade, holding the knife in his fist so tightly that the nails of his fingers cut into the flesh of his palm.

Go away, he said. I have a knife. I do not want any trouble.

The drunkard said he was an American. Twenty-four months in France. Wounded twice. Once in the leg, and once in the thigh. He would not go away. He was afraid of no dirty little yellow-belly Filipino with a knife. Let the Filipino come out, he was an American.

I will kill you, said the boy. I do not want to kill any man. You are drunk. Go away.

Please do not make any trouble, he said earnestly.

He could hear the motor of the boat pounding. It was like his rage pounding. It was a feeling of having been humiliated, chased about and made to hide, and now it was a wish to be free, even if he had to kill. He threw the door open and tried to rush beyond the man, the knife tight in his fist, but the drunkard caught him by the sleeve and drew him back. The sleeve of the boy's coat ripped, and the boy turned and thrust the knife into the side of the drunkard, feeling it scrape against rib-bone. The drunkard shouted and screamed at once, then caught the boy by the throat, and the boy began to thrust the knife into the side of the man many times, as a boxer jabs in the clinches.

When the drunkard could no longer hold him and had fallen to the floor, the boy rushed from the room, the knife still in his hand, blood dripping from the blade, his hat gone, his hair mussed, and the sleeve of his coat badly torn.

Everyone knew what he had done, yet no one moved.

The boy ran to the front of the boat, seeking some place to go, then ran back to a corner, no one daring to speak to him, and everyone aware of his crime.

There was no place to go, and before the officers of the boat arrived he stopped suddenly and began to shout at the people.

I did not want to hurt him, he said. Why didn't you stop him? Is it right to chase a man like a rat? You knew he was drunk. I did not want to hurt him, but he would not let me go. He tore my coat and tried to choke me. I told him I would kill him if he would not go away. It is not my fault. I must go to Oakland to see my brother. He is sick. Do you think I am looking for trouble when my brother is sick? Why didn't you stop him?

Reading for Comprehension

1. How does the drunkard harass the boy in the waiting room?
2. What does the drunkard say about the boy's clothing?
3. Where does the Filipino hide from the drunkard?
4. What does the boy do when the drunkard grabs him?
5. What do the people do when they realize that the boy has killed the drunkard?
6. What words does the boy use to condemn the bystanders?

Reading for Understanding

1. What do you think would have happened if one of the white people had told the boy to go to the other side of the ship and then had tried to calm down the drunkard?

2. Describe a scene where you have witnessed a bully picking on a weaker person and nobody does anything to protect the weaker person. How did that experience make you feel? List three things that you and your friends could have done to prevent the bullying.

Activity

In the past decade, there have been several instances of disturbed students coming to school with weapons and killing their classmates and teachers. Investigate one of these occurrences. Did bullying play a role in this tragedy? What programs or activities do you think could be initiated in schools to insure that all students feel a sense of belonging? What current programs or activities at your school meet this need?

Law of Love

"The Story of the Other Wise Man"
Henry Van Dyke

Amen, I say to you, whatever you did for one of these
least brothers of mine, you did for me.
—Matthew 25:40

Author Background

Henry Van Dyke (1852–1933) was a clergyman, educator, and diplomat.
He taught English Literature at Princeton University from 1899 to 1923.
He was a minister at the Brick Presbyterian Church in New York City. Van
Dyke wrote several books of stories and collections of poetry. He is most famous for the story that follows, which is one of the best-known Christmas
tales ever written. "The Story of the Other Wise Man" has been translated
into numerous foreign languages and has been adapted for children's illustrated books, television, and film.

Before the Reading

"The Story of the Other Wise Man" is a long tale and has been abridged
slightly below. The opening chapters of this tale give the historical background of the Magi, who, through their investigation of the stars and their
reading of ancient prophecies, come to the realization that a king who will
bring justice and peace to the world is to be born in the land of Israel. Three
of these Magi leave immediately to search for the king. The "Other Wise
Man," Artaban, is delayed from leaving with his companions, so he makes
arrangements to meet up with them at a later date. This is where the selection begins, with Artaban and his horse Vasda pressing on the meet up with
the other Magi. This tale was delivered as a Christmas sermon by Henry Van
Dyke and is recounted as if it was given to the narrator in a dream or vision.

267

It teaches about the type of life called for in the Beatitudes (Mt 5:1–12) and illustrates in a most creative way the true meaning of Christmas.

"The Story of the Other Wise Man"

Artaban pressed onward until he arrived at nightfall of the tenth day, beneath the shattered walls of populous Babylon.

Vasda was almost spent, and he would gladly have turned into the city to find rest and refreshment for himself and for her. But he knew that it was three hours journey yet to the Temple of the Seven Spheres, and he must reach the place by midnight if he would find his comrades waiting. So he did not halt, but rode steadily across the stubble-fields.

A grove of date-palms made an island of gloom in the pale yellow sea. As she passed into the shadow Vasda slackened her pace, and began to pick her way more carefully.

Near the farther end of the darkness an excess of caution seemed to fall upon her. She scented some danger or difficulty; it was not in her heart to fly from it—only to be prepared for it, and to meet it wisely, as a good horse should do. The grove was close and silent as the tomb; not a leaf rustled, not a bird sang.

She felt her steps before her delicately, carrying her head low, and sighing now and then with apprehension. At last she gave a quick breath of anxiety and dismay, and stood stock-still, quivering in every muscle, before a dark object in the shadow of the last palm tree.

Artaban dismounted. The dim starlight revealed the form of a man lying across the road. His humble dress and the outline of his haggard face showed that he was probably one of the poor Hebrew exiles who still dwelt in great numbers in the vicinity. His pallid skin, dry and yellow as parchment, bore the mark of the deadly fever which ravaged the marshlands in autumn. The chill of death was in his lean hand, and as Artaban released it the arm fell back inertly upon the motionless breast.

He turned away with a thought of pity, consigning the body to that strange burial which the Magians deemed most fitting—the funeral of the desert, from which the kites and vultures rise on dark wings, and the beasts of prey slink furtively away, leaving only a heap of white bones in the sand.

But, as he turned, a long, faint, ghostly sigh came from the man's lips. The brown, bony fingers closed convulsively on the hem of the Magian's robe and held him fast.

Artaban's heart leaped to his throat, not with fear, but with a dumb resentment at the importunity of this blind delay.

How could he stay, here in the darkness to minister to a dying stranger? What claim had this unknown fragment of human life upon his compassion or his service? If he lingered but for an hour he could hardly reach Borsippa at the appointed time. His companions would think he had given up the journey. They would go without him. He would lose his quest.

But if he went on now, the man would surely die. If he stayed, life might be restored. His spirit throbbed and fluttered with the urgency of the crisis. Should he risk the reward of his divine faith for the sake of a single deed of human love? Should he turn aside, if only for a moment, from the following of the star, to give a cup of cold water to a poor, perishing Hebrew?

"God of truth and purity," he prayed, "direct me in the holy path, the way of wisdom which Thou only knowest."

Then he turned back to the sick man. Loosening the grasp of his hand, he carried him to a little mound at the foot of the palm-tree. He unbound the thick folds of the turban and opened the garment above the sunken breast. He brought water from one of the small canals near by, and moistened the sufferer's brow and mouth. He mingled a draught of one of those simple but potent remedies which he carried always in his girdle, for the Magians were physicians as well as astrologers—and poured it slowly between the colorless lips. Hour after hour he labored as only a skillful healer of disease can do; and at last the man's strength returned; he sat up and looked about him.

"Who art thou?" he said, in the rude dialect of the country, "and why hast thou sought me here to bring back my life?"

"I am Artaban the Magian, of the city of Ecbatana, and I am going to Jerusalem in search of one who is to be born King of the Jews, a great Prince and Deliverer of all men. I dare not delay any longer upon my journey, for the caravan that has waited for me may depart without me. But see, here is all that I have left of bread and wine, and here is a potion of healing herbs. When thy strength is restored thou canst find the dwellings of the Hebrews among the houses of Babylon."

The Jew raised his trembling hand solemnly to heaven.

"Now may the God of Abraham and Isaac and Jacob bless and prosper the journey of the merciful, and bring him in peace to his desired haven. But stay; I have nothing to give thee in return—only this: that I can tell thee where the Messiah must be sought. For our prophets have said that he should be born not in Jerusalem, but in Bethlehem of Judah. May the Lord bring thee in safety to that place, because thou hast had pity upon the sick."

It was already long past midnight. Artaban rode in haste, and Vasda, restored by the brief rest, ran eagerly through the silent plain and swam the channels of the river. She put forth the remnant of her strength, and fled over the ground like a gazelle.

But the first beam of the sun sent her shadow before her as she entered upon the final stadium of the journey, and the eyes of Artaban, anxiously scanning the great mound of Nimrod and the Temple of the Seven Spheres, could discern no trace of his friends.

The many-colored terraces of black and orange and red and yellow and green and blue and white, shattered by the convulsions of nature, and crumbling under the repeated blows of human violence, still glittered like a ruined rainbow in the morning light.

Artaban rode swiftly around the hill. He dismounted and climbed to the highest terrace, looking out toward the west.

The huge desolation of the marshes stretched away to the horizon and the border of the desert. Bitterns stood by the stagnant pools and jackals skulked through the low bushes; but there was no sign of the caravan of the wise men, far or near.

At the edge of the terrace he saw a little cairn of broken bricks, and under them a piece of parchment. He caught it up and read: "We have waited past the midnight, and can delay no longer. We go to find the King. Follow us across the desert."

Artaban sat down upon the ground and covered his head in despair.

"How can I cross the desert," said he, "with no food and with a spent horse? I must return to Babylon, sell my sapphire, and buy a train of camels, and provision for the journey. I may never overtake my friends. Only God the merciful knows whether I shall not lose the sight of the King because I tarried to show mercy."

For the Sake of a Little Child

There was a silence in the Hall of Dreams, where I was listening to the story of the Other Wise Man. And through this silence I saw, but very dimly, his figure passing over the dreary undulations of the desert, high upon the back of his camel, rocking steadily onward like a ship over the waves.

The land of death spread its cruel net around him. The stony wastes bore no fruit but briers and thorns. The dark ledges of rock thrust themselves above the surface here and there, like the bones of perished monsters. Arid and inhospitable mountain ranges rose before him, furrowed with dry channels of ancient torrents, white and ghastly as scars on the face of nature. Shifting hills of treacherous sand were heaped like tombs along the horizon. By day, the fierce heat pressed its intolerable burden on the quivering air; and no living creature moved on the dumb, swooning earth, but tiny jerboas scuttling through the parched bushes, or lizards vanishing in the clefts of the rock. By night the jackals prowled and barked in the distance, and the lion made the black ravines echo with his hollow roaring, while a bitter blighting chill followed the fever of the day. Through heat and cold, the Magian moved steadily onward.

Then I saw the gardens and orchards of Damascus, watered by the streams of Abana and Pharpar with their sloping swards inlaid with bloom, and their thickets of myrrh and roses. I saw also the long, snowy ridge of Hermon, and the dark groves of cedars, and the valley of the Jordan, and the blue waters of the Lake of Galilee, and the fertile plain of Esdraelon, and the hills of Ephraim, and the highlands of Judah. Through all these I followed the figure of Artaban moving steadily onward, until he arrived at Bethlehem. And it was the third day after the three wise men had come to that place and had found Mary and Joseph, with the young child, Jesus, and had laid their gifts of gold and frankincense and myrrh at his feet.

Then the Other Wise Man drew near, weary, but full of hope, bearing his ruby and his pearl to offer to the King. "For now at last," he said, "I shall surely find him, though it be alone, and later than my brethren. This is the place of which the Hebrew exile told me that the prophets had spoken, and here I shall behold the rising of the great light. But I must inquire about the visit of my brethren, and to what house the star directed them, and to whom they presented their tribute." The streets of the village seemed to be deserted, and Artaban wondered whether the men had all gone up to the hill-pastures to bring down their sheep. From the open door of a low stone cottage he heard the sound of a woman's voice singing softly. He entered and found a young mother hushing her baby to rest. She told him of the strangers from the far East who had appeared in the village three days ago, and how they said that a star had guided them to the place where Joseph of Nazareth was lodging with his wife and her newborn child, and how they had paid reverence to the child and given him many rich gifts.

"But the travelers disappeared again," she continued, "as suddenly as they had come. We were afraid at the strangeness of their visit. We could not understand it. The man of Nazareth took the babe and his mother and fled away that same night secretly, and it was whispered that they were going far away to Egypt. Ever since, there has been a spell upon the village; something evil hangs over it. They say that the Roman soldiers are coming from Jerusalem to force a new tax from us, and the men have driven the flocks and herds far back among the hills, and hidden themselves to escape it."

Artaban listened to her gentle, timid speech, and the child in her arms looked up in his face and smiled, stretching out its rosy hands to grasp at the winged circle of gold on his breast. His heart warmed to the touch. It seemed like a greeting of love and trust to one who had journeyed long in loneliness and perplexity, fighting with his own doubts and fears, and following a light that was veiled in clouds.

"Might not this child have been the promised Prince?" he asked within himself, as he touched its soft cheek. "Kings have been born here now in lowlier houses than this, and the favorite of the stars may rise even from a cottage. But it has not seemed good to the God of Wisdom to reward my search so soon and so easily. The one whom I seek has gone before me; and now I must follow the King to Egypt."

The young mother laid the babe in its cradle, and rose to minister to the wants of the strange guest that fate had brought into her house. She set food before him, the plain fare of peasants, but willingly offered, and therefore full of refreshment for the soul as well as for the body. Artaban accepted it gratefully; and, as he ate, the child fell into a happy slumber, and murmured sweetly in its dreams, and a great peace filled the quiet room.

But suddenly there came the noise of a wild confusion and uproar in the streets of the village, a shrieking and wailing of women's voices, a clangor of brazen trumpets and a clashing of swords, and a desperate cry: "The soldiers; the soldiers of Herod! They are killing our children."

The young mother's face grew white with terror. She clasped her child to her bosom, and crouched motionless in the darkest corner of the room, covering him with the folds of her robe, lest he should wake and cry.

But Artaban went quickly and stood in the doorway of the house. His broad shoulders filled the portal from side to side, and the peak of his white cap all but touched the lintel.

The soldiers came hurrying down the street with bloody hands and dripping swords. At the sight of the stranger in his imposing dress they hesitated with surprise. The captain of the band approached the threshold to thrust him aside. But Artaban did not stir. His face was as calm as though he were watching the stars, and in his eyes there burned that steady radiance before which even the half-tamed hunting leopard shrinks and the fierce bloodhound pauses in his leap. He held the soldier silently for an instant, and then said in a low voice:

"I am all alone in this place, and I am waiting to give this jewel to the prudent captain who will leave me in peace."

He showed the ruby, glistening in the hollow of his hand like a great drop of blood. The captain was amazed at the splendor of the gem. The pupils of his eyes expanded with desire, and the hard lines of greed wrinkled around his lips. He stretched out his hand and took the ruby.

"March on!" he cried to his men, "there is no child here. The house is still."

The clamor and the clang of arms passed down the street as the headlong fury of the chase sweeps by the secret covert where the trembling deer is hidden. Artaban re-entered the cottage. He turned his face to the east and prayed:

"God of truth, forgive my sin! I have said the thing that is not, to save the life of a child. And two of my gifts are gone. I have spent for man that which was meant for God. Shall I ever be worthy to see the face of the King?"

But the voice of the woman, weeping for joy in the shadow behind him, said very gently:

"Because thou hast saved the life of my little one, may the Lord bless thee and keep thee; the Lord make his face to shine upon thee and be gracious unto thee; the Lord lift up his countenance upon thee and give thee peace."

In the Hidden Way of Sorrow

Then again there was a silence in the Hall of Dreams, deeper and more mysterious than the first interval, and I understood that the years of Artaban were flowing very swiftly under the stillness of that clinging fog, and I caught only a glimpse, here and there, of the river of his life shining through the shadows that concealed its course.

I saw him moving among the throngs of men in populous Egypt, seeking everywhere for traces of the household that had come down from Bethlehem, and finding them under the spreading sycamore trees of Heliopolis, and beneath the walls of the Roman fortress of New Babylon beside the Nile—traces so faint and dim that they vanished before him continually, as footprints on the hard river-sand glisten for a moment with moisture and then disappear.

I saw him again at the foot of the pyramids, which lifted their sharp points into the intense saffron glow of the sunset sky, changeless monuments of the perishable glory and the imperishable hope of man. He looked up into the vast countenance of the crouching Sphinx, and vainly tried to read the meaning of the calm eyes and smiling mouth. Was it, indeed, the mockery of all effort and all aspiration, as Tigranes had said—the cruel jest of a riddle that has no answer, a search that never can succeed? Or was there a touch of pity and encouragement in that inscrutable smile—a promise that even the defeated should attain a victory, and the disappointed should discover a prize, and the ignorant should be made wise, and the blind should see, and the wandering should come into the haven at last?

I saw him again in an obscure house of Alexandria, taking counsel with a Hebrew rabbi. The venerable man, bending over the rolls of parchment on which the prophecies of Israel were written, read aloud the pathetic words which foretold the sufferings of the promised Messiah—the despised and rejected of men, the man of sorrows and the acquaintance of grief.

"And remember, my son," said he, fixing his deep-set eyes upon the face of Artaban, "the one whom you are seeking is not to be found in a palace, nor among the rich and powerful. If the light of the world and the glory of Israel had been appointed to come with the greatness of earthly splendor, it must have appeared long ago. For no son of Abraham will ever again rival the power which Joseph had in the palaces of Egypt, or the magnificence of Solomon throned between the lions in Jerusalem. But the light for which the world is waiting is a new light, the glory that shall rise out of patient and triumphant suffering. And the kingdom which is to be established forever is a new kingdom, the royalty of perfect and unconquerable love.

"I do not know how this shall come to pass, nor how the turbulent kings and peoples of earth shall be brought to acknowledge the Messiah and pay homage to him. But this I know. Those who seek him will do well to look among the poor and the lowly, the sorrowful and the oppressed."

So I saw the other wise man again and again, traveling from place to place, and searching among the people of the dispersion, with whom the little family from Bethlehem might, perhaps, have found a refuge. He passed through countries where famine lay heavy upon the land and the poor were crying for bread. He made his dwelling in plague-stricken cities where the sick were languishing in the bitter companionship of helpless misery. He visited the oppressed and the afflicted in the gloom of subterranean prisons, and the crowded wretchedness of slave-markets, and the weary toil of galley ships. In all this populous and intricate world of anguish, though he found none to worship, he found many to help. He fed the hungry, and clothed the naked, and healed the sick, and comforted the captive; and his years went by more swiftly than the weaver's shuttle that flashes back and forth through the loom while the web grows and the invisible pattern is completed.

It seemed almost as if he had forgotten his quest. But once I saw him for a moment as he stood alone at sunrise, waiting at the gate of a Roman prison. He had taken from a secret resting-place in his bosom the pearl, the last of his jewels. As he looked at it, a mellow luster, a soft and iridescent light, full of shifting gleams of azure and rose, trembled upon its surface. It seemed to have absorbed some reflection of the colors of the lost sapphire and ruby. So the profound, secret purpose of a noble life draws into itself the memories of past joy and past sorrow. All that has helped it, all that has hindered it, is transfused by a subtle magic into its very essence. It becomes more luminous and precious the longer it is carried close to the warmth of the beating heart.

Then, at last, while I was thinking of this pearl, and of its meaning, I heard the end of the story of the Other Wise Man.

A Pearl of Great Price
Three-and-thirty years of the life of Artaban had passed away, and he was still a pilgrim, and a seeker after light. His hair, once darker than the cliffs of Zagros, was now white as the wintry snow that covered them. His eyes, that once flashed like flames of fire, were dull as embers smouldering among the ashes.

Worn and weary and ready to die, but still looking for the King, he had come for the last time to Jerusalem. He had often visited the holy city before, and had searched through all its lanes and crowded hovels and black prisons without finding any trace of the family of Nazarenes who had fled from Bethlehem long ago. But now it seemed as if he must make one more effort, and something whispered in his heart that, at last, he might succeed.

It was the season of the Passover. The city was thronged with strangers. The children of Israel, scattered in far lands all over the world, had returned to the Temple for the great feast, and there had been a confusion of tongues in the narrow streets for many days.

But on this day there was a singular agitation visible in the multitude. The sky was veiled with a portentous gloom, and currents of excitement seemed to flash through the crowd like the thrill which shakes the forest on the eve of a storm. A secret tide was sweeping them all one way. The clatter of sandals, and the soft, thick sound of thousands of bare feet shuffling over the stones, flowed unceasingly along the street that leads to the Damascus gate.

Artaban joined company with a group of people from his own country, Parthian Jews who had come up to keep the Passover, and inquired of them the cause of the tumult, and where they were going.

"We are going," they answered, "to the place called Golgotha, outside the city walls, where there is to be an execution. Have you not heard what has happened? Two famous robbers are to be crucified, and with them another, called Jesus of Nazareth, a man who has done many wonderful works among the people, so that they love him greatly. But the priests and elders have said that he must die, because he gave himself out to be the Son of God. And Pilate has sent him to the cross because he said that he was the "King of the Jews.""

How strangely these familiar words fell upon the tired heart of Artaban! They had led him for a lifetime over land and sea. And now they came to him darkly and mysteriously like a message of despair. The King had arisen, but he had been denied and cast out. He was about to perish. Perhaps he was already dying. Could it be the same who had been born in Bethlehem thirty-three years ago, at whose birth the star had appeared in heaven, and of whose coming the prophets had spoken?

Artaban's heart beat unsteadily with that troubled, doubtful apprehension which is the excitement of old age. But he said within himself: "The ways of God are stranger than the thoughts of men, and it may be that I shall find the King, at last, in the hands of his enemies, and shall come in time to offer my pearl for his ransom before he dies."

So the old man followed the multitude with slow and painful steps toward the Damascus gate of the city. Just beyond the entrance of the guardhouse a troop of Macedonian soldiers came down the street, dragging a young girl with torn dress and dishevelled hair. As the Magian paused to look at her with compassion, she broke suddenly from the hands of her tormentors and threw herself at his feet, clasping him around the knees. She had seen his white cap and the winged circle on his breast.

"Have pity on me," she cried, "and save me, for the sake of the God of purity! I also am a daughter of the true religion which is taught by the Magi. My father was a merchant of Parthia, but he is dead, and I am seized for his debts to be sold as a slave. Save me from worse than death."

Artaban trembled.

It was the old conflict in his soul, which had come to him in the palm grove of Babylon and in the cottage at Bethlehem—the conflict between the expectation of faith and the impulse of love. Twice the gift which he had consecrated to the worship of religion had been drawn from his hand to the service of humanity. This was the third trial, the ultimate probation, the final and irrevocable choice.

Was it his great opportunity or his last temptation? He could not tell. One thing only was clear in the darkness of his mind—it was inevitable. And does not the inevitable come from God?

One thing only was sure to his divided heart—to rescue this helpless girl would be a true deed of love. And is not love the light of the soul?

He took the pearl from his bosom. Never had it seemed so luminous, so radiant, so full of tender, living lustre. He laid it in the hand of the slave.

"This is thy ransom, daughter! It is the last of my treasures which I kept for the King."

While he spoke the darkness of the sky thickened, and shuddering tremors ran through the earth, heaving convulsively like the breast of one who struggles with mighty grief.

The walls of the houses rocked to and fro. Stones were loosened and crashed into the street. Dust clouds filled the air. The soldiers fled in terror, reeling like drunken men. But Artaban and the girl whom he had ransomed crouched helpless beneath the wall of the Praetorium.

What had he to fear? What had he to live for? He had given away the last remnant of his tribute for the King. He had parted with the last hope of finding him. The quest was over, and it had failed. But even in that thought, accepted and embraced, there was peace. It was not resignation. It was not submission. It was something more profound and searching. He knew that all was well, because he had done the best that he could, from day to day. He had been true to the light that had been given to him. He had looked for more. And if he had not found it, if a failure was all that came out of his life, doubtless that was the best that was possible. He had not seen the revelation of "life everlasting, incorruptible and immortal." But he knew that even if he could live his earthly life over again, it could not be otherwise than it had been.

One more lingering pulsation of the earthquake quivered through the ground. A heavy tile, shaken from the roof, fell and struck the old man on the temple. He lay breathless and pale, with his gray head resting on the young girl's shoulder, and the blood trickling from the wound. As she bent over him, fearing that he was dead, there came a voice through the twilight, very small and still, like music sounding from a distance, in which the notes are clear but the words are lost. The girl turned to see if someone had spoken from the window above them, but she saw no one.

Then the old man's lips began to move, as if in answer, and she heard him say in the Parthian tongue:

"Not so, my Lord: For when saw I thee a hungered and fed thee? Or thirsty, and gave thee drink? When saw I thee a stranger, and took thee in? Or naked, and clothed thee? When saw I thee sick or in prison, and came unto thee? Three-and-thirty years have I looked for thee; but I have never seen thy face, nor ministered to thee, my King."

He ceased, and the sweet voice came again. And again the maid heard it, very faintly and far away. But now it seemed as though she understood the words:

"Verily I say unto thee, Inasmuch as thou hast done it unto one of the least of these my brethren, thou hast done it unto me."

A calm radiance of wonder and joy lighted the pale face of Artaban like the first ray of dawn on a snowy mountain-peak. One long, last breath of relief exhaled gently from his lips. His journey was ended. His treasures were accepted. The Other Wise Man had found the King.

Reading for Comprehension

1. Why did Artaban miss his planned meeting with the other Magi?
2. What does Artaban do with his first gift for the king, the sapphire?
3. Why does he give his second gift, the ruby, to the Roman captain?
4. What does Artaban do with his final gift, the pearl?
5. What accident befalls Artaban at the end of the story?
6. What does the servant girl hear the mysterious voice saying to Artaban?

Reading for Understanding

1. What is meant by the final sentences of the story: "His journey was ended. His treasures were accepted. The Other Wise Man had found the King"?
2. In what way is the message in the story, "The Other Wise Man," similar to the message in Tolstoy's tale, "Where Love Is, God Is" (pages 101–113)?

Activity

The concept of a journey is an ancient and very compelling metaphor for the idea of seeking God with all of our hearts. In reality, however, it is God who seeks us and not we who seek him. Look up and read the poem "The Hound of Heaven," by Francis Thompson. Explain how it dramatizes the manner in which people seek to flee from the God of Love who always pursues them.

Law of Love

"The Bishop's Candlesticks"
from *Les Misérables*

Victor Hugo (translated by Isabel Florence Hapgood)

Turn away from sin and be faithful to the Gospel.
—Prayer on the Reception of Ashes on Ash Wednesday

Author Background

Victor Hugo (1802–1885) is one of the greatest French writers of the nineteenth century. Two of his novels, *Les Misérables* and *The Hunchback of Notre Dame*, are world classics that have been translated into many, many languages. Hugo's novels also are social documents that directly confront the exploitation of the poor, the barbarity of the penal system, the evils of female prostitution, and the horrors of child abuse. His heroes, Jean Valjean in *Les Misérables*, and the Hunchback, Quasimodo, in *The Hunchback of Notre Dame*, represent by their lives the triumph of human values over hatred and evil.

Before the Reading

Les Misérables tells the story of Jean Valjean, a man who is sentenced to nineteen years of imprisonment for stealing a piece of bread to feed his sister's starving children. Released from prison he is treated with indifference and contempt because of his prison record. He is filled with bitterness and hatred and vows to revenge himself because of the injustice shown to him. Admitted to the home of a saintly bishop, he takes advantage of his host and steals the bishop's silverware. Caught by the police, he expects to be returned to prison but the bishop's pardon enables him to go free. This incident changes his whole life and the remainder of the novel shows how Jean Valjean is transformed into an angel of mercy in a world filled with violence and hatred. The excerpt that follows, "The Bishop's Candlesticks," recounts the incident that set Valjean free and shows the power of Christian mercy and love to soften and change the most hardened heart.

"The Bishop's Candlesticks"

Chapter X
The Man Awakened

As the Cathedral clock struck two in the morning, Jean Valjean awoke.

What woke him was that his bed was too good. It was nearly twenty years since he had slept in a bed, and, although he had not undressed, the sensation was too novel not to disturb his slumbers.

He had slept more than four hours. His fatigue had passed away. He was accustomed not to devote many hours to repose.

He opened his eyes and stared into the gloom which surrounded him; then he closed them again, with the intention of going to sleep once more.

When many varied sensations have agitated the day, when various matters preoccupy the mind, one falls asleep once, but not a second time. Sleep comes more easily than it returns. This is what happened to Jean Valjean. He could not get to sleep again, and he fell to thinking.

He was at one of those moments when the thoughts which one has in one's mind are troubled. There was a sort of dark confusion in his brain. His memories of the olden time and of the immediate present floated there pell-mell and mingled confusedly, losing their proper forms, becoming disproportionately large, then suddenly disappearing, as in a muddy and perturbed pool. Many thoughts occurred to him; but there was one which kept constantly presenting itself afresh, and which drove away all others. We will mention this thought at once: he had observed the six sets of silver forks and spoons and the ladle which Madame Magloire had placed on the table.

Those six sets of silver haunted him. They were there. A few paces distant. Just as he was traversing the adjoining room to reach the one in which he then was, the old servant-woman had been in the act of placing them in a little cupboard near the head of the bed. He had taken careful note of this cupboard. On the right, as you entered from the dining room. They were solid. And old silver. From the ladle one could get at least two hundred francs. Double what he had earned in nineteen years. It is true that he would have earned more if "the administration had not robbed him."

His mind wavered for a whole hour in fluctuations with which there was certainly mingled some struggle. Three o'clock struck. He opened his eyes again, drew himself up abruptly into a sitting posture, stretched out his arm and felt for his knapsack, which he had thrown down on a corner of the alcove; then he hung his legs over the edge of the bed, and placed his feet on the floor, and thus found himself, almost without knowing it, seated on his bed.

He remained for a time thoughtfully in this attitude, which would have been suggestive of something sinister for any one who had seen him thus in the dark, the only person awake in that house where all were sleeping. All of a sudden he stooped down, removed his shoes and placed them softly on the mat beside the bed; then he resumed his thoughtful attitude, and became motionless once more.

Throughout this hideous meditation, the thoughts which we have above indicated moved incessantly through his brain; entered, withdrew, re-entered, and in a manner oppressed him; and then he thought, also, without knowing why, and with the mechanical persistence of reverie, of a convict named Brevet, whom he had known in the galleys, and whose trousers had been upheld by a single suspender of knitted cotton. The checkered pattern of that suspender recurred incessantly to his mind.

He remained in this situation, and would have so remained indefinitely, even until daybreak, had not the clock struck one—the half or quarter hour. It seemed to him that that stroke said to him, "Come on!"

He rose to his feet, hesitated still another moment, and listened; all was quiet in the house; then he walked straight ahead, with short steps, to the window, of which he caught a glimpse. The night was not very dark; there was a full moon, across which coursed large clouds driven by the wind. This created, outdoors, alternate shadow and gleams of light, eclipses, then bright openings of the clouds; and indoors a sort of twilight. This twilight, sufficient to enable a person to see his way, intermittent on account of the clouds, resembled the sort of livid light which falls through an air-hole in a cellar, before which the passersby come and go. On arriving at the window, Jean Valjean examined it. It had no grating; it opened in the garden and was fastened, according to the fashion of the country, only by a small pin. He opened it; but as a rush of cold and piercing air penetrated the room abruptly, he closed it again immediately. He scrutinized the garden with that attentive gaze which studies rather than looks. The garden was enclosed by a tolerably low white wall, easy to climb. Far away, at the extremity, he perceived tops of trees, spaced at regular intervals, which indicated that the wall separated the garden from an avenue or lane planted with trees.

Having taken this survey, he executed a movement like that of a man who has made up his mind, strode to his alcove, grasped his knapsack, opened it, fumbled in it, pulled out of it something which he placed on the bed, put his shoes into one of his pockets, shut the whole thing up again, threw the knapsack on his shoulders, put on his cap, drew the visor down over his eyes, felt for his cudgel, went and placed it in the angle of the window; then returned to the bed, and resolutely seized the object which he had deposited there. It resembled a short bar of iron, pointed like a pike at one end. It would have been difficult to distinguish in that darkness for what employment that bit of iron could have been designed. Perhaps it was a lever; possibly it was a club.

In the daytime it would have been possible to recognize it as nothing more than a miner's candlestick. Convicts were, at that period, sometimes employed in quarrying stone from the lofty hills which environ Toulon, and it was not rare for them to have miners' tools at their command. These miners' candlesticks are of massive iron, terminated at the lower extremity by a point, by means of which they are stuck into the rock.

He took the candlestick in his right hand; holding his breath and trying to deaden the sound of his tread, he directed his steps to the door of the adjoining room, occupied by the Bishop, as we already know.

On arriving at this door, he found it ajar. The Bishop had not closed it.

Chapter XI
What He Does

Jean Valjean listened. Not a sound.

He gave the door a push.

He pushed it gently with the tip of his finger, lightly, with the furtive and uneasy gentleness of a cat which is desirous of entering.

The door yielded to this pressure, and made an imperceptible and silent movement, which enlarged the opening a little.

He waited a moment; then gave the door a second and a bolder push.

It continued to yield in silence. The opening was now large enough to allow him to pass. But near the door there stood a little table, which formed an embarrassing angle with it, and barred the entrance.

Jean Valjean recognized the difficulty. It was necessary, at any cost, to enlarge the aperture still further.

He decided on his course of action, and gave the door a third push, more energetic than the two preceding. This time a badly oiled hinge suddenly emitted amid the silence a hoarse and prolonged cry.

Jean Valjean shuddered. The noise of the hinge rang in his ears with something of the piercing and formidable sound of the trumpet of the Day of Judgment.

In the fantastic exaggerations of the first moment he almost imagined that that hinge had just become animated, and had suddenly assumed a terrible life, and that it was barking like a dog to arouse every one, and warn and to wake those who were asleep. He halted, shuddering, bewildered, and fell back from the tips of his toes upon his heels. He heard the arteries in his temples beating like two forge hammers, and it seemed to him that his breath issued from his breast with the roar of the wind issuing from a cavern. It seemed impossible to him that the horrible clamor of that irritated hinge should not have disturbed the entire household, like the shock of an earthquake; the door, pushed by him, had taken the alarm, and had shouted; the old man would rise at once; the two old women would shriek out; people would come to their assistance; in less than a quarter of an hour the town would be in an uproar, and the gendarmerie on hand. For a moment he thought himself lost.

He remained where he was, petrified like the statue of salt, not daring to make a movement. Several minutes elapsed. The door had fallen wide open. He ventured to peep into the next room. Nothing had stirred there. He lent an ear. Nothing was moving in the house. The noise made by the rusty hinge had not awakened anyone.

This first danger was past; but there still reigned a frightful tumult within him. Nevertheless, he did not retreat. Even when he had thought himself lost, he had not drawn back. His only thought now was to finish as soon as possible. He took a step and entered the room.

This room was in a state of perfect calm. Here and there vague and confused forms were distinguishable, which in the daylight were papers scattered on a table, open folios, volumes piled upon a stool, an arm-chair heaped with clothing, a *prie-Dieu*, and which at that hour were only shadowy corners and whitish spots. Jean Valjean advanced with precaution, taking care not to knock against the furniture. He could hear, at the extremity of the room, the even and tranquil breathing of the sleeping Bishop.

He suddenly came to a halt. He was near the bed. He had arrived there sooner than he had thought for. Nature sometimes mingles her effects and her spectacles with our actions with sombre and intelligent appropriateness, as though she desired to make us reflect. For the last half-hour a large cloud had covered the heavens. At the moment when Jean Valjean paused in front of the bed, this cloud parted, as though on purpose, and a ray of light, traversing the long window, suddenly illuminated the Bishop's pale face. He was sleeping peacefully. He lay in his bed almost completely dressed, on account of the cold of the Basses-Alps, in a garment of brown wool, which covered his arms to the wrists. His head was thrown back on the pillow, in the careless attitude of repose; his hand, adorned with the pastoral ring, and whence had fallen so many good deeds and so many holy actions, was hanging over the edge of the bed. His whole face was illumined with a vague expression of satisfaction, of hope, and of felicity. It was more than a smile, and almost a radiance. He bore upon his brow the indescribable reflection of a light which was invisible. The soul of the just contemplates in sleep a mysterious heaven.

A reflection of that heaven rested on the Bishop.

It was, at the same time, a luminous transparency, for that heaven was within him. That heaven was his conscience.

At the moment when the ray of moonlight superposed itself, so to speak, upon that inward radiance, the sleeping Bishop seemed as in a glory. It remained, however, gentle and veiled in an ineffable half-light. That moon in the sky, that slumbering nature, that garden without a quiver, that house which was so calm, the hour, the moment, the silence, added some solemn and unspeakable quality to the venerable repose of this man, and enveloped in a sort of serene and majestic aureole that white hair, those closed eyes, that face in which all was hope and all was confidence, that head of an old man, and that slumber of an infant.

There was something almost divine in this man, who was thus august, without being himself aware of it.

Jean Valjean was in the shadow, and stood motionless, with his iron candlestick in his hand, frightened by this luminous old man. Never had he beheld anything like this. This confidence terrified him. The moral world has no grander spectacle than this: a troubled and uneasy conscience, which has arrived on the brink of an evil action, contemplating the slumber of the just. That slumber in that isolation, and with a neighbor like himself, had about it something sublime, of which he was vaguely but imperiously conscious.

No one could have told what was passing within him, not even himself. In order to attempt to form an idea of it, it is necessary to think of the most violent of things in the presence of the most gentle. Even on his visage it would have been impossible to distinguish anything with certainty. It was a sort of haggard astonishment. He gazed at it, and that was all. But what was his thought? It would have been impossible to divine it. What was evident was, that he was touched and astounded. But what was the nature of this emotion?

His eye never quitted the old man. The only thing which was clearly to be inferred from his attitude and his physiognomy was a strange indecision. One would have said that he was hesitating between the two abysses, the one in which one loses one's self and that in which one saves one's self. He seemed prepared to crush that skull or to kiss that hand.

At the expiration of a few minutes his left arm rose slowly towards his brow, and he took off his cap; then his arm fell back with the same deliberation, and Jean Valjean fell to meditating once more, his cap in his left hand, his club in his right hand, his hair bristling all over his savage head.

The Bishop continued to sleep in profound peace beneath that terrifying gaze.

The gleam of the moon rendered confusedly visible the crucifix over the chimney-piece, which seemed to be extending its arms to both of them, with a benediction for one and pardon for the other.

Suddenly Jean Valjean replaced his cap on his brow; then stepped rapidly past the bed, without glancing at the Bishop, straight to the cupboard, which he saw near the head; he raised his iron candlestick as though to force the lock; the key was there; he opened it; the first thing which presented itself to him was the basket of silverware; he seized it, traversed the chamber with long strides, without taking any precautions and without troubling himself about the noise, gained the door, re-entered the oratory, opened the window, seized his cudgel, bestrode the window-sill of the ground-floor, put the silver into his knapsack, threw away the basket, crossed the garden, leaped over the wall like a tiger, and fled.

Chapter XII
The Bishop Works

The next morning at sunrise Monseigneur Bienvenu was strolling in his garden. Madame Magloire ran up to him in utter consternation.

"Monseigneur, Monseigneur" she exclaimed, "does your Grace know where the basket of silver is?"

"Yes," replied the Bishop.

"Jesus the Lord be blessed!" she resumed; "I did not know what had become of it."

The Bishop had just picked up the basket in a flower-bed. He presented it to Madame Magloire.

"Here it is."

"Well!" said she. "Nothing in it! And the silver?"

"Ah," returned the Bishop, "so it is the silver which troubles you? I don't know where it is."

"Great, good God! It is stolen! That man who was here last night has stolen it."

In a twinkling, with all the vivacity of an alert old woman, Madame Magloire had rushed to the oratory, entered the alcove, and returned to the Bishop. The Bishop had just bent down, and was sighing as he examined a plant of cochlearia des Guillons, which the basket had broken as it fell across the bed. He rose up at Madame Magloire's cry.

"Monseigneur, the man is gone! The silver has been stolen!"

As she uttered this exclamation, her eyes fell upon a corner of the garden, where traces of the wall having been scaled were visible. The coping of the wall had been torn away.

"Stay! Yonder is the way he went. He jumped over into Cochefilet Lane. Ah, the abomination! He has stolen our silver!"

The Bishop remained silent for a moment; then he raised his grave eyes, and said gently to Madame Magloire:

"And, in the first place, was that silver ours?"

Madame Magloire was speechless. Another silence ensued; then the Bishop went on:

"Madame Magloire, I have for a long time detained that silver wrongfully. It belonged to the poor. Who was that man? A poor man, evidently."

"Alas! Jesus!" returned Madame Magloire. "It is not for my sake, nor for Mademoiselle's. It makes no difference to us. But it is for the sake of Monseigneur. What is Monseigneur to eat with now?"

The Bishop gazed at her with an air of amazement.

"Ah, come! Are there no such things as pewter forks and spoons?"

Madame Magloire shrugged her shoulders.

"Pewter has an odor."

"Iron forks and spoons, then."

Madame Magloire made an expressive grimace. Iron has a taste."

"Very well," said the Bishop; "wooden ones then."

A few moments later he was breakfasting at the very table at which Jean Valjean had sat on the previous evening. As he ate his breakfast, Monseigneur Welcome remarked gaily to his sister, who said nothing, and to Madame Magloire, who was grumbling under her breath, that one really does not need either fork or spoon, even of wood, in order to dip a bit of bread in a cup of milk.

"A pretty idea, truly," said Madame Magloire to herself, as she went and came, "to take in a man like that! and to lodge him close to one's self! And how fortunate that he did nothing but steal! Ah, *mon Dieu*! it makes one shudder to think of it!"

As the brother and sister were about to rise from the table, there came a knock at the door.

"Come in," said the Bishop.

The door opened. A singular and violent group made its appearance on the threshold. Three men were holding a fourth man by the collar. The three men were gendarmes; the other was Jean Valjean.

A brigadier of gendarmes, who seemed to be in command of the group, was standing near the door. He entered and advanced to the Bishop, making a military salute.

"Monseigneur" said he.

At this word, Jean Valjean, who was dejected and seemed overwhelmed, raised his head with an air of stupefaction.

"Monseigneur!" he murmured. "So he is not the curé?"

"Silence!" said the gendarme. "He is Monseigneur the Bishop."

In the meantime, Monseigneur Bienvenu had advanced as quickly as his great age permitted.

"Ah! here you are!" he exclaimed, looking at Jean Valjean. "I am glad to see you. Well, but how is this? I gave you the candlesticks too, which are of silver like the rest, and for which you can certainly get two hundred francs. Why did you not carry them away with your forks and spoons?"

Jean Valjean opened his eyes wide, and stared at the venerable Bishop with an expression which no human tongue can render any account of.

"Monseigneur," said the brigadier of gendarmes, "so what this man said is true, then? We came across him. He was walking like a man who is running away. We stopped him to look into the matter. He had this silver—"

"And he told you," interposed the Bishop with a smile, "that it had been given to him by a kind old fellow of a priest with whom he had passed the night? I see how the matter stands. And you have brought him back here? It is a mistake."

"In that case," replied the brigadier, "we can let him go?"

"Certainly," replied the Bishop.

The gendarmes released Jean Valjean, who recoiled.

"Is it true that I am to be released?" he said, in an almost inarticulate voice, and as though he were talking in his sleep.

"Yes, thou art released; dost thou not understand?" said one of the gendarmes.

"My friend," resumed the Bishop, "before you go, here are your candlesticks. Take them."

He stepped to the chimney-piece, took the two silver candlesticks, and brought them to Jean Valjean. The two women looked on without uttering a word, without a gesture, without a look which could disconcert the Bishop.

Jean Valjean was trembling in every limb. He took the two candlesticks mechanically, and with a bewildered air.

"Now," said the Bishop, "go in peace. By the way, when you return, my friend, it is not necessary to pass through the garden. You can always enter and depart through the street door. It is never fastened with anything but a latch, either by day or by night."

Then, turning to the gendarmes:

"You may retire, gentlemen."

The gendarmes retired.

Jean Valjean was like a man on the point of fainting.

The Bishop drew near to him, and said in a low voice:

"Do not forget, never forget, that you have promised to use this money in becoming an honest man."

Jean Valjean, who had no recollection of ever having promised anything, remained speechless. The Bishop had emphasized the words when he uttered them. He resumed with solemnity:

"Jean Valjean, my brother, you no longer belong to evil, but to good. It is your soul that I buy from you; I withdraw it from black thoughts and the spirit of perdition, and I give it to God."

Chapter XIII
Little Gervais

When Jean Valjean left the Bishop's house, he was, as we have seen, quite thrown out of everything that had been his thought hitherto. He could not yield to the evidence of what was going on within him. He hardened himself against the angelic action and the gentle words of the old man. "You have promised me to become an honest man. I buy your soul. I take it away from the spirit of perversity; I give it to the good God."

This recurred to his mind unceasingly. To this celestial kindness he opposed pride, which is the fortress of evil within us. He was indistinctly conscious that the pardon of this priest was the greatest assault and the most formidable attack which had moved him yet; that his obduracy was finally settled if he resisted this clemency; that if he yielded, he should be obliged to renounce that hatred with which the actions of other men had filled his soul through so many years, and which pleased him; that this time it was necessary to conquer or to be conquered; and that a struggle, a colossal and final struggle, had been begun between his viciousness and the goodness of that man. . . .

Thus he contemplated himself, so to speak, face to face, and at the same time, athwart this hallucination, he perceived in a mysterious depth a sort of light which he at first took for a torch. On scrutinizing this light which appeared to his conscience with more attention, he recognized the fact that it possessed a human form and that this torch was the Bishop.

His conscience weighed in turn these two men thus placed before it, the Bishop and Jean Valjean. Nothing less than the first was required to soften the second. By one of those singular effects, which are peculiar to this sort of ecstasies, in proportion as his reverie continued, as the Bishop grew great and resplendent in his eyes, so did Jean Valjean grow less and vanish. After a certain time he was no longer anything more than a shade. All at once he disappeared. The Bishop alone remained; he filled the whole soul of this wretched man with a magnificent radiance.

Jean Valjean wept for a long time. He wept burning tears, he sobbed with more weakness than a woman, with more fright than a child.

As he wept, daylight penetrated more and more clearly into his soul; an extraordinary light; a light at once ravishing and terrible. His past life, his first fault, his long expiation, his external brutishness, his internal hardness, his dismissal to liberty, rejoicing in manifold plans of vengeance, what had happened to him at the Bishop's, the last thing that he had done, that theft of forty sous from a child, a crime all the more cowardly, and all the more monstrous since it had come after the Bishop's pardon, all this recurred to his mind and appeared clearly to him, but with a clearness which he had never hitherto witnessed. He examined his life, and it seemed horrible to him; his soul, and it seemed frightful to him. In the meantime a gentle light rested over this life and this soul. It seemed to him that he beheld Satan by the light of Paradise.

How many hours did he weep thus? What did he do after he had wept? Whither did he go? No one ever knew. The only thing which seems to be authenticated is that that same night the carrier who served Grenoble at that epoch, and who arrived at about three o'clock in the morning, saw, as he traversed the street in which the Bishop's residence was situated, a man in the attitude of prayer, kneeling on the pavement in the shadow, in front of the door of Monseigneur Welcome.

Reading for Comprehension

1. What did Jean Valjean see when he broke into Monseigneur Welcome's bedroom?

2. What does Valjean do after stealing the silver?

3. What does Madame Magloire tell the bishop in the morning?

4. What does the Bishop tell Valjean never to forget?

5. What is Jean Valjean doing at the end of this selected reading?

Reading for Understanding

1. *Metanoia* is a Greek word that means turning around from one direction and facing a new direction. Spiritual writers use this term

to describe the spiritual experience that occurs when a person turns from sin and comes to God. How is the incident of Valjean with the bishop an occasion of *metanoia*?

2. Jean Valjean was sent to prison because he was a poor man. In prison, he became a bitter, brutal man. In the depiction of the Last Judgment (see Matthew 25:31–46), Christ says, "Come, you who are blessed by my father. Inherit the kingdom prepared for you from the foundation of the world. For I was . . . in prison and you visited me." What do you think is the Church's responsibility to those who are incarcerated? What is *your* responsibility to the imprisoned?

Activity

One of the most popular musical dramas in the world was based on the novel, *Les Misérables*, by Victor Hugo. Listen to the musical score of the play and explain how the song that Jean Valjean sings over the body of a wounded student, "Let Him Live," shows the depth of his love of God and man.

Law of Love

"Helen" from
The Junkie Priest: Father Daniel Egan, S.A.
John D. Harris

Come, you who are blessed by my Father. . . . For I was in prison
and you visited me.
—Matthew 25:34, 36

Author Background
John D. Harris was a respected writer for the Hearst newspapers when
he wrote *The Junkie Priest: Father Daniel Egan, S.A.*, published in 1965.
Although not a Catholic, Harris was impressed with the redemptive work
performed by Fr. Egan and his associates at the halfway houses for drug
abusers in the metropolitan New York area, beginning in the 1950s.

Before the Reading
The abuse of drugs is one of the greatest scourges of contemporary American
society. The vast majority of prisoners in the United States are drug abusers
and have been arrested for drug-related crimes. What is the Christian response in the face of this tremendous human tragedy? Fr. Daniel Egan, S.A.
(1915–2000), was a Franciscan priest of the Atonement who spent most of
his life working with those who suffered from drug abuse. He founded the
Village Haven for drug addicts in Greenwich Village in 1962 and New Hope
Manor at Graymoor, New York, for drug-addicted girls in 1970. He was a
member of the first White House Conference on Drugs. This excerpt from
Harris's account details the origins of Fr. Egan's ministry.

Helen

It began without warning.

The dim interior of the church seemed empty. But a woman sat alone beside one of the white stone pillars that rose, culminating in graceful arcs, to the high ceiling.

Father Egan had been preaching a Lenten mission there for several days and had heard confessions throughout the evening. It was after 11 p.m. and he decided to say a few prayers and go to the rectory and sleep. He was close to the woman before he saw her. He paused, then approached her and spoke in a whisper. Could he help her?

She was young and attractive with slim, well-kept hands. She wore no rings and her head was closely wrapped in a black silk scarf. She looked up at him for an instant, then burst into tears and buried her face in her hands. He was not alarmed; it happened often. He sat down and spoke consolingly, urging her to be calm and to stop crying. When her sobs died she stared at him. Behind the tears he saw a neatly shaped face with wide gray eyes. She seemed to hesitate before she spoke, then blurted out her words.

"Father," she said, "I'm a drug addict."

His eyebrows rose. He peered at her closely. To his knowledge he had never met an addict. He searched his mind for what he knew about addiction. It came to little. He was, in fact, forced to admit it was confined to newspaper accounts of arrests and drug seizures and generally that drugs were detrimental to physical and mental well-being. But he was conditioned to show no surprise when informed of the most peculiar matters. He smiled reassuringly. Maybe he could still help her, he said.

The girl dabbed at her eyes and her tearful expression dissolved into a tight, bitter smile. She looked at him almost pityingly.

"How?" she asked. "Can you get me off drugs? I'm a nurse—I was a nurse—and I know what's wrong with me."

The tears returned and she began to cry quietly. Father Egan sighed. He asked her if she needed emergency treatment and was further puzzled when she told him she needed months of treatment. She added that the only place where that was available was at the federal hospital at Lexington, Kentucky. Yet she knew people who had been to Lexington four and five times and were still addicts. It was hopeless, she said.

In spite of his sympathy Father Egan felt skeptical. Anyway it was late and there was nothing he could do now. In as kindly a manner as he knew he told her to return in the morning at 10 a.m. when he would try to give her problem some attention. The girl shrugged and promised to come back. He watched her leave, a trimly dressed figure with her hands thrust deeply into her raincoat pockets.

In the morning there was a mission sermon to be preached at six o'clock and he rose early. He heard some confessions before Mass, gave the instruction after it, then heard more confessions. Another mission Mass was said at nine with further confessions before, during, and after. It was a busy morning and he began to tire as the hours passed. As the time neared 10 a.m. he found himself looking repeatedly at his watch. Following the last confession after nine o'clock Mass he went back to the rectory for coffee.

When he returned she was sitting by the pillar in the same seat she had occupied the night before. She wore last night's raincoat and scarf but he could see her face had higher color. She was gazing curiously about the church. As he approached her she smiled in recognition. He greeted her and told her she seemed in a better mood than the night before.

"Father," she said solemnly, "you're a square."

He grunted and sat down. In the section of New York where he had been raised they practically ate squares. But he said nothing. The girl was cheerful, even if her buoyancy seemed vaguely fragile. He decided not to hurry matters; he would let her tell him what she wanted him to do. Then, if he could, he would do it. He did not have to wait long. Her mood became serious and she looked down at her lap before, speaking slowly and evenly.

"Do you realize," she asked, "that I'm spending fifty dollars a day on heroin?"

His skepticism returned.

"Fifty dollars a day," he repeated. "Where d'you get that kind of money?"

"I'm a prostitute."

"Oh."

He rubbed his chin to give himself time to think. Not that what she said disturbed him. It was mild compared to some of the human behavior he encountered. He merely wanted to handle the situation as effectively as possible. He grinned at her and raised his shoulders expressively.

"All right, I'm a square," he said. "Now, how did you get into this jam?"

She sighed. There was really nothing to tell, she said.

"I was a nurse and I was dating this guy, a musician. He was very nice. How should I know he was an addict when I met him? But then he made me steal drugs from the hospital. After a while I experimented myself and became addicted too."

She hesitated and bit her lip.

"Go on," he said.

"I used to take drugs out of the patients' medications and inject them with sterile water instead. I guess it was lucky for someone the head nurse found out in time. I was fired and I lost my license. She could have had me arrested but she just told me to get out."

Father Egan listened without expression as the girl's dry and unemotional voice told him how she had tried to get a job and had failed; employers wanted references. Her musician left her. She became depressed and her craving for drugs intensified. She had sold everything she owned to raise money, her clothes, her television set, furniture, and spent it on drugs. One day she had tried to steal clothing from a department store in the hope of selling it and had been caught. The judge had released her on probation. A week later she stood before him again. This time he hadn't even looked at her as he sentenced her to sixty days.

"Since then," she said dully, "I've been to jail four other times. When I get out I pick up the first guy I can. Sometimes I get fifty, sometimes ten. I've been a prostitute for two years now. Sometimes I've hustled just for drugs. I can't think about anything but drugs, Father. I've got to stop but I can't. I've thought about getting treatment but nobody cares about a junkie, especially a junkie prostitute. I've—"

Father Egan had been listening in fascination but at these words he interrupted. What did she mean, nobody cared? If she was sick she was sick and that was all there was to it. He was surprised by the vehemence of her reply.

"That's not so, Father," she whispered fiercely. "You don't know anything about this. Addicts can't get medical treatment unless they're in jail."

He eyed her thoughtfully. She couldn't possibly be telling the truth, not in New York in 1952. And even if she was, there had to be an explanation. But he was intrigued and he had an idea. He stood up.

"We're going for a ride," he said. "I know a place that treats anybody for anything."

"Where?"

"Bellevue."

She shook her head but he grasped her arm firmly and strode with her out of the church. On Fourteenth Street he flagged a taxi. During the ride he asked her name.

"Helen."

"When did you take drugs last, Helen?"

"An hour ago. That's why I feel so good."

The taxi headed east and north and finally halted at the huge hospital's main entrance. Perhaps he was being naive, Father Egan thought. But his curiosity was aroused and he had to find out whether Helen was telling the truth.

To his astonishment a doctor in the hospital's admissions office convinced him she was. Addicts were not admitted merely for detoxification, to cure them physically of addiction. If they became ill, however, due to use of drugs or for other reasons, they could of course be admitted to the hospital. Many prisoners in the city's jails were sent to Bellevue's prison wards under those conditions. Some jailed addicts were, in addition, admitted to the hospital's psychiatric wards.

Father Egan listened with some annoyance, a flush creeping up his face. The doctor noticed this and shrugged.

"It's not my doing, Father," she said. "It's the procedure of the hospital."

Father Egan led Helen to the hospital's main lobby. He told her to sit down and marched to a coin telephone. He dialed three other New York hospitals and received the same answers each time. If she needed emergency treatment she should be brought in at once. If she was experiencing severe withdrawal symptoms—he noted the term—she should be brought in and they would see. Was she in convulsions? Was she in a coma? No, they were sorry but they did not admit drug addicts for simple detoxification.

He hung up and looked across the lobby at Helen. These hospitals ought to know what they're doing, he thought. He wasn't a doctor.

When he rejoined Helen he saw the color had mysteriously vanished from her face. Her eyes had become deep, luminous pools, giving her an oddly transparent, defenseless appearance. She sneezed.

"Don't worry, Father," she said in a tone so resigned that he winced. "I knew this would happen but you just couldn't believe me. Anyway, I've got to go now. I'll call you."

Before he could stop her she rose and walked quickly through the door.

In following weeks the memory of Helen and the peculiar visit to the hospital rarely left his mind. It was inconceivable that she was the victim of injustice. Drug addiction could only be some kind of illness. Why was it apparently shunned in hospitals? Helen was a prostitute and of course addiction was mixed up with crime and police and so on. But that was no excuse for ignoring her condition. And how many others were in a similar plight? Almost by chance he was given the opportunity to find out.

He was assigned to preach at a women's prison. The institution was close to New York, in a New England state. He delivered his sermon to the rows of silent inmates seated before him, his words flowing in clear, ringing phrases. His effect on the assembled prisoners was not lost on prison officials. They were absorbed by the ease with which this priest made the most depressed, tense inmates relax and even laugh.

He was asked to come again. Invitations from similar jails followed and Father Egan became a familiar figure among drably dressed women behind bars.

He ached at what he saw. Each visit to each institution left him more disturbed than the last. He watched inmates in barren prison yards standing aimlessly, some slack-jawed, some screeching with laughter, and bitterly resented such denials of womanly dignity. What chance, he wondered, was there of rehabilitation in such environments? The widespread homosexuality grieved him and he was appalled to learn that so many women were serving their fourth, fifth and even sixth terms in jail. But it was their apathy that bruised him more than anything else. As time behind the walls stretched into dreary months and years many women degenerated into a dullness and stagnation that seemed tragically inimical to womanhood itself.

He made a startling discovery, one that instantly returned the image of Helen to his mind. A huge proportion of the women in each institution was made up of drug addicts, regardless of the crime for which they were imprisoned. In some jails the ratio was as high as 80 percent.

While touring one prison he observed to a silent official at his side: "It seems that the most that's being done for these people is keeping them out of sight. It's as if society considers them garbage and puts them in a can and slams the lid. Then society can't see them. But they're still there."

The addiction question nagged constantly at his mind. To learn more about it he questioned women in each jail he visited.

If you become ill on the outside, he asked, due to lack of drugs, what do you do?

Nothing, Father. Nobody helps junkies.

Can you get jobs if you want to live square?

Pretty tough. Lots of places require medical examinations. Like restaurants if you want to be a waitress. But the veins in our arms, where we've been sticking needles for years, are a giveaway. They make us self-conscious. We're scared of being turned down.

What happens then?

We go back to drugs.

How do you get the money?

We steal. We hustle.

Then?

We get busted, arrested.

And?

We come back here.

Father Egan was convinced the only way to break this circle was to aid prison inmates after they were released. He knew, of course, that the idea was not new. Sociologists and criminologists had been saying the same thing for years. But he was not conditioned by failure and he had too little experience to be disillusioned. In even his meager reading of penal literature the term "halfway house" occurred repeatedly and Father Egan's thoughts soon became polarized around this aspect of rehabilitation. His ideas were still vague. But he felt certain that the tragic inmates he encountered in prisons should at least be granted a transitional stage between life behind the walls and life in so-called normal society. Without this stage the change was too abrupt. It posed overwhelming problems of adjustment for the many unstable, immature, uneducated and unskilled persons held in jails. Women especially needed a brief, protective pause before venturing again into the world.

Father Egan communicated his thoughts to women convicts. They responded with cynical shrugs. The drug addicts, who needed some form of post-discharge care more desperately than anyone, were the most emphatic in their conviction that society would never take an active role in establishing halfway houses. They told Father Egan he was wasting his time.

Nothing could have been more calculated to heighten his obsession with the halfway house idea. And it was at this time that Father Egan met Lois.

He first saw her, a dark-haired, tight-lipped girl, during a prison visit. She told him she had been an aspiring actress and had modeled for fashion magazines in New York. With a hard smile she said she had once won second place in a beauty contest. She had graduated from one of California's best women's colleges and could quote at length from Shakespeare and Shelley. Her stately features were immobile as she added that she was nearing the end of a three-year sentence for prostitution.

His face framed the question: Why?

The hard smile reappeared. She explained that nothing had come of her dogged attempts at professional acting. She had run out of money and turned to prostitution. In a final gesture of hopelessness she had succumbed to heroin.

"Don't tell my mother," she said cynically.

Father Egan made Lois promise she would keep in touch with him after her release.

He was surprised to receive a letter from her a few weeks later while he was preaching in Toronto. The envelope showed the letter had been sent to him at his New York address, then forwarded. The girl had written, with apparent melodrama:

Dear Father:

I don't know if this will reach you in time, but please try to help me. I cannot stand it much longer. I may not be at the above address when you return to New York, but please try to find me wherever I am. I have reached the end of my rope. I have to be out all night and it is bitterly cold. My heroin habit is now costing me $50 a day. I do not know where to turn.

Respectfully,
Lois

He hastily replied:

Dear Lois:

Even if you are at the end of your rope please hang on for dear life, hang on until I get back. When I do I'll try to find you. I deeply regret being unable to tell you where to wait until then, but you and I both know the situation only too well. I wish indeed that there was somewhere in the city where you could go and feel safe and protected. Some day, though, we will have a halfway house. In the meantime, Lois, remember you can never wander so far away from God that you can't come back at the last minute. Remember your hands can never be so dirty with sin that God won't wash them clean, even at the last moment.

Always your priest friend,
Father Egan

Forty-eight hours later Father Egan was back in New York, Lois uppermost in his mind. Immediately on leaving the airline terminal he boarded a subway train and twenty minutes later was knocking on Lois' door, in a seamy West Nineties building off Amsterdam Avenue. There was no answer. He questioned the building superintendent. The man shrugged. Yes, he knew Lois. She came and went. But he had not seen her for several days. No, he had no idea where she would be. He shrugged again and closed his door. Father Egan questioned neighbors and two patrolmen in a parked prowl car with the same result. Lois had vanished.

It was late when he reached the Graymoor house in Greenwich Village. On the bulletin board was a message. He read it, and dread rose within him.

> Fr. Daniel—a detective from Missing Persons called. Will you please go to Bellevue Morgue to identify a body?

He borrowed a car and drove to the vast hospital on the East River. In the Missing Persons office, near the door that led down to the morgue, a plainclothesman handed him a small sheet of notepaper.

"We got this out of a dead girl's bra, Father," he said. "It's a letter from you. We found her in a basement off Amsterdam, uptown. Looks like a drug overdose. Maybe you can identify her."

Father Egan looked at the letter he had written to Lois. He nodded slowly. Yes, he said, he believed he could identify her.

After silently viewing Lois' body on the morgue slab for a few moments, Father Egan turned to go. He was stopped by a touch on his arm.

"You know, Father," the detective said, "I've been around this morgue a long time and I don't remember anything hittin' me just like this. I read that letter and I can't help feeling that if there had been something in town like that halfway house you wrote about, maybe that girl would be alive today. I hope you get it."

Father Egan stared at the detective for a moment. He thanked him and walked out. The words echoed in his ears, maybe that girl would be alive today. He slammed his car into gear and his mouth formed an angry, determined line. He would get it, he vowed, he would establish a halfway house in New York, if only for Lois. Somehow, somewhere, he would find a way.

Reading for Comprehension

1. How did Helen become a drug addict and how did she earn the money to pay for her drugs?

2. What happened when Fr. Egan tried to get Helen admitted to a hospital?

3. Why did Lois write to Fr. Egan that she was desperate?

4. What did Fr. Egan discover had happened to Lois?

Reading for Understanding

1. What is a halfway house?

2. Why do you think Helen and Lois each sought out a Catholic priest for help?

Activities

1. Research and summarize the operation of a halfway house in your areas.

2. How prevalent is drug use among teens today? Why do teens feel they cannot become addicted to drugs? How would you counsel someone who has come to you seeking help for drug addiction?

The Voice of Conscience

"The Merit of a Young Priest"
from *Hasidic Tales of the Holocaust*

Yaffa Eliach

The Church reproves, as foreign to the mind of Christ,
any discrimination against men or harassment of them because
of their race, color, condition of life, or religion.

—*Nostra Aetate* **5, from Documents of the Second Vatican Council**

Author Background

As a child, Yaffa Eliach survived the Nazi campaign to exterminate the
Jewish people. In the years since, she has written extensively about the
Holocaust and has worked with many universities in developing Holocaust
Studies Programs. Eliach was a key advisor in the program that resulted in
the building of the Holocaust Museum in Washington, D.C. Most recently
she served as professor emeritus at Brooklyn College in New York City. Her
collection of stories, *Hasidic Tales of the Holocaust*, is considered a masterpiece in the extensive literature on the Holocaust.

Before the Reading

During the period of Nazi dominance in Europe during the 1930s and
1940s, it is estimated that more than six million Jews were killed in the
death camps of Germany and Eastern Europe. Although most of the Jewish
people did not survive the war, some young children were saved with the
help of Catholics who hid them from the Nazi murderers. At the conclusion
of the war, the parents of many of these Jewish children were dead, and
the children were for all intents and purposes members of Catholic families who had protected them. A problem in these cases was: in what religion
should these children be raised, Catholic or Jewish? In this tale, a Hasidic
rabbi of great learning reflects on the decision of a young Catholic priest
not to baptize a Jewish child.

"The Merit of a Young Priest"

It was June 1942; the murder of Jews in the Krakow ghetto was at its height. About 5,000 victims were deported to the Belzec death camp. Hundreds were being murdered in the ghetto itself, shot on its streets on the way to deportation. Among them were Dr. Arthur Rosenzweig, head of the Judenrat, the famous Yiddish poet Mordechai Gebirtig, and the distinguished old artist Abraham Neumann.

The Hiller family realized that their days in the Krakow ghetto were numbered; they too would soon be swept away in one of the frequent Aktions. Yet there was still a glimmer of hope. They were young and skilled laborers; if they were deported to a labor camp, perhaps they would still have a chance of survival. But the fate of their little son Shachne was a different matter. Small children had become a rare sight in the ghetto; starvation, disease, and the ever-increasing selections took their constant toll. Helen and Moses Hiller began feverishly to plan the rescue of their little Shachne. After considering various possibilities they decided to contact family friends on the Aryan side in the small town of Dombrowa, childless Gentile people named Yachowitch.

Helen Hiller, with the help of the Jewish underground, made her way to Dombrowa. She went to Mr. and Mrs. Joseph Yachowitch and begged them to take care of her little son. Although they could do so only at great risk to their own lives, the Christian friends agreed to take the child.

Despite the ever-increasing dangers of the ghetto, the young parents could not bring themselves to part from their only child. Only after the large Aktion of October 28, 1942, when 6,000 additional Jews were shipped to Belzec and the patients at the Jewish hospital, the residents of the old-age home, and three hundred children at the orphanage were murdered on the spot, did the Hiller family decide to act.

On November 15, 1942, Helen Hiller smuggled her little boy out of the ghetto. Along with her son, she gave her Christian friends two large envelopes. One envelope contained all the Hillers' precious valuables; the other, letters and a will. One of the letters was addressed to Mr. and Mrs. Yachowitch, entrusting them with little Shachne, and asking them to bring up the child as a Jew and to return him to his people in case of his parents' deaths. The Hillers thanked the Yachowitch family for their humanitarian act and promised to reward them for their goodness. The letter also included the names and addresses of relatives in Montreal and Washington, D.C.

The second letter was addressed to Shachne himself, telling him how much his parents loved him, that it was this love that had prompted them to leave him alone with strangers, good and noble people. They told him of his Jewishness and how they hoped that he would grow up to be a man proud of his Jewish heritage.

The third letter contained a will written by Helen's mother, Mrs. Reizel Wurtzel. It was addressed to her sister-in-law Jenny Berger in Washington. She wrote to her of the horrible conditions in the ghetto, the deportations, the death of family members, and of the impending doom. She wrote: "Our grandson, by the name of Shachne Hiller, born on the 18th day of Av, August 22,1940, was given to good people. I beg you, if none of us will return, take the child to you; bring him up righteously. Reward the good people for their efforts and may God grant life to the parents of the child. Regards and kisses, your sister, Reizel Wurtzel."

As Helen was handing the letters to Mrs. Yachowitch, she once more stated her instructions: "If I or my husband do not return when this madness is over, please mail this letter to America to our relatives. They will surely respond and take the child. Regardless of the fates of my husband or myself, I want my son to grow up as a Jew." The two women embraced and Mrs. Yachowitch promised that she would do her best. The young mother hurriedly kissed her little child and left, fearing that her emotions would betray her and she would not be able to leave her little son behind in this strange house, but, instead, would take him back with her to the ghetto.

It was a beautiful autumn day. The Vistula's waters reflected the foliage of a Polish autumn. The Wavel, the ancient castle of the Polish kings, looked as majestic as ever. Mothers strolled with their children and she, the young Jewish mother, was trying to hold back her tears. She slowed her hasty, nervous steps so as not to betray herself and changed her hurried pace to a leisurely stroll, as if she too were out to enjoy the sights of ancient Krakow. To thwart all suspicion, Helen displayed a huge cross hanging around her neck and stepped in for a moment to the Holy Virgin Church in the Old Square.

Smuggling little Shachne out from the ghetto to the Aryan side was indeed timely. In March 1943, the Krakow ghetto was liquidated. People in the work camp adjacent to the ghetto were transferred to nearby Plaszow and to the more distant Auschwitz. Anyone found hiding was shot on the spot. Krakow, the first Jewish settlement on Polish soil, dating back to the thirteenth century, was Judenrein!

Mr. and Mrs. Joseph Yachowitch constantly inquired about the boy's young parents. Eventually they learned that the Hillers had shared the fate of most of Krakow's Jews. Both of them were consumed by the flames of the Holocaust.

The Yachowitches, too, faced many perilous days. They moved to a new home in a different town. From time to time, they had to hide in barns and haystacks. When little Shachne suffered from one of his crying spells, calling for his mother and father, they feared that unfriendly, suspicious neighbors would betray them to the Gestapo. But time is the greatest healer. Little Shachne stopped crying. Mrs. Yachowitch became very attached to the child and loved him like her own. She took great pride in her "son" and loved him dearly. His big, bright, wise eyes were always alert and inquiring. She and little Shachne never missed a Sunday service and he soon knew by heart all the church hymns. A devout Catholic herself, Mrs. Yachowitch decided to baptize the child and, indeed, make him into a full-fledged Catholic.

She went to see a young, newly ordained parish priest who had a reputation for being wise and trustworthy. Mrs. Yachowitch revealed to him her secret about the true identity of the little boy who was entrusted to her and her husband, Joseph, and told him of her wish to have him baptized so that he might become a true Christian and a devout Catholic like herself. The young priest listened intently to the woman's story. When she finished her tale, he asked, "And what was the parents' wish when they entrusted their only child to you and your husband?" Mrs. Yachowitch told the priest about the letters and the mother's last request that the child be told of his Jewish origins and returned to his people in the event of the parents' death.

The young priest explained to Mrs. Yachowitch that it would be unfair to baptize the child while there was still hope that the relatives of the child might take him. He did not perform the ceremony. This was in 1946.

Some time later, Mr. Yachowitch mailed the letters to the United States and Canada. Both Jenny Berger, from Washington, D.C., and Mr. and Mrs. H. Aron from Montreal responded, stating their readiness to bring the child to the U.S.A. and Canada immediately. But then a legal battle began on both sides of the Atlantic that was to last for four years! Polish law forbade Polish orphan children to leave the country. The immigration laws of the United States and Canada were strict, and no visa was issued to little Shachne. Finally, in 1949, the Canadian Jewish Congress obtained permission from the Canadian Government to bring 1,210 orphans to the country. It was arranged for Shachne to be included in this group, the only one in the group to come directly from Poland. Meantime a court action was instituted in Krakow, and Shachne was awarded, by a judge in Poland, to the representatives of the Canadian-American relatives.

In June 1949, Shachne Hiller boarded the Polish liner MS Batory. The parting from Mrs. Yachowitch was a painful one. Both cried, but Mrs. Yachowitch comforted little Shachne that it was the will of his real mother that one day he should be returned to his own people. On July 3, 1949, the Batory arrived at Pier 88 at the foot of West 48th Street in New York City. Aboard was little Shachne, first-class passenger of cabin No. 228. He was met by his relatives, Mrs. Berger and Mrs. Aron. For the next year, Shachne lived in Montreal. On December 19,

1950, after two years of lobbying by Jenny Berger, President Harry S. Truman signed a bill into law making Shachne Hiller a ward of the Berger family. When Shachne arrived at the Bergers' home on Friday, February 9, 1951, there was a front-page story in the Washington Post. It was more than eight years since Shachne's maternal grandmother Reizel Wurtzel, in the ghetto of Krakow, had written the letter to her sister-in-law (his great aunt) Jenny Berger, asking her to take her little grandson to her home and heart. Her will and testament were finally carried out.

Years passed. Young Shachne was educated in American universities and grew up to be a successful man, vice-president of a company, as well as an observant Jew. The bond between him and Mrs. Yachowitch was a lasting one. They corresponded, and both Shachne and his great aunt Jenny Berger continually sent her parcels and money, and tried as much as possible to comfort her in her old age. He preferred not to discuss the Holocaust with his wife, twin sons, family, or friends. Yet all of them knew about the wonderful Mr. and Mrs. Joseph Yachowitch who saved the life of a Jewish child and made sure to return him to his people.

In October 1978, Shachne, now Stanley, received a letter from Mrs. Yachowitch. In it she revealed to him, for the first time, her inclination to baptize him and raise him as a Catholic. She also went on to describe, at length her meeting with the young parish priest on that fateful day. Indeed, that young parish priest was none other than the man who became Cardinal Karol Wojtyla of Krakow, and, on October 16,1978, was elected by the College of Cardinals as Pope—Pope John Paul II!

When the Grand Rabbi of Bluzhov, Rabbi Israel Spira, heard the above story, he said, "God has mysterious, wonderful ways unknown to men. Perhaps it was the merit of saving a single Jewish soul that brought about his election as Pope. It is a story that must be told."

Based upon several of my conversations with Shachne Hiller (Stanley Berger), his family, and his mother-in-law, Mrs. Anne Wolozin. September 1977–October 1, 1981.

Reading for Comprehension

1. Why was the sight of small children so rare in the Krakow Ghetto?
2. What took place during the German Aktion of October 28, 1942?
3. What did Shachne's mother and father write in the letter they left for him in the event of their deaths?
4. What happened to Shachne's mother and father?
5. Who was the parish priest?
6. What did Rabbi Spira say when he was told this story?

Reading for Understanding

1. Why did the young priest refuse to baptize little Shachne?
2. As Pope John Paul II, Karol Wojtyla visited the major synagogue of Rome to meet with the Jewish people there. At that meeting, as head of the Catholic Church he called the Jewish people "our older brother." What do you think he meant by that phrase?

Activity

When Pope John Paul II visited the nation of Israel in 2000, he brought with him a formal letter of apology to the Jewish people which he placed in a niche of the Wailing Wall in Jerusalem. It read:

God of our fathers,
You chose Abraham and his descendants to bring your Name to the Nations:
We are deeply saddened by the behavior of those who in the course of history have caused these children of yours to suffer, and asking your forgiveness we wish to commit ourselves to genuine brotherhood with the people of the Covenant.
Jerusalem 26, March 2000
Signed: John Paul II

Why do you think that the pope felt that it was necessary to perform this penitential task?

The Voice of Conscience

"The Mysterious Visitor"
from *The Brothers Karamazov*

Fyodor Dostoyevsky

The confession (or disclosure) of sins, even from a simply human
point of view, frees us and facilitates our reconciliation with others.
—*Catechism of the Catholic Church*, **1455**

Author Background

The life of Dostoyevsky is detailed in the selection, "A Woman of Little
Faith" (page 115).

Before the Reading

The Brothers Karamazov ranks with the greatest of modern novels. In this
tale of intrigue, Dostoyevsky explores the problems facing contemporary
humanity and uses each of the brothers to give voice to the various answers
to those problems. A central character of the novel is the Elder Zosima, a
Russian monk who is renowned for his wisdom and holiness. In this selection, Fr. Zosima tells of an incident in his youth that illustrates a central
concern of Dostoyevsky: He who sins will be tormented by his conscience
and will be unable to give or receive love. The selection begins with Fr.
Zosima receiving a visit from a mysterious stranger.

"The Mysterious Visitor"

One day, quite unexpectedly, after he had been talking with great
fervor a long time, I saw him suddenly turn pale, and his face worked
convulsively while he stared persistently at me.

"What's the matter?" I said; "do you feel ill?"—he had just been
complaining of headache.

"I . . . do you know . . . I murdered someone."

316

He said this and smiled with a face as white as chalk. "Why is it he is smiling?" The thought flashed through my mind before I realized anything else. I too turned pale.

"What are you saying?" I cried.

"You see," he said with a pale smile, "how much it has cost me to say the first word. Now that I have said it, I feel I've taken the first step, and I shall go on."

For a long while I could not believe him, and I did not believe him at that time but only after he had been to see me three days running and told me all about it. At first I thought he was mad, but I ended by being convinced, to my great grief and amazement. His crime was a great and terrible one.

Fourteen years before, he had murdered the widow of a landowner, a wealthy and handsome young woman who had a house in our town. He had fallen passionately in love with her, declared his feeling, and tried to persuade her to marry him. But she had already given her heart to another man, an officer of noble birth and high rank in the service, who was at that time away at the front, though she was expecting him soon to return. She refused his offer and begged him not to come and see her. After he had ceased to visit her, he took advantage of his knowledge of the house to enter at night through the garden by the roof, at great risk of discovery. But as often happens, a crime committed with extraordinary audacity is more successful than others.

Entering the garret through the skylight, he went down the ladder, knowing that the door at the bottom of it was sometimes, through the negligence of the servants, left unlocked. He hoped to find it so, and so it was. He made his way in the dark to her bedroom, where a light was burning. As though on purpose, both her maids had gone off to a birthday party in the same street, without asking leave. The other servants slept in the servants' quarters or in the kitchen on the ground floor. His passion flamed up at the sight of her asleep, and then vindictive, jealous anger took possession of his heart, and beside himself, like a drunken man, he thrust a knife into her heart, so that she did not even cry out. Then with devilish and criminal cunning he contrived that suspicion should fall on the servants. He was so base as to take her purse, to open her chest with keys from under her pillow, and to take some things from it, doing it all as it might have been done by an ignorant servant, leaving valuable papers and taking only money. He took some of the larger gold things, but left smaller articles that were ten times as valuable. He took with him, too, some things for himself as remembrances, but of that later. Having done this awful deed, he returned by the way he had come.

Neither the next day, when the alarm was raised, nor at any time after in his life, did any one dream of suspecting that he was the criminal. In fact, no one knew of his love for her, for he was always reserved and silent and had no friend to whom he would have opened his heart. He was looked upon simply as an acquaintance, and not a very intimate one, of the murdered woman, since for the previous fortnight he had not even visited her. A serf of hers called Pyotr was at once suspected, and every circumstance confirmed the suspicion. The man knew—indeed his mistress did not conceal the fact—that having to send one of her serfs as a recruit, she had decided to send him, as he had no relations and his conduct was unsatisfactory. People had heard him angrily threatening to murder her when he was drunk in a tavern. Two days before her death, he had run away, staying no one knew where in the town. The day after the murder, he was found on the road leading out of the town, dead drunk, with a knife in his pocket and his right hand stained with blood for some reason. He declared that his nose had been bleeding, but no one believed him. The maids confessed that they had gone to a party and that the street door had been left open till they returned. And a number of similar details came to light, throwing suspicion on the innocent servant.

They arrested him, and he was tried for the murder; but a week after the arrest, the prisoner fell sick of a fever and died in the hospital while unconscious. There the matter ended, and the judges and the authorities and everyone in the town remained convinced that the crime had been committed by no one but the servant who had died in the hospital. And after that the punishment began.

My mysterious visitor, now my friend, told me that at first he was not in the least troubled by pangs of conscience. He was miserable a long time, but not for that reason; only from regret that he had killed the woman he loved, that she was no more, that in killing her he had killed his love, while the fire of passion was still in his veins. But of the innocent blood he had shed, of the murder of a fellow human, he scarcely thought. The thought that his victim might have become the wife of another man was unendurable to him, and so for a long time he was convinced in his conscience that he could not have acted otherwise.

At first he was worried at the arrest of the servant, but his illness and death soon set his mind at rest, for the man's death was apparently (so he reflected at the time) not owing to his arrest or his fright but to a chill he had taken on the day he ran away, when he had lain all night dead drunk on the damp ground. The theft of the money and other things troubled him little, for he argued that the theft had not been committed for gain but to avert suspicion. The sum stolen was small, and he shortly afterwards subscribed the whole of it, and much more, towards the funds for maintaining an almshouse in the town. He did this on purpose to set his conscience at rest about the theft, and it's a remarkable fact that for a long time he really was at peace—he told me this himself. He entered then upon a career of great activity in the service, volunteered for a difficult and arduous duty, which occupied him two years, and being a man of strong will almost forgot the past. Whenever he recalled it, he tried not to think of it at all. He became active in philanthropy too, founded and helped to maintain many institutions in the town, did a good deal in the two capitals, and was elected a member of philanthropic societies in both Moscow and Petersburg.

At last, however, he began brooding over the past, and the strain of it was too much for him. Then he was attracted by a fine and intelligent girl and soon after married her, hoping that marriage would dispel his lonely depression and that by entering on a new life and scrupulously doing his duty to his wife and children, he would escape from old memories altogether. But the very opposite of what he expected happened. He began, even in the first month of his marriage, to be continually fretted by the thought, "My wife loves me—but what if she knew?" When she first told him that she would soon bear him a child, he was troubled. "I am giving life, but I have taken life." Children came. "How dare I love them, teach and educate them; how can I talk to them of virtue? I have shed blood." They were splendid children, and he longed to caress them: "But I can't look at their fair and innocent faces, I am unworthy."

At last he began to be bitterly and ominously haunted by the blood of his murdered victim, by the young life he had destroyed, by the blood that cried out for vengeance. He began to have terrible dreams. But being a man of fortitude, he bore his suffering a long time, thinking, "I shall expiate everything by this secret agony." But that hope too was vain; the longer it went on, the more intense was his suffering.

He was respected in society for his active benevolence, though everyone was overawed by his stern and gloomy character. But the more he was respected, the more intolerable it was for him. He confessed to me that he had thoughts of killing himself. But he began to be haunted by another idea—an idea which he had at first regarded as impossible and unthinkable, though at last it got such a hold on his heart that he could not shake it off. He dreamed of rising up, going out, and confessing in the face of all men that he had committed murder. For three years this dream had pursued him, haunting him in different forms. At last he believed with his whole heart that if he confessed his crime, he would heal his soul and be at peace forever. But this belief filled his heart with terror, for how could he carry it out? And then came the occurrence of my duel.

"Looking at you, I have made up my mind."

I looked at him.

"Is it possible," I cried, clasping my hands, "that such a trivial incident could give rise to such a resolution in you?"

"My resolution has been growing for the last three years," he answered, "and your story only gave the last touch to it. Looking at you, I reproached myself and envied you," he said to me almost harshly.

"But you won't be believed," I observed; "it's fourteen years ago."

"I have proofs, great proofs, I shall show them."

Then I cried and kissed him.

"Tell me one thing, one thing," he said (as though it all depended upon me), "my wife, my children! My wife may die of grief, and though my children won't lose their rank and property, they'll be a convict's children—forever! And what a memory, what a memory of me I shall leave in their hearts!"

I said nothing.

"And to part from them, to leave them forever? It's forever, you know, forever!"

I sat still and repeated a silent prayer. I got up at last. I felt afraid.

"Well? "He looked at me.

"Go!" said I, "Confess. Everything passes, only the truth remains. Your children will understand when they grow up, the nobility of your resolution."

He left me that time as though he had made up his mind. Yet for more than a fortnight afterward, he came to me every evening still preparing himself, still unable to bring himself to the point. He made my heart ache. One day he would come determined and say fervently:

"I know it will be heaven for me, heaven, the moment I confess. Fourteen years I've been in hell. I want to suffer. I will take my punishment and begin to live. You can pass through the world doing wrong, but there's no turning back. Now I dare not love my neighbor nor even my own children. Good God, my children will understand, perhaps, what my punishment has cost me and will not condemn me! God is not in strength but in truth."

"All will understand your sacrifice," I said to him, "if not at once, they will understand later; for you have served truth, the higher truth, not of the earth."

And he would go away seeming comforted, but next day he would come again, bitter, pale, sarcastic.

"Every time I come to you, you look at me so inquisitively as though to say, 'He has still not confessed!' Wait a bit longer—don't despise me too much. It's not such an easy thing to do as you think. Perhaps I shall not do it at all. You won't go and inform against me then, will you?"

And far from looking at him with indiscreet curiosity, I was afraid to look at him at all. I was quite ill from anxiety, and my heart was full of tears. I could not sleep at night.

"I have just come from my wife," he went on. "Do you understand what the word 'wife' means? When I went out the children called to me, 'Good-bye, Father, come back quickly to read *The Children's Magazine* with us.' No, you don't understand that! No one is wise from another man's woe."

His eyes were glittering, his lips were twitching. Suddenly he struck the table with his fist so that everything on it danced—it was the first time he had done such a thing; he was such a mild man.

"But need I?" he exclaimed, "Must I? No one has been condemned, no one has been sent to Siberia in my place, the man died of fever. And I've been punished by my sufferings for the blood I shed. And I shan't be believed; they won't believe my proofs. Need I confess, need I? I am ready to go on suffering all my life for the blood I have shed if only my wife and children may be spared. Will it be justice to ruin them along with myself? Aren't we making a mistake? What is right in this case? And will people recognize it, will they appreciate it, will they respect it?"

"Good Lord!" I thought to myself, "he is thinking of other people's respect at such a moment!" And I felt so sorry for him then, that I believe I would have shared his fate if it could have comforted him.

I saw he was beside himself. I was aghast, realizing with my heart as well as my mind what such a resolution meant.

"Decide my fate!" he exclaimed again.

"Go and confess," I whispered to him. My voice failed me, but I whispered it firmly. I took up the New Testament from the table, the Russian translation, and showed him the Gospel of St. John, Chapter 12, Verse 24:

"Verily, verily, I say unto you, except a corn of wheat fall into the ground and die, it abideth alone: but if it die, it bringeth forth much fruit."

I had just been reading that verse when he came in. He read it.

"That's true," he said, but he smiled bitterly. "It's terrible the things you find in those books," he said after a pause. "It's easy enough to thrust them upon one. And who wrote them? Can they have been written by men?"

"The Holy Spirit wrote them," said I.

"It's easy for you to prate," he smiled again, this time almost with hatred.

I took the book again, opened it in another place and showed him the Epistle to the Hebrews, Chapter 10, Verse 31. He read:

"It is a fearful thing to fall into the hands of the living God."

He read it and simply flung down the book. He was trembling all over.

"An awful text," he said. "There's no denying you've picked out fitting ones." He rose from the chair. "Well!" he said, "good-bye, perhaps I shan't come again . . . we shall meet in heaven. So I have been fourteen years 'in the hands of the living God.' That's how one must think of those fourteen years. Tomorrow I will beseech those hands to let me go."

I wanted to take him in my arms and kiss him, but I did not dare—his face was contorted and sombre. He went away.

"Good God," I thought, "what has he gone to face!" I fell on my knees before the ikon and wept for him before the Holy Mother of God, our swift defender and helper. I was half an hour praying in tears, and it was late, about midnight. Suddenly I saw the door open and he came in again. I was surprised.

"Where have you been?" I asked him.

"I think," he said, "I've forgotten something . . . my handkerchief, I think . . . Well, even if I've not forgotten anything, let me stay a little."

He sat down. I stood over him.

"You sit down, too," said he.

I sat down. We sat still for two minutes; he looked intently at me and suddenly smiled—I remembered that—then he got up, embraced me warmly, and kissed me.

"Remember," he said, "how I came to you a second time. Do you hear? Remember it!"

And he went out.

"Tomorrow," I thought.

And so it was. I did not know that evening that the next day was his birthday. I had not been out for the last few days so I had no chance of hearing it from anyone. On that day he always had a great gathering; everyone in the town went to it. It was the same this time. After dinner he walked into the middle of the room with a paper in his hand—a formal declaration to the chief of his department who was present. This declaration he read aloud to the whole assembly. It contained a full account of the crime, in every detail.

"I cut myself off from men as a monster. God has visited me," he said in conclusion. "I want to suffer for my sin!"

Then he brought out and laid on the table all the things he had been keeping for fourteen years that he thought would prove his crime: the jewels belonging to the murdered woman that he had stolen to divert suspicion; a cross and a locket taken from her neck with a portrait of her betrothed in the locket; her notebook and two letters, one from her betrothed telling her that he would soon be with her, and her unfinished answer left on the table to be sent off next day. He had carried off these two letters—what for? Why had he kept them for fourteen years instead of destroying them as evidence against him?

And this is what happened: everyone was amazed and horrified, everyone refused to believe it and thought that he was deranged, though all listened with intense curiosity. A few days later it was fully decided and agreed in every house that the unhappy man was mad. The legal authorities could not refuse to take the case up, but they too dropped it. Though the trinkets and letters made them ponder, they decided that even if they did turn out to be authentic, no charge could be based on those alone. Besides, she might have given him those things as a friend or asked him to take care of them for her. I heard afterwards, however, that the genuineness of the things was proved by the friends and relations of the murdered woman and that there was no doubt about them. Yet nothing was destined to come of it, after all.

Five days later all had heard that he was ill and that his life was in danger. The nature of his illness I can't explain; they said it was a malady of the heart. But it became known that the doctors had been induced by his wife to investigate his mental condition also and had come to the conclusion that it was a case of insanity. I betrayed nothing, though people ran to question me. But when I wanted to visit him, I was for a long while forbidden to do so, above all by his wife.

"It's you who have caused his illness," she said to me; "he was always gloomy, but for the last year people noticed that he was peculiarly excited and did strange things, and now you have been the ruin of him. Your preaching has brought him to this; for the last month he was always with you."

Indeed, not only his wife but the whole town were down upon me and blamed me. "It's all your doing," they said. I was silent but rejoiced at heart, for I saw plainly God's mercy to the man who had turned against himself and punished himself. I could not believe in his insanity.

They let me see him at last; he insisted upon saying goodbye to me. I went in to him and saw at once that not only his days but his hours were numbered. He was weak and yellow, his hands trembled, and he gasped for breath, but his face was full of tender and happy feeling.

"It is done!" he said. "I've long been yearning to see you; why didn't you come?"

I did not tell him that they would not let me see him.

"God has had pity on me and is calling me to Himself. I know I am dying, but I feel joy and peace for the first time after so many years. There was heaven in my heart from the moment I had done what I had to do. Now I dare to love my children and to kiss them. Neither my wife nor the judges nor anyone else has believed it. My children will never believe it either. I see in that God's mercy to them. I shall die, and my name will be without a stain for them. And now I feel God near, my heart rejoices as in Heaven . . . I have done my duty."

He could not speak, he gasped for breath, he pressed my hand warmly, looking fervently at me. We did not talk for long; his wife kept peeping in at us. But he had time to whisper to me:

"Do you remember how I came back to you that second time at midnight? I told you to remember it. You know what I came back for? I came to kill you!"

I started.

"I went out from you then into the darkness; I wandered about the streets, struggling with myself. And suddenly I hated you so that I could hardly bear it. Now, I thought, he is all that binds me, and he is my judge. I can't refuse to face my punishment tomorrow, for he knows all. It was not that I was afraid you would betray me (I never even thought of that) but I thought, 'How can I look him in the face if I don't confess?' And if you had been at the other end of the earth, but alive, it would have been all the same; the thought was unendurable that you were alive, knowing everything and condemning me. I hated you as though you were the cause, as though you were to blame for everything. I came back to you then, remembering that you had a dagger lying on your table. I sat down and asked you to sit down, and for a whole minute I pondered. If I had killed you, I should have been ruined by that murder even if I had not confessed the other. But I didn't think about that at all, and I didn't want to think of it at that moment. I only hated you and longed to revenge myself on you for everything. The Lord vanquished the devil in my heart. But let me tell you, you were never nearer death."

A week later he died. The whole town followed him to the grave. The chief priest made a speech full of feeling. All lamented the terrible illness that had cut short his days. But all the town was up in arms against me after the funeral, and people even refused to see me. Some, at first a few and afterwards more, began to believe in the truth of his story, and they visited me and questioned me with great interest and eagerness, for man loves to see the downfall and disgrace of the righteous. But I held my tongue, and very shortly after, I left the town, and five months later by God's grace I entered upon the safe and blessed path, praising the unseen finger which had guided me so clearly to it. But I remember in my prayer to this day the servant of God, Mihail, who suffered so greatly.

Reading for Comprehension

1. Why did the stranger commit murder?

2. What happened to the servant who was blamed for the murder?

3. What Bible verse does Fr. Zosima show the man when he protests against confessing his crime?

4. What did the stranger tell Fr. Zosima about what he planned to do when he visited Zosima for the last time?

5. What was the reaction of the townspeople to Fr. Zosima after the man died?

Reading for Understanding

1. What does the stranger do to quiet his conscience?

2. How did the voice of the murderer's conscience impact his family life?

3. How did the stranger believe that his children would benefit by the thought that he was insane?

Activities

1. Research and summarize the plot of Nathaniel Hawthorne's novel, *The Scarlet Letter*. How is the behavior of the minister in that story similar to the behavior of the main character in this story told by Dostoyevsky?

2. The judgment of conscience against a person who has committed a great sin or crime is a central motif in Dostoyevsky's writings. Again and again he returns to the idea that it is the voice of God in man's conscience that condemns him for his sin that is the greatest punishment for the evil-doer. This idea of the role of conscience is seen most thoroughly in Dostoyevsky's great novel, *Crime and Punishment*. This novel, which tells of a crime committed by a poor student and the punishment that he suffers through his conscience, is one of the greatest novels of the nineteenth century. Read the novel and write a paper that describes how the student who has committed the murders is unable to escape the voice of his conscience. *Option*: View and report on the Woody Allen film, *Crimes and Misdemeanors*, and explicate the theme: "the eyes of God are on us always." The Allen film investigates Dostoyevsky's themes in a modern context, arriving perhaps at different conclusions.

Right Judgment and Action

"The Little Match Girl"

Hans Christian Andersen

And whoever receives one child such as this in my name receives me.
—Matthew 18:5

Author Background

Danish author and poet Hans Christian Andersen (1805–1875) is world renowned for his fairy tales. Among his best-known stories are *The Snow Queen*, *The Little Mermaid*, and *The Ugly Duckling*. Many of his stories have been adapted for the theater or ballet.

Before the Reading

One of the most frightening effects of Original Sin is seen in the exploitation and suffering of children. Throughout history, children have been victimized because of their defenselessness and innocence. On farms, in sweatshops and brothels, young boys and girls are victimized because they have no one to defend them. In this story by Andersen, and in the next story by Anton Chekhov, we see examples of the victimization of children that existed in Europe at the end of the nineteenth century.

The Little Match Girl

It was very, very cold; it snowed and it grew dark; it was the last evening of the year, New Year's Eve. In the cold and dark a poor little girl, with bare head and bare feet, was walking through the streets. When she left her own house she certainly had had slippers on; but what could they do? They were very big slippers, and her mother had used them till then, so big were they. The little maid lost them as she slipped across the road, where two carriages were rattling by terribly fast. One slipper was not to be found again, and a boy ran away with the other. He said he could use it for a cradle when he had children of his own.

So now the little girl went with her little naked feet, which were quite red and blue with the cold. In an old apron she carried a number of matches, and a bundle of them in her hand. No one had bought anything of her all day; no one had given her a copper. Hungry and cold she went, and drew herself together, poor little thing! The snow-flakes fell on her long yellow hair, which curled prettily over her neck; but she did not think of that now. In all the windows lights were shining, and there was a glorious smell of roast goose out there in the street; it was no doubt New Year's Eve. Yes, she thought of that!

In a corner formed by two houses, one of which was a little farther from the street than the other, she sat down and crept close. She had drawn up her little feet, but she was still colder, and she did not dare to go home, for she had sold no matches, and she had not a single cent; her father would beat her; and besides, it was cold at home, for they had nothing over the them but a roof through which the wind whistled, though straw and rags stopped the largest holes.

Her small hands were quite numb with the cold. Ah! a little match might do her good if she only dared draw one from the bundle, and strike it against the wall, and warm her fingers at it. She drew one out. R-r-atch! how it spluttered and burned! It was a warm bright flame, like a little candle, when she held her hands over it; it was a wonderful little light! It really seemed to the little girl as if she sat before a great polished stove, with bright brass feet and a brass cover. The fire burned so nicely; it warmed her so well,—the little girl was just putting out her feet to warm these, too, when out went the flame; the stove was gone; she sat with only the end of the burned match in her hand.

She struck another; it burned; it gave a light; and where it shone on the wall, the wall became thin like a veil, and she could see through it into the room where a table stood, spread with a white cloth, and with china on it; and the roast goose smoked gloriously, stuffed with apples and dried plums. And what was still more splendid to behold, the goose hopped down from the dish, and waddled along the floor, with a knife and fork in its breast; straight to the little girl he came. Then the match went out, and only the thick, damp, cold wall was before her.

She lighted another. Then she was sitting under a beautiful Christmas tree; it was greater and finer than the one she had seen through the glass door at the rich merchant's. Thousands of candles burned upon the green branches, and colored pictures like those in the shop windows looked down upon them. The little girl stretched forth both hands toward them; then the match went out. The Christmas lights went higher and higher. She saw that now they were stars in the sky: one of them fell and made a long line of fire.

"Now someone is dying," said the little girl, for her old grandmother, the only person who had been good to her, but who was now dead, had said: "When a star falls a soul mounts up to God."

She rubbed another match against the wall; it became bright again, and in the light there stood the old grandmother clear and shining, mild and lovely.

"Grandmother!" cried the child. "Oh, take me with you! I know you will go when the match is burned out. You will go away like the warm stove, the nice roast goose, and the great glorious Christmas tree!"

And she hastily rubbed the whole bundle of matches, for she wished to hold her grandmother fast. And the matches burned with such a glow that it became brighter than in the middle of the day; grandmother had never been so large or so beautiful. She took the little girl up in her arms, and both flew in the light and the joy so high, so high! and up there was no cold, nor hunger, nor care—they were with God.

But in the corner by the house sat the little girl, with red cheeks and smiling mouth, frozen to death on the last evening of the Old Year. The New Year's sun rose upon the little body, that sat there with the matches, of which one bundle was burned. She wanted to warm herself, the people said. No one knew what fine things she had seen, and in what glory she had gone in with her grandmother to the New Year's Day.

Reading for Comprehension

1. What happened to the little girl's slippers?
2. How many matchsticks had the little girl sold that day?
3. Why was the little girl afraid to go home?
4. What did the little girl's grandmother say about the meaning of a falling star?
5. What happens to the little girl at the conclusion of the story?

Reading for Understanding

1. What was the last thing that the little match girl saw? Was this vision a reality or fantasy?
2. Who are children today who live like the little match girl in misery?

Activity

"The Little Match Girl" has been adapted several times, including onto video and film. Look up the adaptations of the story. Choose and view one of the videos or films that illustrate the story. Summarize: How was the version different than how you imagined the story? How was it similar to your imagination?

Right Judgment and Action

"Vanka"

Anton Chekhov (translated by Constance Garnett)

Author Background

Anton Chekhov (1860–1904) was one of the greatest dramatists of the Western world. His four great plays, *The Seagull*, *Uncle Vanya*, *The Cherry Orchard*, and *The Three Sisters*, are masterpieces of dramatic art. Chekhov was also a prolific short story writer who was most adept at defining and illuminating the character of the subjects of his stories.

Before the Reading

"Vanka," written in 1886, is the story of an unhappy orphan who has been apprenticed to a shoemaker named Alyahin in Moscow. The plot of this story underscores Chekhov's writings that often dealt with pain, grief, and human suffering. On Christmas Eve, while alone in his master's house, Vanka writes a letter of appeal to his only relative, his grandfather.

"Vanka"

Vanka Zhukov, a boy of nine, who had been for three months apprenticed to Alyahin the shoemaker, was sitting up on Christmas Eve. Waiting till his master and mistress and their workmen had gone to the midnight service, he took out of his master's cupboard a bottle of ink and a pen with a rusty nib, and, spreading out a crumpled sheet of paper in front of him, began writing. Before forming the first letter he several times looked round fearfully at the door and the windows, stole a glance at the dark ikon, on both sides of which stretched shelves full, and heaved a broken sigh. The paper lay on the bench while he knelt before it.

"Dear grandfather, Konstantin Makaritch," he wrote, "I am writing you a letter. I wish you a happy Christmas, and all blessings from

God Almighty. I have neither father nor mother, you are the only one left me."

Vanka raised his eyes to the dark ikon on which the light of his candle was reflected, and vividly recalled his grandfather, Konstantin Makaritch, who was night watchman to a family called Zhivarev. He was a thin but extraordinarily nimble and lively little old man of sixty-five, with an everlastingly laughing face and drunken eyes. By day he slept in the servants' kitchen, or made jokes with the cooks; at night, wrapped in an ample sheepskin, he walked round the grounds and tapped with his little mallet. Old Kashtanka and Eel, so-called on account of his dark colour and his long body like a weasel's, followed him with hanging heads. This Eel was exceptionally polite and affectionate, and looked with equal kindness on strangers and his own masters, but had not a very good reputation. Under his politeness and meekness was hidden the most Jesuitical cunning. No one knew better how to creep up on occasion and snap at one's legs, to slip into the store-room, or steal a hen from a peasant. His hind legs had been nearly pulled off more than once, twice he had been hanged, every week he was thrashed till he was half dead, but he always revived.

At this moment grandfather was, no doubt, standing at the gate, screwing up his eyes at the red windows of the church, stamping with his high felt boots, and joking with the servants. His little mallet was hanging on his belt. He was clasping his hands, shrugging with the cold, and, with an aged chuckle, pinching first the housemaid, then the cook.

"How about a pinch of snuff?" he was saying, offering the women his snuff-box.

The women would take a sniff and sneeze. Grandfather would be indescribably delighted, go off into a merry chuckle, and cry:

"Tear it off, it has frozen on!"

They give the dogs a sniff of snuff too. Kashtanka sneezes, wriggles her head, and walks away offended. Eel does not sneeze, from politeness, but wags his tail. And the weather is glorious. The air is still, fresh, and transparent. The night is dark, but one can see the whole village with its white roofs and coils of smoke coming from the chimneys, the trees silvered with hoar frost, the snowdrifts. The whole sky spangled with gay twinkling stars, and the Milky Way is as distinct as though it had been washed and rubbed with snow for a holiday. . . .

Vanka sighed, dipped his pen, and went on writing:

"And yesterday I had a wigging. The master pulled me out into the yard by my hair, and whacked me with a boot-stretcher because I accidentally fell asleep while I was rocking their brat in the cradle. And a week ago the mistress told me to clean a herring, and I began from the tail end, and she took the herring and thrust its head in my face. The workmen laugh at me and send me to the tavern for vodka, and tell me to steal the master's cucumbers for them, and the master beats me with anything that comes to hand. And there is nothing to eat in the morning they give me bread, for dinner, porridge, and in the evening, bread again; but as for tea, or soup, the master and mistress gobble it all up themselves. And I am put to sleep in the passage, and when their wretched brat cries I get no sleep at all, but have to rock the cradle. Dear grandfather, show the divine mercy, take me away from here, home to the village. It's more than I can bear. I bow down to your feet, and will pray to God for you for ever, take me away from here or I shall die."

Vanka's mouth worked, he rubbed his eyes with his black fist, and gave a sob.

"I will powder your snuff for you," he went on. "I will pray for you, and if I do anything you can thrash me like Sidor's goat. And if you think I've no job, then I will beg the steward for Christ's sake to let me clean his boots, or I'll go for a shepherd-boy instead of Fedka. Dear grandfather, it is more than I can bear, it's simply no life at all. I wanted to run away to the village, but I have no boots, and I am afraid of the frost. When I grow up big I will take care of you for this, and not let anyone annoy you, and when you die I will pray for the rest of your soul, just as for my mammy's.

"Moscow is a big town. It's all gentlemen's houses, and there are lots of horses, but there are no sheep, and the dogs are not spiteful. The lads here don't go out with the star, and they don't let anyone go into the choir, and once I saw in a shop window fishing-hooks for sale, fitted ready with the line and for all sorts of fish, awfully good ones, there was even one hook that would hold a forty-pound sheat-fish. And I have seen shops where there are guns of all sorts, after the pattern of the master's guns at home, so that I shouldn't wonder if they are a hundred roubles each. . . . And in the butchers' shops there are grouse and woodcocks and fish and hares, but the shop-men don't say where they shoot them.

"Dear grandfather, when they have the Christmas tree at the big house, get me a gilt walnut, and put it away in the green trunk. Ask the young lady Olga Ignatyevna, say it's for Vanka."

Vanka gave a tremulous sigh, and again stared at the window. He remembered how his grandfather always went into the forest to get the Christmas tree for his master's family, and took his grandson with him. It was a merry time! Grandfather made a noise in his throat, the forest crackled with the frost, and looking at them Vanka chortled too. Before chopping down the Christmas tree, grandfather would smoke a pipe, slowly take a pinch of snuff, and laugh at frozen Vanka. . . . The young fir trees, covered with hoar frost, stood motionless, waiting to see which of them was to die. Wherever one looked, a hare flew like an arrow over the snowdrifts. . . . Grandfather could not refrain from shouting: "Hold him, hold him. . . . hold him! Ah, the bob-tailed devil!"

When he had cut down the Christmas tree, grandfather used to drag it to the big house, and there set to work to decorate it. . . . The young lady, who was Vanka's favourite, Olga Ignatyevna, was the busiest of all. When Vanka's mother Pelageya was alive, and a servant in the big house, Olga Ignatyevna used to give him goodies, and having nothing better to do, taught him to read and write, to count up to a hundred, and even to dance a quadrille. When Pelageya died,

Vanka had been transferred to the servants' kitchen to be with his grandfather, and from the kitchen to the shoemaker's in Moscow.

"Do come, dear grandfather," Vanka went on with his letter. "For Christ's sake, I beg you, take me away. Have pity on an unhappy orphan like me; here everyone knocks me about, and I am fearfully hungry; I can't tell you what misery it is, I am always crying. And the other day the master hit me on the head with a fist, so that I fell down. My life is wretched, worse than any dog's. . . . I send greetings to Alyona, one-eyed Yegorka, and the coachman, and don't give my concertina to anyone. I remain, your grandson, Ivan Zhukov. Dear grandfather, do come."

Vanka folded the sheet of writing-paper twice, and put it into an envelope he had bought the day before for a kopeck. . . . After thinking a little, he dipped the pen and wrote the address:

To grandfather in the village.

Then he scratched his head, thought a little, and added: Konstantin Makaritch. Glad that he had not been prevented from writing, he put on his cap and, without putting on his little greatcoat, ran out into the street as he was in his shirt. . . .

The shopmen at the butcher's, whom he had questioned the day before, told him that letters were put in post-boxes, and from the boxes were carried about all over the earth in mailcarts with drunken drivers and ringing bells. Vanka ran to the nearest post-box, and thrust the precious letter in the slit. . . .

An hour later, lulled by sweet hopes, he was sound asleep. . . . He dreamed of the stove. On the stove was sitting his grandfather, swinging his bare legs, and reading the letter to the cooks. . . .

By the stove was Eel, wagging his tail.

Reading for Comprehension

1. What was the name of Vanka's grandfather's playful and mischievous dog?

2. What does Vanka's master do to him when he falls asleep while watching the baby?
3. What does Vanka ask of his grandfather?
4. What had happened to Vanka after the death of his mother?
5. To whom does Vanka address his letter?

Reading for Understanding

1. What does this tale, and "The Little Match Girl," reveal about the condition of poor children at the end of the nineteenth century?
2. Why do you think Chekhov and Andersen set their stories at Christmastime?

Activity

Research the service organization Covenant House. What is its mission? How does it seek to address the problem of child abuse?

Right Judgment and Action

"The Trouble"

J.F. Powers

With this faith we will be able to transform the jangling discords of our nation into a beautiful symphony of brotherhood.

—Martin Luther King, Jr.

Author Background

J.F. Powers (1917–1999), a Catholic who grew up in the Midwest, was a conscientious objector during World War II. He subsequently worked as a hospital orderly. As an author, Powers wrote on several subjects, but he is best known for his stories (especially *The Prince of Darkness and Other Stories*) and novels that deal with the lives of American Catholic priests. His brilliant novel *Morte D'Urban*, which follows the rise, fall, and redemption of a flawed but charismatic priest, won the National Book Award in 1963.

Before the Reading

In "The Trouble," a story of racial strife, J.F. Powers reflects on the need of Catholics to speak out in the face of prejudice and oppression. The title of the story aptly describes those who bear the name "Catholic" but who do not put their faith into action. It is set in the South in the first half of the twentieth century.

"The Trouble"

Neither the slavers' whip nor the lynchers' rope nor the bayonet could kill our black belief.

—Margaret Walker "For My People"

We watched at the window all that afternoon. Old Gramma came out of her room and said, "Now you kids get away from there this minute." And we would until she went back to her room. We could hear her old rocking chair creak when she got up or sat down, and so we always ran away from the window before she came into the room to see if we were minding her good or looking out. Except once she went back to her room and didn't sit down, or maybe she did and got up easy so the chair didn't creak, or maybe we got our signals mixed, because she caught us all there and shooed us away and pulled down the green shade. The next time we were real sure she wasn't foxing us before we went to the window and lifted the shade just enough to peek out.

It was like waiting for rats as big as cats to run out from under a tenement so you could pick them off with a .22. Rats are about the biggest live game you can find in ordinary times and you see more of them than white folks in our neighborhood—in ordinary times. But the rats we waited for today were white ones, and they were doing most of the shooting themselves. Sometimes some coloreds would come by with guns, but not often; they mostly had clubs. This morning we'd seen the whites catch up with a shot-in-the-leg colored and throw bricks and stones at his black head till it got all red and he was dead. I could still see the wet places in the alley. That's why we kept looking out the window. We wanted to see some whites get killed for a change, but we didn't much think we would, and I guess what we really expected to see was nothing, or maybe them killing another colored.

There was a rumpus downstairs in front, and I could hear a mess of people tramping up the stairs. They kept on coming after the second floor and my sister Carrie, my twin, said maybe they were whites come to get us because we saw what they did to the shot-in-the-leg colored in the alley. I was scared for a minute, I admit, but when I heard their voices plainer I knew they were coloreds and it was all right, only I didn't see why there were so many of them.

Then I got scared again, only different now, empty scared all over, when they came down the hall on our floor, not stopping at anybody else's door. And then there they were, banging on our door, of all the doors in the building. They tried to come right on in, but the door was locked.

Old Gramma was the one who locked it and she said she'd clean house if one of us kids so much as looked at the knob even, and she threw the key down her neck somewhere. I went and told her that was our door the people were pounding on and where was the key. She reached down her neck and there was the key all right. But she didn't act much like she intended to open the door. She just stood there staring at it like it was somebody alive, saying the litany to the Blessed Virgin: *Mere du Christ, priezpour nous, Secours des cretins, priez.* . . . Then all of a sudden she was crying; tears were blurry in her old yellow eyes, and she put the key in the lock, her veiny hands shaking, and unlocked the door.

They had Mama in their arms. I forgot all about Old Gramma, but I guess she passed out. Anyway, she was on the floor and a couple of men were picking her up and a couple of women were saying, "Put her here, put her there." I wasn't worried as much about Old Gramma as I was about Mama. A bone—God, it made me sick—had poked through the flesh of Mama's arm, all bloody like a sharp stick, and something terrible was wrong with her chest. I couldn't look any more and Carrie was screaming. That started me crying. Tears got in the way, but still I could see the baby, one and a half, and brother George, four and a half, and they had their eyes wide-open at what they saw and weren't crying a bit, too young to know what the hell. They put Old Gramma in her room on the cot and closed the door on her and some old woman friend of hers that kept dipping a handkerchief in cold water and laying it on Old Gramma's head. They put Mama on the bed in the room where everybody was standing around and talking lower and lower until pretty soon they were just whispering.

Somebody came in with a doctor, a colored one, and he had a little black bag like they have in the movies. I don't think our family ever had a doctor come to see us before. Maybe before I was born Mama and Daddy did. I heard the doctor tell Mr. Purine, that works in the same mill Daddy does, only the night shift, that he ought to set the bone, but honest to God he thought he might as well wait, as he didn't want to hurt Mama if it wasn't going to make any difference.

He wasn't nearly as brisk now with his little black bag as he had been when he came in. He touched Mama's forehead a couple of times and it didn't feel good to him, I guess, because he looked tired after he did it. He held his hand on the wrist of her good arm, but I couldn't tell what this meant from his face. It mustn't have been any worse than the forehead, or maybe his face had nothing to do with what he thought, and I was imagining all this from seeing the shape Mama was in. Finally he said, "I'll try," and he began calling for hot water and other things, and pretty soon Mama was all bandaged up white.

The doctor stepped away from Mama and over to some men and women, six or seven of them now—a lot more had gone—and asked them what had happened. He didn't ask all the questions I wanted to ask—I guess he already knew some of the answers—but I did find out Mama was on a streetcar coming home from the plant—Mama works now and we're saving for a cranberry farm—when the riot broke out in that section. Mr. Purine said he called the mill and told Daddy to come home. But Mr. Purine said he wasn't going to work tonight himself, the way the riot was spreading and the way the coloreds were getting the worst of it.

"As usual," said a man with glasses on. "The Negroes ought to organize and fight the thing to a finish." The doctor frowned at that. Mr. Purine said he didn't know. But one woman and another man said that was the right idea.

"If we must die," said the man with glasses on, "let it not be like hogs hunted and penned in an inglorious spot!" The doctor said, "Yes, we all know that." But the man with glasses on went on, because the others were listening to him, and I was glad he did, because I was listening to him too. "We must meet the common foe; though far outnumbered, let us still be brave, and for their thousand blows deal one deathblow! What, though before us lies the open grave?

Like men we'll face the murderous, cowardly pack, pressed to the wall, dying, but—fighting back!"

They all thought it was fine, and a woman said that it was poetry, and I thought if that is what it is I know what I want to be now—a poetryman. I asked the man with glasses on if that was his poetry, though I did not think it was for some reason, and the men and women all looked at me like they were surprised to see me there and like I ought not hear such things—except the man with glasses on, and he said, No, son, it was not his poetry; he wished it was, but it was Claude McKay's, a Negro, and I could find it in the public library. I decided I would go to the public library when the riot was over, and it was the first time in my life I ever thought of the public library the way I did then.

They all left about this time, except the doctor and the old woman friend of Old Gramma's. She came out of Old Gramma's room, and when the door opened I saw Old Gramma lying on the cot with her eyes closed. The old woman asked me if I could work a can opener, and I said, "Yes, I can," and she handed me a can of vegetable soup from the shelf. She got a meal together and us kids sat down to eat. Not Carrie, though. She sat in our good chair with her legs under her and her eyes closed. Mama was sleeping and the doctor rolled up the shade at the window and looked out while we ate. I mean brother George and the baby. I couldn't eat, I just drank my glass of water. The old woman said, Here, here, I hadn't ought to let good food go to waste and was that any way to act at the table and I wasn't the first boy in the world to lose his mother.

I wondered was she crazy and I yelled I wasn't going to lose my mother and I looked to see and I was right. Mama was just sleeping and the doctor was there in case she needed him and everything was taken care of and . . . everything. The doctor didn't even turn away from the window when I yelled at the old woman, and I thought at least he'd say I'd wake my mother up shouting that way, or maybe that I was right and the old woman was wrong. I got up from the table and stood by the doctor at the window. He only stayed there a minute more then and went over to feel Mama's wrist again. He did not touch her forehead this time.

Old Gramma came out of her room and said to me, "Was that you raising so much cain in here, boy?"

I said, "Yes, it was," and just when I was going to tell her what the old woman said about losing Mama I couldn't. I didn't want to hear it out loud again. I didn't even want to think it in my mind.

Old Gramma went over and gazed down at Mama. She turned away quickly and told the old woman, "Please, I'll just have a cup of hot water, that's all, I'm so upset." Then she went over to the doctor by the window and whispered something to him and he whispered something back and it must've been only one or two words, because he was looking out the window the next moment.

Old Gramma said she'd be back in a minute and went out the door, slipslapping down the hall. I went to the window, the evening sun was going down, and I saw Old Gramma come out the back entrance of our building. She crossed the alley and went in the back door of the grocery store.

A lot of racket cut loose about a block up the alley. It was still empty, though. Old Gramma came out of the grocery store with something in a brown bag. She stopped in the middle of the alley and seemed to be watching the orange evening sun going down behind the buildings. The sun got in her hair and somehow under her skin, kind of, and it did a wonderful thing to her. She looked so young for a moment that I saw Mama in her, both of them beautiful New Orleans ladies.

The racket cut loose again, nearer now, and a pack of men came running down the alley, about three dozen whites chasing two coloreds. One of the whites was blowing a bugle—tan tidy, tan civvy, tan tidy—like the white folks do when they go fox hunting in the movies or Virginia. I looked down, quick, to see if Old Gramma had enough sense to come inside, and I guess she did because she wasn't there. The two coloreds ran between two buildings, the whites ran after them, and then the alley was quiet again. Old Gramma stepped out, and I watched her stoop and pick up the brown bag that she had dropped before.

Another big noise made her drop it again. A whole smear of men swarmed out of the used-car lot and came galloping down the alley like wild buffaloes. Old Gramma scooted inside our building and the brown bag stayed there in the alley. This time I couldn't believe my eyes; I saw what I thought I'd never see; I saw what us kids had been waiting to see ever since the riot broke out—a white man that was fixing to get himself nice and killed. A white man running—running, God Almighty, from about a million coloreds. And he was the one with the tan-tidy bugle, too. I hoped the coloreds would do the job up right.

The closer the white man came the worse it got for him, because the alley comes to a dead end when it hits our building. All at once— I don't know why—I was praying for that fool white man with the bugle to get away. But I didn't think he had a Chinaman's chance, the way he was going now, and maybe that's what made me pray for him.

Then he did a smart thing. He whipped the bugle over his shoulder, like you do with a horseshoe for good luck, and it hit the first colored behind him smack in the head, knocking him out, and that slowed up the others. The white man turned into the junk yard behind the furniture warehouse and the Victory Ballroom. Another smart thing, if he used his head. The space between the warehouse and the Victory is just wide enough for a man to run through. It's a long piece to the street, but if he made it there, he'd be safe probably.

The long passageway must've looked too narrow to him, though, because the fool came rushing around the garage next to our building. For a moment he was the only one in the alley. The coloreds had followed him through the junk yard and probably got themselves all tangled up in garbage cans and rusty bed springs and ash piles. But the white man was a goner just the same. In a minute they'd be coming for him for real. He'd have to run the length of the alley again to get away and the coloreds have got the best legs.

Then Old Gramma opened our back door and saved him.

I was very glad for the white man, until suddenly I remembered poor Mama all broken to pieces on the bed, and then I was sorry Old Gramma did it. The next moment I was glad again that she did. I understood now I did not care one way or the other about the white man. Now I was thinking of Mama—not of myself. I did not see what difference it could make to Mama if the white man lived or died. It only had something to do with us and him.

Then I got hold of a funny idea. I told myself the trouble is somebody gets cheated or insulted or killed and everybody else tries to make it come out even by cheating and insulting and killing the cheaters and insulters and killers. Only they never do. I did not think they ever would. I told myself that I had a very big idea there, and when the riot was over I would go to the public library and sit in the reading room and think about it. Or I would speak to Old Gramma about it, because it seemed like she had the same big idea and like she had it a long time, too.

The doctor was standing by me at the window all the time. He said nothing about what Old Gramma did, and now he stepped away from the window and so did I. I guess he felt the same way I did about the white man and that's why he stepped away from the window. The big idea again. He was afraid the coloreds down below would yell up at us, did we see the white man pass by. The coloreds were crazy mad all right. One of them had the white man's bugle and he banged on our door with it. I was worried Old Gramma had forgot to lock it and they might walk right in, and that would be the end of the white man and the big idea.

But Old Gramma pulled another fast one. She ran out into the alley and pointed her old yellow finger in about three wrong directions. In a second the alley was quiet and empty, except for Old Gramma. She walked slowly over against our building, where somebody had kicked the brown bag, and picked it up.

Old Gramma brought the white man right into our room, told him to sit down, and poured herself a cup of hot water. She sipped it and said the white man could leave whenever he wanted to, but it might be better to wait a bit. The white man said he was much obliged, he hated to give us any trouble, and, "Oh, oh, is somebody sick over there?" when he saw Mama, and that he'd just been passing by when a hundred nig . . . —when he was attacked.

Old Gramma sipped her hot water. The doctor turned away from the window and said, "Here they come again," took another look, and said, "No, they're going back." He went over to Mama and held her wrist. I couldn't tell anything about her from his face. She was sleeping just the same. The doctor asked the white man, still standing, to sit down. Carrie only opened her eyes once and closed them. She hadn't changed her position in the good chair. Brother George and the baby stood in a corner with their eyes on the white man. The baby's legs buckled then—she'd only been walking about a week— and she collapsed softly to the floor. She worked her way up again without taking her eyes off the white man. He even looked funny and out of place to me in our room. I guess the man for the rent and Father Egan were the only white people come to see us since I could remember; and now it was only the man for the rent since Father Egan died.

The doctor asked the white man did he work or own a business in this neighborhood. The white man said, "No," glancing down at his feet; no, he just happened to be passing by when he was suddenly attacked like he said before. The doctor told Old Gramma she might wash Mama's face and neck again with warm water.

There was noise again in the alley—windows breaking and fences being pushed over. The doctor said to the white man, "You could leave now; it's a white mob this time; you'd be safe."

"No," the white man said, "I should say not; I wouldn't be seen with them; they're as bad as the others almost."

"It is quite possible," the doctor said.

Old Gramma asked the white man if he would like a cup of tea.

"Tea? No," he said, "I don't drink tea; I didn't know you drank it."

"I didn't know you knew her," the doctor said, looking at Old Gramma and the white man.

"You colored folks, I mean," the white man said, "Americans, I mean. Me, I don't drink tea—always considered it an English drink and bad for the kidneys."

The doctor did not answer. Old Gramma brought him a cup of tea.

And then Daddy came in. He ran over to Mama and fell down on his knees like he was dead—like seeing Mama with her arm broke and her chest so pushed in killed him on the spot. He lifted his face from the bed and kissed Mama on the lips; and then, Daddy, I could see, was crying—the strongest man in the world was crying with tears in his big dark eyes and coming down the side of his big hard face. Mama called him her John Henry sometimes and there he was, her John Henry, the strongest man, black or white, in the whole damn world, crying.

He put his head down on the bed again. Nobody in the room moved until the baby toddled over to Daddy and patted him on the ear like she wanted to play the games those two make up with her little hands and his big ears and eyes and nose. But Daddy didn't move or say anything, if he even knew she was there, and the baby got a blank look in her eyes and walked away from Daddy and sat down, plump, on the floor across the room, staring at Daddy and the white man, back and forth. Daddy and the white man.

Daddy got up after a while and walked very slowly across the room and got himself a drink of water at the sink. For the first time he noticed the white man in the room. "Who's he?" he said. "Who's he?" None of us said anything. "Who the hell's he?" Daddy wanted to know, thunder in his throat like there always is when he's extra mad or happy.

The doctor said the white man was Mr. German, and went over to Daddy and told him something in a low voice.

"Innocent! What's he doing in this neighborhood then?"

Daddy said, loud as before. "What's an innocent white man doing in this neighborhood now? Answer me that!" He looked at all of us in the room and none of us that knew what the white man was doing in this neighborhood wanted to explain to Daddy. Old Gramma and the doctor and me—none of us that knew—would tell.

"I was just passing by," the white man said, "as they can tell you."

The scared way he said it almost made me laugh. Was this a white man, I asked myself. Alongside Daddy's voice the white man's sounded plain foolish and weak—a little old tug squeaking at a big ocean liner about the right of way. Daddy seemed to forget all about him and began asking the doctor a lot of questions about Mama in a hoarse whisper I couldn't hear very well. Daddy's face got harder and harder and it didn't look like he'd ever crack a smile or shed a tear or anything soft again. Just hard, it got, hard as four spikes.

Old Gramma came and stood by Daddy's side and said she had called the priest when she was downstairs a while ago getting some candles. She was worried that the candles weren't blessed ones. She opened the brown bag then, and that's what was inside—two white candles. I didn't know grocery stores carried them.

Old Gramma went to her room and took down the picture of the Sacred Heart all bleeding and put it on the little table by Mama's bed and set the candles in sticks on each side of it. She lit the candles and it made the Sacred Heart, punctured by the wreath of thorns, look bloodier than ever, and made me think of that song, "To Jesus' Heart All Burning," the kids sing at Our Saviour's on Sundays.

The white man went up to the doctor and said, "I'm a Catholic, too." But the doctor didn't say anything back, only nodded. He probably wasn't one himself, I thought; not many of the race are. Our family wouldn't be if Old Gramma and Mama didn't come from New Orleans, where Catholics are thicker than flies or Baptists.

Daddy got up from the table and said to the white man, "So help me God, mister, I'll kill you in this room if my wife dies!" The baby started crying and the doctor went to Daddy's side and turned him

349

away from the white man, and it wasn't hard to do because now Daddy was kind of limp and didn't look like he remembered anything about the white man or what he said he'd do to him if Mama . . . or anything.

"I'll bet the priest won't show up," Daddy said.

"The priest will come," Old Gramma said. "The priest will always come when you need him; just wait." Her old lips were praying in French.

I hoped he would come like Old Gramma said, but I wasn't so sure. Some of the priests weren't much different from anybody else. They knew how to keep their necks in. Daddy said to Mama once if you only wanted to hear about social justice you could turn on the radio or go to the nearest stadium on the Fourth of July, and there'd be an old white man in a new black suit saying it was a good thing and everybody ought to get some, and if they'd just kick in more they might and, anyway, they'd be saved. One came to Our Saviour's last year, and Father Egan said this is our new assistant and the next Sunday our new assistant was gone—poor health. But Daddy said he was transferred to a church in a white neighborhood because he couldn't stand to save black souls. Father Egan would've come a-flying, riot or no riot, but he was dead now and we didn't know much about the one that took his place.

Then he came, by God; the priest from Our Saviour's came to our room while the riot was going on. Old Gramma got all excited and said over and over she knew the priest would come. He was kind of young and skinny and pale, even for a white man, and he said, "I'm Father Crowe," to everybody in the room and looked around to see who was who.

The doctor introduced himself and said Old Gramma was Old Gramma, Daddy was Daddy, we were the children, that was Mr. German, who was just passing by, and over there was poor Mama. He missed Old Gramma's old woman friend; I guess he didn't know what to call her. The priest went over and took a look at Mama and nodded to the doctor and they went into Old Gramma's room together. The priest had a little black bag, too, and he took it with him. I suppose he was getting ready to give Mama Extreme Unction. I didn't think they would wake her up for Confession or Holy Communion; she was so weak and needed the rest.

Daddy got up from the table mad as a bull and said to the white man, "Remember what I said, mister."

"But why me?" the white man asked, "Just because I'm white?"

Daddy looked over at Mama on the bed and said, "Yeah, just because you're white; yeah, that's why. . . ." Old Gramma took Daddy by the arm and steered him over to the table again and he sat down.

The priest and the doctor came out of Old Gramma's room, and right away the priest faced the white man, like they'd been talking about him in Old Gramma's room, and asked him why he didn't go home. The white man said he'd heard some shouting in the alley a while ago that didn't sound so good to him and he didn't think it was safe yet and that was why.

"I see," the priest said.

"I'm a Catholic too, Father," the white man said.

"That's the trouble," the priest said.

The priest took some cotton from his little black bag, dipped his fingers in holy oil, and made the Sign of the Cross on Mama's eyes, nose, ears, mouth, and hands, rubbing the oil off with the cotton, and said prayers in Latin all the time he was doing it.

"I want you all to kneel down now," the priest said, "and we'll say a rosary. But we mustn't say it too loud because she is sleeping."

We all knelt down except the baby and Carrie. Carrie said she'd never kneel down to God again. "Now Carrie," Old Gramma said, almost crying. She told Carrie it was for poor Mama and wouldn't Carrie kneel down if it was for poor Mama?

"No!" Carrie said. "It must be a white God too!" Then she began crying and she did kneel down after all.

Even the white man knelt down and the doctor and the old woman friend of Old Gramma's, a solid Baptist if I ever saw one, and we all said the rosary of the five sorrowful mysteries.

Afterwards the white man said to the priest, "Do you mind if I leave when you do, Father?" The priest didn't answer, and the white man said, "I think I'll be leaving now, Father. I wonder if you'd be going my way?"

The priest finally said, "All right, all right, come along. You won't be the first one to hide behind a Roman collar."

The white man said, "I'm sure I don't know what you mean by that, Father." The priest didn't hear him, I guess, or want to explain, because he went over to Mama's bed.

The priest knelt once more by Mama and said a prayer in Latin out loud and made the Sign of the Cross over Mama: *In nomine Patris et Filii et Spiritus Sancti.* He looked closer at Mama and motioned to the doctor. The doctor stepped over to the bed, felt Mama's wrist, put his head to her chest, where it wasn't pushed in, and stood up slowly.

Daddy and all of us had been watching the doctor when the priest motioned him over, and now Daddy got up from the table, kicking the chair over he got up so fast, and ran to the bed. Shaking all over, he sank to his knees, and I believe he must've been crying again, although I thought he never would again and his head was down and I couldn't see for sure.

I began to get an awful bulging pain in my stomach. The doctor left the bed and grabbed the white man by the arm and was taking him to the door when Daddy jumped up, like he knew where they were going, and said, "Wait a minute, mister!"

The doctor and the white man stopped at the door. Daddy walked draggily over to them and stood in front of the white man, took a deep breath, and said in the stillest kind of whisper, "I wouldn't touch you." That was all. He moved slowly back to Mama's bed and his big shoulders were sagged down like I never saw them before.

Old Gramma said, "Jesus!" and stumbled down on her knees by Mama. Then the awful bulging pain in my stomach exploded, and I knew that Mama wasn't just sleeping now, and I couldn't breathe for a long while, and then when I finally could I was crying like the baby and brother George, and so was Carrie.

Reading for Comprehension

1. What do the whites do to the black man who is shot in the leg?
2. What has happened to the boy's mother?
3. What does the doctor say about setting the mother's broken bones?
4. How was the white man saved?
5. What does the white man tell the doctor and the priest about his religious affiliation?
6. What did the priest do for the boy's mother?
7. What does the boy's father tell the white man when the white man is at the door preparing to leave?

Reading for Understanding

1. One of the signs of the Church is that it is catholic (universal). How does the story illustrate this doctrine?
2. What does the priest say to the white man when the white man informs him that he is a Catholic? What is the meaning of the priest's answer?
3. Morality deals with social evil as well as individual sin. How does "The Trouble" illustrate the point that individuals share in the sins of society?

Activity

Tell three ways in which the word "trouble" is used to describe the events that occur in this story. What is the meaning of the priest's comments about Catholics and the trouble?

Right Judgment and Action

"On Opening a Page in *Time Magazine*"
Cothrai Gogan

> "There is one thing left for you: sell all that you have
> and distribute it to the poor, and you will have a
> treasure in heaven. Then come, follow me."
> **—Luke 18: 22**

Author Background
Fr. Cothrai Gogan is a Holy Ghost priest of Irish descent who ministered for many years in Africa. During his years as a missionary he witnessed the horrors of war, famine, and genocide. Fr. Gogan recorded the impact of these experiences in several books of poetry: *God Knows: A Journal of Sorrow* (1971), *Poems of Prayer* (1975), *Come Deaf Now Hear* (1978), and *Something Else* (1988).

Before the Reading
Civil wars taking place on the continent of Africa during the 1960s and 1970s were among the causes of mass starvation of thousands of people. During that period, newspapers and magazines were filled with pictures of emaciated men and women and malnourished children. In the following poem, Cothrai Gogan reflects on the image shock that results when one two-page spread of an American magazine advertises a life of ease and luxury on one side, while the facing page portrays a horrific image of famine.

On Opening a Page in Time Magazine
Sunshine beauty bathed in the tumbling surf
of warm south seas, breathing the full clear air
of distant oceans, radiating health and grace
from your soft cosmetic skin. . . . But why do you

flaunt your grace and health and beauty
before the despairing eyes of those poor refugees
on the opposite page? Shaming their near-nakedness
their dried-up skin with bones protruding, ribs
countable, their eyes already dead. . . . and you,
the sparkle in your glad youthful eyes reflects
the blue-quick-silver sheen of smooth summer waves. . . .
so hateful now! so shameful now! for how can you be so
    happy
amid such gross unhappiness? (only a quick nightflight
    away
in the plane you advertise so. . . .what shall I say? So
gracefully or so barefacedly? or simply so forgetfully?)
Why don't you take a flight yourself?
Forget the clump of rich young men, bronzed, well-fed
who gaze at you with such interest and appreciation
from the other pages. Long cigarettes hang from their
    languid lips.
Long cars await behind. (This is not a sales promotion.)
Forget them all and stretch your hand across the page!
Discover for yourself the thrill to see a smile
dawn again in the eyes of a once-starved child.
What new joys you would discover in giving just a little
of your own to those poor sad old men.
How peacefully they'd die holding your soft long fingers
in their knotted claws, despairing hands now full of hope
convinced by you that amid the hate and ugliness and fear
of all those long horrible years—that beauty still exists!
Love is! And happiness is possible!

Turn the page. And take that dead child from
his ravaged father's arms. Or must he carry it without
    you forever?

Reading for Comprehension

1. What words does the poet use to criticize the young girl in the magazine advertisement?

2. How does Gogan describe the refugees pictured on the page opposite the girl?

3. What does he ask the girl to do with the dead child?

Reading for Understanding

1. When have you encountered a vivid contrast between poverty and materialism?

2. Read the Gospel account of the man with many possessions (Lk 18:18–25). In what way is this poem a contemporary commentary on that gospel passage?

Activities

1. Search through several popular pictorial magazines and make a collage of pictures from these magazines that show, on one hand, the materialism and consumerism of modern America and, on the other hand, illustrate the misery and pain of the poor of this world.

2. Locate and listen to the song "Driven to Tears" written by Sting and performed by the Police. How does the message of the song compare with the message of this poem?

Right Judgment and Action

Salvador Witness:
The Life and Calling of Jean Donovan

Ana Carrigan

Actually what I've learned here is that death is not the worst evil.
We live with these evils, hate, manipulation, selfishness.
We look death in the face every day. But the cause of the death
is evil. That's what we have to wrestle and fight against.

—Sr. Ita Ford

Author Background

Ana Carrigan is a contemporary journalist and documentary filmmaker who has focused on human rights in El Salvador, Colombia, and other areas of Latin America. She has written for the *New York Times*, the *Boston Globe*, the *Nation*, and the *Irish Times*. She is the author of *The Palace of Justice: A Columbian Tragedy* and she directed the film, *Roses in December*, which explored the themes covered in her book, *Salvador Witness: The Life and Calling of Jean Donovan*.

Before the Reading

Four American missionaries—Maryknoll nuns Sr. Maura Clark and Sr. Ita Ford, Ursuline nun Sr. Dorothy Kazel, and lay missionary volunteer Jean Donovan—were known as the "rescue squad" by other Americans working in El Salvador during the period of intense political fighting during the 1970s and 1980s. Despite facing the threat of death, these women risked their lives to assist and protect the peasant refugees who were caught in the civil war between left-wing revolutionaries and right-wing militarists. On December 2, 1980, all four women were all murdered by members of the El Salvadoran national guard. The following selections, drawn from Carrigan's book, portray the events leading to their deaths, a witness's statement of how they were murdered, and reflections on the aftermath of the discovery of their bodies.

Salvador Witness: The Life and Calling of Jean Donovan

Part II: July–September 1980

In the fall of 1980, Sister Ita Ford wrote to a friend:

> What do we really do?
>
> 1. We continue to seek out dialogue and collaboration with humanitarian groups.
>
> 2. We drive priests to outlying country districts.
>
> 3. We drive food to contacts who will get it to people hiding from the security forces or the popular groups.
>
> 4. We transport refugees and clothes to different hiding places.

In her diary, Jean began recording the changed focus of her activities:

> July 26: Two children and a few others shot in Chalatenango. The others died. Got the children out to San Salvador on Monday. 18-year-old killed in the hospital. Nuns and priests threatened and fired on during Mass in Chalatenango. Man killed near the church in Santa Cruz.
>
> August 5: Meeting with the International Red Cross. Saw 3,000 people on the river border with 17 weapons keeping Orden at bay. Have chosen to die because they have arms. 200 people say they want to come down for the Red Cross bus on Friday.

August 6: Maryknollers here are having an area meeting at the house (Laragoza) but Carla was very late arriving this night. Was trying to arrange for 300 to come down to Red Cross bus.

August 7: Chris and I drive up to Chalatenango to stay with Carla for the night because we leave at dawn for Dulce de Maria. Ron has 23 children in his house to be evacuated.

August 8: No gas in Chalatenango. Change for Ephraim's jeep. Not much gas. Fly to Dulce de Maria. Learn 26 have been killed on Guardia side. Pack kids up in jeep and leave. At entrance to Chalate I'm out of gas. Transfer kids and go for gas. Guardia calls to talk to Carla. They are moving 90 families into Ron's church. No one has wheels. International Red Cross takes 31 people (3 women, the rest kids).

August 9: Ita trying to arrange transportation for a kid shot in Chalatenango hospital. Four families talk to Carla for relocation. Five bodies found on the road to the airport.

August 13: Talk to Carla and Ita. Violence bad in Chalatenango. They took food to 50 people in Ron Potter's house. 40 soldiers killed in a truck in San Antonio Abad.

August 14: Helicopters, trucks and soldiers very active in Chalatenango.

"Chalatenango is absolutely civil war at the moment," Jean told Crowley. "They've got bodies lying all over—no one can bury them because they get shot at if they try. Some nuns were up there. Orden just really turned on the nuns. They got a message to leave in six days

359

or you're going to be killed, and they burned their jeep to prove it. So they believed it, and left. People don't have liberty to do anything. They have to take a side. And it's very hard not to take a particular side. It's so much harder to fight for your liberty in a nonviolent way than it is with a gun. It's funny—people very close to me have been killed now, and yet I still think that. So I'm starting to think maybe I really do believe it. At the moment, the only nonviolent voice in the whole country is the Church, and I think they have to remain in a neutral position."

That neutral position was a very lonely one. It was also, inevitably, misunderstood, misinterpreted and fatally lacking in any credibility among the partisans of the Right. Yet they held fast to their commitment to all of the victims of the violence—that desolate population of old men and women, young girls and boys, mere children themselves, carrying the smaller children in their arms as they wandered the roads and mountain paths, dazed with fear and exhaustion and weakened by hunger. Carla and Ita, Jean and Dorothy never stopped to ask which side had driven these shattered people from their homes. They just pitched in and found them food, transport, and shelter in one or another of the refugee camps that were expanding daily under the jurisdiction of the archdiocese. And when Ita learned that an eight-year-old boy, wounded in a fire fight between the army and the guerrillas, had been machine-gunned as he lay in his hospital bed early one morning, she and Carla instantly became involved in rescuing two other wounded "guerrillas"—eleven and twelve years old respectively—from the hospital, and made arrangements for them to receive shelter and medical care in a safe house belonging to a middle-class Salvadoran friend in the capital.

The women knew they were vulnerable and defenseless in this no man's land where they had chosen to carry on their work. They understood, only too well, the extent to which they were exposed daily to the hatred and the scrutiny of their enemies. The young priest for whom Carla drove had been personally threatened, and when she would drive him up into the hills to say Mass for the fugitive communities in one of the contested areas, they were both perfectly aware of the risks. Carla described how the young priest would ask her to step on the gas on some mountain road that even the commercials for Toyota jeeps did not adequately portray. For even as they drove past some Orden lookout post, it never occurred to either of them to turn back. Retreat from the people who needed them and who were counting on their support was never even an option.

In their response to a situation they recognized to be growing daily more insane, more irrationally violent, the women were being drawn always closer to the extreme edge of danger without any safety net in sight. They had no map to guide them, no master plan for the future—only their total trust that this was what they were being called upon to do. Each day they put themselves and their lives on the line in the pursuit of a shared faith in what it meant to live as a true follower of Christ. That was all they had to sustain them—that and their friendship and sense of humor. Like Peter, stranded in the Sea of Galilee, Carla was able to tell her friend that in spite of everything she was glad she had jumped out of the boat in answer to God's call. She described how even as she felt herself sinking, even as a part of her began to scream in terror, she could feel herself being held; she knew she was not alone.

"You say you don't want anything to happen to me," Ita wrote her younger sister Rene. "I'd prefer it that way myself—but I don't see that we have control over the forces of madness, and if you choose to enter into other peoples' suffering, or to love others, you at least have to consent in some way to the possible consequences." Among themselves they had grown accustomed to looking those possible consequences in the face. To her sister Ita explained: "Actually what I've learned here is that death is not the worst evil. We live with these evils, hate, manipulation, selfishness. We look death in the face every day. But the cause of the death is evil. That's what we have to wrestle and fight against."

They had always known that the rejection of death, its exclusion from life, diminished and impoverished life itself. Now that death had

invaded their lives, now that its reality faced them daily, they had begun to experience amid all the destruction and evil, the truth of the
age-old paradox: acceptance of death, the admission of its inevitabil-
ity, not only made it easier for them to carry on with their work, it had
given their lives new meaning, richness and intensity.

"What I want to say, some of it isn't too jolly birthday talk, but
it's real," Ita wrote to a favorite niece about to celebrate her sixteenth
birthday. "Yesterday I stood looking down at a sixteen-year-old who
had been killed a few hours earlier. I know a lot of kids even younger
who are dead. This is a terrible time in El Salvador for youth. A lot of
idealism and commitment are getting snuffed out here now.

"The reasons why so many people are being killed are quite
complicated—yet there are a few simple strands. One is that many
people have found a meaning to live, sacrifice, and even die. And,
whether their life-span is sixteen years, sixty, or ninety, for them their
life has had a purpose. In many ways, they are fortunate people.

"Brooklyn is not passing through the drama of El Salvador but
some things hold true wherever one is—and at whatever price. What
I'm saying is I hope you come to find that which gives life a deep
meaning for you. Something worth living for—maybe even worth
dying for—something that energizes you, enthuses you and enables
you to keep moving ahead."

Chapter xi
They Were Subversives
Questioned about the accusations made against him, the accused
National Guardsman, Joaquin Contreras Palacios, twenty-five, mar-
ried, recalled taking part in the murder of four women on the night of
December 2, 1980, and stated that the following was what occurred:

> On December 2, 1980, he was on guard duty at the
> International Airport in El Salvador. At about 6 p.m. his
> immediate supervisor, Sub-Sergeant Colindres Alemdn,
> the officer in charge of the post, ordered him to put

on civilian clothes. Guardsmen Francisco Orlando Contreras, Jose Roberto Moreno Canjura, Salvador Rivera Franco and Daniel Canales Ramirez were ordered to do the same. Colindres Alemdn also put on civilian clothes and told the aforementioned guardsmen that they were going out on assignment, but did not specify where. He also ordered these men to take their G-3 rifles and appropriate ammunition. At 7 p.m. Colindres Alemdn accompanied by the witness and other guardsmen in civilian clothes got into a jeep that belonged to the post and started out of the airport. When they got to the control booth, Colindres Alemdn got out to give some orders to the guards on duty there. He then got back in the jeep and they continued on.

When they reached the vicinity of the first tollbooth, Colindres ordered the jeep to halt. Everyone got out and took up separate positions on the road. Approximately twenty-five minutes later, a white microbus approached and was given the order to stop. The witness observed that there were four women in the vehicle. The witness and the others got into the microbus and began driving.

When they reached the crossing with the road to San Pedro Nonualco, Colindres Alemdn told the driver to take that road. After they had gone about six kilometers they came to a turn off onto a secondary road and Colindres told the driver to go down there. The witness noted that it was a deserted area.

Then Colindres told all of the guardsmen to fire their weapons and kill the four women. The order was obeyed by the witness and the others in the jeep. The witness recalled that Colindres Alemdn had to use the rifle of one of the guardsmen because his own rifle had jammed. Before they killed the women the witness and the others abused them sexually.

When it was all over Colindres said he had done it this way because the women were subversives.

—From the confession of the accused, as witnessed, heard in full, read, ratified and signed by the accused at National Guard Headquarters, San Salvador, 8:00 a.m. , on February 9, 1982.

The Aftermath

"We parked the cars and went into the field, and there was this campesino who was telling Paul that yes, he lived there on the property, and two nights before he had heard shots, and on the next morning, the milkman who was delivering milk had come along and found these bodies. And then the National Guard had arrived and ordered the people to bury them. The grave was just inside the fence, beside the road, and there was a very rustic cross made of two pieces of twigs that the people had placed over the grave to mark it. So White said, 'Four women, look like gringos, this has got to be them. We've got to dig them up.'

"But the campesinos were afraid. They told us that without permission from the justice of the peace they would be breaking the law. So two of the embassy security men went into town to fetch the justice of the peace, and they brought him back, and he showed us the entry in his book where the burial had been reported and gave permission to dig them up.

"By the time we started to open the grave it was twelve or one o'clock, and there were press and people all over the place. . . . They dug quite a way down, and the thought occurred to me that we were on a wild goose chase, that there had to be some reason that the women had not been able to contact us. . . . Well, when they reached a depth of I guess three feet, one of the diggers signaled us over: he had uncovered what turned out to be Jean's hip. All you could see were the blue jeans and just a section of her hip. So then we said to proceed. And we stepped back. And that's when the thing just turned into a total nightmare.

"They kept digging. And the first thing I knew was, they pulled Jean up with ropes. They had a rope around her shoulders and one around her legs, and they pulled her up over the edge of the grave, they pulled her body out, and pulled her with the ropes like they were hauling a sack of alfalfa or something, across the dirt, across the weeds, away from the grave; and the whole time they were pulling her I was thinking to myself. Oh how awful! They're going to scratch her face, you know, they're going to mar her skin. Later I realized—what a dumb thought. She was dead. It didn't hurt her. And they were not doing it out of disrespect, they were just doing a job, unearthing a dead body and pulling it away from the grave.

"So they laid her out. She was the first one. And she was so disfigured, you really couldn't be sure it was Jean because her face was so disfigured. It appears the bullet had collapsed the bone structure of her face and she was unrecognizable.

"Then they proceeded to pull the next body out—I think it was Maura. They pulled her over to the side and some of the people came over and broke branches off the trees and covered the two bodies so that people couldn't stare at them. I remember the stench was terrible. Oh God, it was awful. They pulled up Dorothy. She was dressed in jeans but she had her jeans on backward. Subsequently, the campesinos told us that they found them without their jeans on; they had put their jeans back on but put hers on backward. And then they brought up Ita. Of course Ita was a very tiny person, it was very easy for them to bring her up. It was like practically bringing up a child. But her body was crumbled and broken. Jean and Ita were very badly bruised; the least was Maura. Maura and Dorothy. Then they laid them all out there and the people covered the rest of the bodies with branches.

"I remember, somewhere during the whole time they were digging them up they were throwing things out of the grave, and at one point I walked over and picked up one of these things just to see what it was, and it was one of their panties. And the whole thing just hit me with disgust, what had happened to them. I could not believe I had seen these women, well two of them anyway, just two days before. And they were so alive, and so vibrant . . . and then here was testimony to the fact that they had been through a terrible experience. All the evidence was around to testify to that fact.

I remember at one point we knelt, I was kneeling beside Maddie, and we said some prayers. I don't know whether we prayed for them or for those who were responsible for this terrible thing. . . ."

In keeping with Maryknoll tradition Ita and Maura were buried among the people for whom they worked and died in Chalatenango. There, in the small, overgrown and overcrowded country cemetery that lies at the bottom of the hill leading into the town, their bodies were laid to rest beside Carla's on Saturday, December 6.

On the same day, the bodies of Jean and Dorothy were flown home to their families in the States. But not before the people of La Libertad had an opportunity to say their own goodbyes. On the evening of Friday, December 5, after the celebration of the joint funeral Mass for all four in San Salvador, Paul, Chris and Ken brought Jean and Dorothy back to La Libertad one final time. A wake was held through the night in their own parish church. At 4:30 the following morning, Paul celebrated a second funeral Mass. When it was ended, and Jean and Dorothy's coworkers lifted their caskets and prepared to carry them from the church to the waiting limousine, the people inside the crowded church lined up to take their places. As the two caskets passed through the crowd, from hand to hand, from shoulder to shoulder, the congregation climbed onto the benches and started to applaud.

Outside in the early dawn the applause was picked up by the waiting crowd. In the square beyond the church, along the street outside the windows of Jean's apartment, and down the narrow streets of the port, the people of La Libertad and Zaragoza, of Santa Cruz and the surrounding communities, had arrived to line the route leading out of town to the airport road. They loaded the caskets. Then the small cavalcade of vehicles started out along the final stretch of Jean's and Dorothy's Salvadoran journey, moving slowly through the dense lines of defiant, triumphant applause.

Reading for Comprehension

1. What did Jean Donovan tell Father Crowley about the situation in Chalatenago?
2. What did Sr. Ita Ford learn about the fate of an eight-year-old boy who had been wounded?
3. What sustained the women in the midst of all this violence and death?
4. What did Sr. Ita hope for her niece who lived in Brooklyn?
5. How were the four women slain?
6. What did the congregation do at the conclusion of the funeral mass for Sr. Dorothy Kazel and Jean Donovan?

Reading for Understanding

1. What did Jean Donovan mean when she said, "It's so much harder to fight for your liberty in a nonviolent way than it is with a gun"?
2. What did Sr. Ita Ford mean when she wrote to her niece that the young and older people who had been slain were in many ways fortunate?
3. A Christian martyr is someone who dies as a witness to his or her belief in Christ and his Church. What values of Christ and the Church did these women act as witnesses for?
4. What did Carla mean when she compared herself to St. Peter when he jumped out of the boat to meet Christ who was walking on the water (Mt 15:22–33)?

Activity

Archbishop Oscar Romero spoke out against the violence in El Salvador. He was a true shepherd trying to protect his flock. Because of his stance against violence, he was shot to death while saying Mass in San Salvador on March 24, 1980. View and review the film *Romero*. Compare it to the story of Jean Donovan and the other women missionaries.

HOW WE SHOULD LIVE

(Life in Christ)

SEEING WITH THE ARTIST

Use an Internet search engine to locate the following artwork. Take your time to view each piece in combination with the background information provided below. Reflect on how the focus of the paintings apply to living a life in Jesus Christ. In a journal or notebook, write your impressions of each piece. Also see Activities 1 and 2 on pages 379–380.

The Paintings

Adam and Eve Banished from Paradise—Domenichino (1581–1641)

A frightened and cowardly Adam is portrayed blaming Eve for the sin that has led to their expulsion. An interesting aspect of the painting is the attitude of the animals who look on Adam and Eve with sorrow because they understand the consequences of their sin: The effects will spread to all of nature. Henceforth, humans will have to fight nature to gain their livelihood and not live in the harmony that existed in the Garden of Eden.

Adam and Eve Driven Out of the Garden of Eden —Caspar Luiken (1672–1708)

This is an engraving that depicts the anger of the hosts of heaven at the sin of Adam and Eve. An angel with a flaming sword expels a frightened Eve and a weeping Adam from paradise.

The Scream—Edvard Munch (1863–1944)

This is one of the iconic images of modern art. The horrific expression of a man screaming shows in visual terms the isolation and terror of man alienated from God. He represents a man who has been cast out of paradise.

Cain and Abel—Pietro Novelli (1603–1647)

The effects of the Original Sin are immediately shared with the sons of Adam and Eve. This painting shows Cain being driven away by God as the body of his slain brother, Abel, lies in the foreground of the painting. The hideous gash on Abel's neck highlights the monstrosity of Cain's sin. The representation of God, his hand raised in judgment as he emerges from an ominous cloud, can be understood as a visual representation of the voice of conscience.

The Return of the Prodigal Son—Rembrandt van Rijn (1606–1669)

This is a famous representation of the scene in the great parable of the Prodigal Son when the sinful son kneels before his elderly father, who embraces him. This scene has been represented by many great painters, some of whom emphasize the repentance of the son. Note how this painting instead focuses on the merciful father and his joy at having his son returned to him.

The Return of the Prodigal Son—Sir Edward Poynter (1836–1919)

This is another perspective of the parable, in which our attention is drawn not so much to the figure of the father as it is to the face and crushed demeanor of the son who has wasted his father's resources.

Christ and the Woman Taken in Adultery
—Guercino (1591–1666)

This painting is based on the moment when Christ confronts the accusers of the woman taken in adultery (Jn 8:3–11). A youthful Christ stares intently at those who wish to have the woman killed. The women, her arm held harshly by a soldier, stands silently alongside Christ. The woman does not raise her eyes but seems to be looking into her own soul as she hears the accusations of her accusers and the forgiving response of Jesus.

LOOKING AT FILM

Moral dilemmas, lessons, and decisions form part of the plots of many films. Character development often reveals the personal and collective difficulties in choosing right from wrong. The following films portray the lives of those who live according to an inner light of goodness and justice. They also illustrate the effect of sin and corruption on the individual and society. Some of the films focus specifically on how humans deal with the issue of greed while balancing their own needs with the needs of the poor. Read the synopses of each film. Note the moral issue that is presented. Watch one or more of the films and complete the appropriate activities on page 380.

The Films

It's A Wonderful Life (1946)—Directed by Frank Capra

Rating: Vatican Top Forty-five Films

This classic film tells the story of an ordinary man (James Stewart) who is about to commit suicide because of his feelings of inadequacy and failure. An angel appears to him and allows him to see what would have happened to his friends, his family, and his community if he had never lived. The man sees that his goodness and his fair play have influenced all those about him and that, had he never lived, the world would be a poorer place.

Keys of the Kingdom (1944)—Directed by John Stahl

Rating: A-1

The life of a Scottish missionary priest (Gregory Peck) is explored as he labors to bring the message of Christ through word and deed to the people of China. This is a wonderful adaptation of A. J. Cronin's novel, which explores the peace and goodness that are brought into this world by the humble life of this simple priest.

Cool Hand Luke (1967)—Directed by Stuart Rosenberg

Rating: A-IV

Paul Newman portrays a prisoner serving a jail sentence on a southern chain gang. But the story has a much deeper level, as it recreates the story of the Life and Passion of Christ in a contemporary setting. The imagery and symbolism of the film point directly to the Life, Death, and Resurrection of Christ while pointing to the consequences of leading a Christian life in the midst of a rigid, rule-obsessed world.

Les Misérables (1935)—Directed by Richard Boleslawski
Les Misérables (1998)—Directed by Bille August

Ratings: A-II

Both of these films are splendid adaptations of the great novel by Victor Hugo. Recall that *Les Misérables* is the story of the redemption of a man who has served nineteen years as a prisoner for stealing food to feed his sister's children. Note that the 1935 version is in black and white.

The Tree of Wooden Clogs (1978)—Directed by Ermanno Olmi

Rating A-II, Vatican Top Forty-five Films

An Italian film with subtitles, *The Tree of Wooden Clogs* tells the story of peasant tenant farmers at the end of the nineteenth century as they cope with the needs of daily life while trying to understand the coming age of industrialization and de-Christianization that will destroy their way of life. This film is a masterpiece in its depiction of the organic and integrated quality of life of those who make their decisions in the light of the Gospel and Church teaching.

David and Lisa (1962)—Directed by Frank Perry

Rating: A-II

In this film, two emotionally disturbed teenagers reside at a psychiatric institution that cares for young people with severe emotional problems. The boy (Keir Dullea) is brilliant, analytic, and cold. His disorder is manifested in his horror at being physically touched. Even a casual touch by another person sends him into fits of rage. The girl (Janet Margolin) is a teenage schizophrenic who has withdrawn into her own private world. She speaks only in rhyme and nobody can communicate with her. Together these two young people enter into a loving friendship that results in each gaining emotional stability. This beautiful film is based on a true story and represents well what it means to "love your neighbor."

Au Revoir Les Enfants (1987)—Directed by Louis Malle

Rating: A-II, Vatican Top Forty-five Films

When director Louis Malle was a schoolboy, he witnessed an act of courage by a priest who taught in his school that he never forgot. In this French film with subtitles, he tells the story of a priest who attempts to hide three Jewish boys from the Nazis. It explores our moral obligations in the midst of an evil political system.

Cry, the Beloved Country (1951)—Directed by Zoltan Korda

Rating: A-II

This production of Alan Paton's novel tells a tale of murder, racial hatred, revenge, and reconciliation during the time of the Apartheid regime in South Africa. This film connects well with the meaning of the Beatitudes, especially regarding the poor in spirit and all people who depend fully on the grace of God for their lives.

On the Waterfront (1954)—Directed by Elia Kazan

Rating: Vatican Top Forty-five Films

One of the greatest American films, the plot involves a young longshoreman (brilliantly portrayed by Marlon Brando) who rises from a life of moral squalor and meaninglessness to a life of Christian heroism. The film explores such topics as the meaning of loyalty, the power of conscience, the evils of organized crime and the oppression of labor, and the power of redemptive love. Karl Malden's role as a parish priest who reluctantly cries out against evil is a beautiful rendition of the nature of the priesthood.

Chariots of Fire (1981)—Directed by Hugh Hudson

Rating: A-I

Set in the context of the 1924 Olympic Games in Paris, this film explores the courage of a young racing champion who refuses to run in the finals because it violates his understanding of the command not to do servile labor on the Sabbath day.

Gandhi *(1982)—Directed by Richard Attenborough*

Rating: A-II

The non-violent tactics of the great Indian leader, Gandhi, are shown in this film. Gandhi's actions resulted in independence, the unification of India, and the end of British colonialism. This film points out Christian opposition to violence and the need to use the highest moral principles to direct our actions in the social and political world.

Romero (1989)—Directed by John Duigan

Rating: A-II

This is the story of a contemporary martyr. This film depicts the final days and the assassination of Archbishop Oscar Romero of El Salvador. The Archbishop was killed by a sniper while he was celebrating Mass, in retaliation for his speaking out for the poor and oppressed and for denouncing the violent actions of the military leadership of the country.

The Mission (1986)—Directed by Roland Joffé

Rating: A-III, Vatican Top Forty-five Films

There are several important lessons in this film. On the one hand it shows the destruction of native South American culture at the hands of ruthless and rapacious Europeans in the 1750s. On the other hand, it depicts the non-violent Jesuit priest (Jeremy Irons) who attempts to preach the Gospel to the natives and to protect them from the greed and cruelty of their European overlords.

Crimes and Misdemeanors (1989) —Directed by Woody Allen

Rating: A-III

Director Woody Allen plays off themes found in the Dostoyevsky novel *Crime and Punishment* in order to explore the dimensions of moral decision-making in a world absent any objective order. The plot involves a successful doctor who, faced with having his affair disclosed to his wife, chooses to have his mistress murdered. Several subplots analyze other moral decision-making situations in a sophisticated and intelligent manner. Allen, like his hero, Charles Chaplin, is fascinated with the act of "seeing." Interestingly, the character of the rabbi, the only man who truly sees the value of moral good over moral evil, is blind. His blindness emphasizes that choosing between right and wrong is primarily a decision of the heart.

The Defiant Ones (1958)—Directed by Stanley Kramer

Rating: A-III

This film was made just at the start of the historic Civil Rights Movement and tells the story of two escaped convicts (Tony Curtis and Sidney Poitier), one white, the other black. They are chained together and therefore must travel together. Their journey to freedom is a metaphor for the need for us to see the humanity of every person rather than their color or creed, and that it is only by traveling together that we will achieve true social and personal liberty.

East of Eden (1955)—Directed by Elia Kazan

Rating: A-III

This brilliant film, a retelling of the story of Cain and Abel that is based on John Steinbeck's award-winning novel, relates the conflict between Cal (James Dean) and his brother Aron (Richard Davelos) in the house of their father, Adam (Raymond Massey). The film, whose title is taken from the book of Genesis, refers to Cain's expulsion from paradise and his making of a new home in the land "east of Eden." Two important questions the film poses are: What becomes of the murderer, Cain? Is he forever cast out of God's presence or does he have a possibility of forgiveness and redemption? *East of Eden* also contains an electrifying performance by the young American actor James Dean, in his first major performance. Dean, who died after making only three pictures, is still regarded today as an icon of the alienated and rebellious teenager.

La Dolce Vita (1960)—Directed by Federico Fellini

Rating: A-IV

La Dolce Vita is a complex, episodic work of art for mature viewers that follows a journalist (Marcello Maistroiani) as he spirals through the "sweet life" of drugs, sex, and celebrity in the Rome of the 1960s. The film portrays the despair that results from living a life totally dedicated to the pleasures of the senses. It is also rich in religious symbolism. The opening sequence shows a helicopter transporting a huge stone statue of Jesus out of the city. The image underscores the emptiness of the lives of those who have cast Jesus and his message out of their minds. The final scene shows the journalist, now exhausted and emptied by his hedonistic pursuits, too deafened to hear the call of grace.

The Little Foxes (1941)—William Wyler

Rating: A-II

This film explores the life of an early-twentieth-century southern family that is consumed by greed. Their obsessive quest for wealth makes them blind to the needs of others and results in the portrayal of the sheer ugliness of sin. Bette Davis plays the lead as the calculating sister who ends up defrauding her husband and her brothers. Her coldness and her growing isolation from humanity shows the price to be paid by those who focus on sin rather than grace as a way of life.

The Decalogue (1988)—Directed by Krzysztof Kieslowski

Rating: A-III, Vatican Top Forty-five Films

This is a series of films (with subtitles) produced for Polish television that deals with the contemporary meaning of the Ten Commandments.

Body and Soul (1947)—Directed by Robert Rossen
The Hustler (1961)—Directed by Robert Rossen

Ratings: A-II

Both of these films by the same director deal with the very American question of success: Who is a winner? What must one do to be a winner? Rossen uses the world of sport to examine the values that motivate us. In *Body and Soul*, a man (John Garfield) abandons his family, his girlfriend, and the values of his youth to become a championship boxer. At the conclusion of the film, he redeems himself by refusing to "throw" a fight. In *The Hustler*, a pool shark (Paul Newman) deserts old friends and his true love in order to succeed in the world of competitive billiards. The film explores sin and corruption while also allowing for the redemptive power of love and friendship.

LISTENING TO SACRED MUSIC

Traditionally, Catholic hymns were sung by the clergy, not the laity. This has changed, especially since the Second Vatican Council's encouragement of the laity to participate in singing at liturgy. There exists today a large collection of newly-composed music meant primarily for the laity. One of the purposes of hymns is to encourage us to practice the Beatitudes, to live Christ-like lives, and to have a passion for justice.

The Music
. . . .

Hymns

Below you will find hymns that call the Christian more deeply into conformity with the radical nature of the teachings of Christ. All these hymns are found in *Today's Missal—Music Issue 2008*, published by Oregon Catholic Press (OCP).

- "The Prayer of St. Francis," by Sebastian Temple
  This hymn expresses St. Francis's plea: "Where there is hatred, let me bring love. Where there is sorrow, joy; where there is injury, pardon!"

- "Let There Be Peace on Earth" by Sy Miller and Jill Jackson
  The lesson is given to bring about peace on earth by first bringing peace to ourselves, our families, and to our neighbors: "Let there be peace on earth and let it begin with me."

- "All That Is Hidden" by Bernadette Farrell
  A theme of the song is "If you would honor me, honor the least of these." This hymn encourages us to look for an encounter with God through our love of the lowly and by embracing the Cross of Christ.

- "Battle Hymn of the Republic" by Julia W. Howe
  This rousing and patriotic American hymn is a call to action in the cause of justice. It was the anthem of the abolitionists, who used it as a rallying cry against slavery during the Civil War era: "As He died to make us holy, let us die that all be free!"

ACTIVITIES

1. What is the main focus of the biblical story of the Prodigal Son (Lk 15:11–32)? Is it the repentance of the son or the merciful forgiveness and joy of the father? Answer that question after you look at

the paintings *The Return of the Prodigal Son,* by Rembrandt, and *The Return of the Prodigal Son*, by Sir Edward Poynter.

2. Compare the story of Cain and Abel as represented in the painting by Pietro Novelli to the story "The Sniper" by Liam O'Flaherty.

3. Redemption often comes as God's gift of friends who love us and stand up for us. How do Lisa (*David and Lisa*) and Abra *(East of Eden)* serve as sources of redemption for David and Cal?

4. Give four examples of how the film *Cool Hand Luke* presents Luke as a figure of Jesus—that is, someone who lives for others.

5. In the film, *On the Waterfront,* how is the anguish of Terry Malloy over his role in the death of a longshoreman similar to the anguish felt by the man who committed murder in the story "The Mysterious Stranger," by Dostoyevsky?

6. Name three themes in the film *The Mission* that are similar to the themes explored in the reading on the four churchwomen in El Salvador by Ana Carrigan.

7. Explore the similarity of the prophetic voices that denounce evil in the characters of the priests in the films *On the Waterfront* and *Au Revoir Les Enfants*.

8. What are the good qualities of George Bailey that make his life so meaningful in the film *It's a Wonderful Life*?

9. How is the process of moral destruction portrayed in the films *The Little Foxes, The Hustler*, and *Body and Soul*?

10. How do the artists represent the horror and misery of the loss of paradise in the painting, *The Scream*, by Munch, and the painting, *Adam and Eve Banished From Paradise*, by Domenichino?

11. Research more about the history of the patriotic hymn, "Battle Hymn of the Republic," and its author, Julia W. Howe. What Christian themes are presented in its lyrics?

UNIT 4

How We Talk to God and How God Talks to Us

(Prayer)

Our Response to God

The *Catechism of the Catholic Church* defines prayer in three parts: as God's gift; as covenant; and as communion (see *CCC*, 2558–2565). Jesus once said to the Samaritan woman he met at the well, "If you knew the gift of God and who is saying to you 'Give me a drink,' you would have asked him and he would have given you living water" (Jn 4:10). God loves us. He thirsts for our response to him. That response is prayer.

Where does prayer come from? The *Catechism* explains further that prayer comes from our heart, the deepest part of our being. The heart is also the place of our covenant with God. "Christian prayer is a covenant relationship between God and man in Christ" (*CCC*, 2564). In the Gospel of Mark, when Jesus' disciples ask him to teach them to pray, he responds with the beautiful words known today as "The Lord's Prayer." Like the disciples, we also wish to know how to pray. We desire a relationship and conversation with the heavenly Father who has made us for himself and who desires that we seek him with all our heart.

When we humbly pray, we establish a communion between God and ourselves. We grow in the presence of our Triune God—Father, Son, and Holy Spirit.

Introducing the Unit

This unit explores themes involving prayer, like the power and majesty of God, along with ways that prayer can connect us with him in a relationship of intimacy and simplicity. The Church has several aids to help us pray and to know and love God even better. Prayer can also help us to know ourselves better.

The Virgin Mary is a great source of inspiration and a model of faith. Holy icons or images are another way we can learn to focus our prayer.

We also pray at times of need, especially when we grieve an illness or a death of someone we love.

The following selections offer illustrations of the meaning of prayer and the prayer experiences of several individuals.

Connecting with God

- In Robert Hugh Benson's "In the Convent Chapel," we are given a mystical view of a nun at prayer; we are able to witness the power and majesty of God as he dialogues and interacts with this contemplative sister.

- In Leo Tolstoy's tale, "The Three Hermits," we see what it means to pray to God with simplicity of heart.

- John Henry Cardinal Newman, one of the greatest theologians of modern times, shares how one man has put into words the desire to discover the meaning of life in "March 7, 1848."

Inspirations to Prayer

- In John Fante's excerpt from *Dago Red*, "Hail Mary," we hear the very personal voice of a young man as he calls on the Blessed Virgin Mary for assistance.

- Throughout the history of the Church, holy images have been used to assist believers in prayer. In the Decree of the Second Council of Nicaea, we see that using images as an aid to prayer is not idolatry but rather a logical extension of the effects of the Incarnation of the Son of God.

Praying in Times of Need

- "An Experience of God at Midnight" shows how Martin Luther King, Jr., called on God in his hour of need and how God responded to him.

- "A Woman's Prayer," by Dorothy Day, shows how the power and intimacy of prayer can be found not only in a convent chapel but in a humble tenement bedroom as well.

- All of us must deal with grief when a loved one dies. In the poem by Daniel Berrigan, "His Cleric's Eye," the poet reflects on the death of a young priest and prays that, in Christ, this young priest will become fully alive.

Connecting with God

"In the Convent Chapel"
from *The Light Invisible*

Robert Hugh Benson

Mental prayer is nothing else than an intimate friendship, a frequent heart-to-heart conversation with Him by whom we know
ourselves to be loved.

—St. Teresa of Avila

Author Background

Msgr. Robert Hugh Benson (1871–1914) was one of the most renowned
and prolific Catholic authors of the early twentieth century. He is best
known for his novel of the English Reformation, *Come Rack, Come Rope!*
One of his earliest books, *The Light Invisible*, deals with the mystical experiences of an elderly country priest. The following selection from that
work had a profound effect on the great Jesuit scientist Pierre Teilhard de
Chardin, whose *Three Stories in the Style of R. H. Benson* are included in the
collection of Father Teilhard's short works, *Hymn of the Universe*.

Before the Reading

In the following selection, Benson describes in a work of fiction the experience of a priest as he watches a contemplative nun at prayer. The priest is
given "a vision" of the conversation between this kneeling sister and the infinite God to whom she addresses her prayers. The priest eventually points
out how this experience gave him a profound insight into the supernatural
nature of reality and the power of prayer. The story is written as if told to
the author.

"In the Convent Chapel"

"Some years ago I took my annual holiday in the form of a solitary walking tour. I will not tell you where I went, as there are others concerned in this story who would dislike intensely to be publicly spoken of in the way that I shall have to speak of them; but it is enough to say that I came at last to a little town towards sunset. My object in coming to this place was to visit a convent of enclosed nuns whose reputation for holiness was very great. I carried with me a letter of introduction to the Reverend Mother, which I knew would admit me to the chapel. I left my bag at the inn, and then walked down to the convent, which stood a little way out of the town.

"The lay sister who opened the door to me asked me to come into the parlor while she told the Reverend Mother; and after waiting a few minutes in the prim room with its beeswaxed floor and its religious engravings and objects, a wonderfully dignified little old lady, with a quiet wrinkled face, came in with my letter open in her hand. We talked a few minutes about various things, and I had a glass of cowslip wine in a thick-lipped wineglass.

"She told me that the convent was a very ancient foundation, that it had been a country house ever since the Dissolution of the Religious Houses, until about twenty years ago, when it had been acquired for the community. There still remained of the old buildings part of the cloisters, with the south transept of the old church, which was not the chapel; the whole, with a wall or two, forming the courtyard through which I had come. Behind the house lay the garden, on to which the window of the parlor looked; and as I sat I could see a black cross or two marking the nuns' graveyard. I made inquiries as to the way the time of the community was spent.

"'Our object,' said the old lady, 'is perpetual intercession for sinners. We have the great joy of the Blessed Sacrament amongst us in the chapel, and, except during the choir offices and Mass there is always a nun kneeling before It. We look after one or two ladies incurably ill, who have come to end their days with us, and we make our living by embroidery.'

"I asked how it was that she could receive strangers if the order was an enclosed one."

"'The lay sisters and myself alone can receive strangers. We find that necessary.'

"After a little more talk I asked whether I might see the chapel, and she took me out into the courtyard immediately.

"As we walked across the grass she pointed out to me the cloisters, now built up into a corridor, and the long ruined wall of the old nave which formed one side of the quadrangle. A grave-faced and stout collie dog had joined us at the door, and we three went together slowly towards the door in the centre of the west wall of the restored transept. The evening sun lay golden on the wall before us and on the ruined base of the central tower of the old church, round which jackdaws wheeled and croaked."

The old priest broke off and turned to me, with his eyes burning:

"What a marvelous thing the Religious Life is," he said, "and above all the Contemplative Life! Here were these nuns as no doubt they and their younger sisters are still, without one single thing that in the world's opinion makes life worth living. There is practically perpetual silence, there are hours to be spent in the chapel, no luxuries, no amusements, no power of choice, they are always rather hungry and rather tired, at the very least. And yet they are not sacrificing present happiness to future happiness, as the world always supposes, but they are intensely and radiantly happy now in this present time. I don't know what further proof any one wants of Who our Lord is than that men and women find the keenest, and in fact their only joy, in serving Him and belonging to Him."

"Well, I remember that something of this sort was in my mind as I went across the courtyard beside this motherly old lady with her happy quiet face. She had been over fifty years in Religion, my friend had told me.

"At the door she stopped.

"'I will not come in,' she said, 'but you will find me in the parlor when you come out.'

"And she turned and went back, with the collie walking slowly beside her, his golden plumed tail raised high against her black habit.

"The door was partly open, but a thick curtain hung beyond. I pushed it quietly aside and stepped in. It seemed very dark at first, in contrast to the brilliant sunshine outside; but I presently saw that I was kneeling before a high iron-barred screen, in which there was no door. On the left, in the further corner of the chapel, glimmered a blue light in a silver lamp before a statue of our Lady.

"Opposite me rose up the steps before the high altar; but not far away, because, as you remember, the chapel had once been the transept of a church, and the east wall, in the centre of which the high altar stood, was longer than both the south wall where a second altar stood, and the modern brick wall that closed it on the north. A slender crucifix in black and white and six thin tapers rose above the altar, and high above stood the Tabernacle closed by a white silk curtain, before which flickered a tiny red spark.

"I said a prayer or two, and then I noticed for the first time a dark outline rising in the centre of the space before the altar. For a moment I was perplexed, and then I saw that it was the nun whose hour it was for intercession. Her back was turned to me as she knelt at the footstool, and her black veil fell in rigid lines on to her shoulders, and mingled with her black serge habit below. There she knelt perfectly motionless, praying. I had not, and have not, a notion as to her age. She might have been twenty-five or seventy.

"As I knelt there I thought deeply, wondering as to the nun's age, how long she had been professed, when she would die, whether she was happy; and, I am afraid, I thought more of her than of Him Who was so near. Then a kind of anger seized me, as I compared in my mind the life of a happy good woman in the world with that of this poor creature. I pictured the life, as one so often sees it in homes, of a mother with her children growing up about her, her hands busy with healthy home work, her life glorified by a good man's love; as she grows older, passing from happy stage to happy stage, comforting, helping, sweetening every soul she meets. Was it not for this that women—and men, too, I thought, rebuking myself—were made? Then think of the sour life of the cloister—as loveless and desolate as the cold walls themselves! And even, I thought, even if there is a strange peculiar joy in the Religious Life, even if there is an absence of sorrows and anxieties such as spoil the happiness of many lives in the world—yet, after all, surely the Contemplative Life is useless and barren. The Active Life may be well enough, if the prayers and the discipline issue in greater efficiency, if the priest is more fervent when he ministers outside, and the Sister of Charity more charitable. Yes, I thought, the active Religious Life is reasonable enough; but the Contemplative . . . ! After all it is essentially selfish, it is a sin against society. Possibly it was necessary when the wickedness of the world was more fierce, to protest against it by this retirement; but not now, not now! How can the lump be leavened if the leaven be withdrawn? How can a soul serve God by forsaking the world which He made and loves . . . ?"

"And so," said the priest, turning to me again, "I went on—poor ignorant fool—thinking that the woman who knelt in front of me was less useful than myself, and that my words and actions and sermons and life did more to advance God's kingdom than her prayers! And then—then—at the moment when I reached that climax of folly and pride, God was good to me and gave me a little light.

"Now, I do not know how to put it—I have never put it into words before, except to myself— but I became aware, in my intellect alone, of one or two clear facts. In order to tell you what those facts were I must use picture language; but remember they are only translations or paraphrases of what I perceived.

"First I became aware suddenly that there ran a vital connection from the Tabernacle to the woman. You may think of it as one of those bands you see in machinery connecting two wheels, so that when either wheel moves the other moves too. Or you may think of it as an electric wire, joining the instrument the telegraph operator uses with the pointer at the other end. At any rate there was this vital band or wire of life.

"Now in the Tabernacle I became aware that there was a mighty stirring and movement. Something within it beat like a vast Heart, and the vibrations of each pulse seemed to quiver through all the ground. Or you may picture it as the movement of a clear deep pool when the basin that contains it is jarred—it seemed like the movement of circular ripples crossing and recrossing in swift thrills. Or you may think of it as that faint movement of light and shade that may be seen in the heart of a white-hot furnace. Or again you may picture it as sound—as the sound of a high ship-mast with the rigging, in a steady wind; or the sound of deep woods in a July noon."

The priest's face was working, and his hands moved nervously.

"How hopeless it is," he said, "to express all this! Remember that all these pictures are not in the least what I perceived. They are only grotesque paraphrases of a spiritual fact that was shown me.

"Now I was aware that there was something of the same activity in the heart of the woman, but I did not know which was the controlling power. I did not know whether the initiative sprang from the Tabernacle and communicated itself to the nun's will; or whether she, by bending herself upon the Tabernacle, set in motion a huge dormant power. It appeared to me possible that the solution lay in the fact that two wills cooperated, each reacting upon the other. This, in a kind of way, appears to me now true as regards the whole mystery of free will and prayer and grace.

"At any rate the union of these two represented itself to me, as I have said, as forming a kind of engine that radiated an immense light or sound or movement. And then I perceived something else too.

"I once fell asleep in one of those fast trains from the north, and did not awake until we had reached the terminus. The last thing I had seen before falling asleep had been the quiet darkening woods and fields through which we were sliding, and it was a shock to awake in the bright humming terminus and to drive through the crowded streets, under the electric glare from the lamps and windows. Now I felt something of that sort now. A moment ago I had fancied myself apart from movement and activity in this quiet convent; but I seemed somehow to have stepped into a centre of busy, rushing life. I can scarcely put the sensation more clearly than that. I was aware that the atmosphere was charged with energy; great powers seemed to be astir, and I to be close to the whirling center of it all.

"Or think of it like this. Have you ever had to wait in a City office? If you have done that you will know how intense quiet can coexist with intense activity. There are quiet figures here and there round the room. Or it may be there is only one such figure—a great financier—and he is sitting there almost motionless. Yet you know that every movement tingles, as it were, out from that still room all over the world. You can picture to yourself how people leap to obey or to resist—how lives rise and fall, and fortunes are made and lost, at the gentle movements of this lonely quiet man in his office. Well, so it was here. I perceived that this black figure knelt at the centre of reality and force, and with the movements of her will and lips controlled spiritual destinies for eternity. There ran out from this peaceful chapel lines of spiritual power that lost themselves in the distance, bewildering in their profusion and terrible in the intensity of their hidden fire. Souls leaped up and renewed the conflict as this tense will strove for them. Souls even at that moment leaving the body struggled from death into spiritual life, and fell panting and saved at the feet of the Redeemer on the other side of death. Others, acquiescent and swooning in sin, woke and snarled at the merciful stab of this poor nun's prayers."

The priest was trembling now with excitement.

'Yes," he said; "yes, and I in my stupid arrogance had thought that my life was more active in God's world than hers. So a small provincial shopkeeper, bustling to and fro behind the counter, might think, if only he were mad enough, that his life was more active and alive than the life of a director who sits at his table in the City. Yes, that is a vulgar simile; but the only one that I can think of which in the least expresses what I knew to be true. There lay my little foolish narrow life behind me, made up of spiritless prayers and efforts and feeble dealings with souls; and how complacent I had been with it all, how self-centered, how out of the real tide of spiritual movement! And meanwhile, for years probably, this nun had toiled behind these walls in the silence of grace, with the hum of the world coming faintly to her ears, and the cries of peoples and nations, and of persons whom the world accounts important, sounding like the voices of children at play in the muddy street outside; and indeed that is all that they are, compared to her—children making mud-pies or playing at shop outside the financier's office."

The priest was silent, and his face became quieter again. Then in a moment he spoke again.

"Well," he said, "that is what I believe to have been an intellectual vision. There was no form or appearance or sound; but I can only express what was shown to me to be true, under those images. It almost seems to me as I look back now as if the air in the chapel were full of a murmurous sound and a luminous mist as the currents of need and grace went to and fro. But I know really that the silence was deep and the air dim."

Then I made a foolish remark.

"If you feel like that about the Contemplative Life, I wonder you did not try to enter it yourself."

The priest looked at me for a moment.

"It would be rash, surely, for a little shopkeeper of no particular ability to compete with Rothschild."

Reading for Comprehension

1. What did the old nun tell the priest about the purpose of their religious order?

2. Who were the two members of the religious community able to greet someone from the public?

3. What did the priest notice in the chapel as he was praying?

4. What vision does the priest have of the relationship between the nun and the tabernacle?

Reading for Understanding

1. What thoughts does the priest have as he compares the value of the married life of a woman in the world and the contemplative life of a cloistered sister?

2. How does the priest describe what he sees as the effects of the nun's prayer for people whom she has never seen?

3. What is the source of the energy that the priest experiences in the chapel?

4. How does the priest compare the quiet work of a great financial director sitting alone at his desk making financial decisions (Rothschild) with the effects of the solitary prayer of the nun on the lives of people in the world?

Activity

The practice of mental prayer, as practiced by contemplatives, is available to all people. Read the following definition of prayer by St. Teresa of Avila:

> Mental prayer is nothing else than an intimate friendship, a frequent heart-to-heart conversation with Him by whom we know ourselves to be loved.

Then sit quietly for ten minutes and talk to Jesus, knowing that he loves you with an eternal love. After ten minutes, write a short reflection of the experience.

Connecting with God

"The Three Hermits"

Leo Tolstoy

This is how you are to pray:
Our Father in heaven, hallowed be your name . . .

—Matthew 6:9

Author Background

Leo Tolstoy (see page 100 for his biography) became obsessed with the meaning and purpose of life. In 1866 he wrote a tale of a bishop and three old men that reflects his quest to answer these deep questions.

Before the Reading

Throughout the history of the Church, there have been men and women who have withdrawn from society to wild and barren places so that they can be alone with God and enter into uninterrupted conversation with him. In this story, Leo Tolstoy describes the encounter between three such hermits and a bishop. Tolstoy had very firm ideas about why love was superior to knowledge for the religious person. For him, one's relationship with God and the manifestation of this love in the love of our neighbor was the essence of religion. Tolstoy's attraction to the life of simple, prayerful love is seen in the following story.

"The Three Hermits"
An Old Legend Current in the Volga District

A Bishop was sailing from Archangel to the Solovetsk Monastery; and on the same vessel were a number of pilgrims on their way to visit the shrines at that place. The voyage was a smooth one—the wind favorable, and the weather fair. The pilgrims lay on deck, eating, or sat in groups talking to one another. The Bishop, too, came on deck, and as he was pacing up and down, he noticed a group of men standing near the prow and listening to a fisherman who was pointing to the sea and telling them something. The Bishop stopped, and looked in the direction in which the man was pointing. He could see nothing however, but the sea glistening in the sunshine. He drew nearer to listen, but when the man saw him, he took off his cap and was silent. The rest of the people also took off their caps, and bowed.

"Do not let me disturb you, friends," said the Bishop. "I came to hear what this good man was saying."

"The fisherman was telling us about the hermits," replied one, a tradesman, rather bolder than the rest.

"What hermits?" asked the Bishop, going to the side of the vessel and seating himself on a box. "Tell me about them. I should like to hear. What were you pointing at?"

"Why, that little island you can just see over there," answered the man, pointing to a spot ahead and a little to the right. "That is the island where the hermits live for the salvation of their souls."

"Where is the island?" asked the Bishop. "I see nothing."

"There, in the distance, if you will please look along my hand. Do you see that little cloud? Below it and a bit to the left, there is just a faint streak. That is the island."

The Bishop looked carefully, but his unaccustomed eyes could make out nothing but the water shimmering in the sun.

"I cannot see it," he said. "But who are the hermits that live there?"

"They are holy men," answered the fisherman. "I had long heard tell of them, but never chanced to see them myself till the year before last."

And the fisherman related how once, when he was out fishing, he had been stranded at night upon that island, not knowing where he was. In the morning, as he wandered about the island, he came across an earth hut, and met an old man standing near it. Presently two others came out, and after having fed him, and dried his things, they helped him mend his boat.

"And what are they like?" asked the Bishop.

"One is a small man and his back is bent. He wears a priest's cassock and is very old; he must be more than a hundred, I should say. He is so old that the white of his beard is taking a greenish tinge, but he is always smiling, and his face is as bright as an angel's from heaven. The second is taller, but he also is very old. He wears a tattered peasant coat. His beard is broad, and of a yellowish gray color. He is a strong man. Before I had time to help him, he turned my boat over as if it were only a pail. He too, is kindly and cheerful. The third is tall, and has a beard as white as snow and reaching to his knees. He is stern, with overhanging eyebrows; and he wears nothing but a mat tied round his waist."

"And did they speak to you?" asked the Bishop.

"For the most part they did everything in silence and spoke but little even to one another. One of them would just give a glance, and the others would understand him. I asked the tallest whether they had lived there long. He frowned, and muttered something as if he were angry; but the oldest one took his hand and smiled, and then the tall one was quiet. The oldest one only said: 'Have mercy upon us,' and smiled."

While the fisherman was talking, the ship had drawn nearer to the island.

"There, now you can see it plainly, if your Grace will please to look," said the tradesman, pointing with his hand.

The Bishop looked, and now he really saw a dark streak—which was the island. Having looked at it a while, he left the prow of the vessel, and going to the stern, asked the helmsman:

"What island is that?"

"That one," replied the man, "has no name. There are many such in this sea."

"Is it true that there are hermits who live there for the salvation of their souls?"

"So it is said, your Grace, but I don't know if it's true. Fishermen say they have seen them; but of course they may only be spinning yarns."

"I should like to land on the island and see these men," said the Bishop. "How could I manage it?"

"The ship cannot get close to the island," replied the helmsman, "but you might be rowed there in a boat. You had better speak to the captain."

The captain was sent for and came.

"I should like to see these hermits," said the Bishop. "Could I not be rowed ashore?"

The captain tried to dissuade him.

"Of course it could be done," said he, "but we should lose much time. And if I might venture to say so to your Grace, the old men are not worth your pains. I have heard say that they are foolish old fellows, who understand nothing, and never speak a word, any more than the fish in the sea."

"I wish to see them," said the Bishop, "and I will pay you for your trouble and loss of time. Please let me have a boat."

There was no help for it; so the order was given. The sailors trimmed the sails, the steersman put up the helm, and the ship's course was set for the island. A chair was placed at the prow for the Bishop, and he sat there, looking ahead. The passengers all collected at the prow, and gazed at the island. Those who had the sharpest eyes could presently make out the rocks on it, and then a mud hut was seen. At last one man saw the hermits themselves. The captain brought a telescope and, after looking through it, handed it to the Bishop.

"It's right enough. There are three men standing on the shore. There, a little to the right of that big rock."

The Bishop took the telescope, got it into position, and he saw the three men: a tall one, a shorter one, and one very small and bent, standing on the shore and holding each other by the hand.

The captain turned to the Bishop.

398

"The vessel can get no nearer in than this, your Grace. If you wish to go ashore, we must ask you to go in the boat, while we anchor here."

The cable was quickly let out, the anchor cast, and the sails furled. There was a jerk, and the vessel shook. Then a boat having been lowered, the oarsmen jumped in, and the Bishop descended the ladder and took his seat. The men pulled at their oars, and the boat moved rapidly towards the island. When they came within a stone's throw they saw three old men: a tall one with only a mat tied round his waist: a shorter one in a tattered peasant coat, and a very old one bent with age and wearing an old cassock—all three standing hand in hand.

The oarsmen pulled in to the shore, and held on with the boat-hook while the Bishop got out.

The old men bowed to him, and he gave them his benediction, at which they bowed still lower. Then the Bishop began to speak to them.

"I have heard," he said, "that you, godly men, live here saving your own souls, and praying to our Lord Christ for your fellow men. I, an unworthy servant of Christ, am called, by God's mercy, to keep and teach His flock. I wished to see you, servants of God, and to do what I can to teach you, also."

The old men looked at each other smiling, but remained silent.

"Tell me," said the Bishop, "what you are doing to save your souls, and how you serve God on this island."

The second hermit sighed, and looked at the oldest, the very ancient one. The latter smiled, and said:

"We do not know how to serve God. We only serve and support ourselves, servant of God."

"But how do you pray to God?" asked the Bishop.

"We pray in this way," replied the hermit. "Three are ye, three are we, have mercy upon us."

And when the old man said this, all three raised their eyes to heaven, and repeated:

"Three are ye, three are we, have mercy upon us!"

The Bishop smiled.

"You have evidently heard something about the Holy Trinity," said he. "But you do not pray aright. You have won my affection, godly men. I see you wish to please the Lord, but you do not know how to serve Him. That is not the way to pray; but listen to me, and I will teach you. I will teach you, not a way of my own, but the way in which God in the Holy Scriptures has commanded all men to pray to Him."

And the Bishop began explaining to the hermits how God had revealed Himself to men; telling them of God the Father, and God the Son, and God the Holy Ghost.

"God the Son came down on earth," said he, "to save men, and this is how He taught us all to pray. Listen and repeat after me: 'Our Father.'"

And the first old man repeated after him, "Our Father," and the second said, "Our Father," and the third said, "Our Father."

"Which art in heaven," continued the Bishop.

The first hermit repeated, "Which art in heaven," but the second blundered over the words, and the tall hermit could not say them properly. His hair had grown over his mouth so that he could not speak plainly. The very old hermit, having no teeth, also mumbled indistinctly.

The Bishop repeated the words again, and the old men repeated them after him. The Bishop sat down on a stone, and the old men stood before him, watching his mouth, and repeating the words as he uttered them. And all day long the Bishop labored, saying a word twenty, thirty, a hundred times over, and the old men repeated it after him. They blundered, and he corrected them, and made them begin again.

The Bishop did not leave off till he had taught them the whole of the Lord's Prayer so that they could not only repeat it after him, but could say it by themselves. The middle one was the first to know it, and to repeat the whole of it alone. The Bishop made him say it again and again, and at last the others could say it too.

It was getting dark, and the moon was appearing over the water, before the Bishop rose to return to the vessel. When he took leave of the old men, they all bowed down to the ground before him. He raised them, and kissed each of them, telling them to pray as he had taught them. Then he got into the boat and returned to the ship.

And as he sat in the boat and was rowed to the ship he could hear the three voices of the hermits loudly repeating the Lord's Prayer. As the boat drew near the vessel their voices could no longer be heard, but they could still be seen in the moonlight, standing as he had left them on the shore, the shortest in the middle, the tallest on the right, the middle one on the left. As soon as the Bishop had reached the vessel and got on board, the anchor was weighed and the sails un-furled. The wind filled them, and the ship sailed away, and the Bishop took a seat in the stern and watched the island they had left. For a time he could still see the hermits, but presently they disappeared from sight, though the island was still visible. At last it too vanished, and only the sea was to be seen, rippling in the moonlight.

The pilgrims lay down to sleep, and all was quiet on deck. The Bishop did not wish to sleep, but sat alone at the stern, gazing at the sea where the island was no longer visible, and thinking of the good old men. He thought how pleased they had been to learn the Lord's prayer; and he thanked God for having sent him to teach and help such godly men.

So the Bishop sat, thinking, and gazing at the sea where the is-land had disappeared. And the moonlight flickered before his eyes, sparkling, now here, now there, upon the waves. Suddenly he saw something white and shining, on the bright path which the moon cast across the sea. Was it a seagull, or the little gleaming sail of some small boat? The Bishop fixed his eyes on it, wondering.

"It must be a boat sailing after us," thought he, "but it is overtak-ing us very rapidly. It was far, far away a minute ago, but now it is much nearer. It cannot be a boat, for I can see no sail; but whatever it may be, it is following us, and catching us up."

And he could not make out what it was. Not a boat, nor a bird, nor a fish! It was too large for a man, and besides a man could not be out there in the midst of the sea. The Bishop rose, and said to the helmsman:

"Look there, what is that, my friend? What is it?" the Bishop repeated, though he could now see plainly what it was—the three hermits running upon the water, all gleaming white, their gray beards shining, and approaching the ship as quickly as though it were not moving.

The steersman looked and let go the helm in terror.

"Oh Lord! The hermits are running after us on the water as though it were dry land!"

The passengers hearing him, jumped up, and crowded to the stern. They saw the hermits coming along hand in hand, and the two outer ones beckoning the ship to stop. All three were gliding along upon the water without moving their feet. Before the ship could be stopped, the hermits had reached it, and raising their heads, all three as with one voice, began to say:

"We have forgotten your teaching, servant of God. As long as we kept repeating it we remembered, but when we stopped saying it for a time, a word dropped out, and now it has all gone to pieces. We can remember nothing of it. Teach us again."

The Bishop crossed himself, and leaning over the ship's side, said:

"Your own prayer will reach the Lord, men of God. It is not for me to teach you. Pray for us sinners."

And the Bishop bowed low before the old men; and they turned and went back across the sea. And a light shone until daybreak on the spot where they were lost to sight.

Reading for Comprehension

1. What did the fisherman tell the pilgrims and the bishop about the small island that they were passing?

2. How did the fisherman describe the three hermits?

3. What prayer does the elder hermit recite for the bishop?

4. How does the bishop instruct the three hermits?

5. What does the bishop see after he has left the island and is gazing on the sea?

6. What does the bishop tell the hermits when they ask him to re-teach them the Lord's Prayer?

Reading for Understanding

1. Do you think that an advanced education and a high social status is a detriment to a fruitful prayer life? How do you think Tolstoy would answer that question?

2. What do you think the second hermit meant when he said "We do not know how to serve God. We only serve and support ourselves"?

3. What is the lesson that the bishop learns from his encounter with the hermits?

Activities

1. Research and report on the "Jesus Prayer." What is the nature of this prayer? How is it practiced?

2. Read the novel *Franny and Zooey,* by J. D. Salinger, and explain the role that the Jesus Prayer plays in it.

Connecting with God

"March 7, 1848"
from *Meditations and Devotions*

John Henry Cardinal Newman

Cor ad cor loquitor (Heart speaks unto heart).
—**Motto of John Henry Newman's Cardinalate**

Author Background

John Henry Cardinal Newman (1801–1890) is one of the giants of Catholic theology. He was trained to be an Anglican priest, but his reading of the Church Fathers and his experience of parish life led him to convert to Roman Catholicism. He also is one of the greatest prose writers of the nineteenth century and his work *The Idea of a University*, his autobiography, *Apologia Pro Vita Sua*, and his *Grammar of Assent* are classics of English and Christian literature. Newman was totally convinced that God spoke to him in the experiences of his daily life and that he had been called by God to do a specific mission for the Church. The following meditation summarizes much of his spiritual writing. Newman is currently being considered for canonization.

Before the Reading

Throughout Scripture, we are given examples of those who have been called by God to do some great work on his behalf. For example, Abraham, Isaac, Jacob, Moses, the prophets, Zachary, the Virgin Mary, St. Joseph, and the Apostles all had visions of angels or heard the voice of God that gave them specific tasks to assist in the building up of the Kingdom of God. In this classic meditation, Cardinal Newman shows how all of us have been called by God to do him a specific service. He points out how the essence of the life of grace is to listen always for his call and to never cease doing his will.

"March 7, 1848"

God has created me
to do him some definite service;
He has committed some work to me
which He has not committed to another.

I have my mission—

I may never know it in this life,
but I shall be told of it in the next.
I am a link in a chain,
a bond of connection between persons.
He has not created me for naught,
I shall do good,
I shall do his work.
I shall be an angel of peace,
a preacher of truth
in my own place
while not intending it—
if I do but keep His Commandments.

Therefore, I will trust Him.

Whatever, wherever I am,
I can never be thrown away.
If I am in sickness,
my sickness may serve Him;
in perplexity,
my perplexity may serve Him;
if I am in sorrow
my sorrow may serve Him.
He does nothing in vain.

He knows what He is about.

He may take away my friends.
He may throw me among strangers.
He may make me feel desolate,
make my spirits sink,
hide my future from me—still

He knows what He is about.

Reading for Comprehension

1. What is the author's mission in life?

2. How does Newman serve God?

Reading for Understanding

1. How do you serve God?

2. What great work do you feel destined for in your life?

Activity

As a spiritual exercise, turn your heart and mind to God and silently listen to the special call that he has for you and no other.

Inspirations to Prayer

"Hail Mary" from *Dago Red*
John Fante

Hail, favored one! The Lord is with you.
—Luke 1:28

Author Background

American writer John Fante (1909–1983) was born to an Italian immigrant father and an Italian-American mother. He produced a large variety of work that included short stories, novels, and screenplays. His work is largely autobiographical and reflects his Catholic faith and upbringing, his rootedness in Italian-American culture, and his life as a struggling writer in Los Angeles. His writing is known for its pungent prose, colorful characters, and searing emotional honesty.

Before the Reading

The term "stream of consciousness" refers to a literary technique that has been used by many modern novelists. It describes the style of writing that allows readers to enter into the inner life of a person while capturing the person's thoughts as they occur. The result is an episodic style of writing that follows the flow of ideas. In this story by John Fante, we enter into the inner conversation of a man who is praying to the Blessed Virgin Mary. His love for the Blessed Mother and his trust in her care for him is beautifully reported in this rushing flow of ideas and images.

"Hail Mary"

Hail Mary, full of grace, the Lord is with thee; blessed art thou among women, and blessed is the fruit of thy womb, Jesus. O Holy Mother Mary, I am now in Hollywood, California, on the corner of Franklin and Argyle, in a house where I rent a room at six a week. Remember,

O Blessed Virgin, remember the night twenty years ago in Colorado when my father went to the hospital for his operation, and I got all my brothers and sisters down on the floor in our bedroom, and I said: "Now by gosh—pray! Papa's sick, so you kids pray." Ah, boy, we prayed, you Virgin Mary, you Honey, we prayed and my blood sang, and I felt big feelings in my chest, the ripple of electricity, the power of cold faith, and we all got up and walked to different parts of the house. I sat in the kitchen and smirked. They had said at the hospital that Papa was going to die, and nobody knew it but me and Mamma and you, you Honey, but we had prayed and I sat smirking, pooh-poohing at death because we had prayed and I knew we had done our share for Papa, and that he would live.

The rest of them wouldn't go to bed that night, they were afraid Papa would die, and they all waited, and already Grandma planned the funeral, but I smirked and went to bed and slept very happy, with your beads in my fingers, kissing the cross a few times and then dozing off because Papa could not die after my prayers, because you were my girl, my queen, and there was no doubt in my heart.

And in the morning there was wild joy to wake me, because Papa had lived and would live some more, a lot of years to come, and there was Mamma back from the hospital, beaming and sticky when she kissed us for joy, and I heard her say to Grandma: "He lived because he has an iron constitution. He is a strong man. You can't kill that man." And when I heard that, I snickered. They didn't know, these people, they didn't know about you and me, you Honey, and I thought of your pale face, your dark hair, your feet on the serpent at the side-altar, and I said, she's wonderful, she's sure wonderful.

Oh, those were the days! Oh, I loved you then! You were the celestial blue, and I looked up at you when I walked to school with books under my arms, and my ecstasy was simple and smashing, crushing and mad and whirling, all these things across my chest, sensations, and you in the blue sky, in my blue shirt, in the covers of my blue-covered book. You were the color blue and I saw you every-where and then I saw the statue in the church, at the side-altar, with your feet on the serpent, and I said and said a thousand times, I said, oh, you Honey, and I wasn't afraid of anything. . . .

Hail Mary, full of grace, the Lord is with thee; blessed art thou among women, and blessed is the fruit of thy womb, Jesus. O Holy Mother Mary, I want to ask a favor of you, but first I want to remind you of something I once did for you.

You will say that I am bragging again, and that you have heard this story before, but I am proud of it, and my heart is beating wildly and there is the rustle of a bird in my throat, and I could cry, and I am crying because I loved you, oh, I loved you so. That hot flash on my cheek is the course of my tears, and I flick it off with the point of my finger, and the finger comes away warm and wet, and I sit here and I am of the living, I am saying this is a dream.

His name was Willie Cox, and he went to Grover Cleveland. He was always razzing me because I was a Catholic. O you Mary! I have told you this before, I admit the braggadocio, but tonight, one day removed from Christmas Eve, I am in Hollywood, California, on the corner of Franklin and Argyle, and the rent is six a week, and I want to ask you a favor, and I cannot ask until I tell you once more about this Willie Cox.

He chewed tobacco, this Willie Cox. He went to Grover Cleveland, and he chewed tobacco, and I went to St. Catherine's and we used to pass one another on the corner, and he used to squirt tobacco juice on my shoes and legs and say: "*That's* for the Catholics. They stink."

Willie Cox, where are you tonight? I am on the corner of Franklin and Argyle, and this is Hollywood, so it is quite possible that you are two blocks away, but wherever you are, Mr. Willie Cox, I call upon you to bear witness to the truth of my narrative. Willie Cox, I took a hell of a lot of your guff that spring. When you said the priests ate the nuns' babies, and then spat on my shoes, I took it. When you said we had human sacrifices at Mass, and the priest drank the blood of young girls, and you spat across my knees, I took that. The truth is, Willie, and tonight I admit, you scared me. You were very tough, and I decided to do as the martyrs did—to do nothing. To take it.

Hail Mary, full of grace! I was a boy then, and there was no love like my love. And there was no tougher boy than Willie Cox, and I feared him. Ah, but my days were celestial blues and my eyes had only to lift and there was my love, and I was not afraid. And yet, in spite of it all, I was afraid of Willie Cox.

How is your nose today, Willie Cox? Did your front teeth grow out again? He was on his way to Grover Cleveland and I was on my way to St. Catherine's and it was eight o'clock in the morning. He shifted the wad in his jaw, and I held my breath.

"Hi, Red Neck."

"Hello, Willie."

"What's your hurry, Catholic?"

"Gotta, Willie. I'm late."

"What'sa matter? Scared of the nunnies?"

"Don't, Willie. You're choking me."

"Scared of the nunnies?"

"Don't, Willie! I can't hardly breathe!"

"I heard somethin', Red Neck. My old man, he tells me you Catlickers think Jesus was borned without his mother having kids like other people have kids. Is that right?"

"It's the Immaculate Conception. Ouch!"

"Immaculate, crap! I bet she was a whore like all Catlickers."

"Willie Cox, you dirty dog!"

Mr. Thomas Holyoke, you are dead now, you died two years later, but even in death you may speak out tonight and tell what you saw from your window, there on the lawn, fourteen years ago one morning in the spring. You may say what you said to the policeman who ran from the courthouse steps, you may say again:

"I saw the dark lad here struggling to get free. The Cox boy was choking him. I thought he'd hurt the boy, and I was about to intervene. All at once the dark lad here swung his fist, and the Cox boy went sprawling across my new spring lawn. I thought they were playing, until I saw the Cox boy didn't move. When I ran out his nose was bleeding and his front teeth were missing."

410

Hail Mary, full of grace! Here in Hollywood, on the corner of Franklin and Argyle, I look through my window and gaze and gaze at an unending pattern of celestial blue. I wait and I remember. O you Honey, where are you now? Oh, endless blue, you have not changed!

In her room next to mine, my landlady sits before the radio. Willie Cox, I know now that you are in Hollywood. Willie Cox, you are the woman in the next room playing the radio. You have given up the vulgar habit of chewing tobacco, but, oh, Willie, you had charm in those days, and you were not nearly so monstrous as you are now, slipping little pieces of paper under my door, telling me over and over that I owe you eighteen dollars.

Hail Mary, full of grace! Today when I talked to my agent he said there was a slump in Hollywood, that the condition was serious. I went down the stairs of his office and into the big, late afternoon. Such a blue sky! Such riotous blue in the Santa Monica mountains! I looked everywhere above, and I sighed, and I said, well, it won't rain tonight, anyway. That was this afternoon. Willie Cox, you are my landlady and you are a Slump in Hollywood.

Mary in the Sky, what has happened to me? O tall queen standing on the serpent at the side-altar, O sweet girl with waxen fingers, there is a Slump in Hollywood, my landlady slips little pieces of paper under my door, and when I gaze at the sky it is to form an opinion about the weather. This is funny. It is probably goddamn funny to the world and it is funny to me, but this gathering dust in my throat, this quiet in my chest where once there was whirling, this cigarette-clenching mouth that once bore a smirk of faith and joy in destiny—there is no laughter in these things. Willie Cox has got me by the throat again.

Willie Cox, I am not afraid of you. I know that I cannot bloody the nose of a Slump in Hollywood or knock the teeth out of my land-lady's mouth, but, Willie Cox, remember that I still look to the sky. Remember that there are nights like these when I pause to listen, to search, to feel, to grope.

Hail Mary, full of grace, the Lord is with thee, and blessed art thou among women. Holy Mary, Mother of God, I was going to ask a favor, I was going to ask boldly about that rent. I see it is not necessary now. I see that you have not deserted me. For in a little while I shall slip this into an envelope and send it off. There is a Slump in Hollywood, and my landlady slips little pieces of paper under my door, and once more I sit in the kitchen of my world, a smirk on my lips.

Reading for Comprehension

1. For whom did the family pray at the beginning of the story?
2. How does Willie Cox harass the boy?
3. What blasphemy does Willie Cox state in his insults against the Blessed Virgin Mary?
4. What does the narrator do to Willie Cox?
5. What is the current status of the narrator?
6. Why does the narrator feel no need to pray to the Blessed Virgin for the money to pay his rent?

Reading for Understanding

1. Who was Willie Cox when the narrator was a boy? Who is Willie Cox for the narrator now?
2. What color does the narrator associate with the Blessed Virgin? Describe three places he sees this color.
3. Why does the narrator have a smirk on his lips at the end of the story?
4. What are your feelings about the familiar way the narrator continually addresses the Blessed Virgin by the name, "Honey?"

Activities

1. One of the most popular prayer devotions of Catholics is to recite the Holy Rosary. List the names of the mysteries found in the Joyful, Luminous, Sorrowful, and Glorious Mysteries of the Holy Rosary.

412

Pray a decade of the Rosary slowly and meditatively. Describe your experience in a journal.

2. A *mantra* is a word or phrase that is used repeatedly in order to come into contact with the divine. Research the use of mantras in Hinduism and Buddhism and explain how the Rosary is likewise a mantra form of prayer.

Inspirations to Prayer

Decree of the Second Council of Nicaea

Christian iconography expresses in images the same Gospel message that Scripture communicates by words.

—*Catechism of the Catholic Church*, 1160

Before the Reading

In an ancient tradition of the Church, the visual images of Jesus, the Blessed Virgin Mary, and the communion of saints were to be used in churches as an aid in worshipping the one true God. This practice was explained and defined by the Second Council of Nicaea in 787, which issued various decrees regarding the use of images or icons.

Decree of the Second Council of Nicaea

The Council formulates for the first time what the Church has always believed regarding icons.

One of these is the production of representational art; this is quite in harmony with the history of the spread of the gospel, as it provides confirmation that the becoming man of the Word of God was real and not just imaginary, and as it brings us a similar benefit. For, things that mutually illustrate one another undoubtedly possess one another's message.

Given this state of affairs and stepping out as though on the royal highway, following as we are the God-spoken teaching of our Holy Fathers and the tradition of the Catholic Church—for we recognize that this tradition comes from the Holy Spirit who dwells in her—we decree with full precision and care that, like the figure of the honored and life-giving cross, the revered and holy images, whether painted or made of mosaic or of other suitable material, are to be exposed in the holy churches of God, on sacred instruments and vestments, on walls and panels, in houses and by public ways, these are the images of our Lord, God and Savior, Jesus Christ, and of our Lady without blemish, the holy God-bearer, and of the revered angels and of any of the saintly holy men.

The more frequently they are seen in representational art, the more are those who see them drawn to remember and long for those who serve as models, and to pay these images the tribute of salutation and respectful veneration. Certainly this is not the full adoration in accordance with our faith, which is properly paid only to the divine nature, but it resembles that given to the figure of the honored and life-giving cross, and also to the holy books of the gospels and to other sacred cult objects. Further, people are drawn to honor these images with the offering of incense and lights, as was piously established by ancient custom. Indeed, the honor paid to an image traverses it, reaching the model, and he who venerates the image, venerates the person represented in that image.

So it is that the teaching of our Holy Fathers is strengthened, namely, the tradition of the Catholic Church which has received the gospel from one end of the earth to the other.

So it is that we really follow Paul, who spoke in Christ, and the entire divine apostolic group and the holiness of the fathers, clinging fast to the traditions which we have received.

So it is that we sing out with the prophets the hymns of victory to the church: *Rejoice exceedingly O daughter of Zion, proclaim O daughter of Jerusalem; enjoy your happiness and gladness with a full heart. The Lord has removed away from you the injustices of your enemies, you have been redeemed from the hand of your foes. The Lord the king is in your midst, you will never more see evil, and peace will be upon you for time eternal.*

Reading for Comprehension

1. What does the council document say about the origin of the veneration of sacred images?

2. Where do the council fathers say that the images of Christ, the Virgin, and the saints are to be displayed?

Reading for Understanding

1. Why do you think the Church had to address the issue of using icons in churches?

Activity

Research and explain a dispute that involved the Byzantine Emperor Leo III's condemnation of the veneration of sacred images, known as *iconoclasm* ("image breaking").

Praying in Times of Need

"An Experience of God at Midnight," from *Bearing the Cross: Martin Luther King, Jr., and the Southern Christian Leadership Conference*

David J. Garrow

> He advanced a little and fell prostrate in prayer, saying, "My Father, if it is possible, let this cup pass from me; yet, not as I will, but as you will."
>
> **—Matthew 26:39**

Author Background

Contemporary American historian David Garrow won the 1987 Pulitzer Prize for Biography for his book, *Bearing the Cross: Martin Luther King, Jr., and the Southern Christian Leadership Conference*. Garrow continues to write frequently about the United States Supreme Court for scholarly journals and has also written for more popular publications such as *The New York Times*, *The New Republic*, and *The Nation*. He is currently a fellow at Cambridge University.

Before the Reading

The segregation of Southern society prior to the Civil Rights Movement included segregation on public transportation. Blacks were not permitted to sit in sections of the bus reserved for whites. In opposition to this policy of segregation, the black community of Montgomery, Alabama, began a boycott of public buses and organized car-pools to transport black workers around the city. Martin Luther King, Jr., who had just assumed the leadership of a parish in Montgomery, was thrust in the role of leadership of this movement for civil rights. The following section describes one of the most momentous experiences in King's life. It tells of the moment when, during a time of prayer for guidance, he heard the voice of Jesus telling him that he was to be a herald for justice.

"An Experience of God at Midnight"

(To end the boycott of public transportation by black citizens, the political leaders of Montgomery introduced policies that would make it illegal for carpools to transport black citizens around the city.)

By late Saturday night, the MIA (Montgomery Improvement Association) had asked all black ministers to tell their congregations the next morning that the protest was not at an end despite the headlines in the *Advertiser*. Other representatives were sent out to pass the word at Saturday nightspots. Acting on the clues Sellers had given Rowan, King and the other MIA principals managed to identify and track down Kind, Mosely, and Rice, all of whom claimed they had made no deal with the commission concerning the buses. A denial in their names was issued to the press, and by Sunday afternoon it was clear that the city's effort at deception had failed miserably.

The embarrassment of that flop only made the city commissioners more determined to best the MIA. On Monday, Mayor Gayle announced that the city was adopting a new, tougher stance. Calling the MIA "a group of Negro radicals who have split asunder the fine relationships" between Montgomery's blacks and whites, Gayle declared that "we have pussyfooted around on this boycott long enough." No further negotiations would take place while the protest remained in force. "Until they are ready to end it, there will be no more discussions." White people, Gayle emphasized, must realize that far more was at stake in the MIA's demands than merely the question of seating practices. "What they are after is the destruction of our social fabric."

The meaning of the new city policy quickly became clear. Sellers ordered policemen to disperse groups of blacks waiting for car pool rides on street corners, and Gayle asked white housewives to stop giving rides to their black domestic workers. Giving a lift to any black person would merely aid "the Negro radicals who lead the boycott." City police also began tailing drivers from the MIA car pool, issuing tickets for trivial or nonexistent traffic violations. The official harassment made some protest supporters pause. "The voluntary pick-up system began to weaken," one MIA leader reported, and "for a moment the protest movement seemed to be wavering."

One of the first motorists to fall victim to this new policy of traffic enforcement was King himself. On Thursday, January 26, King left Dexter church in midafternoon, accompanied by one of his best friends, Robert Williams, and his church secretary, Mrs. Lillie Thomas. Before heading home, King stopped at the MIA's central transportation point to give three other persons a lift. When King pulled out, two motorcycle officers began tailing him. After several blocks, King stopped to drop off the riders. The officers pulled up beside him and told him he was under arrest for going thirty miles per hour in a twenty-five-MPH zone. King stepped out of the car, was frisked and told that he would have to go to the city jail until bond was arranged. King told Williams to take the car home and alert Coretta and the others. Then King himself was placed in a patrol car and driven to the dingy city jail, a long and somewhat fearful ride to a desolate section of northern Montgomery.

King was placed in a filthy group cell with various black criminals. Several minutes later he was taken out and fingerprinted. It was the first time King had been locked in a jail, and the first time he had been fingerprinted. It was not pleasant. In less than thirty minutes, Ralph Abernathy arrived to bail King out. The jailer told Abernathy that for release on a signature bond, he had to have a certified statement showing he owned sufficient property. It was too late in the evening to secure that, the jailer noted, and King would have to stay in jail overnight. Abernathy then asked if cash would be accepted. Reluctantly, the jailer said yes, and Abernathy rushed off to collect the necessary money.

Meanwhile, word of King's arrest had spread rapidly through the black community. Even before Abernathy returned, several dozen others—members of Dexter, MIA colleagues, and friends—began arriving at the jail. The growing crowd worried the white jailers, and while the fingerprinting ink was still being wiped from King's hands, the chief jailer told him he was free to leave upon his own signature. His trial would be Saturday morning. In hardly a moment's time, King was escorted out and driven back to town.

The emotional trauma of the arrest heightened the growing personal tensions King was feeling. He had not wanted to be the focal point of the protest in the first place, and he had erroneously assumed that a negotiated settlement would be obtained in just a few weeks time. With no end in sight, and more attention coming his way, King wondered whether he was up to the rigors of the job. He stressed to everyone that he as an individual was not crucial to the protest, that if something happened to him, or should he step aside, the movement would go on. "If M. L. King had never been born this movement would have taken place," the young minister told one mass meeting. "I just happened to be here. You know there comes a time when time itself is ready for change. That time has come in Montgomery, and I had nothing to do with it."

But others thought King had everything to do with it. The obscene and threatening phone calls continued apace, and they took their toll. "I felt myself faltering and growing in fear," King recalled later. Finally, on Friday night, January 27, the evening after his brief sojourn at the Montgomery jail, King's crisis of confidence peaked. He returned home late after an MIA meeting. Coretta was asleep, and he was about to retire when the phone rang and yet another caller warned him that if he was going to leave Montgomery alive, he had better do so soon. King hung up and went to bed, but found himself unable to sleep. Restless and fearful, he went to the kitchen, made some coffee, and sat down at the table. "I started thinking about many things," he recalled eleven years later. He thought about the difficulties the MIA was facing, and the many threats he was receiving. "I was ready to give up," he said later. "With my cup of coffee sitting untouched before me I tried to think of a way to move out of the picture without appearing a coward," to surrender the leadership to someone else. He thought about his life up until that moment. "The first twenty-five years of my life were very comfortable years, very happy years," King later said, reflecting back on that moment in the most remarkable and self-revealing utterances he ever made publicly:

> I didn't have to worry about anything. I have a marvel-
> ous mother and father. They went out of their way to
> provide everything for their children. . . . I went right
> on through school; I never had to drop out to work
> or anything. And you know, I was about to conclude
> that life had been wrapped up for me in a Christmas
> package.

> Now of course I was religious, I grew up in the church.
> I'm the son of a preacher . . . my grandfather was a
> preacher, my great grandfather was a preacher, my
> only brother is a preacher, my daddy's brother is a
> preacher, so I didn't have much choice, I guess. But
> I had grown up in the church, and the church meant
> something very real to me, but it was a kind of inher-
> ited religion and I had never felt an experience with
> God in the way that you must, and have it, if you're
> going to walk the lonely paths of this life.

That night, for the first time in his life, King felt such an experience as he sought to escape the pressures the MIA presidency had
placed upon him. He thought more about how trouble-free his life
had been until the movement began.

> Everything was done [for me], and if I had a problem
> I could always call Daddy—my earthly father. Things
> were solved. But one day after finishing school, I

was called to a little church, down in Montgomery, Alabama. And I started preaching there. Things were going well in that church, it was a marvelous experience. But one day a year later, a lady by the name of Rosa Parks decided that she wasn't going to take it any longer. . . . It was the beginning of a movement, . . . and the people of Montgomery asked me to serve them as a spokesman, and as the president of the new organization . . . that came into being to lead the boycott. I couldn't say no.

And then we started our struggle together. Things were going well for the first few days but then, about ten or fifteen days later, after the white people in Montgomery knew that we meant business, they started doing some nasty things. They started making nasty telephone calls, and it came to the point that some days more than forty telephone calls would come in, threatening my life, the life of my family, the life of my child. I took it for a while, in a strong manner.

But that night, unable to be at peace with himself, King feared he could take it no longer. It was the most important night of his life, the one he always would think back to in future years when the pressures again seemed to be too great.

"It was around midnight," he said, thinking back on it. "You can have some strange experiences at midnight." The threatening caller had rattled him deeply. "Nigger, we are tired of you and your mess now. And if you aren't out of this town in three days, we're going to blow your brains out, and blow up your house."

I sat there and thought about a beautiful little daughter who had just been born. . . . She was the darling of my life. I'd come in night after night and see that little gentle smile. And I sat at that table thinking about that little girl and thinking about the fact that she could be taken away from me any minute.

And I started thinking about a dedicated, devoted and loyal wife, who was over there asleep. And she could be taken from me, or I could be taken from her. And I got to the point that I couldn't take it any longer. I was weak. Something said to me, you can't call on Daddy now, he's up in Atlanta a hundred and seventy-five miles away. You can't even call on Mama now. You've got to call on that something in that person that your Daddy used to tell you about, that power that can make a way out of no way.

And I discovered then that religion had to become real to me, and I had to know God for myself. And I bowed down over that cup of coffee. I never will forget it. . . . I prayed a prayer, and I prayed out loud that night. I said, "Lord, I'm down here trying to do what's right. I think I'm right. I think the cause that we represent is right. But Lord, I must confess that I'm weak now. I'm faltering. I'm losing my courage. And I can't let the people see me like this because if they see me weak and losing my courage, they will begin to get weak."

Then it happened:

And it seemed at that moment that I could hear an inner voice saying to me, "Martin Luther, stand up for righteousness. Stand up for justice. Stand up for truth. And lo I will be with you, even until the end of the world." . . . I heard the voice of Jesus saying still to fight on. He promised never to leave me, never to leave me alone. No never alone. No never alone. He promised never to leave me, never to leave me alone.

That experience gave King a new strength and courage. "Almost at once my fears began to go. My uncertainty disappeared." He went back to bed no longer worried about the threats of bombings. The next morning he went down to the Montgomery courthouse and was convicted of the Thursday speeding charge. He was fined $10, plus $4 in court costs. Fred Gray filed notice of appeal.

Reading for Comprehension

1. What order was given to the police about black people who were carpooling instead of taking city buses?
2. What reason did the police give Martin Luther King, Jr., for his arrest?
3. How did the black community respond to King's arrest?
4. What happened as King prayed aloud for guidance in this time of crisis?
5. What effect did this hour of prayer have on Martin Luther King, Jr.?

Reading for Understanding

1. Martin Luther King, Jr., talked about beginning a time in his life when he could not depend on his own father to solve his problems. How do you see yourself moving toward this type of independence?
2. What was the difference between King's religious life before his encounter with Christ at midnight and after the encounter?

Activity

Role-play peaceful resolutions to situations that are often marked by racial tensions (e.g., students of different races sharing the same lunchroom).

Praying in Times of Need

"A Woman's Prayer"
Dorothy Day

And though I became oppressed with the problem of poverty
and injustice, though I groaned at the hideous sordidness of man's
lot, though there were years when I clung to the philosophy of
economic determinism as an explanation of man's fate,
still there were moments when, in the midst of misery
and class strife, life was shot through with glory.

—Dorothy Day

Author Background

Dorothy Day (1897–1980) was a co-founder, with Peter Maurin, of the
Catholic Worker Movement. Throughout her life she sought to apply the
Church's teachings on social justice to modern economic conditions. She
founded a group of Catholic Worker homes across the country where
Catholics lived and worked among the poor. Dorothy Day was a lifelong
pacifist and was arrested several times for her anti-war activities. She is
also known for her writings on prayer and the spiritual life.

Before the Reading

In this reading from her autobiography *From Union Square to Rome*, Dorothy
Day makes two points. First, in her description of a neighbor at prayer, she
illustrates that contemplation is not a form of prayer that can only be at-
tained in convents and monasteries. She believed that the highest form of
prayer and the closest union with God occurs in the factory, the office, and
the home. Second, she underscores the fact that material possessions don't
bring satisfaction. She held that our hearts yearn for the infinite riches
that only God can offer, and that the fight for economic justice for all can
help us to attend to the spiritual realities of human life.

"A Woman's Prayer"

It was in Chicago, where we moved to afterward, that I met my first Catholic. It was the first time we had been really poor. We lived in an apartment over a store, on Cottage Grove Avenue. There was no upstairs, no garden, no sense of space. The tenement stretched way down the block and there were back porches and paved courtyards with never a touch of green anywhere. I remember how hungry I became for green fields during the long hot summer that followed. There was a vacant lot over by the lakefront, and I used to walk down there with my sister and stand sniffing ecstatically the hot sweet smell of wild clover and listening to the sleepy sound of the crickets. But that very desire for beauty was a painful delight for me. It sharpened my senses and made me more avid in my search for it. I found it in the lake that stretched steel gray beyond the Illinois Central tracks. I found it in a glimpse of supernatural beauty in Mrs. Barrett, mother of Kathryn and six other little Barretts, who lived upstairs.

It was Mrs. Barrett who gave me my first impulse toward Catholicism. It was around ten o'clock in the morning that I went to Kathryn's to call for her to come out and play. There was no one on the porch or in the kitchen. The breakfast dishes had all been washed. They were long railroad apartments, those flats, and thinking the children must be in the front room, I burst in and ran through the bedrooms.

In the front bedroom Mrs. Barrett was on her knees, saying her prayers. She turned to tell me that Kathryn and the children had all gone to the store and went on with her praying. And I felt a warm burst of love toward Mrs. Barrett that I have never forgotten, a feeling of gratitude and happiness that still warms my heart when I remember her. She had God, and there was beauty and joy in her life.

All through my life, what she was doing remained with me. And though I became oppressed with the problem of poverty and injustice, through I groaned at the hideous sordidness of man's lot, though there were years when I clung to the philosophy of economic determinism as an explanation of man's fate, still there were moments when, in the midst of misery and class strife, life was shot through with glory. Mrs. Barrett in her sordid little tenement flat finished her breakfast dishes at ten o'clock in the morning and got down on her knees and prayed to God.

The Harrington family also lived in that block of tenements, and there were nine children, the eldest a little girl of twelve. She was a hard-working little girl, and naturally I had the greatest admiration for her on account of the rigorous life she led. I had a longing for the rigorous life. But I had a tremendous amount of liberty compared to little Mary Harrington. It was not until after the dishes were done that she could come out to play in the evening. Often she was so tired that we just stretched out on the long back porch, open to the sky. We lay there, gazing up at the only beauty the city had to offer us, and we talked and dreamed.

I don't remember what we talked about, but I do remember one occasion when she told me of the life of some saint. I don't remember which one, nor can I remember any of the incidents of it. I can only remember the feeling of lofty enthusiasm I had, how my heart seemed almost bursting with desire to take part in such high endeavor. One verse of the Psalms often comes to mind: "Enlarge Thou my heart, O Lord, that Thou mayest enter in." This was one of those occasions when my small heart was enlarged. I could feel it swelling with love and gratitude to such a good God for such a friendship as Mary's, for conversation such as hers, and I was filled with lofty ambitions to be a saint, a natural striving, a thrilling recognition of the possibilities of spiritual adventure.

Reading for Comprehension

1. What was it that Dorothy missed most when she moved into her tenement apartment?

2. What did Dorothy discover when she went to her friend's apartment for a visit?

3. What were Dorothy's feelings for Mrs. Barrett?

4. Describe Dorothy's thoughts as she lay on the porch in the evening talking with her friend Mary Harrington.

Reading for Understanding

1. Both Martin Luther King, Jr., and Dorothy Day were giants in bringing about social change in the United States. Where do you think they got the energy and strength to pursue goals of justice and to withstand hatred and imprisonment for their views?

2. Thomas Merton, the great American Trappist monk and writer, wrote a book titled *Contemplation in a World of Action*. How does that title aptly describe the lives of Martin Luther King, Jr., and Dorothy Day?

3. Read Matthew 6:6. How does Jesus' teaching on prayer apply to the actions of Mrs. Barrett?

Activity

A retreat is a time for people to step out of the routine of their daily lives and go away and spend some quiet time with God. Many people go to monasteries in the country for a few days each year for this experience. Research the types of retreats that are available to your school or your parish. Select the one that appeals most to you and explain why it attracted you.

Praying in Times of Need

"His Cleric's Eye"

Daniel Berrigan

> . . . for if he were not expecting the fallen to rise again, it would have been useless and foolish to pray for them in death.
> **—2 Maccabees, 12:44**

Author Background

Daniel Berrigan, S.J. (1921–), is a Jesuit priest who has written numerous volumes of poetry as well as an important drama and several volumes of prose works. His book of poems, *Time Without Number*, was nominated for the National Book Award in 1957. Fr. Berrigan came to national prominence during the Vietnam War. He was a vocal opponent of the war, which he believed contradicted basic Catholic principles of justice and peace. He was tried for activities connected to his opposition to the war and served eighteen months in prison. He expressed his motives for opposing the war in his dramatic piece, *The Trial of the Catonsville Nine*.

Before the Reading

In this poem, Father Berrigan reflects on the life and death of a young priest who was not a man of great vision or passion. The poem is not only a reflection on the priest's life; it is also a prayer for the present and future in hope that this young man will have the opportunity to experience the passion, joy, and suffering that he did not experience while he lived.

"His Cleric's Eye"

A young priest, dead suddenly
at forty years
taught a metaphysic of the world.
His mind was lucid, ingrained. He would say,

The Catholic Spirit

it is deductibly verified
that God is immutable; and,
universal order converges on one being.

So be it. This priest, alas for poetry, love and priests
was neither great nor evil.
The truths he spoke
being inert, fired no mind to a flare;
a remote world order
of essence, cause, finality,
invited submission to his God.

He never conveyed a man, Christ, or himself—
His cleric's eye
forbade singulars, oddments, smells,
sickness, pushcarts, the poor.
He dwelt in the fierce Bronx, among a university's
stone faced acres
hemmed in by trucks and tumbrels. No avail.

Yet it could not be borne
by those who love him, that having passed
from unawareness to light
he should be denied
the suffering that marks man
like a circumcision, like unstanched tears; *saved.*

Heaven is everything earth has withheld.
I wish you, priest, for herald angel,
a phthisic old man
beating a tin can with a mutton bone—
behold he comes!

For savior,
a Coxey's army, a Bowery 2 a.m.
For beatific vision
an end to books, book ends, unbending minds,
tasteless fodder, restrictive order.

For eternal joy
veins casting off, in a moment's
burning transfiguration
the waste and sludge of unrealized time.

Christ make most of you!
stitch you through
the needle's eye, the grudging gate.
Crawl through
that crotch of being;
new eyes, new heart, the runner's burning start.

Reading for Comprehension

1. How old was the priest when he died?

2. What did his cleric's eye forbid?

3. What does Fr. Berrigan say that heaven is?

4. What beatific vision does the poet wish for the priest?

Reading for Understanding

1. What does Fr. Berrigan mean when he says that the priest's worldview "forbade singulars, oddments, smells . . ."?

2. Who will announce the coming of the Lord for the priest?

3. What does the poet see as the danger of book learning?

4. What is the difference in the priest's experience of life and the runner's experience in the last stanza?

Activity

What are five things that you truly enjoy in life? How do these experiences energize you and make you feel fully alive? How do these experiences forge a connection between you and God?

HOW WE TALK TO GOD AND HOW GOD TALKS TO US

(Prayer)

SEEING WITH THE ARTIST

Meditation can be described as "an active turning to God." A person can ponder and reflect on any subject using all the faculties of the mind, including imagination. Almost anything from the simplest object to a Bible passage can be the subject of meditation; everything can speak to the believer who is sensitive to the omnipresent God. The paintings, sculpture, engraving, and fresco referenced here are also sources of meditation. Use an Internet search engine to find links for these artworks. Practice the skills of meditation as you view them. Write a free flowing reflection in the style of John Fante (pages 407–412) for one or more of the pieces of art.

The Paintings

The Agony in the Garden—Giovanni Bellini (1426–1516)

This painting is a representation of the account of Christ's prayer in the garden of Gethsemane recorded in Mark 14:32–43. In the painting, Jesus is kneeling before an angel and praying to his Father in anguish. The disciples James, John, and Peter are seen sleeping in the foreground. In the distance, Judas and a group of soldiers are approaching to arrest Jesus.

La Orana Maria (Ave Maria)—Paul Gauguin (1848–1903)

Gauguin left his home in France to live in the French Colony of Tahiti in the Pacific. He lived among the native population and painted a series of images that expressed his respect for the native people. Gauguin presents here the Virgin Mary and the Christ Child as Polynesian natives. The Virgin is wearing a native dress and the landscape is lush with tropical flowers. The vibrant colors are in stark contrast to the more sedate images of the Virgin found in Renaissance paintings.

The Visitation—Tintoretto (1518–1594)

The Gospel story of the Visitation (Lk 1:39–45) tells us that Elizabeth, upon seeing Mary, cried out, "Most blessed are you among women, and blessed is the fruit of your womb." Mary responded to Elizabeth's greeting with her great song of praise, The Magnificat (Lk 1:46–55). This painting depicts Mary and Elizabeth hugging one another upon their meeting.

St. Jerome in the Wilderness—Lorenzo Sabatini (1520–1576)

St. Jerome the hermit, who is credited with translating the Bible into Latin, is depicted in the desert in order to represent his desire for solitude. He wears a red robe because he was often painted as a cardinal (even though the office of cardinal did not exist in his lifetime) to show his high status as a Doctor of the Church. He holds a rock in his hand, with which he beats his breast as a sign of penance. The lion in the background recalls the legend that he removed a thorn from the paw of a ferocious lion, who thereafter lived with him as a gentle pet.

St. Francis Receiving the Stigmata—Giotto di Bondone (1267–1337)

Giotto is one of the greatest painters of the early Renaissance. He specialized in painting frescos. Frescos are paintings that are painted immediately into wet plaster and are often fused with the interior of churches. This fresco of St. Francis is found in the Upper Church of the Basilica of St. Francis in Assisi. The painting shows St. Francis as he receives the stigmata (an impression of the wounds of Christ) in the isolated mountains of his place of refuge, La Verna. In the foreground his companion, Brother Leo, reads the Scripture about the life of Christ as St. Francis, a true follower of Christ, is made like him, even receiving the wounds of his Passion.

The Sculpture

The Ecstasy of St. Teresa—Gian Lorenzo Bernini (1598–1680)

Bernini was the sculptor for the Basilica of St. Peter's in Rome and is considered the greatest of the High Roman Baroque sculptors. This sculpture of the foundress of the Discalced Carmelite Order and Doctor of the Church shows the saint in a rapture of ecstatic prayer. An angel stands by her as her face and body show the passion of the soul as it encounters the living God.

The Engraving

The Pharisee and the Publican—John Everett Millais (1829–1896)

This engraving is about two men's approaches to prayer. The subjects of the engraving are a Pharisee, who stands proudly and informs God of his goodness, and a Publican, who stands aside and beats his breast as he asks for God's mercy. This is a representation of the Gospel parable in Luke 18:9–14.

LOOKING AT FILM

The two films suggested below speak to the themes of repentance, conversion, contemplation, and new life in Christ. One is an older film from the 1950s, the other, more recent. Make time to reserve and view each of these films. Activity 5 on page 440 provides a source for follow up.

The Films

···

The End of the Affair (1955)—Directed by Edward Dmytryk

Rating: A II

This film, which was adapted from the great Graham Greene novel of the same name, tells the story of an author (Van Johnson) who has an affair with a married woman. During a bombing raid of London during World War II, the author is knocked unconscious. After he awakes and recovers, his lover (Deborah Kerr) abruptly breaks off the affair. Determined to learn the name of her new lover, the novelist hires a private detective to investigate the woman's life. The investigations reveal that she has not gone to a new lover but has instead begun to lead a life of real sanctity. The woman dies but not before the author learns that he was seemingly killed in the bomb blast and that the woman had made a vow to God to end the affair if he was brought back to life. This film offers a gripping portrayal of the supernatural and the grace-filled life. A 1999 film also based on Greene's novel is a less successful adaptation. It concentrates more on the erotic nature of the affair than the spiritual core of the relationship that was the main focus of Greene's novel.

Into Great Silence (2005)—Directed by Philip Gröning

Rating: A I

This is a breathtaking film that follows the rhythm of life of a group of monks at a Carthusian monastery in the French Alps. It is a long film, and with no musical background, there is an eerie quiet, for the monks are vowed to a life of silence. This is not an easy film to watch because, on the surface, it seems as if nothing is happening. As the film progresses, however, you begin to enter into the life of silence and then, like the monks, you begin to realize how wrapped up we are in our own lives and how we do not take time to still ourselves and "contemplate" the universe of God's beauty that surrounds us.

LISTENING TO SACRED MUSIC

The following selection of hymns includes some of the most popular Catholic hymns today. They are intended to encourage an encounter with the God who is Love. Check the latest OCP *Music Issue* for the music and lyrics of each of these songs. Practice singing these songs on your own or join with a friend to offer your praise to God.

The Music
....

Hymns

Each of these songs—mostly contemporary but some traditional—are often included as part of Sunday liturgies:

- "*Ubi Caritas*" (Where True Charity and Love Dwell, God Himself Is There), Gregorian Chant (OCP)
- "On Eagle's Wings" by Michael Joncas (OCP)
- "I Heard the Voice of Jesus" by Ralph Vaughan Williams (OCP)
- "All Creatures of Our God and King" by St. Francis of Assisi (OCP)
- "Rain Down" by Jaime Cortez (OCP)
- "Morning Has Broken" by Eleanor Farjeon (OCP)
- "*Salve Regina*" (Hail, Holy Queen), Gregorian Chant (OCP)
- "*Ave Maria*" (Hail Mary) by Franz Schubert
- "*Jubilate Deo*" (Rejoice in the Lord) by Flor Peeters (A contemporary polyphonic hymn in Latin)

ACTIVITIES

1. How does Bellini's painting *The Agony in the Garden* reflect the experience found in Dr. King's "An Experience of God at Midnight" (pages 418–424)?

2. One of the "marks" of the Church from the Nicene Creed is that the Church is catholic (universal). How is this article of the Creed reflected in the painting *La Orana Maria*, by Gauguin?

3. In his painting of St. Francis, Giotto shows the saint receiving the stigmata. Research the life of St. Padre Pio, a contemporary stigmatic, and explain how he received the marks of Christ's Passion.

4. In Luke 1:46–55, Mary sings her great hymn of praise, The Magnificat, to thank God for all that he has done for her. Look at the painting of Mary and Elizabeth greeting one another by Tintoretto and then read Dorothy Day's account of her friendship with Mary Harrington, "A Woman's Prayer" (pages 426–427). Reflect on your own friendships and write a prayer of thanksgiving to God in the style of Mary's great song of gratitude.

5. After watching the film *Into Great Silence*, write an essay that explains why spiritual writers throughout the centuries have recommended that we go apart into a quiet place and keep silent. What do you think happens when we keep silent? Why is doing this so difficult?

6. How do you rate the singing of the congregation at your parish? What do you think can be done to make congregational participation better?

Acknowledgments

The Catholic Spirit

Acknowledgments

Salvador Witness: The Life and Calling of Jean Donovan by Ana Carrigan. Copyright 1984 by Ana Carrigan, copyright 2005 by Ana Carrigan & Margaret Swedish. Orbis Books.

"She Went By Gently" by Paul Vincent Carroll, from *44 Irish Stories*, edited by Devin A. Garrity. All rights reserved. Copyright and permission to re-print by Devin-Adair, Publishers, Inc., Old Greenwich, CT, 1955.

"The Trouble" by J.F. Powers from *The Prince of Darkness and Other Stories* by J. F. Powers. Copyright 1947; copyright renewal 1975 by J. F. Powers, held by the Powers Family Literary Property Trust.

"Two Letters of St. Thérèse of Lisieux to Abbe Belliere," from *The Collected Letters of St. Thérèse*, translated by Frank Sheed. Copyright 1949. Used by permission of Sheed and Ward, an imprint of Rowman and Littlefield Publishers, Inc. in Lanham, MD.

"Welcome Morning" by Anne Sexton, from *The Awful Rowing Toward God* by Anne Sexton. Copyright 1975 by Loring Conant, Jr., Executor of the Estate of Anne Sexton. Reprinted by permission of Houghton Mifflin Harcourt Publishing Company. All rights reserved.

"A Woman's Prayer" by Dorothy Day, from *By Little and by Little: The Selected Writing of Dorothy Day*, edited by Robert Ellsberg. Copyright 1983 by Robert Ellsberg & Tamar Hennessy. Knopf.

Reference List

An Account of the Martyrdom of St. Blandine and Her Companions In AD 177, from *The Ecclesiastical History* by Eusebius of Caesarea

"Address to the Pontifical Academy of Science" by Pope John Paul II: www.its.caltech.edu/~nmcenter/sci-cp/sci-9211.html

"The Bethlehem Explosion" from *Miracle on 10th Street* by Madeleine L'Engle

"The Bishop's Candlesticks" from *Les Misérables* by Victor Hugo (translated by Isabel Florence Hapgood)

"The Blessed Virgin Mary Compared to a Window" from *The Collected Poems of Thomas Merton* by Thomas Merton

"The Burning Babe" by Robert Southwell

The Cathedral by J. K. Huysmans

"The Creation" from *God's Trombones* by James Weldon Johnson

Decree of the Second Council of Nicaea

The Diary of a Country Priest by Georges Bernanos

"An Experience of God at Midnight," from *Bearing the Cross: Martin Luther King, Jr., and the Southern Christian Leadership Conference* by David J. Garrow

"The Filipino and the Drunkard" from *Love, Here Is My Hat* by William Saroyan

"The Gift of the Magi" by O. Henry

"God's Grandeur" by Gerard Manley Hopkins

"Hail Mary" from *Dago Red* by John Fante

"Helen" from *The Junkie Priest by Father Daniel Egan, S.A.* by John D. Harris

"The Hint of An Explanation" from *Collected Stories of Graham Greene* by Graham Greene

"His Cleric's Eye" from *And the Risen Bread* by Daniel Berrigan

Reference List

"In the Convent Chapel" from *The Light Invisible* by Robert Hugh Benson

"i thank you God for most this amazing" from *The Complete Poems* by e e cummings

The Journey of the Mind into God by St. Bonaventure

Letter to the Grand Duchess Christina of Tuscany by Galileo Galilei

"The Little Match Girl" by Hans Christian Andersen

"Marble Floor" from *The Collected Poems of Karol Wojtyla* by Karol Wojtyla (Pope John Paul II)

"March 7, 1848" from *Meditations and Devotions* by John Henry Cardinal Newman

"The Merit of a Young Priest" from *Hasidic Tales of the Holocaust* by Yaffa Eliach

"The Mysterious Visitor" from *The Brothers Karamazov* by Fyodor Dostoyevsky

"On Opening a Page in *Time Magazine*" by Cothrai Gogan

"Our Lady's Juggler" by Anatole France

"Pigeon Feathers" from *The Early Stories 1953–1975* by John Updike

"Parker's Back" from *The Complete Stories* by Flannery O'Connor

"Questions for Fra Angelico" by Annabelle Mosley

"Richard Cory" by Edward Arlington Robinson

"St. Francis and the Animals," from *The Writings of Thomas of Celano*, adapted by John Feister

Salvador Witness: The Life and Calling of Jean Donovan by Ana Carrigan

"She Went by Gently" by Paul Vincent Carroll from *44 Irish Stories* edited by Devin A. Garrity

"The Sniper" by Liam O'Flaherty

"The Story of the Other Wise Man" by Henry Van Dyke

The Catholic Spirit

"The Teacher of Wisdom" from *Poems in Prose* by Oscar Wilde

"The Three Hermits" by Leo Tolstoy

"The Trouble" from *The Prince of Darkness and Other Stories* by J. F. Powers

Two Letters of St. Thérèse of Lisieux to Abbe Belliere from *The Collected Letters of St. Thérèse* by St. Thérèse of Lisieux

"Vanka" by Anton Chekhov (translated by Constance Garnett)

"Welcome Morning" from *The Awful Rowing Toward God* by Anne Sexton

"Where Love Is, God Is" by Leo Tolstoy

"A Woman of Little Faith" from *The Brothers Karamazov* by Fyodor Dostoyevsky

"A Woman's Prayer" from *From Union Square to Rome* by Dorothy Day

Index

The Catholic Spirit

Photography Credits

Interior photography

p. x © www.sxc.hu and www.jiunlimited.com; p. 8 © PocketAces @ www.sxc.hu; p. 88 © www.jiunlimited.com; p. 136 © www.jiunlimited.com; p. 172 © enrika79 @ www.sxc.hu; p. 178 © www.jiunlimited.com; p. 238 © www.jiunlimited.com; p. 248 © www.sxc.hu and www.jiunlimited.com; p. 368 © www.jiunlimited.com; p. 382 © www.jiunlimited.com; p. 434 © Philip Gröning / VG Bild Kunst / Zeitgeist Films Ltd.

Color insert photo credits:

Georges Rouault, *Et Veronique au tendre lin* © 2009 Artists Rights Society (ARS), NY / ADAGP, Paris

Michelangelo Merisi da Caravaggio, *Supper at Emmaus* © Bridgeman Art Library, London / Superstock

Andy Warhol, *The Last Supper* © Andy Warhol Foundation / CORBIS

Salvador Dali, *The Sacrament of the Last Supper* © 2009 Salvador Dali, Gala-Salvador Dali Foundation / Artists Rights Society (ARS), NY

2001: A Space Odyssey © Sunset Boulevard / CORBIS

Paul Newman in *Cool Hand Luke* © Bettman / CORBIS

Paul Gauguin, *Ia Oriana Maria (Hail Mary)* © The Metropolitan Museum of Art / Art Resource, NY

Giotto Di Bondone, *St. Francis Preaching to the Birds* © Superstock / Superstock

Michelangelo Buonarroti *Creation of Adam* © age footstock / Superstock

Giovanni Bellini *The Agony in the Garden* © Superstock / Superstock

Scene from Alfred Hitchcock's *I Confess* © John Springer Collection / CORBIS

Edvard Munch *The Scream* © 2009 The Munch Museum / The Munch-Ellingsen Group / Artists Right Society (ARS) NY

Raymond Massey, Julie Harris, and James Dean in *East of Eden* © Sunset Boulevard / Sygma / CORBIS

Gian Lorenzo Bernini *Ecstasy of St. Theresa* © Superstock / Superstock

On the Waterfront movie poster © CinemaPhoto / CORBIS